Quantitative Methods for Business and Economics

34823

Longman modular texts in business and economics

··········

Series Editors
Geoff Black and Stuart Wall

Quantitative Methods for Business and Economics

Glyn Burton, George Carrol and Stuart Wall

LONGMAN

Addison Wesley Longman Limited
Edinburgh Gate, Harlow, Essex CM20 2JE, England
and Associated Companies throughout the world

*Published in the United States of America
by Addison Wesley Longman Inc., New York*

Visit Addision Wesley Longman on the world wide web at:
http://www.awl-he.com

© Addison Wesley Longman Limited 1999

First published 1999

ISBN 0 582 311659

British Library Cataloguing-in-Publication Data
A catalogue record for this book isavailable from the British Library

Library of Congress Cataloging-in-Publication Data
Burton, Glyn.
   Quantitative methods for business and economics / Glyn Burton,
George Carrol, and Stuart Wall.
     p. cm. — (Longman modular texts in business and economics)
   Includes bibliographical references and index.
   ISBN 0–582–31165–9 (pbk.)
   1. Industrial management—Statistical methods. 2. Economics—
Statistical methods. 3. Commercial statistics—Methodology.
4. Mathematical statistics. I. Carrol, George. II. Wall, Stuart,
1946– . III. Title. IV. Series.
HD30.215.B87 1998
519.5—dc21   98–27625
                                                 CIP

Typeset by 35 in Stone Serif 9/12pt
Produced by Addison Wesley Longman Singapore (Pte) Ltd.,
Printed in Singapore

Contents

Preface

Quantitative Methods is a key component of a wide range of undergraduate and equivalent courses involving Business, Economics and Management. It takes a variety of titles, including Business Analysis, Business Mathematics and Statistics, Quantitative Methods, etc. Student success in many subsequent modules will depend on the confidence and skills acquired in the first Quantitative Methods course they encounter.

This book seeks to give extensive practice in the key topic areas of any such course. Worked solutions are provided to a wide range of questions in each topic area. The usefulness and importance of statistical packages is fully recognised and various activities are presented for use with such packages. Nevertheless, the underlying theme of this book is that it is vital that students themselves acquire an understanding and facility in the key mathematical and statistical processes so essential to their development in a variety of business, economic and managerial disciplines. Indeed a meaningful interpretation of the results of statistical packages crucially depends upon an understanding of the mathematical and statistical variables which feature in such results. It is our view that extensive, first-hand practice in using and applying such variables in a variety of calculations is a key step in acquiring understanding.

This book contains a number of features to help build experience and confidence.

▶ **Worked examples** throughout each topic area to show the student how a particular idea can be used to resolve business–related problems.
▶ **Self–check questions** (with full solutions) throughout each topic area to give an early opportunity to apply the work covered.
▶ **Review questions** (with full solutions) having a clearly focused business context at the end of each chapter.
▶ **Activities** (with responses) giving opportunities to use and interpret statistical packages.
▶ **Pause for thought** at various points (with suggested responses) encouraging students to think more widely about particular ideas.
▶ **Did you know?** entries which provide fact and information relevant to particular topics.
▶ **Further study and data** at the end of each chapter, giving specific guidance to other key sources of text and information.

Acknowledgements

We are grateful to the following for permission to reproduce copyright material:

Figure 8.1 'Inflation as measured by the RPI' from *Labour Market Trends*, Office for National Statistics, © Crown copyright, 1998; Table 8.13 'General index of retail prices: group weights' from *Employment Gazette* 1998, *Labour Market Trends*, Office for National Statistics, © Crown copyright, 1998.

Whilst every effort has been made to trace the owners of copyright material, in a few cases this has proved impossible and we take this opportunity to offer our apologies to any copyright holders whose rights we may have unwittingly infringed.

CHAPTER 1

Data presentation and collection

Objectives
············

When you have read this chapter you should be able to:

▶ construct tally charts and assemble data in the form of frequency tables;
▶ know the difference between discrete data and continuous data;
▶ present a visual display of frequency tables in the form of equal and unequal width histograms;
▶ use the histogram as a basis for constructing frequency polygons and frequency curves;
▶ develop and interpret cumulative frequency tables and their associated diagrams;
▶ present and use various visual approaches involving bar charts, pie charts, Lorenz curves, etc., which are widely used as a means of communicating patterns and trends in data.

Introduction
···············

Statistics, as a subject, is a study of the various techniques of giving meaning to untreated or *raw* data. In this chapter we consider some simple, visual techniques which will be helpful in identifying patterns and trends in data. These will often involve drawing diagrams such as histograms, frequency curves, bar graphs, pie charts, Lorenz curves, etc. However we start by considering some simple procedures of data collection involving tally charts and the presentation of the data collected in a more 'grouped' form using class intervals and frequency tables. Ideas which involve selecting *samples* from all the data available and interpreting the results from sample data are considered in Chapter 7.

Answers to the 'Self-check questions', responses to each 'Pause for thought' and answers to the 'Review questions' can be found at the end of the book (pp. 320–471).

1.1 Frequency distribution
··································

Frequency is the number of times a certain event has happened, and is often found by means of a *tally chart*. For example, if you were conducting a survey of defective items produced by machines of different ages (in months) in an assembly workshop, you might record your findings as shown in the tally chart of Figure 1.1.

Each time a defective item is identified as coming from a machine of a particular age, a *vertical* line is drawn, and should a fifth such line be needed a *diagonal* line is drawn through the previous four vertical lines. At the end of the data collection period the total number of tally marks are added for each age of machinery and the total placed in the end column marked F for frequency. The total frequency (80) is found by adding these individual (class) frequencies together.

figure 1.1

Tally chart for defective items

Age in months	Tally	Frequency (F)
0 and under 5	II	2
5 and under 10	III	3
10 and under 15	HH II	7
15 and under 20	HH IIII	9
20 and under 25	HH HH HH HH	20
25 and under 30	HH HH HH II	17
30 and under 35	HH HH HH HH II	22
		—
Total		80

1.2 Frequency tables
....

Figure 1.1 is essentially a **frequency table,** and it will be useful at the outset to define a number of terms often encountered when discussing such tables.

▶ *Class intervals*: these are the groups into which we organise the data. There are seven class intervals in Figure 1.1, the first being '0 and under 5' and so on.
▶ *Class boundaries*: these are the values at which the different class intervals meet. For example the second class interval has a lower class boundary (LCB) of 5 and an upper class boundary (UCB) of 10.
▶ *Class limits*: these are the lower and upper values of the class interval *as shown in the frequency table*. In Figure 1.1 the class limits are the same as the class boundaries. However this may not always be the case. Suppose a frequency table contains the following entries.

Marks	Frequency
0 to 9	5
10 to 19	6
20 to 29	14
30 to 39	18

The second class interval has *class limits* of 10 and 19 as shown in the frequency table, but *class boundaries* of 9.5 and 19.5. Where there is a gap in the values between class limits, the mid-point of the gap will be the value at which the class intervals meet, i.e. the class boundary. For example a mark below 9.5 will go into the first class interval, whereas a mark of 9.5 or above will go into the second class interval.

▶ *Class width (or size)*: this is the difference between the upper and lower class boundaries for each class interval. As we can see from Figure 1.1 *all* the class intervals have a class width (or size) of 5.
▶ *Class frequency*: this is the number of observations found to occur in a particular class interval.

A frequency table is useful in giving an immediate impression of how the raw data are distributed. We can see from Figure 1.1 that, although the relationship is not precise, the older the machine the greater the number of defective items that were found to occur.

The following steps may help when you try to construct your own frequency table from raw data.

Step 1 Determine the range of the data:

range = maximum value − minimum value

Step 2 Determine the number of class intervals to be shown in the table. This is largely a matter of opinion – too many class intervals will confuse the data whilst too few class intervals will mean that you lose much of the information. Most published frequency tables use between five and ten class intervals.

Step 3 Determine the width (size) of class intervals. As a general rule the width of each class interval should be approximately equal to the range of the data divided by the number of class intervals.

Sometimes Steps 2 and 3 are best reversed, as when you have already decided on an appropriate width (size) for your class interval.

Step 4 Determine the first lower class limit.

Step 5 Construct the frequency table using a tally chart.

WORKED
EXAMPLE **1.1**
••••••••••••••

The percentage marks scored by 58 candidates seeking promotion in a personnel selection test were recorded as follows:

37	49	58	59	56	79
62	82	53	58	34	45
40	43	44	50	42	61
54	30	49	54	76	47
64	53	64	54	60	39
49	44	47	44	25	38
55	57	54	55	59	40
31	41	53	47	58	55
59	64	56	42	38	37
33	33	47	50		

Construct a frequency table of the data, using class intervals with a class width (size) of ten percentage marks.

Solution

Step 1 Determine the range of the data:

maximum = 82; minimum = 25; range = 57

Steps 2 and 3 Determine the width (size) and number of the class intervals.
Width of class intervals = 10 (e.g. 20.5 to 30.5). Therefore seven class intervals will be required to cover scores 21 to 90 (per cent) should we decide to set the first lower class limit at 21, as in Step 4.

Step 4   First lower class limit = 21

Step 5   Construct the frequency table

figure 1.2

Tally chart for percentage scores

Class	Tally	Frequency
21–30	II	2
31–40	IIII IIII I	11
41–50	IIII IIII IIII III	18
51–60	IIII IIII IIII IIII	20
61–70	IIII	4
71–80	II	2
81–90	I	1

1.3 Discrete or continuous data

Data are either 'discrete' or 'continuous'.

Discrete data

These are data which can only take on a *limited number* of different values. For example:

▶ the number of houses built
▶ the number of goals scored
▶ the number of marks scored in a test

All these examples can only take on a limited or finite number of *integer* (whole number) values.

Continuous data

These are data which can take on an *infinite number* of different values (at least in theory):

▶ your height
▶ your weight
▶ your age
▶ the time taken to do a job

DID YOU KNOW?
There has been a huge increase in the volume of data a firm must process. The OECD has estimated that it has grown sevenfold in the past 20 years. Despite the growth of IT, some 92 million paper documents involving data of one kind or another are produced each year.

All these examples can take on *any* value, subject only to the minimum unit of measurement available. These values need *not* be integers; example, 0.001 cm, 1.24 grams, 4.03 seconds, and so on. Continuous data are often 'rounded off' to a certain number of decimal places even though still smaller measurements might theoretically be possible.

Can you give two more examples of discrete data and two more examples of continuous data?

1.4 Histograms

The **histogram** is a visual means which is often used to display data which have been arranged in the form of a frequency table. The histogram can be used for displaying both *discrete* and *continuous* data. The histogram has a number of properties:

▶ it is a set of rectangles, each of which represents the frequency of a particular class interval;

▶ each rectangle is constructed so that its *area* is in proportion to the frequency of the class interval it represents;

▶ the base of each rectangle represents the width (or size) of the class interval and the height of each rectangle represents the frequency of the class interval;

▶ when all the class intervals have the same width (or size), then the vertical axis which represents the height of each rectangle is the class frequency;

▶ when the class intervals are of *unequal width* (or size), then the height of each rectangle must be adjusted where it differs from the 'standard' class width, i.e. from the class width of the majority of class intervals. For example if the width of a particular class interval *doubles* (and with it the base of the rectangle), then we must *halve* the height of the rectangle used to represent its class frequency. We must do this to keep the *areas* of the rectangles proportional to the class frequencies. The vertical axis is no longer the frequency of the class interval but the *frequency density*, as we shall see below.

Equal-width histograms

Table 1.1 represents the data from our earlier example of defective items produced by machines of varying age.

table 1.1

Frequency table for defective items by age of machine

Age in months	Frequency
0–5	2
5–10	3
10–15	7
15–20	9
20–25	20
25–30	17
30–35	<u>22</u>
	<u>80</u>

figure 1.3
Equal-width histogram

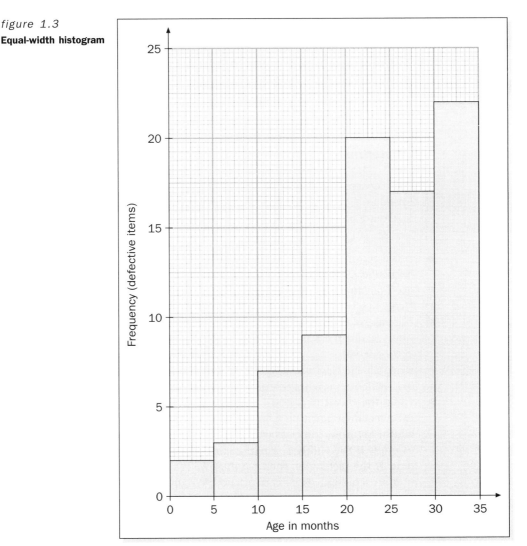

As can be seen, each class interval has an *equal* class width (or size) of five months. This is sometimes called the *standard class width*. The **equal-width histogram** which represents these data is shown in Figure 1.3.

Note that the rectangles are connected together, that the base on each rectangle represents the standard class width (five months) and is the same throughout, and that the height of each rectangle represents the class frequency. As a result the *areas* of the rectangles are in proportion to the respective class frequencies, and so we can see at a glance that the bulk of the frequency distribution is to the right of the histogram, in the rectangles 20–25, 25–30 and 30–35 months. We gain an immediate visual impression from the histogram that the frequency (of defective items) increases broadly in relation to the age of the machinery.

table 1.2 **Frequency table** **for time taken** **by employees to** **complete a task**	

Time (nearest minute)	Frequency
0–1	42
2	35
3	30
4	21
5	15
6–7	15
8–9	6
10	1
	165

table 1.3
Frequency density
for time taken by
employees to
complete a task

Time (nearest minute)	Frequency	Class width (minutes)	Frequency density
0–1	42	1.5	(42 ÷ 1.5) 28
2	35	1	35
3	30	1	30
4	21	1	21
5	15	1	15
6–7	15	2	(15 ÷ 2) 7.5
8–9	6	2	(6 ÷ 2) 3
10	1	1	1

Unequal-width histogram

Sometimes the data will be such that the class intervals are of different widths (or sizes). In the previous example of defective items the width of each class interval was five months. In the next example (Table 1.2) however we have a frequency table in which the widths of the various class intervals vary, being either 1 minute, 1.5 minutes or 2 minutes.

Remembering that the *areas* of the rectangles must be in proportion to the class frequencies, we must adjust the height of any rectangles in line with any variations in the base of that rectangle. So if the base (class width) doubles in length we must halve the height (class frequency) and so on. The value on the vertical axis is no longer frequency, but *frequency density*. These adjustments are shown in Table 1.3 and Figure 1.3.

Remembering that the *class width* is the difference between upper and lower *class boundaries*. we can see that the first class interval has a width of 1.5 minutes, and the sixth and seventh class intervals have class widths of 2 minutes, with all other intervals having a class width of 1 minute. The adjusted frequency densities from Table 1.3 are shown in the **unequal-width** histogram below (Figure 1.4).

The class width which appears most often in an unequal-width frequency table and histogram is often called the *standard class width*. In the above example the standard class width is 1 minute. We derive the **frequency density** by dividing the class frequency by the number of standard class widths in that class interval. So, for example, we divide the six employees in the penultimate class interval by two to give a frequency density of three.

This approach can be seen more clearly in the following worked example.

figure 1.4
Unequal-width
histogram

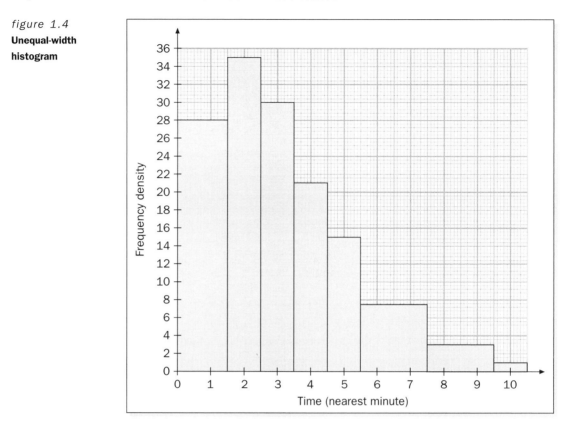

WORKED
EXAMPLE **1.2**
••••••••••••••

A company wishes to review its distribution operation and from its time sheet records it found that 144 vehicles were loaded in a 24 hour period. A frequency distribution table was prepared from the data as follows.

Time to load (minutes)	Number of vehicles
40–45	4
45–50	13
50–55	17
55–60	44
60–70	59
70–80	7

From the above data construct a histogram to represent the data.

Solution

Step 1 From the frequency table decide on a standard class width = 5 minutes.
Step 2 Enlarge the original table, adding columns for class width, number of standard class widths and height (frequency density).

Time	Frequency	Class width	No. of standard class widths	Height (frequency density)
40–45	4	5	1	4
45–50	13	5	1	13
50–55	17	5	1	17
55–60	44	5	1	44
60–70	59	10	2	(59 ÷ 2) 29.5
70–80	7	10	2	(7 ÷ 2) 3.5

Note that where the standard class width has doubled, as in the case of the last two class intervals, we must halve the height (frequency density) of the corresponding rectangle.

Step 3 Construct the histogram

figure 1.5
Histogram showing number of vehicles loaded in a 24 hour period

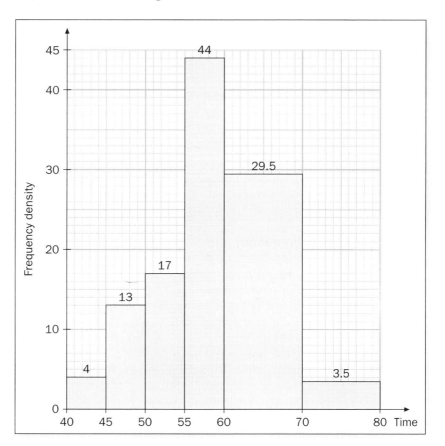

1.5 Frequency polygon

A **frequency polygon** is a straight line diagram which represents exactly the same area (i.e. frequency) as shown in the histogram. The frequency polygon is derived from the histogram by connecting the mid-points of the tops of each

figure 1.6
**Frequency polygon:
area enclosed
identical to
histogram**

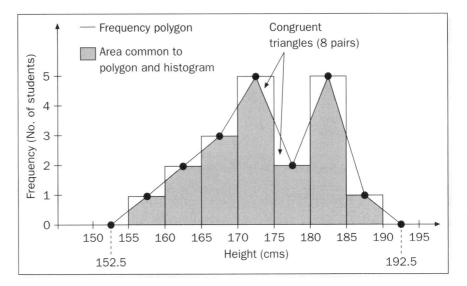

adjacent rectangle by straight lines, as in Figure 1.6. If we then use straight lines to join the mid-points of the tops of the end two rectangles with the horizontal axis, as shown, then a key property of the frequency polygon should quickly become apparent: namely that the area under the histogram is identically equal to the area under the frequency polygon.

The shaded area is common to both polygon and histogram and there are eight respective pairs of congruent triangles (side–angle–side), giving identical areas contained by polygon and histogram.

1.6 Frequency curve
····························

From the previous discussion we can therefore state that the frequency distribution represented by the histogram can equivalently be represented by the straight line polygon known as the **frequency polygon**. Further, if the points to be connected by straight lines were close together then, as an approximation, we could represent the frequency polygon by the **frequency curve** shown in Figure 1.7. Indeed the frequency curve is the most usual way of representing a frequency table visually. However, it is basically an alternative means of displaying visually the properties of a frequency table already captured by the histogram and frequency polygon.

The two peaks indicated by the frequency curve would represent a *bimodal* distribution, as we note in chapter 2.

1.7 Cumulative frequency curves
··

Cumulative frequency is the 'running total' of the figures shown in the frequency column of a frequency table. As we shall see we can draw up cumulative 'more than' and cumulative 'less than' tables to represent data on income,

figure 1.7

Frequency curve as an approximation to the frequency polygon

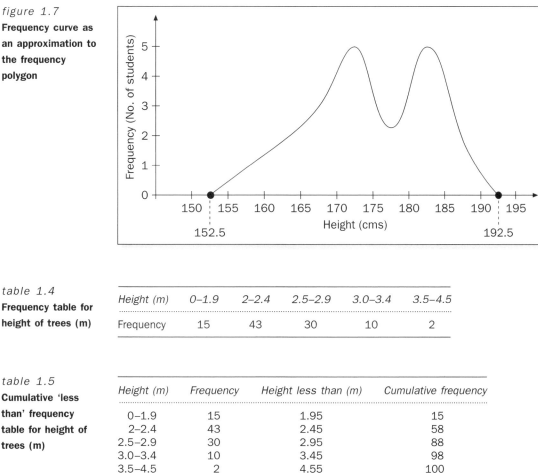

table 1.4

Frequency table for height of trees (m)

Height (m)	0–1.9	2–2.4	2.5–2.9	3.0–3.4	3.5–4.5
Frequency	15	43	30	10	2

table 1.5

Cumulative 'less than' frequency table for height of trees (m)

Height (m)	Frequency	Height less than (m)	Cumulative frequency
0–1.9	15	1.95	15
2–2.4	43	2.45	58
2.5–2.9	30	2.95	88
3.0–3.4	10	3.45	98
3.5–4.5	2	4.55	100

wealth and many other variables. We can then draw cumulative frequency *polygons* or *curves* to give a visual picture of these tables.

Table 1.4 illustrates the frequency distribution of the height of 100 trees in a plantation, each tree being measured to the nearest 0.1 m.

We can, for example, produce a *cumulative 'less than' frequency table* (Table 1.5). This keeps a running total on how many trees are 'less than' a particular height. As we saw with histograms, the width (size) of the class intervals (groups) are slightly wider than the table suggests. For example 2–2.4 is really $1.95 \le$ height < 2.45, i.e. a class width of 0.5 (m).

We now draw a cumulative frequency *curve* from this table by plotting the cumulative frequency (on the vertical axis) against the 'less than' value (on the horizontal axis). Here, we join up the points we have plotted with a smooth curve. This frequency curve is also known as an **'ogive'**. The curve plotted in Figure 1.8 is therefore the cumulative 'less than' curve (or ogive).

You can take note of some useful information from such a curve. For example all but two of the trees (i.e. 98 out of a hundred) have a height less

figure 1.8
Cumulative 'less than' curve or ogive

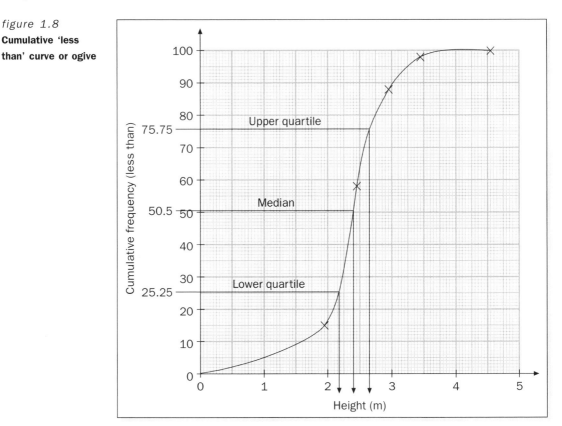

than 3.45 m. On the other hand, only 15 out of a hundred trees are less than 1.95 m in height.

PAUSE FOR THOUGHT 1.2 *Try to construct a 'cumulative more than' frequency table using the data in Table 1.5 but using the lower class boundaries for each class interval.*

Percentiles

We can also use our cumulative 'less than' frequency curve to answer questions involving *percentiles*. A percentile is a particular value below (or above) which a given percentage of the distribution lies.

For example, 'what is the height of tree for which 25 per cent of the distribution will lie below that height?' This height is the **lower quartile** height (or 'first quartile'), shown as 2.15 m in Figure 1.8. Note that since the total frequency is 100, then 25 per cent is 25 trees in this case. However because of the *continuity correction* (see box below) we should strictly regard 25.25 trees as the lower quartile observation. Let us consider the continuity correction for first, second (median) and third quartiles respectively, before using Figure 1.8 to estimate those values.

Continuity correction

Strictly speaking we should make slight adjustments when finding the quartile values of a distribution:

▶ lower (first) quartile position $\frac{1}{4}(n + 1)$

▶ median (second) quartile position $\frac{1}{2}(n + 1)$

▶ upper (third) quartile position $\frac{3}{4}(n + 1)$

where n is the number of observations.

It is perhaps helpful to explain the reason for this continuity correction by starting with the second quartile, the median.

Median

The **median** (second quartile) value is that value for which 50 per cent of the data are below it and 50 per cent above it. If we arrange the items of data in *order* (whether rising or falling in value), we need to find the value corresponding to the middle item. For example, with nine items, the median value will correspond to that of the fifth item arranged in order, i.e. the value 7 in the example below.

2   4   4   5   (7)   10   11   14   18

Note that the median position is given by $\frac{1}{2}(n + 1) = \frac{1}{2}(9 + 1) = $ 5th item arranged in order. However when the number of observations, n, is not an odd number but an even number, then the median value will lie mid-way between two observations. For example, with ten items as a result of adding the number 20 to the previous nine items, the median value will correspond to that of the 5.5th item arranged in order.

median position

2   4   4   5   7 $\updownarrow$ 10   11   14   18   20

5.5th item

Notice that the median position is given by $\frac{1}{2}(n + 1) = \frac{1}{2}(10 + 1) = $ 5.5th item arranged in order.

> We can therefore say that the median position is given by $\frac{1}{2}(n + 1)$, where this expression is known as the continuity correction.

In the previous example with 100 trees, the median item in the cumulative frequency table is the $\frac{1}{2}(100 + 1) = $ 50.5th item.

We can use our cumulative frequency curve (Figure 1.8) to find the median height of trees. We draw a horizontal line from 50.5 on the vertical (cumulative frequency) axis to the curve. We then draw a vertical line from the curve to the horizontal axis and 'read off' the value, i.e. around 2.4 m. So half the number of trees are below 2.4 m in height, and half above 2.4 m in height.

We follow a similar procedure for finding the first and third quartile positions as we do for the second quartile (median). However instead of $\frac{1}{2}$ (i.e. $\frac{2}{4}$) we have $\frac{1}{4}$ and $\frac{3}{4}$ respectively.

PAUSE FOR THOUGHT 1.3 *At what value would you expect a cumulative 'more than' frequency curve to intersect a cumulative 'less than' frequency curve?*

Lower quartile

The **lower quartile** (first quartile) is that value for which a quarter (25 per cent) of the distribution lies *below* it. If there are n items in the distribution, we need to find the value corresponding to the $\frac{1}{4}$ $(n + 1)$th item, when the items are arranged in order. In our 'tree' example, $n = 100$ so $\frac{1}{4}$ $(n + 1) = \frac{101}{4}$ = 25.25.

We can therefore use our cumulative frequency curve to estimate the value of the lower quartile. This time draw the horizontal line from 25.25 on the vertical (cumulative frequency) axis to the curve, and read down to around 2.15 metres on the horizontal axis. So a quarter of the trees are below 2.15 metres in height.

Upper quartile

The **upper quartile** (third quartile) is that value for which a quarter (25 per cent) of the distribution lies *above* it. (We therefore look three-quarters of the way up the distribution, arranged in order, where we find the upper quartile). If there are n items in the distribution, we need to find the value corresponding to the $\frac{3}{4}$ $(n + 1)$th item, when the items are arranged in order. If our 'tree' example, $n = 100$ so $\frac{3}{4}$ $(100 + 1) = \frac{303}{4}$ = 75.75.

In Figure 1.8 we now read across from 75.75 on the vertical (cumulative frequency) axis to the curve, and then down to the horizontal axis. This gives a reading of around 2.65 m. So one-quarter of the trees are above 2.65 metres in height (i.e. three-quarters of trees are below 2.65 metres in height).

We can, in these ways, find the heights of trees at *any percentile* point of the distribution. Here we have used *quartiles* (25 per cents), but we could have used *quintiles* (20 per cents) or *deciles* (10 per cents).

Of course we can use the cumulative 'less than' distribution the other way round, this time starting on the horizontal axis and then moving to the vertical axis. For example, we can read off the number (here percentage) of trees having a height less than a specific value. For example 90 trees (90 per cent) have a height less than 3 m.

We return to the ideas of median and lower and upper quartiles in chapter 2.

1.1 The frequency table below shows the number and value of transactions at a corner shop taking place between the hours of 17.00 and 22.00.

Value of transaction (£)	Frequency
0–3.99	8
4–7.99	18
8–11.99	22
12–15.99	24
16–19.99	13
20–23.99	12
24–27.99	2
28–31.99	1

Construct a histogram of the data.

1.2 Here is the frequency table of the weekly income of 45 people in a survey. Draw a histogram to represent these data (*note*: unequal-width histogram).

Weekly income (£)	Frequency
76–100	6
101–125	8
126–150	17
151–200	8
201–300	6

1.3 The following table shows the distribution of the ages of people attending a public concert.

Age range (yrs)	0–19	20–39	40–59	60–79	80–99
No. of people	8	26	110	128	56

Construct a cumulative frequency (less than) table and draw the corresponding curve on a graph. Use your curve to estimate:

(i) the median age attending the concert,
(ii) the lower and upper quartile ages,
(iii) the percentage of people over 65 attending the concert.

1.4 (a) Complete the cumulative 'more than' table below:

Height (m)	Frequency	Height more than (m)	Cumulative frequency
0–1.9	15	0.0	
2–2.4	43	1.95	
2.5–2.9	30	2.45	
3.0–3.4	10	2.95	
3.5–4.5	2	3.45	
		4.55	

(b) Draw the cumulative 'more than' curve on Figure 1.8.

(c) What do you notice about the point at which the cumulative 'less than' and 'more than' curves intersect?

Note: **Answers can be found on p. 320.**

1.8 Bar charts

There are three main types of **bar chart**:

▶ simple bar chart
▶ component bar chart
▶ multiple bar chart

Simple bar chart

A **simple bar chart** is a set of non-joining bars of equal width whose height or length is proportional to the frequency it is representing. They can be drawn in a vertical or horizontal format and can show negative, as well as positive, values (see Figure 1.9).

Component bar chart

A **component or segmented bar chart** is useful to illustrate a breakdown in the figures, e.g. the total sales of XYZ Co. could be broken down into sales by product (see Figure 1.10a). The constituent parts of each bar are always stacked in the same order with the height of each representing the individual values or frequencies.

figure 1.9
Simple bar charts

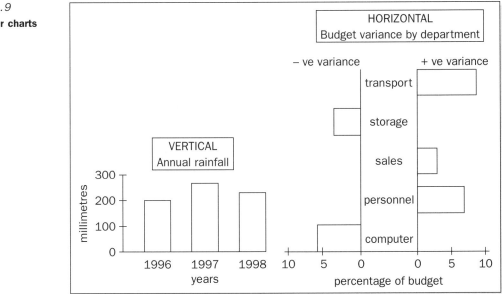

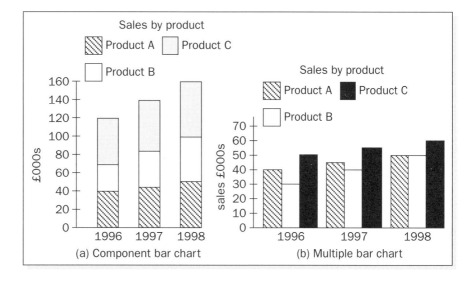

(a) Component bar chart   (b) Multiple bar chart

Multiple bar chart

A **multiple bar chart** uses a separate bar to represent each constituent part of the total. These bars are joined into a set for each class of data (see Figure 1.10b). The data in Figure 1.10a are represented in multiple bar chart form in Figure 1.10b.

1.9 Pie chart

• • • • • • • • • • • • • •

A **pie chart** involves a circle which is used to represent the *whole data*. Sectors of this circle ('pie') are then used to represent the relative frequencies of particular *components* of the data. The size of each sector is found by calculating the proportion of the whole data represented by the component and then multiplying by 360° to obtain the angle of the sector from the centre of the circle.

Pie charts give an immediate visual impression of the relative contribution of particular components to the overall total. They are widely used in company reports and accounts, as in highlighting the relative contribution of different product lines to overall profit or of different types of cost to overall cost. However they are only effective for displaying the contributions of a relatively small number of separate components.

WORKED
EXAMPLE **1.3**
• • • • • • • • • • • • • •

A survey of 12,000 television viewers on a particular evening found the following information as to the channels being watched at 8 p.m. on that evening. You are asked to construct a pie chart to represent these data.

table 1.6

TV viewing figures

Channel	Number
BBC1	3,000
BBC2	1,000
ITV3	5,500
ITV4	2,000
5	500

Solution

To find the angle of the circle ('pie') represented by each channel, we find the proportion of the whole data (12,000 viewers) represented by that channel and then multiply by 360°. This is done in Table 1.7.

table 1.7

Finding the sectors of the 'pie'

Channel	Frequency	Angle
BBC1	3,000	$\dfrac{3,000}{12,000} \times 360° = 90°$
BBC2	1,000	$\dfrac{1,000}{12,000} \times 360° = 30°$
ITV3	5,500	$\dfrac{5,500}{12,000} \times 360° = 165°$
ITV4	2,000	$\dfrac{2,000}{12,000} \times 360° = 60°$
Channel 5	500	$\dfrac{500}{12,000} \times 360° = 15°$

The pie chart is then drawn from this table using a protractor or angle measurer. The completed pie chart is shown in Figure 1.11. We can see at a glance how ITV3 dominated that evening's viewing figures, with channel 5 having the smallest share of viewers.

figure 1.11

Pie chart for viewing figures

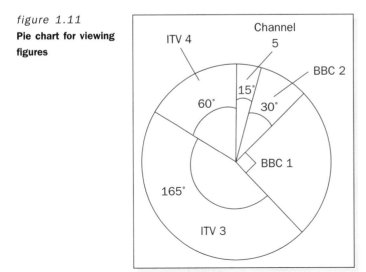

In actually drawing the pie chart it is helpful to draw the smallest sectors first, so that any small inaccuracies in angles will be visually less important when you come to drawing the larger sectors.

ACTIVITY **1**
· · · · · · · · · · · ·

Greece is a major export market for your company. You sell a variety of products, many of which are age specific. You therefore require a demographic breakdown, by age, of the Greek population. Use the information in the following table and a spreadsheet with which you are familiar to plot the graphs mentioned.

Greece: population by age 1996
`000

Age	`000
0–9	1,160
10–19	1,425
20–29	1,544
30–39	1,428
40–49	1,263
50–59	1,305
60–69	1,081
70–79	663
80+	331

1 Construct an ogive (cumulative less than frequency curve) from the data in the table above (the first class [0 to 9] is placed in cell A4).
Remember that an ogive is plotted against the upper class boundary of the class interval therefore: put these upper class boundaries in column C (i.e. 9.5, 19.5, 29.5 . . .).
Calculate the cumulative less than frequency in column D as follows:
(a) in **cell D4** enter **1,160**,
(b) in **cell D5** construct a formula to calculate the cumulative less than frequency,
(c) copy the formula down to cell **D12**.
Plot a graph of the cumulative frequency, i.e. the ogive.
Use the ogive to estimate the population below 25 years of age.
2 Convert your results into a cumulative *percentage* less than ogive.
3 Construct a pie chart from the above data to show the relative importance of the age groups specified within the whole Greek population (total for 1996: 10,200,000).
4 Comment on your results.

A response to this activity can be found on p. 459.

1.10 Lorenz curve
· ·

The **Lorenz curve** is used to contrast the *actual* distribution of a variable with the distribution which would have occurred in a situation of 'perfect equality'. The distribution of variables such as income, wealth, profit, etc. are often displayed visually using Lorenz curves.

figure 1.12
Lorenz curve

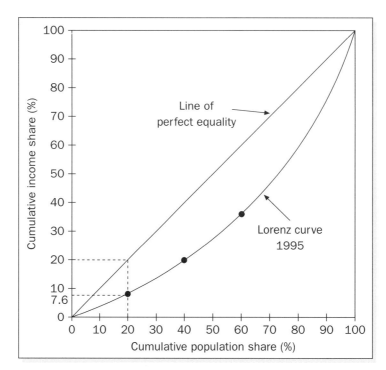

As we can see from Figure 1.12, the Lorenz curve uses *cumulative percentages* for each axis; one axis being the cumulative percentage figure for the *variable* (here income), the other being the cumulative percentage figure for the *frequency* (here people).

▶ The diagonal line represents *perfect equality*; for example 20 per cent of all people have 20 per cent of all incomes, and so on.
▶ The Lorenz curve itself represents the *actual distribution*; for example 20 per cent of all people have only 7.6 per cent of all income, and so on.
▶ The vertical distance between Lorenz curve and the diagonal represents *inequality*; for example the bottom 20 per cent of income earners should have had a further 12.4 per cent of income had perfect equality existed.

The **Gini coefficient** is sometimes used with the Lorenz curve as a measure of inequality. It is the ratio of the area between the Lorenz curve and diagonal to the total area beneath the diagonal:

▶ If there is *perfect equality* (i.e. the plotted Lorenz curve *is* the diagonal), then the Gini coefficient is zero.
▶ If there is *perfect inequality* (i.e. the plotted Lorenz curve is the horizontal axis until the last person who has *all* the variable), then the Gini coefficient is one.
▶ The smaller the Gini coefficient, the greater the equality, and the larger the Gini coefficient the greater the inequality.

As we shall see from Self-check question 1.6 below, the above conclusions may be invalidated should different Lorenz curves intersect one another. In this case we may have to trade-off greater equality at one part of the distribution with greater inequality at another part, which may render the *overall* figure of the Gini coefficient less useful.

SELF-CHECK
QUESTIONS

1.5 Draw a pie chart to display the following data. You can round your result to the nearest degree.

Road accident casualties	1997
Category	*Number killed*
Pedestrians	1,914
Pedal cyclists	323
Two-wheeled motor vehicles	942
Cars & taxis	2,019
Others	226
Total	5,424

1.6 (a) Use the following data to draw a Lorenz curve for 1979 on Figure 1.12 above (p. 20).

Cumulative per cent of income received by deciles of population.

Income receivers	*1979*	*1995*
Bottom 10%	4.7	3.0
Bottom 20%	11.0	7.6
Bottom 30%	17.5	13.9
Bottom 40%	24.2	20.3
Bottom 50%	32.2	27.5
Bottom 60%	41.2	36.2
Bottom 70%	51.8	46.7
Bottom 80%	64.3	59.2
Bottom 90%	79.6	75.0
Bottom 100%	100.0	100.0
Gini coefficient	0.248	0.337

(b) Compare the 1979 and 1995 Lorenz curves and comment on any changes in inequality.

(c) Suppose, for 1995, you were to add an extra 10.0 per cent to the incomes received by the bottom 60 per cent, 70 per cent, 80 per cent and 90 per cent, so that the respective percentage figures become 46.2, 56.7, 69.2, 85.0 (all other figures unchanged). How would this affect your interpretation of income inequality in 1995 as compared with 1979?

Note: Answers can be found on pp. 323–324.

1.1 A local authority is reviewing the amenities of one of the villages in their district. It commissions a survey based on a questionnaire to investigate the age distribution (in years) of the village's population. The results of the investigation are as follows:

<5	5–15	15–25	25–35	35–45	45–55	55–65	>65
41	142	63	70	105	102	177	138

The oldest resident was 95 years.

From the above data construct:

(a) a histogram of the data,
(b) a frequency polygon.

1.2 A survey has been conducted by the personnel department on the distances travelled to work by the production staff, with the results shown below:

Distance travelled to work (in kilometres)

13	1	2	9	27
4	63	7	2	3
12	43	6	4	3
73	26	7	8	2
48	16	42	3	2
8	26	49	21	15
2	53	7	16	21
57	2	55	18	25
6	71	8	2	8
3	4	8	4	3

The aim of the survey is to investigate the effect on the staff of relocating the production facility. The main impact of the move will be determined by investigating the impact on those who travel: 0–5 kilometres; 5–10 kilometres; 10–30 kilometres; >30 kilometres.

Construct:

(a) a frequency table of the data,
(b) draw a histogram of the data.

1.3 A company wishes to review its distribution operation and from its time sheet records it found that 144 vehicles were loaded in a 24 hour period. A frequency distribution table was prepared from the data as follows:

Time to load (minutes)	N° of vehicles
40–45	4
45–50	13
50–55	17
55–60	44
60–70	59
70–80	7

From the above data construct:

(a) a cumulative frequency curve (ogive);
(b) from your ogive estimate:
    (i) the median loading time,
    (ii) the interquartile range (the difference between the upper and lower quartiles),
    (iii) the number of vehicles loaded in under 52 minutes.

1.4 The following total expenditure was incurred by a business in the last financial year:

Cost centre	£
Employees	1,139,410
Premises	69,004
Transport	52,524
Raw materials	83,205
Admin	23,242
Capital financing costs	71,282
Total	1,438,667

Construct a pie chart to illustrate the data.

1.5 Whilst investigating the pattern of imports into a target market, a firm collected the following data:

Year	$ (billion)
1988	308.962
1989	283.724
1990	305.448
1991	292.457
1992	202.743
1993	204.61
1994	226.2
1995	272.981
1996	319.01
1997	303.829

Use a vertical bar chart to illustrate the data.

1.6 The sales volume (units) by geographical area of three types of product in a particular quarter are as follows:

Model	North	South	East	West	Export
Galactic	4,644	4,817	4,055	4,393	1,201
Jupiter	7,884	9,735	6,468	7,089	3,067
Saturn	6,136	6,703	6,497	5,934	1,844

(a) Use a component bar chart to illustrate the data.
(b) Use a multiple bar chart to illustrate the data.

1.7 With the use of suitable graphs/charts illustrate the data in the table:

Airline	No. of passengers (millions)	
	International	Domestic
Delta	8.4	80.5
American	15.2	65.9
United	11.4	62.7
USAir	1.7	57.8
Northwest	7.6	37.9
Continental	3.0	36.9
CAAC	1.4	36.1
Al Nippon	1.7	32.8
Lufthansa	16.9	14.1
Aeroflot	3.8	25.2
British Airways	22.0	5.5
JAL	9.4	16.7
TWA	1.8	19.0
Alitalia	9.1	11.2
SAS	9.8	9.0
America West	–	15.6
Air France	13.8	1.8
Air Inter	0.1	6.8
Japan Air System	0.3	15.1
Malaysia Air	6.4	7.8

Source: ICAO

Note: Answers to Review questions can be found on pp. 376–384.

Further study and data

Texts

Bancroft, G and O'Sullivan, G. (1993), *Quantitative methods for accounting and business studies*, 3rd edn, McGraw Hill, chapter 7.

Curwin, J. and Slater, R. (1996), *Quantitative methods for business decisions*, 4th edn, Chapman and Hall, chapters 1 and 2.

Lawson, M., Hubbard, S. and Pugh, P. (1995), *Maths and statistics for business*, Addison Wesley Longman, chapters 1 and 2.

Morris, C. (1996), *Quantitative approaches in business studies*, 4th edn, Pitman, chapter 5.

Oakshott, L. (1996), *Essential elements of business statistics*, BPP, chapter 2.

Swift, L. (1997), *Mathematics and statistics for business, management and finance*, Macmillan, part C, chapter 1.

Thomas, R. (1997), *Quantitative methods for business studies*, Prentice Hall, chapter 1.

Waters, D. (1997), *Quantitative methods*, 2nd edn, Addison Wesley Longman, chapters 2, 3 and 4.

Wisniewski, M. with Stead, R. (1996), *Foundation quantitative methods for business*, Pitman, chapters 3, 4, 5 and 6.

Sources of information and data

Of course the precise source of data you require will depend on the problem you seek to address. The following list gives a brief summary of the types of data you might find for the UK, Europe and the rest of the world in various statistical sources. Those for the UK are mainly published by the Office for National Statistics (ONS).

▶ **UK National Accounts** (formerly known as *National Income and Expenditure*), more normally referred to simply as the **Blue Book**. Published annually in the Autumn by the ONS, it is the most important source of data for the UK economy. Most of the data presented are annual and the tables usually cover a 20 year period.

▶ **UK Balance of Payments** (known as the **Pink Book**). The sister publication to the Blue Book. Published annually by the ONS.

▶ **Economic Trends** is published monthly by the ONS. Most of the data are quarterly, extending back over, perhaps, five years. It covers a range of areas including output, prices, employment and trade. The **Economic Trends Annual Supplement** is particularly useful for obtaining long series of both annual and quarterly data, some series going back to 1945.

▶ **Regional Trends** is published annually by the ONS. It includes economic and social indicators, broken down by the various regions of the UK.

▶ **Social Trends**, published annually by the ONS, contains data on patterns of household wealth, income and expenditure, together with data on demographic, housing and social trends.

▶ **Annual Abstract of Statistics**. An amalgam of topics are covered. Annual data.

▶ **Monthly Digest of Statistics**. As the name implies, an amalgam of statistics published monthly. It covers a wide range of topics, including economic, social and demographic.

▶ **General Household Survey**. The results of a sample survey of households are published annually in the GHS. Five core topics are covered – education, employment, health, housing and population and family information.

▶ **Labour Market Trends**. A monthly publication covering labour market issues and offering detailed information on wage rates, productivity, hours worked and so on for various sectors of the economy.

▶ **Business Monitor MM23**. The source of detailed information on prices.

▶ **Financial Statistics**. Monthly publication of the ONS relating to financial indices such as interest rates, exchange rates and the money supply.

▶ **Bank of England Quarterly Bulletin**. Published by the Economics Division of the Bank of England, containing a number of articles and statistics about the money supply and the financial sector.

▶ **National Institute Economic Review**. Unlike all of the above, this is *not* an official Government publication. However, it does contain a statistical appendix which is a very useful compilation of UK and international data on a wide range of economic issues. Published quarterly by the National Institute of Economic and Social Research.

▶ **Eurostat**. Published monthly by the Statistical Office of the European Union, this contains comparative data on various aspects of EU countries. There are also annual publications under the Eurostat heading covering specific issues.

▶ **OECD Main Economic Indicators**. Published monthly by the Organisation for Economic Co-operation and Development, this contains annual and quarterly data on OECD countries. Very useful for purposes of comparison.

▶ **International Financial Statistics**. Published monthly by the IMF it covers a larger number of countries than *OECD Main Economic Indicators*. Statistics relating to all member countries of the International Monetary Fund (IMF) are included. The data are annual, quarterly and monthly where appropriate. The **IFS Yearbook** is published annually and has annual data going back over a longer period.

Electronic Media

Many series of data and sources of information can now be accessed directly on-line or are available on disk or tape.

ONS Databank, ONS Sales Desk, Room 131/4, Office for National Statistics, Government Offices, Great George Street, London SW1P 3AQ

The ONS Databank contains major series such as GDP, PSBR, RPI, Balance of Payments, National Accounts, index of production, etc. Time series data for these items are available on disk or paper.

NOMIS Unit 3P, Mountjoy Research Centre, University of Durham, Durham DH1 3SW

The National Online Manpower Information Service (NOMIS) is a database of labour statistics run on behalf of the ONS by the University of Durham. It contains a range of official statistics relating to the labour market.

ESRC Data Archive, University of Essex, Colchester, Essex CO4 3SQ

This archive provides data across the full range of the social sciences and humanities and contains information about most areas of social and economic life including Family Expenditure Surveys, Labour Force Surveys, census data, etc. The Data Archive will endeavour to locate and obtain research data for those interested.

SINES Help Line, Room 285, Ordnance Survey, Romsey Road, Southampton, Hants SO16 4GU.

This source contains information about specific datasets through printouts, floppy disks or E-mail. It states the purpose, the sources, and frequency of update, etc. of major economic, environmental and industrial, and other datasets.

CD-Rom Many colleges and public libraries now provide CD-Rom access to a range of UK and EU databases and information sources. The following items are indicative of what may well be available to you via this resource.

1 ABI/INFORM   Gives 150 word abstracts and indexing to over 800 international academic business, economics and management journals.

2 ANBAR ABSTRACTS   Abstracts and indexes articles covering business, management and IT topics from mainly UK and European journals.

3 BOOKBANK   Gives bibliographic information on over 600,000 books from UK publishers and English language titles from overseas, which are available in the UK.

4 BOOKFIND   Includes over 2 million books, currently in print, from publishers in the UK, the US, Canada and other English speaking countries.

5 DISCLOSURE/ WORLDSCOPE EUROPE   Contains company accounts and financial information on over 10,000 companies in 27 countries. This information enables comparisons to be made between the major companies trading in Europe.

6 EC/EU INFODISK   Contains the official bibliographic database of the European Union (SCAD) and detailed briefings on Britain's implementation of EU legislation prepared by the DTI (Spearhead).

7 FINANCIAL TIMES   Full text of back issues of this newspaper.

8 THE GUARDIAN   Full text of back issues of this newspaper.

9 JUSTIC   This is the official legal database of the European Union. It contains the full text of most of the Treaties, regulations, directives, preparatory work, case law and parliamentary questions dealt with by the EU.

10 THE TIMES   Full text of back issues of this newspaper.

CHAPTER 2

Central location and dispersion

Objectives
. . . .

When you have read this chapter you should be able to:

▶ understand and use simple short-hand notation widely used in statistics;

▶ identify and calculate the various measures of central location, such as arithmetic mean, median and mode;

▶ find measures of central location for both ungrouped and grouped data;

▶ be aware of the circumstances under which the various measures of central location will be similar and under which they will differ;

▶ identify and calculate the various measures of dispersion, such as range, interquartile range, mean deviation, variance and standard deviation;

▶ find measures of dispersion for both ungrouped and grouped data;

▶ understand and interpret measures which combine aspects of central location and dispersion, such as the coefficient of variation.

Introduction
. . . .

We saw in Chapter 1 that the use of tables and charts can help by giving a visual impression of patterns and trends in data. Meaning can also be given to the original (raw) data by calculating various measures of central location (average) and dispersion (spread of data around the average).

Answers to the 'Self-check questions', responses to each 'Pause for thought' and answers to the 'Review questions' can be found at the end of the book.

2.1 Notation
. . . .

At least three types of average are in common use when seeking to describe raw data, namely arithmetic mean, median and mode. The formulae used in their derivation (and indeed elsewhere) make use of a type of notation with which you should become familiar.

$$\Sigma = \text{Greek letter sigma} = \text{sum of}$$

When applied to some variable X_i the values of the variable which are to be summed are indicated by the numbers imposed below and above the sigma sign. For example, suppose X_i refers to the throws of a dice, and we wish to sum (add together) the scores on the first three throws, we would write:

$$\sum_{i=1}^{3} X_i = X_1 + X_2 + X_3$$

$$= 3 + 5 + 1 \text{ (say)}$$

Other possibilities might include the following:

$$\sum_{i=2}^{4} X_i = X_2 + X_3 + X_4$$

$$= 5 + 1 + 6 \text{ (say)}$$

More generally, when we wish to sum over n values of the variable we write:

$$\sum_{i=1}^{n} X_i = X_1 + X_2 + X_3 + \ldots X_n$$

where n can be any number (here the number of throws of the dice).

Sometimes a particular score on the dice might occur once or more than once; in other words that particular score might occur with a *frequency* F_i. For *n* throws of the dice we might obtain *j* different scores. We would then write the total score as being given by:

$$\sum_{i=1}^{j} F_i X_i = F_1 X_1 + F_2 X_2 + F_3 X_3 + \ldots F_j X_j$$

where *j* is the number of different scores observed in the *n* throws.

For example, suppose we are faced with the following results from 12 throws of the dice:

5, 2, 6, 6, 2, 1, 6, 3, 5, 3, 2, 1

As chance would have it only five of the six possible scores on the dice have appeared (no scores of 4 obtained) in the 12 throws. Here $j = 5$ and $n = 12$.

If we let: $X_1 = 1$, occurs with frequency $F_1 = 2$
$X_2 = 2$, occurs with frequency $F_2 = 3$
$X_3 = 3$, occurs with frequency $F_3 = 2$
$X_4 = 5$, occurs with frequency $F_4 = 2$
$X_5 = 6$, occurs with frequency $F_5 = 3$

Note that if we sum the individual frequencies over the five different scores observed we get:

$$\sum_{i=1}^{5} F_i = F_1 + F_2 + F_3 + F_4 + F_5$$

$$\sum_{i=1}^{5} F_i = 2 + 3 + 2 + 2 + 3$$

$$\sum_{i=1}^{5} F_i = 12$$

So the sum of the individual frequencies for each of the five different scores equals the total number of observations, *n*, which in this case equals 12.

As already mentioned we only have five different numbers, so $j = 5$ in our earlier formula:

$$\sum_{i=1}^{5} F_i X_i = F_1 X_1 + F_2 X_2 + F_3 X_3 + F_4 X_4 + F_5 X_5$$

$$= (2 \times 1) + (3 \times 2) + (2 \times 3) + (2 \times 5) + (3 \times 6)$$

$$= 2 + 6 + 6 + 10 + 18$$

$$\sum_{i=1}^{5} F_i X_i = 42$$

You will come across the use of this shorthand notation involving the sigma sign throughout this chapter and in subsequent chapters. It will therefore be helpful to practice *using* the notation before going any further.

SELF-CHECK QUESTIONS

2.1 Expand (write out fully) each of the following expressions:

(a) $\sum_{i=1}^{4} X_i$ (b) $\sum_{i=2}^{5} X_i$ (c) $\sum_{i=1}^{3} F_i X_i$ (d) $\sum_{i=3}^{6} F_i X_i$

2.2 Write out each of the following expressions using sigma notation:

(a) $X_1 + X_2 + X_3 + X_4 + X_5$
(b) $X_5 + X_6 + X_7$
(c) $F_1 X_1 + F_2 X_2 + F_3 X_3 + F_4 X_4$
(d) $F_2 X_2 + F_3 X_3 + F_4 X_4$

2.3 The following scores are obtained for 15 throws of a dice:

5, 6, 4, 3, 6, 5, 1, 1, 2, 4, 3, 1, 2, 4, 6

Find $\sum_{i=1}^{j} F_i X_i$

where j = the number of different scores observed
   F_i = frequency of a particular score
   X_i = particular score

Note: Answers can be found on p. 325.

2.2 Measures of central location
....

A number of measures of central location or 'average' are widely used in an attempt to give meaning to raw data. Here we consider the arithmetic mean, median and mode for both *ungrouped data* (all individual items known) and *grouped data* (items only identified within class intervals).

The arithmetic mean

This is the simple average of everyday use, and is often represented by the symbol $\bar{X}$.

Ungrouped data

Where individual or *ungrouped* data are available, the following formula is commonly used:

$$\bar{X} = \frac{\sum_{i=1}^{n} X_i}{n}$$

where $\bar{X}$ = arithmetic mean

X_i = nalue of each item of data

n = number of items of data

WORKED
EXAMPLE **2.1**
•••••••••••••

Suppose the daily takings of a small corner shop are as shown below:

	Mon.	Tue.	Wed.	Thur.	Fri.
Daily sales	£620	£660	£600	£480	£710

Solution

Using the formula:

$$\bar{X} = \frac{\sum_{i=1}^{n} X_i}{5} = \frac{X_1 + X_2 + X_3 + X_4 + X_5}{5} = \frac{620 + 660 + 600 + 480 + 710}{5}$$

$$= \frac{3{,}070}{5} = £614$$

The average daily sales are £614 and this represents a typical figure around which the rest of the data will cluster.

Grouped data

More usually, as we noted in chapter 1, data are *grouped* into a frequency table with various class intervals. To deal with such data the simplifying assumption must be made that *within any given class interval* the items of data fall on the *class mid-point*. This is equivalent to assuming that the items of data are evenly spread within any given class interval.

We may now make use of the following formulae:

$$\bar{X} = \frac{\sum_{i=1}^{j} F_i X_i}{\sum_{i=1}^{j} F_i} = \frac{F_1 X_1 + F_2 X_2 + \dots F_j X_j}{F_1 + F_2 + \dots F_j}$$

where F_i = frequency of ith class interval
X_i = mid-point of ith class interval
j = number of class intervals

Suppose that a survey of the prices of 60 items sold in a shop gives the results below (five class intervals for prices):

Price of item (£)	Number of items sold
1.5–2.5	15
2.5–3.5	2
3.5–4.5	19
4.5–5.5	10
5.5–6.5	14

Solution

We can use our formula for grouped data to calculate the average (arithmetic mean) price of the items sold (see Table 2.1).

table 2.1
**The average
(arithmetic mean)
price of items sold**

Price of items (£)	Class mid-points X_i	Number of items sold F_i	F_iX_i
1.5–2.5	2	15	30
2.5–3.5	3	2	6
3.5–4.5	4	19	76
4.5–5.5	5	10	50
5.5–6.5	6	14	84
		$\sum\limits_{i=1}^{5}F_i = 60$	$\sum\limits_{i=1}^{5}F_iX_i = 246$

$$\bar{X} = \frac{\sum\limits_{i=1}^{5}F_iX_i}{\sum\limits_{i=1}^{5}F_i} = \frac{246}{60} = 4.1$$

In other words the average price of the items sold in the shop was £4.10 pence.

The median

This is that value which divides the data set into two equal halves; 50 per cent of values lying below the median, and 50 per cent of values lying above the median.

The approach we consider below uses *arithmetical* methods for estimating the median value for both grouped and ungrouped data.

Ungrouped data

To find the median:

(i) Construct an *array* (i.e. place the data in numerical order – whether rising or falling).

(ii) Find the median *position* $\dfrac{n+1}{2}$ where n = number of values.

(iii) Find the median *value*.

WORKED
EXAMPLE **2.3**
••••••••••••••

Find the median value of machine output over a five day period:

	Daily output			
310	340	360	320	330

Solution

Step 1 Place in an array 310 320 330 340 360.

Step 2 Find the median position using the equation $\dfrac{n+1}{2}$ where n = the number of values. Median position $= \dfrac{5+1}{2}$ = third item.

Step 3 Read the value of the third item in the array, i.e. 330 units.

Note: Where there is an *even* number of items there will be *two* middle items. If so, take the *average* of these two middle items.

Grouped data

The following steps can be used to calculate arithmetically the median value for data presented in a frequency table:

▶ Find the median *position*.
▶ Find the *class-interval* in which the median observation lies.
▶ Assume that all items in this class-interval are equally spaced.
▶ Estimate the median.

WORKED
EXAMPLE **2.4**
••••••••••••••

Find the median height of students from the data given in Table 2.2 (p. 34).

Solution

Median position $= \dfrac{n+1}{2}$

$\qquad\qquad = \dfrac{20+1}{2}$

$\qquad\qquad = 10.5$

The class interval in which this median position lies is 170–175.

table 2.2
The height of students

X_i Heights (cm)	F_i Frequency (number of students)
150 and under 155	1
155 and under 160	1
160 and under 165	2
165 and under 170	3
170 and under 175	6
175 and under 180	2
180 and under 185	4
185 and under 190	1
	20

The median value can be found using the formula:

$$\text{LCB} + \text{class width} \times \frac{\text{number of observations to median position}}{\text{total number of observations in median class interval}}$$

Where LCB = lower class boundary (of median class interval).

$$\text{Median} = 170 \text{ cm} + (5 \text{ cm} \times \frac{3.5}{6})$$

$$\text{Median} = 172.9 \text{ cm}$$

Figure 2.1 gives a visual picture of the use of our formula in finding the median height.

figure 2.1
Median class interval for table 2.2

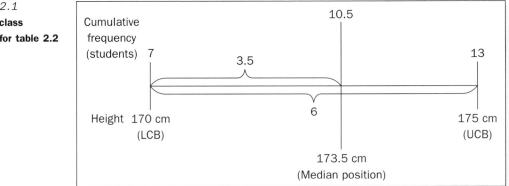

The class interval in which the median position falls has a lower class boundary (LCB) of 170 cm and an upper class boundary (UCB) of 175 cm, giving a *class width* of 5 cm. Now the cumulative frequency up to the LCB is seven students, which is less than the median position which occurs with a cumulative frequency of 10.5 students.

Clearly the median value is larger than 170 cm as we wish to go a further 3.5 students (observations) to reach the median position. However there are six students assumed to be equally spaced along this class interval of 5 cm. We therefore wish to go 3.5/6ths of the way along the 5 cm interval in order to find the median height. This gives the formula:

$$170 \text{ cm} + (5 \text{ cm} \times \frac{3.5}{6}) = 172.9 \text{ cm which we noted above.}$$

We have already noted in Chapter 1 (p. 12) how the use of *cumulative frequency curves* (or ogives) can help find the median value by *graphical* methods.

The mode

This is that value which occurs with greatest frequency. When data are grouped, then the *class interval* with the highest frequency is referred to as the modal class interval. In Table 2.2 above the class interval 170–175 cm is the modal class interval, with six students in the interval.

2.3 Normal and skewed distribution
....

When the set of data is distributed in a perfectly symmetrical way, as in Figure 2.2(a), then all three types of average have the same value. Such a symmetrical distribution is often referred to as a **normal distribution**. However when, as is more usually the case, the set of data is skewed in one direction or another, as in Figures 2.2(b) and (c), then the three types of average will cease to be identical. In fact the arithmetic mean will always be most heavily influenced by the direction of skew, i.e. the direction being described by the tail of the distribution, which represents the side of the distribution with fewest observations. In other words, the arithmetic mean will be most affected by a *few* extreme values, whether higher values (skewed to the right) or lower values (skewed to the left).

figure 2.2
Normal and skewed frequency distributions and measures of central location

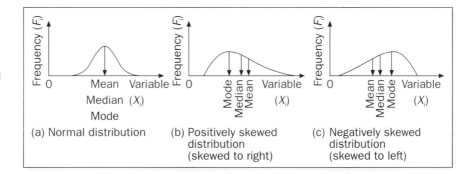

(a) Normal distribution

(b) Positively skewed distribution (skewed to right)

(c) Negatively skewed distribution (skewed to left)

When data are skewed to the right or left, you must be careful in interpreting any loose talk of 'average' values. For example if the distribution of wages in a firm is skewed to the right, as in Figure 2.2(b), the employers might claim an 'average' wage of, say, £180 per week and the trade union an 'average' wage of, say, £160 a week and both might be right! However the employers may be selecting the type of 'average' (arithmetic mean) most favourable to showing them as a high paying company and the union may be selecting the type of average (median) most favourable as a basis for pressing for higher wages.

PAUSE FOR THOUGHT 2.1 *In what direction would you expect the UK income distribution to be skewed? How might this affect median and mean incomes?*

WORKED
EXAMPLE **2.5**
....

The following distribution shows the weekly output of production workers in the company:

table 2.3
Weekly output of production workers

Output (units)	Number of employees
100–160	1
160–180	5
180–200	10
200–220	35
220–240	55
240–260	74
260–300	20
	200

(i)   Find the arithmetic mean of the weekly output.
(ii) Find the median weekly output.
(iii) Why do (i) and (ii) differ?

Solution

(i)   Since we are dealing with grouped data we must take *class mid-points* for the variable X_i. We then use the formula:

$$\bar{X} = \frac{\sum\limits_{i=1}^{j} F_i X_i}{\sum\limits_{i=1}^{j} F_i}$$

where F_i = class frequency
X_i = class mid-point
j = number of class intervals

X_i (class mid-points)	F_i (class frequency)	F_iX_i
130	1	130
170	5	850
190	10	1,900
210	35	7,350
230	55	12,650
250	74	18,500
280	20	5,600
	$\sum_{i=1}^{7} F_i = 200$	$\sum_{i=1}^{7} F_iX_i = 46,980$

$$\bar{X} = \frac{\sum_{i=1}^{7} F_iX_i}{\sum_{i=1}^{7} F_i} = \frac{46,980}{200} = 234.9$$

The arithmetic mean of the weekly output is 234.9 units.

(ii) The median position $= \dfrac{n+1}{2} = \dfrac{201}{2} = 100.5$ employees.

The median class interval for output is 220–240 units, as shown in Figure 2.3

figure 2.3

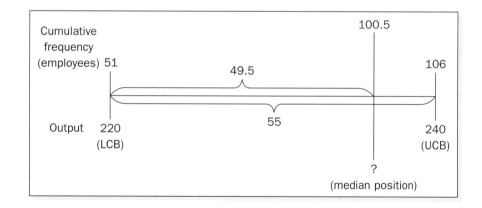

Using our formula for the median, and assuming an equal spacing of the 55 employees along the median class interval of 20 units of output, we have:

$$\text{LCB} + \text{class width} \times \frac{\text{number of observations to median position}}{\text{total number of observations in class interval}}$$

i.e.

$$\text{Median} = 220 + (20 \times \frac{49.5}{55}) = 238 \text{ units}$$

(iii) The arithmetical mean output (234.9 units) is lower than the median output (238 units). We would expect this to be the case since the data are clearly skewed to the left. It is similar to Figure 2.2(c) and the arithmetic mean (simple average) will be pulled down by the few extremely low values.

PAUSE FOR THOUGHT 2.2 *Before calculating the solution to Self-check question 2.6 below, look briefly at the table of data and decide on the direction of skew and the likely impact this will have on the mean and median values.*

SELF-CHECK QUESTIONS

2.4 Passenger cars produced for export (X_i) in thousands in each month during the past year were as follows:

| 69.3 | 75.5 | 76.3 | 94.4 | 88.7 | 77.2 | 86.4 | 75.5 | 79.0 | 83.3 | 82.2 | 78.1 |

(a) What is the value of X_i when:
  (i) $i = 4$
  (ii) $i = 7$
  (iii) $i = 10$
(b) What is the mean monthly production of cars?
(c) What is the mean monthly production of cars over the final six months?
(d) What is the mean monthly production of cars during months 4–9 inclusive?

2.5 The following figures show the annual salaries in £s of 20 workers in a small firm. Calculate the arithmetic mean, median and mode salary and comment on your results:

15,180	19,870	14,375	15,767	15,870	15,180	14,375	36,938
15,180	46,132	15,525	19,600	14,375	23,069	16,767	16,767
17,880	14,375	14,375	14,375

2.6 An investment analyst receives the following table of data showing the percentage changes in labour costs of senior managers in a multi-national company over a 12 month period. The highest change observed was + 172 per cent for a senior manager in one of the plants in Latin America.

Percentage change		Frequency
−5 to under	0	2
0 to under	5	32
5 to under	10	25
10 to under	15	10
15 to under	20	8
20 to under	25	3
25 to under	30	2
30 to under	35	5
35 to under	40	4
40 to under	100	3
100 to	172	4

(a) What is the mean annual percentage change in labour costs for senior managers in this company?

(b) What is the estimate of the median value?

(c) What is the modal class interval?

Note: Answers can be found on pp. 325–328.

2.4 Measures of dispersion

As well as measures of central tendency or average, it is helpful to have a measure of the extent of **dispersion** or spread around that average. The formulae and brief outlines for the most widely used measures of dispersion are presented here.

As we can see from Figure 2.4, two distributions showing the prices of items sold in a shop may have similar measures of central location but may be very different in terms of dispersion around any 'average'. Clearly distribution B is more widely dispersed than distribution A around the same arithmetic mean $\bar{X}$.

▶ **Range** Perhaps the simplest measure of dispersion is to take the absolute difference between the highest and lowest value of the raw data. In Figure 2.4 the range for distribution A is £30, but the range for distribution B is higher at £50.

▶ **Interquartile range** This is the absolute difference between the upper and lower quartiles of the distribution. We saw how to calculate these quartiles in Chapter 1, p. 12.

$$\text{Interquartile range} = \text{upper quartile} - \text{lower quartile}$$

figure 2.4
Same mean ($\bar{X}$), different dispersion for two distributions A and B

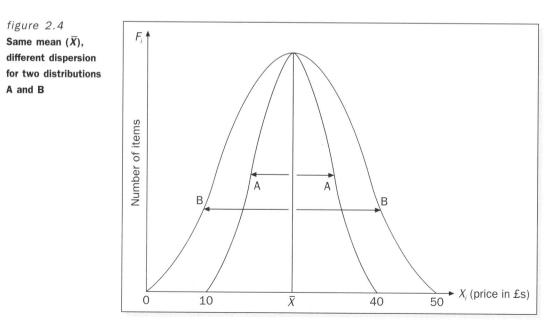

▶ **Semi-interquartile range** This is half the interquartile range. It is sometimes called the *quartile deviation*.

$$\text{Semi-interquartile range} = \frac{\text{upper quartile} - \text{lower quartile}}{2}$$

All the measures of dispersion considered so far have involved comparing two different points on the respective frequency distributions, such as the maximum and minimum points (the range) or the upper and lower quartiles (the interquartile range). We now turn to more useful measures of dispersion which compare *all* the points on the respective frequency distributions.

Mean deviation

This is the average of the absolute deviations from the arithmetic mean, ignoring the sign. Of course if we did *not* ignore the sign, the average deviation from the arithmetic mean would always be zero! When two straight lines (rather than curved brackets) surround a number or variable it is referred to as the *modulus* and means ignore the sign.

The mean deviation is only rarely used as a measure of dispersion. However it is worth some consideration as it is the basis for the more widely used measures of variance and standard deviation.

Ungrouped data

Suppose three throws of a dice yield the following values:

$X_1 = 2, X_2 = 4, X_3 = 3$

Clearly the arithmetic mean, $\bar{X}$, is 3. To find the **mean deviation** (MD) we need to find the average deviation from the mean, ignoring the sign:

$$\text{MD} = \frac{|X_1 - \bar{X}| + |X_2 - \bar{X}| + |X_3 - \bar{X}|}{n}$$

$$\text{MD} = \frac{|2 - 3| + |4 - 3| + |3 - 3|}{3} = \frac{|-1| + |+1| + |0|}{3} = \frac{2}{3}$$

On average, each score on the three throws of the dice is $\frac{2}{3}$ of a unit away from the average score of 3.

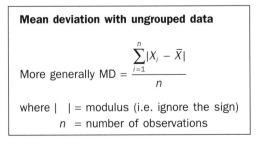

Mean deviation with ungrouped data

$$\text{More generally MD} = \frac{\sum\limits_{i=1}^{n} |X_i - \bar{X}|}{n}$$

where | | = modulus (i.e. ignore the sign)
   n = number of observations

Grouped data

If we return to our example of the prices of 60 items bought in a shop (Table 2.1), we can now use the mean deviation to give a measure of dispersion. We noted (p. 32) that the average price ($\bar{X}$) was £4.1 per item sold. We now apply the formula for mean deviation with grouped data:

Mean deviation with grouped data

$$MD = \frac{\sum_{i=1}^{j} F_i |X_i - \bar{X}|}{\sum_{i=1}^{j} F_i}$$

where F_i = class frequency
X_i = class mid-point
$\bar{X}$ = arithmetic mean
j = number of class intervals
$|\ \ |$ = modulus (i.e. ignore sign)

PAUSE FOR THOUGHT 2.3 *How might you expect the mean deviation for the age of the UK population to change over time?*

WORKED EXAMPLE **2.6**
••••••••••••••

Find the mean deviation for the data shown in Table 2.1 (p. 32).

Solution

Price of item (£)	Class mid-point X_i	Number of items F_i	$|X_i - \bar{X}|$	$F_i|X_i - \bar{X}|$
1.5–2.5	2	15	$|-2.1|$	$|-31.5|$
2.5–3.5	3	2	$|-1.1|$	$|-2.2|$
3.5–4.5	4	19	$|-0.1|$	$|-1.9|$
4.5–5.5	5	10	$|0.9|$	$|9.0|$
5.5–6.5	6	14	$|1.9|$	$|26.6|$
		60		71.2

Note: $\bar{X}$ = 4.1.

$$MD = \frac{\sum_{i=1}^{5} F_i |X_i - \bar{X}|}{\sum_{i=1}^{5} F_i} = \frac{71.2}{60} = 1.19$$

The average deviation from the arithmetic mean price is £1.19 per item.

Variance

If we square all the deviations from the arithmetic mean, then we no longer need to bother with the signs since all the values will be positive. We can then replace the straight line brackets (modulus) for the mean deviation with the more usual round brackets.

The resulting measure is now called the **variance**, which can then be regarded as the average of the *squared* deviations from the mean. Note that all the units are squared, e.g. square pounds, square metres, etc.

Ungrouped data

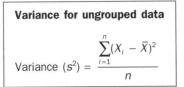

Variance for ungrouped data

$$\text{Variance } (s^2) = \frac{\sum\limits_{i=1}^{n}(X_i - \bar{X})^2}{n}$$

WORKED EXAMPLE **2.7**

Suppose we have to find the variance of the following eight items of raw data.

8, 10, 12, 14, 16, 18, 20, 22

Solution

$$\bar{X} = \frac{\sum\limits_{i=1}^{n}X_i}{n} = \frac{120}{8} = 15$$

X_i	$(X_i - \bar{X})$	$(X_i - \bar{X})^2$
8	(−7)	49
10	(−5)	25
12	(−3)	9
14	(−1)	1
16	(1)	1
18	(3)	9
20	(5)	25
22	(7)	49
		168

$$s^2 = \frac{\sum\limits_{i=1}^{8}(X_i - \bar{X})^2}{n} = \frac{168}{8} = 21 \text{ square units}$$

Variance (s^2) = 21 square units

Grouped data

The formula for calculating the variance when data are grouped is as follows:

Variance for grouped data

$$\text{Variance } (s^2) = \frac{\sum_{i=1}^{j} F_i (X_i - \bar{X})^2}{\sum_{i=1}^{j} F_i}$$

where F_i = class frequency
X_i = class mid-point
$\bar{X}$ = arithmetic mean
j = number of class intervals

However it can be shown (see p. 47) that this formula simplifies to the following:

Variance for grouped data: operational formula

$$\text{Variance } (s^2) = \frac{\sum_{i=1}^{j} F_i X_i^2}{\sum_{i=1}^{j} F_i} - \left(\frac{\sum_{i=1}^{j} F_i X_i}{\sum_{i=1}^{j} F_i} \right)^2$$

$$\text{Variance } (s^2) = \frac{\sum_{i=1}^{j} F_i X_i^2}{\sum_{i=1}^{j} F_i} - (\bar{X})^2$$

This is a useful formula for finding the *variance* since we will already have found the second term when calculating the *arithmetic mean*.

WORKED
EXAMPLE **2.8**
··············

Let us apply this formula to our earlier problem involving prices of items sold in Worked example 2.6.

Price of item (£)	Class mid-points X_i	Number of items F_i	$F_i X_i$	$F_i X_i^2$
1.5–2.5	2	15	30	60
2.5–3.5	3	2	6	18
3.5–4.5	4	19	76	304
4.5–5.5	5	10	50	250
5.5–6.5	6	14	84	504
		60	246	1,136

$$s^2 = \frac{\sum F_i X_i^2}{\sum F_i} - \left(\frac{\sum F_i X_i}{\sum F_i} \right)^2$$

$$s^2 = \frac{1{,}136}{60} - \left(\frac{246}{60}\right)^2 = 18.9 - (4.1)^2$$

$\underline{s^2 = 2.1 \text{ square pounds}}$

Note: $\displaystyle\sum_{i=1}^{j} F_i X_i^2 = F_1 X_1^2 + F_2 X_2^2 + \ldots F_j X_j^2$

In other words the square is only on the X_i term and *not* on $F_i X_i$.

We can obtain the column $F_i X_i^2$ by *either* multiplying the $F_i X_i$ column by the corresponding X_i *or* by multiplying the F_i column by the corresponding X_i^2. Check this yourself in the table above.

Standard deviation

Rather than use square units, it is more realistic to express solutions in terms of single units. The **standard deviation** does this by taking the square root of the variance.

The standard deviation (s) is then the square root of the average of the squared deviations from the mean. The following formula applies to both ungrouped and grouped data:

Standard deviation $= \sqrt{\text{variance}}$

i.e. $\qquad s \qquad = \sqrt{s^2}$

WORKED
EXAMPLE **2.9**
·············

We can use our earlier data on 20 student heights to illustrate the calculation of both the variance and the standard deviation as measures of dispersion.

Solution

Heights (cm)	Number F_i	Mid-points X_i	$F_i X_i$	$F_i X_i^2$
150 and under 155	1	152.5	152.5	23,256.25
155 and under 160	1	157.5	157.5	24,806.25
160 and under 165	2	162.5	325	52,812.50
165 and under 170	3	167.5	502.5	84,168.75
170 and under 175	6	172.5	1,035	178,537.50
175 and under 180	2	177.5	355	63,012.50
180 and under 185	4	182.5	730	133,225.00
185 and under 190	1	187.5	187.5	35,156.25
	20		3,445	594,975

$$\bar{X} = \frac{\displaystyle\sum_{i=1}^{8} F_i X_i}{\displaystyle\sum_{i=1}^{8} F_i} = \frac{3{,}445}{20} = 172.25 \text{ cm}$$

$$s^2 = \frac{\sum\limits_{i=1}^{8} F_i X_i^2}{\sum\limits_{i=1}^{8} F_i} - \left(\frac{\sum\limits_{i=1}^{8} F_i X_i}{\sum\limits_{i=1}^{8} F_i} \right)^2$$

$$s^2 = \frac{594{,}975}{20} - \left(\frac{3{,}445}{20} \right)^2$$

$s^2 = 29{,}748.75 - 29{,}670.06$

$s^2 =$ Variance $= 78.69$ square cm

$s =$ Standard deviation $= \sqrt{78.69}$

i.e. $s = 8.87$ cm

ACTIVITY 2

You have been commissioned by a manufacturing company to examine the potential of the Greek market. Part of the investigation requires work on the demography of Greece. Use a spreadsheet with which you are familiar to derive the following information and data. Here the formulae and functions are given in terms of *Microsoft Excel*.

1 Preparation

Type the following data and headings exactly as shown below

	A	B	C	D
1	**Greece: Population 1983–1996**			
2				
3	Area (sq km)	131,908		
4				
5		**population**	**% change**	**Pop. density**
6				
7	1983	9,642,505		
8	1984	9,729,350		
9	1985	9,789,513		
10	1986	9,846,627		
11	1987	9,895,801		
12	1988	9,934,249		
13	1989	9,963,604		
14	1990	9,983,490		
15	1991	10,004,401		
16	1992	10,038,672		
17	1993	10,088,700		
18	1994	10,200,000		
19	1995	10,311,300		
20	1996	10,422,600		

2 Calculate the percentage change in population

(a) Create a formula in **C8** (*not* **C7**) to give the percentage change of population from 1983 to 1984.

(b) Copy this formula down the column in order to calculate the percentage change for all the years up to and including 1996.

The formula in **C8** needs to be a relative reference (cell references that adjust when copied to new locations).

3 Calculate the population density

A In cell **D7** create a formula, by referencing cell **B3** to calculate the population per sq. km (population density). Before this formula is copied down make cell **B3** an absolute reference. Cell references in formulae must be made absolute if they are not to be adjusted when copied. To create an absolute cell reference in *Excel* do the following:

1 enter the formula in the usual way;

2 position the cursor within the formula bar to the right of the cell reference that is to be made absolute (it will change from a cross to an 'I' shape);

3 press the F4 key once and a $ sign will appear with the cell reference ($B$3).

B Copy the formula down the column.

A formula containing an absolute cell reference can be copied anywhere in the spreadsheet and it will continue to refer back to the absolute cell (in this case **B3**).

4 Construct a graph

Construct a graph showing both the population and the percentage change in population.

5 Calculate the mean percentage change in population for the period.

6 Estimate the future population

(a) Use the mean percentage change in population to estimate the population for 1997, 1998 and 1999.

(b) Put these projections on to your graph.

A response to this activity can be found on p. 461.

2.5 Coefficient of variation (CofV)
....

This is a widely used measure of *relative dispersion*. It relates an *absolute* measure of dispersion (the standard deviation) to the *absolute* value of the arithmetic mean around which the dispersion takes place. Clearly a data set A with a standard deviation (s) of ten units and mean ($\overline{X}$) of ten units has a *greater* relative dispersion than a data set B with a higher absolute standard deviation of 20 units but a still higher absolute mean ($\overline{X}$) of 50 units.

We would say that:

$$\text{C of V}_A = \frac{s}{\overline{X}} = \frac{10}{10} = 1.0$$

$$\text{C of V}_B = \frac{s}{\overline{X}} = \frac{20}{50} = 0.4$$

The coefficient of variation can be expressed (as here) as a decimal, or as a percentage. To obtain a percentage we simply multiply by 100, giving 100 per cent and 40 per cent for this example. The data set with the highest coefficient of variation has the greatest relative dispersion.

Proof of operational formula for variance

The formula for the variance (p. 43) can be made more useful by simplifying, as follows:

$$s^2 = \frac{\sum F_i (X_i - \bar{X})^2}{\sum F_i}$$

$$s^2 = \frac{\sum F_i (X_i^2 - 2X_i\bar{X} + \bar{X}^2)}{\sum F_i} \text{ (expanding the bracket)}$$

$$s^2 = \frac{\sum F_i X_i^2}{\sum F_i} - 2\bar{X}\frac{\sum F_i X_i}{\sum F_i} + \frac{\bar{X}^2 \sum F_i}{\sum F_i}$$

$$s^2 = \frac{\sum F_i X_i^2}{\sum F_i} - 2\bar{X}^2 + \bar{X}^2$$

$$s^2 = \frac{\sum F_i X_i^2}{\sum F_i} - \bar{X}^2$$

$$s^2 = \frac{\sum F_i X_i^2}{\sum F_i} - \left(\frac{\sum F_i X_i}{\sum F_i}\right)^2$$

SELF-CHECK QUESTIONS

2.7 Look back to the data in Self-check question 2.4 (p. 38). Find the variance and standard deviation for monthly production of passenger cars for export.

2.8 Look back to the data in Self-check question 2.6 (p. 38). Find the variance and standard deviation for the percentage change in labour costs of senior managers throughout the multinational company.

Note: **Answers can be found on p. 326.**

REVIEW QUESTIONS

2.1 A frozen food company has a contract with Farm A, to provide peas for their processing plant. The daily supply of peas (in tonnes) over the past two weeks from Farm A has been as follows:

Farm A

357.38 262.80 319.95 412.90 398.46 330.33 341.27
329.33 332.04 309.42 229.88 259.43 337.99 383.31

The frozen food company also contracts with Farm B, The daily supply of peas (in tonnes) over the past two weeks from Farm B has been as follows:

Farm B

364.32   295.18   352.92   380.14   314.39   343.87   290.43
291.21   306.03   348.88   333.81   291.99   324.79   315.25

Calculate the respective values for each farm in terms of:

(a) the mean;
(b) the range;
(c) the interquartile range;
(d) the semi-interquartile range.

Use your calculations to compare and contrast the relative contributions of each farm to the frozen food company.

2.2 Use the data for Farm A and Farm B in question 2.1 above to calculate the mean deviations for both data sets. What do your results show?

2.3 A company requires that chilled food cabinets in its supermarkets must maintain an average hourly temperature of 3.75°C ± 0.5°C. The manager at one of the supermarkets suspects that the performance of one of the shop's cabinets fails to meet this standard and therefore decides to monitor its performance hourly over a 30 day period with the following results:

Temperature (°C)	Frequency
0–1	1
1–2	11
2–3	123
3–4	322
5–5	223
6–6	39
6–7	1

Find the arithmetic mean hourly temperature and the mean deviation (for grouped data) to assess whether the equipment conforms to the company's policy.

2.4 The number of visitors, in thousands, to an amusement park over a summer season were recorded as follows:

Visitors (000)	Frequency
6–8	4
8–10	17
10–12	61
12–14	47
14–16	18
16–18	3

Calculate the mean attendance during the summer season and the variance and standard deviation for that attendance. Comment on your results.

2.5 A new production line had a mean daily rejection rate of 196 units with a standard deviation of 21.48 units in the first three months of operation. In the next three months the mean daily rejection rate was 94 units with a standard deviation of 12.62 units. Find the coefficient of variation in each case and use it to comment on the relative dispersion of the production line over the two time periods.

2.6 A brewing company wishes to launch a new canned lager. It has close links with a major supermarket chain which will only permit a promotion of the lager in two of its stores. The selected stores monitor their sales of all brands of canned lager over a weekend period with the following results, which were communicated to the brewery:

Sales value of lager (£)	Frequency	
	Store A	Store B
0–2.5	27	1
2.5–5	114	3
5–7.5	333	31
7.5–10	530	142
10–12.5	504	328
12.5–15	334	498
15–17.5	121	504
17.5–20	29	351
20–22.5	5	110
22.5–25	2	29
25–27.5	1	3
	2,000	2,000

What advice would you give the management of the brewery on the differences and similarities in the pattern of expenditure in stores A and B. You may wish to consider:

(a) Illustrating the data graphically – using the same axes for each store.
(b) The mean consumer expenditure in each store.
(c) The variability of customer expenditure.
(d) Which supermarket provides the best opportunity for a successful promotion of the new lager.

Answers to Review questions can be found on pp. 384–392.

Further study and data

Texts

Bancroft, G. and O'Sullivan, G. (1993), *Quantitative methods for accounting and business studies*, 3rd edn, McGraw Hill, chapter 8.

Curwin, J. and Slater, R. (1996), *Quantitative methods for business decisions*, 4th edn, Chapman and Hall, chapters 3 and 4.

Lawson, M., Hubbard, S. and Pugh, P. (1995), *Maths and statistics for business*, Addison Wesley Longman, chapter 3.

Morris, C. (1996), *Quantitative approaches in business studies*, 4th edn, Pitman, chapter 6.

Oakshott, L. (1996), *Essential elements of business statistics*, BPP, chapter 2.

Swift, L. (1997), *Mathematics and statistics for business, management and finance*, Macmillan, part C1.

Thomas, R. (1997), *Quantitative methods for business studies*, Prentice Hall, chapter 1.

Waters, D. (1997), *Quantitative methods*, 2nd edn, Addison Wesley Longman, chapter 5.

Wisniewski, M. with Stead, R. (1996), *Foundation quantitative methods for business*, Pitman, chapter 7.

Sources of information and data

See list at end of Chapter 1, p. 25.

CHAPTER 3

Regression and correlation

Objectives
············

By the end of this chapter you should be able to:

▶ calculate the unique 'line of best fit' (**least squares line**) between a dependent variable (Y) and an independent variable (X). In other words you should be able to find the equation of that unique line $Y = mX + c$ which minimises the sum of squared deviations from the line. This is sometimes called the linear regression line.

▶ calculate the **coefficient of determination (R^2)** and Pearson's **coefficient of correlation (R)** between the two variables, thereby helping to establish the 'goodness of fit' of your least squares line.

▶ calculate and interpret Spearman's '**coefficient of rank correlation**'. This seeks to establish whether or not there is a strong linear relationship between two sets of ranked data.

▶ appreciate the approach to finding the regression line (linear or non-linear) which best fits more than two variables. In other words be broadly familiar with the techniques and problems of **multiple regression analysis**.

Introduction
···············

Business activity is an aggregate of tens of thousands of decisions taken daily by small and large firms alike. Decisions bring about change and, hopefully, such change will benefit the firm and the wider economy. For example, 'If I spend more on advertising, sales volume will grow', 'If I invest in the latest equipment, productivity will increase'.

The cornerstone of many of these expectations is usually past experience by the firm in question, or the widely reported experiences of other firms. Of course we can be more confident that the expected outcome will in fact occur, if it is supported by the recorded experiences of a *large number* of decision takers.

The statistical techniques of regression and correlation are important in helping determine whether such relationships can be established. Usually the firm is interested in whether changing some independent variable (say advertising) will have the desired effect on some dependent variable (say sales volume). As we shall see, the section on **regression** will help us identify the equation of the line or curve which 'best fits' the recorded data, often displayed in the form of a scatter diagram. The section on **correlation** will help us determine 'how well' that line or curve actually fits that recorded data.

Throughout this chapter we shall present two alternative approaches to calculation. The first will use the *original data* for the dependent and independent variables, Y and X respectively. The second will use *redefined data* for these variables, giving us the opportunity to use much simpler 'coding formulae' for our calculations. Although both approaches will be presented, you can concentrate on that approach followed by your lecture course (or the approach you find the easiest!)

Answers to the 'Self-check question', responses to each 'Pause for thought' and answers to the 'Review questions' can be found at the end of the book.

3.1 Regression analysis
· ·

Regression analysis involves establishing a relationship between two or more variables. Here we initially illustrate in terms of a *linear* relationship, although more sophisticated approaches can establish similar *non-linear* relationships. In 'simple' regression analysis we assume two variables only, Y the dependent variable and X the independent variable.

Simple linear regression

We consider the equation of a straight line (linear equation) in more detail in Appendix 1 (p. 306). Here we note that the general equation of a straight line is:

$$Y = mX + c$$
where Y = dependent variable
X = independent variable
m = gradient of the line
c = point where the line intersects the Y axis

Figure 3.1 shows a scatter diagram with dots representing the different co-ordinates (X,Y) plotted on the diagram. Our aim is to find an estimated line $(\hat{Y} = mX + c)$ which best fits the data. We use the symbol $\hat{Y}$ to refer to the *estimated* value of Y from the least squares line.

figure 3.1
Finding the least squares line (LSL)
$\hat{Y} = mX + c$

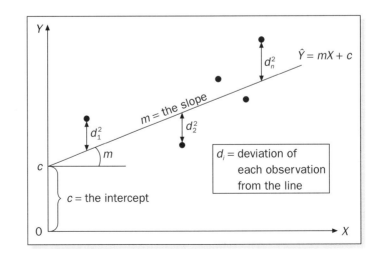

One possibility would be to find that line which minimises the sum of deviations (d_i) of each observation from the line. However some observations would have positive deviations (above the line) and some would have negative deviations (below the line). We would then be faced with the same problem noted in Chapter 2 for the mean deviation (p. 40) of identifying these signs ± and then ignoring them (i.e. taking the *modulus*). It is much easier to *square* all these deviations so that all the signs will be positive.

We shall therefore use the least squares line as our line of best fit, i.e. that (straight) line which minimises the sum of the squared deviations of the actual observations from the line.

In other words the least squares line is that (unique) line for which:

$d_1^2 + d_2^2 + \ldots d_n^2$ is a minimum.

In terms of Figure 3.1, the least squares line will be such that $\sum_{i=1}^{n} d_i^2$ is a minimum.

The slope(m) and intercept (c) of this unique line can be found using *either* of the following two approaches. In each case the formula outlined is obtained via differentiating expressions in order to find those values of m and c which will minimise the sum of squared deviations from the (straight) line containing those values. Proofs of these formulae can be found elsewhere (see 'Further study', p. 76).

Here we present both types of approach in solving regression problems. Remember to use the approach followed by your course or the approach you find the easiest.

Approach 1: Using original data (X, Y)

If we use the data given in the question as they stand (*original data*), then the following formulae will help us calculate m and c for the least squares line. These formulae make use of the sigma notation discussed in Chapter 2, p. 28.

Original data formulae

$$m = \frac{n\sum_{i=1}^{n} X_i Y_i - \sum_{i=1}^{n} X_i \sum_{i=1}^{n} Y_i}{n\sum_{i=1}^{n} X_i^2 - \left(\sum_{i=1}^{n} X_i\right)^2}$$

$$c = \bar{Y} - m\bar{X}$$

where n = number of observations
$\bar{X}, \bar{Y}$ = Arithmetic means of X_i, Y_i

WORKED
EXAMPLE **3.1**
················

Suppose we wish to calculate the least squares line for the four observations shown on the scatter diagram (Figure 3.2a).

figure 3.2

Using original data
(X_i, Y_i) to calculate
least squares line

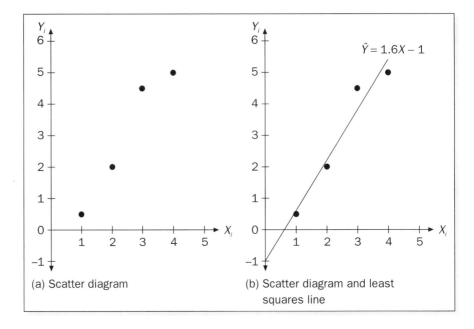

(a) Scatter diagram

(b) Scatter diagram and least
squares line

Solution

We can set the data out in the columns needed to calculate m and c using the above formulae, as follows:

X_i	Y_i	X_iY_i	X_i^2
1	0.5	0.5	1
2	2	4	4
3	4.5	13.5	9
4	5	20	16
$\Sigma X = 10$	$\Sigma Y = 12$	$\Sigma XY = 38$	$\Sigma X^2 = 30$

Note: For simplicity we omit subscripts, etc. in the formulae.

$n = 4$ observations

$$\bar{X} = \frac{\Sigma X}{n} = \frac{10}{4} = 2.5$$

$$\bar{Y} = \frac{\Sigma Y}{n} = \frac{12}{4} = 3$$

$$m = \frac{n\sum XY - \sum X \sum Y}{n\sum X^2 - \left(\sum X\right)^2}$$

$$m = \frac{4(38) - (10)(12)}{4(30) - (10)^2} = \frac{152 - 120}{120 - 100} = \frac{32}{20} = 1.6$$

$$m = 1.6$$

$$c = \bar{Y} - m\bar{X}$$

i.e. $c = 3 - 1.6\ (2.5)$

$c = 3 - 4$

$c = -1$

i.e. $\hat{Y} = 1.6X - 1$

Here the least squares line has a gradient (m) of +1.6, in other words the estimated value of Y is rising by 1.6 units for every 1 unit rise in X. The intercept (c) on the vertical axis is −1, in other words when X is 0 the estimated value of Y is −1. This least squares line is plotted in Figure 3.2(b).

Approach 2: Using redefined data

This approach can be missed out if your course uses Approach 1. In this case move directly to p. 57.

Rather simpler coding formulae can be derived using the fact that the regression (least squares) line must go through the point of means $(\bar{X}, \bar{Y})$. For those interested, this fact is explained in selected sources in 'Further study' (p. 76). We can usefully redefine the origin from zero to the point of means $(\bar{X}, \bar{Y})$, as in Figure 3.3, and use the resulting new axes (x_i, y_i) as the basis for our coding formulae. We can then calculate m at this new origin $(\bar{X}, \bar{Y})$ more easily since the least squares line *goes through* the point of means $(\bar{X}, \bar{Y})$ so that we no longer have any problem in calculating the vertical intercept at this origin. Of course we can then go back to the 'true' zero origin and find c once we have found m at the new origin $(\bar{X}, \bar{Y})$.

If we use the *redefined data* for $x_i(X_i - \bar{X})$ and $y_i(Y_i - \bar{Y})$, then the following formulae will help us calculate m and c for the least squares line.

Coding formulae

Here we change the origin from zero to the point of means $(\bar{X}, \bar{Y})$ and express new axes and data, $x_i\ (X_i - \bar{X})$ and $y_i\ (Y_i - \bar{Y})$

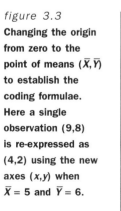

figure 3.3

Changing the origin from zero to the point of means $(\bar{X}, \bar{Y})$ to establish the coding formulae. Here a single observation (9,8) is re-expressed as (4,2) using the new axes (x,y) when $\bar{X} = 5$ and $\bar{Y} = 6$.

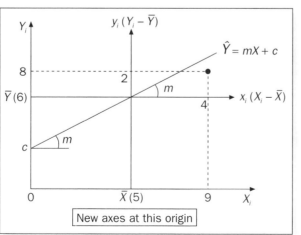

$$m = \frac{\sum_{i=1}^{n} x_i y_i}{\sum_{i=1}^{n} x_i^2}$$

$$c = \bar{Y} - m\bar{X}$$

Having calculated m (the slope of the least squares line) at the new origin $(\bar{X}, \bar{Y})$ we revert to the zero origin to calculate c (the intercept). The slope, m, is of course identical at each of these origins for the linear least squares line.

Let us follow through our previous worked example, but this time using *redefined data*. The two approaches should give us the same result. Let us check that this is the case!

WORKED
EXAMPLE **3.2**
·············
Calculate the least squares line for the same four observations shown on the scatter diagram in Figure 3.2a (p. 54).

Solution

Here we use the new origin $(\bar{X}, \bar{Y})$, namely (2.5,3) and *redefine* the data using the axes x_i $(X_i - 2.5)$ and y_i $(Y_i - 3)$.

figure 3.4
Using redefined data
($x_i y_i$) to calculate
the least squares
line

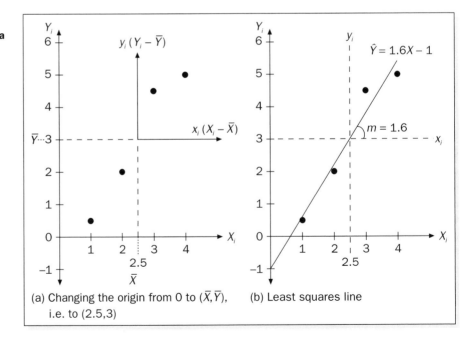

(a) Changing the origin from 0 to $(\bar{X}, \bar{Y})$, i.e. to (2.5,3)

(b) Least squares line

We can set the data out in the columns needed to calculate m and c using the coding formula for redefined data, as follows:

X_i	Y_i	x_i $(X_i - \bar{X})$	y_i $(Y_i - \bar{Y})$	$x_i y_i$	x_i^2
1	0.5	−1.5	−2.5	3.75	2.25
2	2	−0.5	−1	0.50	0.25
3	4.5	0.5	1.5	0.75	0.25
4	5	1.5	2	3.00	2.25
$\sum X = 10$	$\sum Y = 12$			$\sum xy = 8.00$	$\sum x^2 = 5.00$

$$\bar{X} = \frac{\sum X}{4} = \frac{10}{4} = 2.5$$

$$\bar{Y} = \frac{\sum Y}{4} = \frac{12}{4} = 3$$

$$m = \frac{\sum xy}{\sum x^2}$$

$$m = \frac{8.00}{5.00} = 1.6$$

$$\underline{m = 1.6}$$

We have now calculated m for the least squares line at the new origin, which is of course the same as m at the 'true' zero origin. We now revert to the zero origin to find c, the vertical intercept.

$$c = \bar{Y} - m\bar{X}$$

i.e. $c = 3 - 1.6(2.5)$
$c = 3 - 4$

$$\underline{c = -1}$$

i.e. $\underline{\hat{Y} = 1.6X - 1}$

We have the same result for the least squares line as in Approach 1, using the same data in each case. Clearly these two approaches are alternatives, yielding the same results.

DID YOU KNOW?

The founder of the 'least squares' regression technique was a French mathematician, Adrien-Marie Legendre. Born in 1752, he was awarded degrees in mathematics and physics. Having lost his wealth in the French Revolution in 1789 he was forced to 'work' for a living, lecturing in maths in Paris, working at the Greenwich Observatory in London and writing books. He developed the least squares technique in 1805, which was further developed by UK statistician Rober Gauss.

Prediction

Of course, once we have obtained our estimated least squares line we can use it for **prediction (forecasting)**. We can insert values of the independent variable (X_i) not yet experienced and predict values of the dependent variable (Y_i). Of course the confidence we can have in any such prediction will depend upon:

▶ the past relationship between Y and X continuing into the future,
▶ the estimated least squares line ($\hat{Y}$) fitting the past data rather well.

We return to the 'goodness of fit' of the least squares line in the next section. In our previous example we could substitute the value $X_i = 10$ into our equation:

$\hat{Y} = 1.6X - 1$
$\hat{Y} = 1.6(10) - 1$
$\hat{Y} = 16 - 1 = 15$

Hence our predicted value for Y is 15, should X be given the value of 10. We consider forecasting in more detail in Chapter 4.

PAUSE FOR THOUGHT 3.1 *Under what circumstances would you be reasonably confident in using your least squares line for prediction? Can you think of any problems that might arise to make these predictions unreliable?*

SELF-CHECK QUESTIONS

3.1 (a) Use the data below to create a scatter diagram.

X	1	2	3	4	5	6	7	8
Y	2	5	6	7	9	12	15	16

(b) Find the regression line relating Y (as dependent variable) to X (as independent variable).

(c) Comment on your results.

3.2 (a) Use the data below to create a scatter diagram.

X	1	2	3	4	5	6	7	8	9	10
Y	19	18	16	16	20	13	6	6	11	9

(b) Find the regression line relating Y (as dependent variable) to X (as independent variable).

(c) Comment on your results.

3.3 Find the 'line of best fit' (least squares line) for the following data.

X	4	5	6	12	13	13	16	16	17	17	18	19
Y	47	111	124	240	211	205	276	305	309	302	259	334

X	20	22	24
Y	302	371	241

Note: Answers can be found on pp. 328–331.

3.2 Correlation

The idea here is to measure how well the regression line fits the actual data. Two key measures are frequently used in this respect.

▶ the coefficient of determination (R^2)
▶ Pearson's coefficient of correlation (R)

figure 3.5

Deviation for each observation (d_i) is the actual value (Y_i) minus the arithmetic mean ($\bar{Y}$). This can be split into two parts: explained deviation (d_e) and unexplained deviation (d_u)

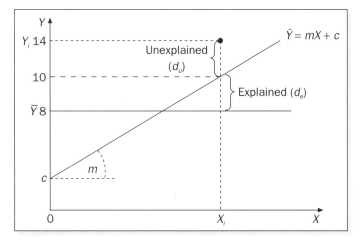

Before considering *formulae* for calculating these measures, it will be helpful to define the concepts of deviation and variation which underpin them. Figure 3.5 will be used for illustration.

Deviation (d_i) is the difference between the actual value of an observation (Y_i) and its arithmetic mean ($\bar{Y}$). This deviation can be split into two separate parts. An explained part (d_e) which is predicted or accounted for by the regression line. An unexplained part (d_u) which is *not* predicted or accounted for by the regression line.

Deviation = $d_i = Y_i - \bar{Y}$
Deviation = explained deviation + unexplained deviation
Deviation = $d_i = d_e + d_u$

Summing such deviations across all *n* observations gives *total deviation*.

$$\sum_{i=1}^{n} d_i = \sum_{i=1}^{n} d_e + \sum_{i=1}^{n} d_u$$

i.e. total deviation $=$ explained deviation $+$ unexplained deviation

Variation (d_i^2) is the square of the difference between the actual value of an observation (Y_i) and its arithmetic mean ($\bar{Y}$). As before, squaring the deviations avoids the problem of first identifying, then dropping the sign $\pm$ of each deviation.

Summing the squared deviations across all *n* observations gives *total variation*.
  It can be shown that:

$$\sum_{i=1}^{n} d_i^2 = \sum_{i=1}^{n} d_e^2 + \sum_{i=1}^{n} d_u^2$$

i.e. total variation $=$ explained variation $+$ unexplained variation

figure 3.6

Coefficient of determination (R^2)

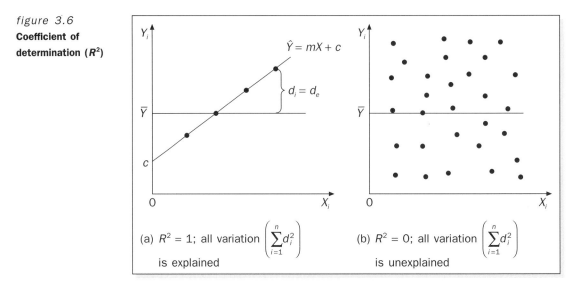

(a) $R^2 = 1$; all variation $\left(\sum\limits_{i=1}^{n} d_i^2\right)$ is explained

(b) $R^2 = 0$; all variation $\left(\sum\limits_{i=1}^{n} d_i^2\right)$ is unexplained

PAUSE FOR THOUGHT 3.2 *How does* total variation *differ from the* variance *discussed in Chapter 2?*

Coefficient of determination (R^2)

$$R^2 = \frac{\text{explained variation}}{\text{total variation}}$$

The **coefficient of determination** (R^2) is the ratio of 'explained variation' to 'total variation'. Clearly when $R^2 = 1$ as in Figure 3.6a, then all the deviation and therefore variation can be explained or accounted for by the regression line. We have a perfect fit.

Similarly when $R^2 = 0$ (or close to 0) as in Figure 3.6b, none of the deviation and therefore variation can be explained or accounted for by the regression line. We effectively have a random scatter of points to which any regression line fits as well as any other. ·

The closer R^2 is to 1, the better the fit of the least squares line to the actual data.

Pearson's coefficient of correlation (R)

$$R = \sqrt{\frac{\text{explained variation}}{\text{total variation}}}$$

Pearson's coefficient of correlation (R) is the square root of the coefficient of determination (R^2)

Just as R^2 varies between 1 and 0, so R varies between ±1 and 0. 'Perfect correlation' implies a value for R of +1 when the relationship between Y and X is direct, and −1 when the relationship between Y and X is indirect (inverse).

figure 3.7
**Coefficient of
correlation (*R*)**

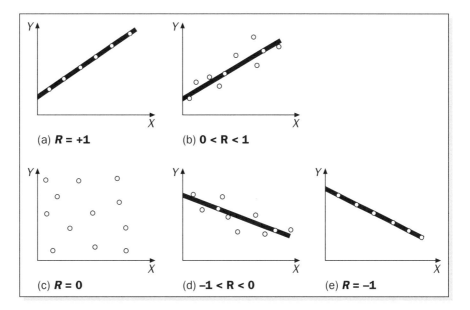

Figure 3.7 outlines the various possible values for *R*, the coefficient of correlation. This is often called Pearson's coefficient of correlation and can have values between +1 and –1.

(a) **R = +1**

This is perfect positive correlation. Here the relationship between *Y* and *X* is direct (positive), as both variables rise or fall together. The sign for *R* is therefore positive, and the value is +1 since the fit of the least squares line is perfect (all the variation is explained).

(b) **R > 0 but < 1**

Again a direct (positive) relationship between *Y* and *X*, so the sign is positive for *R*. Value for *R* is < 1, since not all of the variation is explained.

(c) **R = 0 (random scatter)**

Essentially no relationship between *Y* and *X*. All the variation is unexplained.

(d) **R < 0 but > –1**

Here the relationship between *Y* and *X* is indirect (negative or inverse) as each variable moves in the opposite direction; when one variable rises the other falls, and vice verse. The sign for *R* is therefore negative but the value is greater than –1 since not all of the variation is explained.

(e) **R = –1**

This is perfect negative correlation. The relationship between *Y* and *X* is indirect (negative or inverse) and the value is –1 since the fit of the least squares line is perfect (all the variation is explained).

DID YOU KNOW?

The easiest way to interpret the meaning of a particular value of R, the Pearson coefficient of correlation, is to square it. For example a value R = +0.8 means that $R^2 = (+0.8)^2 = 0.64$, i.e. 64 per cent of total variation can be 'explained' or accounted for by your regression line.

Calculating R^2 and R

As when calculating the least squares line, two alternative approaches can be used to derive formulae for calculating R^2 and R. Be consistent, and follow the same approach here as you have done for calculating the regression line.

Approach 1: Using original data (X,Y)

Finding R^2 and R using original data

$$R^2 = \left[\frac{n\sum_{i=1}^{n}X_iY_i - \sum_{i=1}^{n}X_i\sum_{i=1}^{n}Y_i}{\sqrt{\left[n\sum_{i=1}^{n}X_i^2 - \left(\sum_{i=1}^{n}X_i\right)^2 \right] \times \left[n\sum_{i=1}^{n}Y_i^2 - \left(\sum_{i=1}^{n}Y_i\right)^2 \right]}} \right]^2$$

where n = number of observations

$$R = \sqrt{R^2}$$

WORKED
EXAMPLE **3.3**
....

Here we apply our formula to the data and calculations already presented on p. 54. We reproduce this below, noting that we need an *extra column* for Y_i^2.

X_i	Y_i	X_iY_i	X_i^2	Y_i^2
1	0.5	0.5	1	0.25
2	2	4	4	4
3	4.5	13.5	9	20.25
4	5	20	16	25
$\sum X = 10$	$\sum Y = 12$	$\sum XY = 38$	$\sum X^2 = 30$	$\sum Y^2 = 49.50$

$$R^2 = \left[\frac{4(38) - (10)(12)}{\sqrt{\left[4(30) - (10)^2\right] \times \left[4(49.5) - (12)^2\right]}} \right]^2$$

$$R^2 = \left[\frac{152 - 120}{\sqrt{\left[120 - 100\right] \times \left[198 - 144\right]}} \right]^2$$

$$R^2 = \left[\frac{32}{\sqrt{20 \times 54}} \right]^2 = \left[\frac{32}{\sqrt{1080}} \right]^2 = \left[\frac{32}{32.86} \right]^2$$

$$R^2 = 0.948$$

In other words 0.948 or, as a percentage, 94.8 per cent of the total variation is 'explained' or accounted for by our regression line. This indicates a very good fit of our least squares line to the data, giving us greater confidence should we use our regression line for prediction (forecasting).

Approach 2: Using redefined data

Alternatively, we can transfer the origin from zero to the point of means $(\overline{X},\overline{Y})$ and use a coding formula for R^2 and R. In this case we make use of new axes $x_i = X_i - \overline{X}$, $y_i = Y_i - \overline{Y}$.

Finding R^2 and R using the coding formula

Here we can make use of calculations already undertaken in finding m and c for the regression line $Y = mX + c$ when using the coding formula

$$R^2 = \frac{\left[\sum_{i=1}^{n} x_i y_i\right]^2}{\left[\sum_{i=1}^{n} x_i^2\right]\left[\sum_{i=1}^{n} y_i^2\right]}$$

where $x_i = X_i - \overline{X}$
$y_i = Y_i - \overline{Y}$

$$R = \sqrt{R^2}$$

WORKED
EXAMPLE **3.4**
• • • • • • • • • • • • • • •

Here we apply our coding formula to the data and calculations already presented on p. 57. We reproduce this below, noting that this time we need an *extra column* for y_i^2.

Solution

X_i	Y_i	x_i $(X_i - \overline{X})$	y_i $(Y_i - \overline{Y})$	$x_i y_i$	x_i^2	y_i^2
1	0.5	−1.5	−2.5	3.75	2.25	6.25
2	2	−0.5	−1	0.50	0.25	1
3	4.5	0.5	1.5	0.75	0.25	2.25
4	5	1.5	2	3.00	2.25	4
$\sum X = 10$	$\sum Y = 12$			$\sum xy = 8.00$	$\sum x^2 = 5.00$	$\sum y^2 = 13.50$

$$\overline{X} = \frac{\sum X}{4} = \frac{10}{4} = 2.5$$

$$\overline{Y} = \frac{\sum Y}{4} = \frac{12}{4} = 3$$

Using our coding formula

$$R^2 = \frac{\left[\sum xy\right]^2}{\left[\sum x^2\right]\left[\sum y^2\right]} = \frac{(8.00)^2}{(5.00)(13.50)} = \frac{64.00}{67.50} = 0.948$$

$$\underline{R^2 = 0.948}$$

Again, note that either approach will give the same solution.

WORKED
EXAMPLE **3.5**
• • • • • • • • • • • • • •

The following worked example uses *both* approaches to calculate the regression line and the coefficients of determination and correlation for a data set containing six observations.

Approach 1 solution: Using original data

X_i	Y_i	X_iY_i	X_i^2	Y_i^2
0	−4	0	0	16
1	−3	−3	1	9
2	−1	−2	4	1
3	2	6	9	4
4	3	12	16	9
5	6	30	25	36
$\sum X = 15$	$\sum Y = 3$	$\sum XY = 43$	$\sum X^2 = 55$	$\sum Y^2 = 75$

$$m = \frac{n\sum XY - \sum X\sum Y}{n\sum X^2 - \left(\sum X\right)^2} \qquad\qquad c = \bar{Y} - m\bar{X}$$

$$\bar{Y} = 0.5, \quad \bar{X} = 2.5$$

$$m = \frac{6(43) - (15)(3)}{6(55) - (15)^2} = \frac{258 - 45}{330 - 225} = \frac{213}{105} \qquad c = 0.5 - 2.03(2.5)$$

$$\underline{m = +2.03} \qquad\qquad\qquad\qquad \underline{c = -4.6}$$

$$\underline{\hat{Y} = 2.03X - 4.6}$$

$$R^2 = \left[\frac{n\sum XY - \sum X\sum Y}{\sqrt{\left[n\sum X^2 - \left(\sum X\right)^2\right] \times \left[n\sum Y^2 - \left(\sum Y\right)^2\right]}}\right]^2$$

$$R^2 = \left[\frac{6(43) - (15)(3)}{\sqrt{\left[6(55) - (15)^2\right] \times \left[6(75) - (3)^2\right]}}\right]^2$$

$$R^2 = \left[\frac{258 - 45}{\sqrt{\left[105\right] \times \left[441\right]}}\right]^2$$

$$R^2 = \left[\frac{213}{\sqrt{46{,}305}} \right]^2$$

$$R^2 = \left[\frac{213}{215.2} \right]^2$$

$$\underline{R^2 = 0.98}$$

$$R = \sqrt{0.98}$$

$$\underline{R = 0.99}$$

PAUSE FOR THOUGHT 3.3   *Plot the scatter diagram from the data for this Worked example. Now impose the least squares line on your scatter diagram. Would you have expected to find a high R^2?*

Approach 2 solution: Using redefined data

X_i	Y_i	x_i $(X_i - \bar{X})$	y_i $(Y_i - \bar{Y})$	$x_i y_i$	x_i^2	y_i^2
0	−4	−2.5	−4.5	11.25	6.25	20.25
1	−3	−1.5	−3.5	5.25	2.25	12.25
2	−1	−0.5	−1.5	0.75	0.25	2.25
3	2	0.5	1.5	0.75	0.25	2.25
4	3	1.5	2.5	3.75	2.25	6.25
5	6	2.5	5.5	13.75	6.25	30.25
$\Sigma X = 15$	$\Sigma Y = 3$			$\Sigma xy = 35.5$	$\Sigma x^2 = 17.50$	$\Sigma y^2 = 73.50$
$\bar{X} = 2.5$	$\bar{Y} = 0.5$					

$$m = \frac{\Sigma xy}{\Sigma x^2} \qquad c = \bar{Y} - m\bar{X} \qquad R^2 = \frac{\left(\Sigma x_i y_i \right)^2}{\left(\Sigma x_i^2 \right)\left(\Sigma y_i^2 \right)}$$

$$m = \frac{35.5}{17.5} \qquad c = 0.5 - (2.03)2.5 \qquad R^2 = \frac{1{,}260.25}{1{,}286.25}$$

$$R^2 = 0.98$$

$$\underline{m = 2.03} \qquad \underline{c = -4.6}$$

$$R = \sqrt{0.98}$$

$$\underline{\hat{Y} = 2.03X - 4.6} \qquad \underline{R = 0.99}$$

ACTIVITY 3

The intention here is to derive a regression (least squares) line relating the population of Greece (Y) to time (X). This is important to the long-term planning of our company which sees Greece as a major export market.

You can use the data of Activity 2 (Chapter 2, pp. 45–46) and a spreadsheet with which you are familiar. The approach used involves the coding formula (see p. 55). You can solve either from first principles or use the in-built functions of your spreadsheet.

Solving from first principles

1 Set up your worksheet as follows:

Either load your original data of the Greek population – from Activity 2 (Chapter 2, pp. 45–46) and copy the data from your original sheet to a new clean sheet or re-enter the data into a new spreadsheet. You should end up with something similar to Figure A3.1 but without the formulae.

figure A3.1

	A	B	C	D	E	F	G	H	I
1									
2			Xbar	Ybar		m (slope)	c (intercept)		R^2
3			=AVERAGE(C6:C19)	→		=G20/H20	=D3–(F3*C3)		=G20^2/(H20*I20)
4			X	Y					
5		y hat	year	population	xi	yi	xiyi	xi^2	yi^2
6		=$G$3+($F$3*C6)	1983	9,642,505	=C6–$C$3	=D6–$D$3	=E6*F6	=E6^2	=F6^2
7			1984	9,729,350					
8			1985	9,789,513					
9			1986	9,846,627					
10			1987	9,895,801					
11			1988	9,934,249					
12			1989	9,963,604					
13			1990	9,983,490					
14			1991	10,004,401					
15			1992	10,038,672					
16			1993	10,088,700					
17			1994	10,200,000					
18			1995	10,311,300					
19			1996	10,422,600	▼	▼	▼	▼	▼
20			1997			Sums	=SUM(G6:G19)		→
21			1998						
22		▼	1999						

2 Find the value of m (slope)

$$m = \frac{\sum\limits_{i=1}^{n} x_i y_i}{\sum\limits_{i=1}^{n} x_i^2}$$

(a) In cells **C3 & D3** find the mean of the X and Y values.
(b) In cell **E6** calculate x_i – where $x_i = X_i - \bar{X}$.
(c) In cell **F6** calculate y_i where $y_i = Y_i - \bar{Y}$.
(d) In cell **G6** multiply x_i by y_i.
(e) In cell **H6** square x_i.

(f) Highlight cells **E6 to H6** and copy the formulae down to **Row 19**.

(g) In cell **G20 & H20** find the sums of $x_i y_i$ and x_i^2.

(h) In cell **F3** calculate m by dividing the sum of $x_i y_i$ by the sum of x_i^2.

3 *Find the value of c (intercept) where:* $c = \overline{Y} - m\overline{X}$.

Your table already contains all the values needed to substitute in the above equation, therefore, enter the formula in Figure A3.1 cell G3 to calculate the intercept.

4 *Calculate the coefficient of determination R^2.*

Use the equation:

$$R^2 = \frac{\left(\sum\limits_{i=1}^{n} x_i y_i\right)^2}{\left(\sum\limits_{i=1}^{n} x_i^2\right)\left(\sum\limits_{i=1}^{n} y_i^2\right)}$$

Here we can make use of the calculations already undertaken in finding m and c for the regression line.

(a) Extend your table by adding the heading $yi{\wedge}2$ in cell **I5**.

(b) In cell **I6** calculate y_i^2.

(c) Copy the formula down to cell **I19**.

(d) In cell **I20** find the sum of y_i^2.

(e) In cell **I3** enter the formula for R^2.

5 *Forecast the values of X using the equation:* $\hat{Y} = c + mX$.

(a) Add the heading **yhat** in cell **B5** and the years to be predicted in cells **C20 to C22**.

(b) In cell **B6** calculate $\hat{Y}$ for $X = 1983$.

(c) Copy the formulae down to cell **B22**.

Cells **B6 to B22** hold the predicted values from the equation:

$\hat{Y} = -90037801.5 + 50277.5(X)$

B20 to B22 hold the predictions for the years 1997–1999.

Figure A3.3 (on p. 465) shows the complete solution.

Using in-built functions

1 *Select a new unused worksheet and enter the following labels:*

	B	C	D
2	Slope	Intercept	R^2
3			
4			
5	Y	X	
6	Population	Year	Y hat

Copy the dependent data (Y) – the Greek population data into cells **B7 to B20**.

Enter the independent data (X) 1983–1999 into cells **C7 to C23**.

You should end up with something similar to Figure A3.2 below.

figure A3.2

	A	B	C	D
1				
2		**slope**	**intercept**	**R^2**
3		=SLOPE(B7:B20,C7:C20)	=INTERCEPT(B7:B20,C7:C20)	=RSQ(B7:B20,C7:C20)
4				
5		Y	X	
6		population	year	Y hat
7		9,642,505	1983	=$B$3*C7+$C$3
8		9,729,350	1984	
9		9,789,513	1985	
10		9,846,627	1986	
11		9,895,801	1987	
12		9,934,249	1988	
13		9,963,604	1989	
14		9,983,490	1990	
15		10,004,401	1991	
16		10,038,672	1992	
17		10,088,700	1993	
18		10,200,000	1994	
19		10,311,300	1995	
20		10,422,600	1996	
21			1997	
22			1998	
23			1999	

2 **Calculate m, c and R^2.**
In cells **B3:D3** use the in-built functions to calculate the slope or gradient, intercept and R^2. In *Microsoft's Excel*, for example, the following functions and their arguments are used:

= **Slope (known Ys,known Xs)**
= **Intercept (known Ys,known Xs)**
= **RSQ (known Ys,known Xs)**

3 **Calculate $\hat{Y}$ where $\hat{Y} = c + mX$**
   (a) Add the years to be predicted (1997, 1998, 1999) into cells **B21 to B23**
   (b) In cell **D7** substitute the values for *m and c* into the equation
   (c) Copy the formulae down to cell **B23**

Cells **D7 to D23** hold the predicted values from the equation:

$$\hat{Y} = -90037801.5 + 50277.5(X)$$

Thus cells **D21 to D23** hold the predicted values for the years 1997–1999. Figure A3.4 (p. 465) shows the complete solution.

3.3 Spearman's coefficient of rank correlation
••

Sometimes data are presented in *rank order*, whether descending (first to last) or ascending (last to first). It may be that the ranking comes from two separate sources, as when applicants for a post are ranked both by interview and by psychological tests. We might then wish to check to what extent the different rankings agree!

In such situations **Spearman's coefficient of rank correlation** (R_s) might be calculated. The formula for R_s is as follows:

$$R_s = 1 - \frac{6\sum_{i=1}^{n} d_i^2}{n^3 - n}$$

where R_s = Spearman's rank correlation coefficient
d_i = difference in ranking of a given observation
n = number of observations

If $R_s = 1$, then clearly we have perfect agreement between the respective rankings. This follows from the fact that each d_i would be zero when the respective rankings are identical, giving $R_s = 1 - 0$ in the above expression. The closer to 1 the value of R_s, the better the agreement between the respective rankings.

WORKED
EXAMPLE **3.6**
············

Ten candidates for a managerial post were ranked by interview and psychological test in the following manner:

	A	*B*	*C*	*D*	*E*	*F*	*G*	*H*	*I*	*J*
					Candidates rankings					
I Interview	4	2	7	1	5	6	9	3	10	8
II Psychological test	3	2	5	1	4	9	6	7	8	10

Calculate Spearman's rank correlation coefficient and discuss whether it represents a measure of agreement between the two types of test.

Solution

The first step is to take the difference in the ranks (d_i); the second step is to square each of these differences; the third step is to sum the squares of the differences. We then substitute the result into the formula

d_i 1 0 2 0 1 3 3 4 2 2
d_i^2 1 0 4 0 1 9 9 16 4 4

$$\sum_{i=1}^{10} d_i^2 = 48$$

$$R_s = 1 - \frac{6\sum d_i^2}{n^3 - n} = 1 - \frac{6 \times 48}{10^3 - 10} = 1 - \frac{288}{990} = 0.709$$

The Spearman's rank correlation coefficient shows *some* agreement in ranking between the two types of procedure.

We can use Spearman's coefficient of rank correlation (R_s) whenever the data for two variables are given in *rank order* (i.e. the data are **ordinal**). Whenever data are given in terms of *absolute values* (i.e. the data are **cardinal**) we would usually use the earlier coefficient of correlation (R). However we can *convert* two sets of data which are given in absolute values into rank order should we wish to calculate R_s. Further, should one set of data be given in terms of absolute values (cardinal) and the other in terms of rank order (ordinal) then only by converting the cardinal data to ordinal and calculating R_s might we be able to establish a measure of 'goodness of fit' between the two types of data.

SELF-CHECK QUESTIONS

3.4 Using the data for Self-check question 3.1 (p. 58)

    (a) Find the coefficient of determination.
    (b) Find Pearson's coefficient of correlation.
    (c) Comment on your results.

3.5 Using the data for Self-check question 3.2 (p. 58)

    (a) Find the coefficient of determination.
    (b) Find Pearson's coefficient of correlation.
    (c) Comment on your results.

3.6 The data below give the actual sales of a company (£000s) in each of eight regions of a country together with the forecast of sales by two different methods.

Region	Actual sales (£000)	Forecast: Method 1	Forecast: Method 2
A	15	13	16
B	19	25	19
C	30	23	26
D	12	26	14
E	58	48	65
F	10	15	19
G	23	28	27
H	17	10	22

    (i) Calculate the rank correlation coefficient between
        (1) Actual sales and forecast 1
        (2) Actual sales and forecast 2

    (ii) Which forecasting method would you recommend next year?

Note: **Answers can be found on pp. 331–334.**

3.4 Multiple regression
....

Our analysis has, until this point, concentrated on relationships involving only two variables: a dependent variable Y and an independent variable X. In reality many relationships involve more than two variables, and attempts to fit lines (or surfaces) of 'best fit' to such variables is termed **multiple regression** analysis. Here we merely touch upon a few of the issues involved, with more detailed sources of information indicated on p. 76.

Win Hornby *et al.* (1997) provide a useful illustration of the application of multiple regression analysis in their review of a study seeking to relate the demand for beer in the UK to as many as *seven* separate independent variables, namely:

1 P_b the real price of beer (i.e. the price of beer in relation to the rate of inflation).
2 A_b the real level of advertising on beer (i.e. the level of advertising in relation to an advertising index of TV and press).
3 A_a the real level of advertising on other alcoholic drinks.
4 W the daily mean temperature
5 Y_r the real level of personal disposable income
6 P_c the real price of other alcoholic drink.
7 S a seasonal factor to reflect the higher consumption of beer in the summer months and at Christmas.

Clearly we no longer have a two-dimensional scatter diagram. Instead of a line of 'best fit' we now have a plane or surface which 'best fits' a multi-dimensional scatter diagram. Figure 11.9 (p. 272) gives an idea of a 'surface' in a three dimensional situation. Statistical packages are frequently used to calculate such relationships.

Using quarterly data stretching back over a 15 year period the authors of this study, W. D. Reekie and C. Blight, established the following results from 60 data observations:

$$Q = 3.18 - 1.355P_b + 0.004A_b + 0.019A_a + 0.057W + 0.085Y_r + 0.371P_c + 0.0195S$$
$$\ (0.287)\quad (0.64)\quad\ (0.32)\quad\ (2.66)*\quad (5.84)*\quad (0.10)\quad\ (0.173)$$

where Q = demand for beer in the UK (millions of barrels per year)

$R^2 = 0.57$

t-ratios are in brackets. * indicates the statistically significant variables.

▶ Notice that the *signs* in front of six of the independent variables are *positive*, suggesting that a rise in those variables will *increase* the demand for beer in the UK (shift the demand curve to the right).
▶ However the sign in front of P_b, the real price of beer, is negative, suggesting that a rise in the price of beer will result in a *fall* in the demand for beer (i.e. a contraction in demand, moving up the demand curve from right to left).
▶ The numbers (coefficients) in front of each independent variable indicate the *magnitude* of the respective relationships. For example, any given

percentage change in the price of beer will have the largest (here negative) impact on the demand for beer as compared to changes in the other independent variables.

▶ The large 'intercept' term of 3.18 indicates that should these seven independent variables have zero values, there would still be a sizeable demand for beer in the UK (3.18 million barrels per year).

▶ The R^2 figures of 0.57 indicates that this specified relationship only explains (accounts for) some 57 per cent of the total variation (see p. 60 above). This means that some 43 per cent of the total variation is unexplained. For example we may have omitted one or more independent variables which really do have an impact on the demand for beer in the UK.

▶ The figures in brackets refer to the t statistic scores (or t ratios) discussed in Chapters 6 and 7. The null hypothesis (see p. 159) for the t test conducted on each independent variable is that the coefficient in front of that independent variable is zero. The larger the t score, the more confident we can be in *rejecting* the null hypothesis, i.e. accepting the alternative hypothesis, namely that the independent variable in question really does have a non-zero coefficient. Put another way, the larger the t score, the more confident we can be in concluding that the particular independent variable is 'significant' in influencing the dependent variable. In the results presented above, we can be most confident about the influence on the demand for beer of expenditure on advertising on other alcoholic drinks and the daily mean temperature.

Note: Perhaps surprisingly the sign of the coefficient in front of A_a is positive; suggesting that as more is spent on advertising *other* alcoholic drinks, the demand for beer increases. This suggests positive 'spillover' effects, namely that alcoholic drinks are a generic product, and as one type is advertised so other types of alcoholic drinks also benefit.

REVIEW QUESTIONS

3.1 Sales of products for the past 12 months are shown below. Use linear regression to forecast sales for the next three months.

Month	Jan.	Feb.	March	April	May	June	July	Aug.	Sept.	Oct.	Nov.	Dec.
Sales	89	74	92	123	102	139	152	128	183	148	166	179

Comment on the reliability of your prediction.

3.2 The weather was considered an important element in the sales pattern of a certain product. Over a four month period the average daily air temperature was recorded and the average daily sales of the product were calculated for each temperature. The results were as follows:

Temp (°C)	10	11	12	13	14	15	16	17	18	19	20	21	22	23	24
Average daily sales	103	104	95	83	81	75	68	47	53	40	43	40	38	39	35

(a) Plot a scatter diagram of the data. What does this suggest?
(b) Calculate the linear regression equation that best fits the data.
(c) Plot the least squares regression line on your scatter diagram.
(d) Use the regression equation to estimate the number of products that will be sold if the temperature reaches 25°C.

3.3 The data below show the lateness of trains (in minutes) arriving at a terminus station and the number of passengers alighting from those trains. The train operator believes that the number of passengers (Y) will be greater if the train arrives a little later (X) than scheduled.

Minutes late	No. of passengers
1	1,459
3	395
0	534
2	641
7	927
3	650
4	447
5	392
0	569
11	713
1	401
12	2,691
1	443
7	883
12	1,577
11	147
7	568
2	455
3	632
4	531

(a) Plot a scatter diagram of the data.
(b) Calculate the linear regression equation that best fits the data.
(c) Plot the least squares regression line on your scatter diagram.
(d) Is their any evidence to suggest that there is a relationship between the number of passengers and the punctuality of the train.

3.4 A manager needs to determine the relationship between the company's advertising expenditure and its sales revenue. If the relationship is a strong one, then the company will be able to forecast the sales revenue for a given advertising expenditure. The following data have been collected over the past eight years.

Advertising (£000s)	Sales (£000s)
8.73	40.285
8.78	39.423
9.25	47.389
9.54	45.707
10.29	47.711
11.22	52.500
12.92	53.727
13.99	64.389

(a) Plot a scatter diagram of the data.
(b) Calculate the linear regression equation that best fits the data.
(c) Estimate the sales revenue when advertising is:
    £11,000
    £13,500
    £15,000
(d) Is the relationship sufficiently strong to use as a predictive method?

3.5 The data below show a hypothetical index of economic activity and the sales revenue for a firm over a 14 year period.

Index of economic activity	Sales revenue (£000)
103	1,188
104	1,224
104	1,243
105	1,239
105	1,242
107	1,138
108	1,481
108	1,562
109	1,554
109	1,566
110	1,598
111	1,562
112	1,609
112	1,499

(a) Calculate the regression line relating the two sets of data. Let sales revenue be the dependent variable. Comment on your result.
(b) How well does your regression line fit the data.

3.6 A quality control manager believes that the number of rejected items on an assembly line is related to the length of time between breaks (the work period) for the assembly staff. The period between breaks is measured as well as the percentage of rejects produced by the operatives with the following results:

Work period (minutes)	Rejects %
60	2.3
65	2.5
70	2.7
75	2.9
80	3.2
85	3.6
90	3.5
95	3.7
100	4.0
105	4.4
110	4.3
115	4.6
120	4.7
125	3.3
130	5.1
135	5.2

(a) Calculate the regression line and use it to consider if there is any evidence to support the quality control manager's theory.
(b) Given the above data, is there a case to suggest that work periods not exceeding two hours would reduce the number of rejects below 5 per cent?
(c) How well does your regression line fit the data?

3.7 The marketing department believes that consumer tastes for beer are related to geographical area. They have therefore commissioned research to investigate the popularity of six leading brands of beer. Two different panels, one from the north the other from the south, tasted the products and ranked them in their order of preference. To avoid bias, the name of the products was withheld and substituted with the labels A–F. The results of the blind tasting were as follows:

Product	Northern panel	Southern panel
A	3	2
B	4	4
C	5	3
D	2	6
E	6	5
F	1	1

Is there any statistical evidence to suggest that the tastes of consumers are related to geographical region?

3.8 A motoring organisation commissioned two independent testing laboratories to assess the safety of eight of the best-selling models of car in the midrange family saloon market. The laboratories used different testing procedures and methods before ranking the models in order of safety (where 1 = safest, 8 = least safe) as follows:

Product	Lab 1	Lab 2
Chimera 205	1	2
Apollo T7	6	5
Pastiche	7	8
Ganymede	4	6
Callisto LX	3	4
QM4	5	3
Alfredo GTi	8	7
Arctura	2	1

Is there any correlation between the two sets of results?

Note: Answers can be found on pp. 392–402.

Further study and data
••••••••••••••••••••••••

Texts

Bancroft, G. and O'Sullivan, G. (1993), *Quantitative methods for accounting and business studies*, 3rd edn, McGraw Hill, chapter 9.

Curwin, J. and Slater, R. (1996), *Quantitative methods for business decisions*, 4th edn, Chapman and Hall, chapters 17, 18 and 19.

Hornby, W., Gammie, B. and Wall, S. (1997), *Business Economics*, Longman Modular Texts, Addison Wesley Longman, chapter 6.

Lawson, M., Hubbard, S. and Pugh, P. (1995), *Maths and statistics for business*, Addison Wesley Longman.

Morris, C. (1996), *Quantitative approaches in business studies*, 4th edn, Pitman, chapters 13 and 14.

Oakshott, L. (1996), *Essential elements of business statistics*, BPP, chapter 8.

Swift, L. (1997), *Mathematics and statistics for business, management and Finance*, MacMillan, part C8.

Thomas, R. (1997), *Quantitative methods for business studies*, Prentice Hall, chapter 3.

Waters, D. (1997), *Quantitative methods*, 2nd edn, Addison Wesley Longman, chapter 8.

Wisniewski, M. with Stead, R. (1996), *Foundation quantitative methods for business*, Pitman, chapter 12.

Sources of information and data

See list at end of Chapter 1 (p. 25).

CHAPTER **4**
....

Time series and forecasting

Objectives
....

By the end of this chapter you should be able to:

▶ use time series data to find both trend and seasonal variation as a basis for forecasting;

▶ apply the technique of moving averages to help in the calculation of trend lines and seasonal factors;

▶ combine time series and regression analysis for purposes of forecasting;

▶ apply exponential smoothing as a forecasting technique;

▶ be aware of the use of other approaches to forecasting in contemporary business practice.

Introduction
....

Data can be collected for purposes of analysis in a number of ways. For example data for household expenditure on food can be collected in different locations (nation, region, city, etc.) at a *single point of time*. These are called **cross-sectional data**. Alternatively data for household expenditure on food can be collected for a given location (nation, region, city, etc.) at *different points in time*. This is called **time series data**.

In this chapter we consider the use of such **time series** data as a basis for estimating both trend and seasonal variation. As we shall see, such estimates can then be used as a basis for **forecasting**.

In fact we have already touched on forecasting in Chapter 3 when we used the least squares line to predict values of the dependent variable (Y) for as yet unobtained values of the independent variable (X). We take this aspect of forecasting using regression analysis a little further in this chapter. Indeed we see how we can usefully *combine* regression analysis with the results of our time series analysis to forecast future outcomes.

The chapter concludes with a more general review of forecasting techniques, including **exponential smoothing** and other widely used techniques in current business practice.

Answers to the 'Self-check questions', responses to each 'Pause for thought' and answers to the 'Review Questions' can be found at the end of the book.

4.1 Time series analysis
....

Many types of data have been recorded through time, such as monthly, quarterly or annual data for output, sales revenue, profit, employment, unemployment, prices, etc.

Components of time series

Typically such **time series** data exhibit one or more of the following components.

▶ A **trend component (*T*)**, whereby the variable appears to broadly rise or fall (or remain unchanged) through time.

▶ A **seasonal component (*S*)**, whereby the variable moves in regular cycles *within a year* around that trend line. For example within a broadly rising value of sales through time (trend), an ice cream manufacturer may regularly experience peaks for sales in summer months and troughs for sales in winter months (seasonal).

Note that although the term 'seasonal' has been applied to such short-term cycles, these may involve any units of time within a year; for example days within a week (e.g. high sales on Fridays and low sales on Mondays), weeks within a month, months or quarters or 'seasons' within a year.

PAUSE FOR THOUGHT 4.1   *Can you list six products (goods or services) other than the ice cream already mentioned, the demand for which you might expect to experience seasonal variation within a year?*

▶ A **cyclical component (C)**, whereby the variable moves in a rather less regular cycle over the medium to longer term around the trend line. For example some have claimed to observe a *business cycle* of some eight to ten years between periods of 'boom' and 'bust' in modern industrialised economies. Others have claimed to observe still longer cycles over 50 years, with the peaks of such cycles related to new technological breakthroughs, such as water power, steam, electricity, microelectronics, etc. These have sometimes been referred to as *Kondratief cycles*, after a Russian economist of that name.

Note that the **period** of a cycle is often referred to as the time between successive peaks or successive troughs.

▶ An **irregular component (I)**, which is entirely unpredictable. The stock market crash of 1987 was, for example, a dramatic and unexpected departure from trend in terms of share prices.

PAUSE FOR THOUGHT 4.2   *Can you name three other irregular components which have influenced a wide range of UK producers in the past ten years?*

Figure 4.1 presents two possible time series profiles for the value of a dependent variable (*Y*).

figure 4.1

**Some time series
profiles**

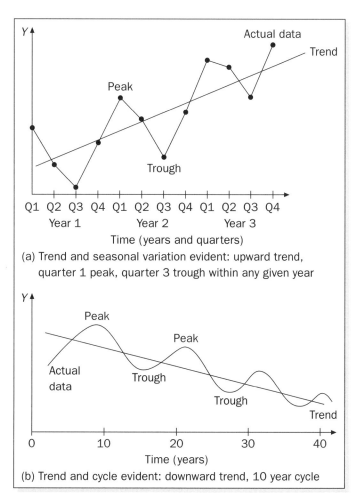

(a) Trend and seasonal variation evident: upward trend,
    quarter 1 peak, quarter 3 trough within any given year

(b) Trend and cycle evident: downward trend, 10 year cycle

In Figure 4.1(a) a clear upward trend is evident, around which there is
seasonal variation, with quarter 1 representing successive peaks and quarter 3
successive troughs within each year. In Figure 4.1(b) a clear downward trend is
evident, around which there is a *cyclical component* with a period of around ten
years between successive peaks or successive troughs.

Of course many variants are possible for such profiles. We may, for example,
have a shorter-term seasonal variation (e.g. quarterly or monthly) superimposed on
a time series showing both a cycle and trend using longer-term (e.g. annual) data.

DID YOU KNOW?
*The construction industry is widely regarded as a
barometer for economic prospects throughout the
economy. Traditionally it is one of the earliest sectors
to be affected by economic recession and one of the
earliest sectors to experience higher demand when
economic recovery occurs.*

Additive or multiplicative model

We can represent or 'model' our time
series using the four components already
identified. We can do this in one of two
ways; either *adding* or *multiplying* the respective components.

figure 4.2

**Choosing an
appropriate time
series model**

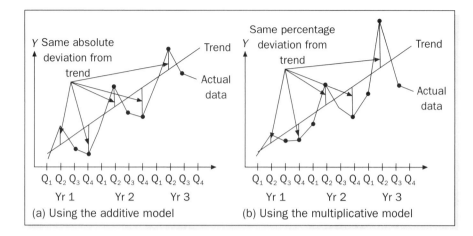

(a) Using the additive model

(b) Using the multiplicative model

▶ $Y = T + S + C + I$ **Additive model**
▶ $Y = T \times S \times C \times I$ **Multiplicative model**

As we shall see, we can use either of these models to calculate any trend line or seasonal variation. However there may be circumstances where one approach is more appropriate than another!

As we see in Figure 4.2(a), the **additive model** is the most appropriate where deviations from the trend line are of a similar *absolute magnitude* from one peak (or trough) to another. This is shown in Figure 4.2(a) as occurring for short-term cycles (e.g. seasonal variations, with Q2 providing peaks and Q4 troughs). The same principle would equally apply if we were using annual data and comparing successive peaks or troughs in a business cycle over, say, an eight to ten year period.

However as we see in Figure 4.2(b), the **multiplicative model** is the most appropriate where deviations from the trend line are of a similar *percentage* from one peak (or trough) to another. We can see that the absolute magnitude of the deviations from the trend line grows over time as the dependent variable (Y) rises, but that the percentage deviations remain roughly constant.

4.2 Moving average
·······················

As we shall see in the next section, we can use the idea of a **moving average** to find the **trend** of the data. To find the moving average we initially find the simple average (arithmetic mean) for a specified number of items of data. We then recalculate that average having dropped the initial item of data and added a subsequent item of data.

In the worked example below involving quarterly data for sales value, we initially find the simple average for four items of data, and then *move* that average along.

WORKED
EXAMPLE **4.1**
••••••••••••

Find a four quarter centred moving average for the following data on sales value (£000):

Solution

(1) Year and	Quarter	(2) Sales value (£000)	(3) 4 quarter moving total	(4) 4 quarter moving average	(5) Centred 4 quarter moving average
1995	1	87.5			
	2	73.2			
			314.0	78.5	
	3	64.8			78.9
			316.8	79.2	
	4	88.5			79.6
			319.6	79.9	
1996	1	90.3			80.5
			324.0	81.0	
	2	76.0			81.8
			330.2	82.6	
	3	69.2			83.1
			333.8	83.5	
	4	94.7			83.8
			336.2	84.1	
1997	1	93.9			84.5
			339.0	84.8	
	2	78.4			85.5
			344.6	86.2	
	3	72.0			
	4	100.3			

It is often helpful to find the four quarter centred moving average in stages.

▶ **Four quarter moving total (column 3).** Here we simply sum the data for the initial four quarters in column (2) to find the four quarter *moving total*. Notice that the moving totals fall in between the actual quarterly data in column (2). For example the first moving total falls in between quarters 2 and 3 for 1995.

▶ **Four quarter moving average (column 4).** We then divide the respective four quarter *moving totals* in column (3) by 4 to find the four quarter *moving average.*

▶ **Four quarter centred moving average (column 5).** It will help to *align* the moving averages with the specific quarterly data in column (2). For this reason we *centre* the data in column (4) by summing respective pairs of data and dividing by 2.

4.3 Finding the trend
••••••••••••••••••••••••••

In practice we are often presented with monthly or quarterly data over a number of years for which no obvious business cycle (C) of eight to ten years is present. We can therefore regard the *actual data*, Y, as having only three of the four components previously mentioned

i.e. $Y = T + S + I$ (Additive)

or $Y = T \times S \times I$ (Multiplicative)

If we calculate an appropriate *moving average* for the monthly or quarterly data, then we can *eliminate* both the seasonal variation component (S) and the irregular component (I) from the actual data. This will leave us with T, the required trend line.

▶ Using a four quarter moving average in column (4) of the worked example above means that we can *eliminate any seasonal variation* (S) as regards high or low quarters. For example in column (3) after our initial calculation of 314 we drop the first quarter of 1995 but add the first quarter of 1996 to get 316.8. Our four quarter moving total which is the basis for the subsequent centred four quarter moving average in column (5) therefore continually takes in *all* quarters, both high (as for quarter 1) and low (as for quarter 3). In this way column (5) continually eliminates S, the seasonal variation component.

▶ In calculating columns (4) and (5) we are *averaging*, and any averaging helps eliminate any irregular component. In this way column (5) helps eliminate I, the irregular component.

If $Y = T + S + I$

or $Y = T \times S \times I$

then column (5), having eliminated S and I, leaves us with T, the trend line.

Figure 4.3 plots the original quarterly data (Y) of column (2) and the trend line (T) of column (5) for the worked example.

Notice how we use the four quarter centred moving average for the trend line and use straight lines to connect successive points. An alternative approach would, of course, be to draw a single least squares line (see p. 52) which 'best fits' the points which correspond to the trend. We consider this alternative approach below (p. 87).

PAUSE FOR THOUGHT 4.3   *Can you name three products (goods or services) for which an upward sales trend is well established, and three products for which a downward sales trend is well established?*

The nature of the data will define the *type* of moving average required to eliminate S and I and therefore leave only the trend line, T.

Using moving averages to find trend (*T*)

▶ **Quarterly data**: use four quarter centred moving average to eliminate S and I, and leave T.

▶ **Monthly data**: use 12 month centred moving average to eliminate S and I, and leave T.

figure 4.3
Plotting the trend line

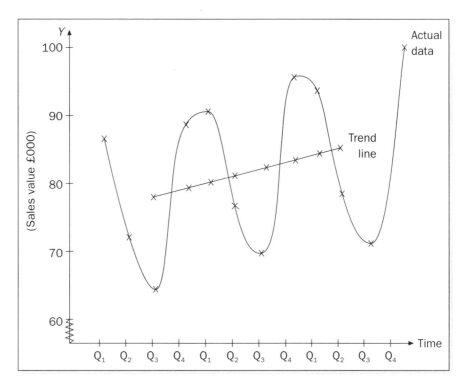

SELF-CHECK QUESTION

4.1 UK passenger movements by air are shown in the table below (data in 100,000 passengers):

Year	Q1	Q2	Q3	Q4
1995	44	80	120	60
1996	52	88	126	62
1997	60	98	140	68

Use an appropriate moving average to find the trend of the data. Plot the original data and your trend line on a graph.

Note: **An answer can be found on p. 334.**

4.4 Finding and eliminating the seasonal variation
••

When the original data (Y) has no obvious longer-term business cycle in evidence, we have already noted that it can be represented as either:

$$Y = T + S + I \quad \text{(additive model)}$$

or $\quad Y = T \times S \times I \quad$ (multiplicative model)

Finding the seasonal variation (S)

We can easily extend our work in using moving averages to find T, the trend component, so that we can find S, the seasonal variation component. Essentially we need only add an extra column to the calculations already undertaken to find T. This extra column which gives us S (and I) will be $(Y - T)$ in the case of the *additive model* or $\left(\dfrac{Y}{T}\right)$ in the case of the multiplicative model, for the following reasons:

$Y = T + S + I$ (additive model)

$MA = T$

$\underline{Y - MA = S + I}$

or $Y = T \times S \times I$ (multiplicative model)

$MA = T$

$\dfrac{Y}{MA} = S \times I$

As we shall see, a further simple averaging process will remove I, leaving S, the seasonal variation which we require.

WORKED
EXAMPLE **4.2**
··············

We can demonstrate this approach by using the earlier calculations (p. 81) for sales value in Worked example 4.1. Here we shall use the *additive* model.

Solution

table 4.1
Time series of quarterly sales value (£000)

		Y (original data)	T Four quarter centred moving average	S + I (Y − T)
1995	Q1	87.5		
	Q2	73.2		
	Q3	64.8	78.9	−14.1
	Q4	88.5	79.6	8.9
1996	Q1	90.3	80.5	9.8
	Q2	76.0	81.8	−5.8
	Q3	69.2	83.1	−13.9
	Q4	94.7	83.8	10.9
1997	Q1	93.9	84.5	9.4
	Q2	78.4	85.5	−7.1
	Q3	72.0		
	Q4	100.3		

Subtracting our trend values (*T*) from the corresponding quarterly sales values (Y) gives us *S* + *I* over successive quarters. The averaging process will then tend to remove *I*, leaving us with *S* as required.

A simple table can usefully illustrate this process.

table 4.2
Finding the seasonal variation factors (£000)

	Q1	Q2	Q3	Q4
1995			−14.1	8.9
1996	9.8	−5.8	−13.9	10.9
1997	9.4	−7.1		
Total	19.2	−12.9	−28.0	19.8
average (*S*)	9.6	−6.45	−14	9.9

The averaging process for each quarter leaves us with *S*, the seasonal variation for that quarter. Clearly quarters 1 and 4 are high sales quarters for this product, whereas quarter 2 and especially quarter 3 are low sales quarters.

Adjusted S

The data shown in the 'average' row for *S* are actually *unadjusted*. If we sum the plus values we have +19.5 (9.6 + 9.9) but if we sum the negative values we have −20.45 (−6.45 + −14.0). In other words there is a *net value* for *S* of −0.95.

Strictly speaking the plus and minus values should cancel out. We can compensate for the −0.95 by adding +0.95/4 (i.e. +0.24) to *each* of the four quarterly values for *S*. These values would then be the **adjusted values** for *S*.

table 4.3
Finding the adjusted seasonal variation factors (£000)

	Q1	Q2	Q3	Q4
Unadjusted *S* (0.95 net)	+9.6	−6.45	−14.0	+9.9
Adjusted *S (zero net)	+9.84	−6.21	−13.76	+10.14

$* + \left(\dfrac{0.95}{4} \right)$ i.e. +0.24 added to each quarter

It is these adjusted values for *S* that we usually refer to as the seasonal variation components. Here we can see that sales are normally +9.84 above trend for Q1, but −6.21 below trend for Q2, and so on (all values in £000).

Eliminating the seasonal variations (S)

Having found *S*, the seasonal variation component our next step is to *eliminate* *S* from the original data, *Y*. We will then have an estimate of *Y* without any 'distortion' resulting from seasonal influences on *Y*. Such data with the seasonal variation removed is sometimes called **deseasonalised data**.

table 4.4

Eliminating the seasonal variation from the original data (i.e. deseasonalising the data)

		Y (original data)	S (adjusted seasonal variation)	Y – S (deseasonalised data)
1995	Q1	87.5	+9.84	77.66
	Q2	73.2	–6.21	79.41
	Q3	64.8	–13.76	78.56
	Q4	88.5	+10.14	78.36
1996	Q1	90.3	+ 9.84	80.46
	Q2	76.0	–6.21	82.21
	Q3	69.2	–13.76	82.96
	Q4	94.7	+10.14	84.56
1997	Q1	93.9	+9.84	84.06
	Q2	78.4	–6.21	84.61
	Q3	72.0	–13.76	85.76
	Q4	100.3	+10.14	90.16

Notice that in eliminating S by subtracting S from Y, we sometimes have – – = +, as in Q2 of 1995 when 73.2 – – 6.21 = 79.41.

Using the adjusted seasonal variation component, *S*, calculated above we can easily eliminate *S* from the original data, *Y*. Here we use the *additive* model for illustration purposes and therefore *subtract S* from *Y* for each quarter (in the multiplicative model we would *divide S* into *Y* for each quarter).

ACTIVITY **4**

It can be an involved process calculating the components of time series data. The spreadsheet (p. 467) provides a template for such calculations with the values of the respective quarterly data entered in column D and the calculations and results carried out automatically. Although the layout is for quarterly data, the concept can be adapted for any time series data. The values 2 and two in cells **I1** and **J1** determine the number of decimal places in selected columns.

The layout and formulae for the spreadsheet are shown in Figure A4.2 (p. 467).

As you will see, you are using the technique of a four quarter centred moving average to estimate the trend of the data (had the data been monthly, you would have used a twelve month centred moving average to estimate trend). You are also finding the (adjusted) seasonal factors. If you are using your trend values for *forecasting* you will need to subtract the seasonal factors from each quarterly trend estimate to get a more accurate forecast for that quarter.

Set up your spreadsheet and then enter the quarterly data values shown below.

Year	Q1	Q2	Q3	Q4
Year 1	196.9	295.5	349.4	389.3
Year 2	324.1	418.0	447.5	456.4
Year 3	415.2	528.6	550.6	615.3
Year 4	513.6	650.8	670.6	754.4

▶ Comment on your results

▶ Check your solution with the response on p. 466

▶ Repeat the procedure using the quarterly data values in the various Self-check and Review questions involving moving averages.

4.5 Forecasting: time series

We have already looked at prediction (forecasting) using the simple regression analysis of Chapter 3 (p. 52). Here we *combine* the idea of finding a least squares line (line of 'best fit') with our analysis of time series components. We can then *extrapolate* (take forward) the regression line which best fits the trend estimates to derive a forecast of future sales, etc.

Forecasting: trend value only

For example we can fit a single *least squares line* to the trend estimates on the earlier scatter diagrams (e.g. Figure 4.3, p. 83), instead of merely linking successive trend estimates by a sequence of straight lines. This regression line, once calculated, can then be used for prediction (forecasting) of future trend values.

We must initially calculate the regression line for the eight trend estimates shown in Figure 4.3 and Table 4.1. We can use *either* of the two approaches considered in Chapter 3 for calculating a regression line. Here we use the 'original data' formula (p. 53), with the dependent variable Y standing for the trend value and the independent variable X standing for time (quarters). With trend estimates available for eight successive quarters, we let $X = 1$ for the first available quarter for a trend estimate (Q3, 1995), rising to $X = 8$ for the eighth available quarter for a trend estimate (Q3, 1997).

From Table 4.1 above (p. 84) we can then construct a new table allowing the application of our regression formula:

X (quarter of data)	Y (trend value)	XY	X^2	Y^2
1	78.9	78.9	1	6,225.2
2	79.6	159.2	4	6,336.2
3	80.5	241.5	9	6,480.3
4	81.8	327.2	16	6,691.2
5	83.1	415.5	25	6,905.6
6	83.8	502.8	36	7,022.4
7	84.5	591.5	49	7,140.3
8	85.5	684.0	64	7,310.3
$\Sigma X = 36$	$\Sigma Y = 657.7$	$\Sigma XY = 3{,}000.6$	$\Sigma X^2 = 204$	$\Sigma Y^2 = 54{,}111.5$

$$\bar{X} = \frac{36}{8} = 4.5 \quad \bar{Y} = \frac{657.7}{8} = 82.2$$

We noted (p. 53) that, using original data, the formula for the regression (least squares) line is:

$$\hat{Y} = mX + c$$

where $m = \dfrac{n\sum XY - \sum X \sum Y}{n\sum X^2 - \left(\sum X\right)^2}$

and $\quad c = \bar{Y} - m\bar{X}$

where $\quad n$ = the number of observations

i.e. $\quad m = \dfrac{8(3{,}000.6) - (36)(657.7)}{8(204) - (36)^2}$

$$m = \frac{24{,}004.8 - 23{,}677.2}{1632 - 1296}$$

$$m = \frac{327.6}{336}$$

$$\underline{m = +0.975}$$

$$c = \bar{Y} - m\bar{X}$$

i.e. $\quad c = 82.2 - 0.975(4.5)$

$$\underline{c = 77.8}$$

$$\underline{\hat{Y}_T = 0.975X + 77.8}$$

where $\hat{Y}_T$ = trend sales value (£000)

X = quarterly time period (Q2, 1995 = 0)

We can now use this regression line to **predict** or **forecast** future trend values should this past relationship hold into the future.

Figure 4.4 plots this regression line for the trend and extrapolates the trend line into the future.

The dashed part of the trend line indicates where the extrapolation occurs, i.e. where the line is extended beyond that for which data are currently available.

We can use the regression line for forecasting. For example we can see from Figure 4.4 that:

when $X = 12$ (i.e. Q2, 1998)

$$\hat{Y}_T = 0.975(12) + 77.8$$

$$\hat{Y}_T = 11.7 + 77.8$$

i.e. $\quad \underline{\hat{Y}_T = 89.5 \text{ (to 1 d.p.)}}$

Similarly, when $X = 20$ (i.e. Q2, 2,000)

$$\hat{Y}_T = 0.975(20) + 77.8$$

$$\hat{Y}_T = 19.5 + 77.8$$

$$\underline{\hat{Y}_T = 97.3 \text{ (to 1 d.p.)}}$$

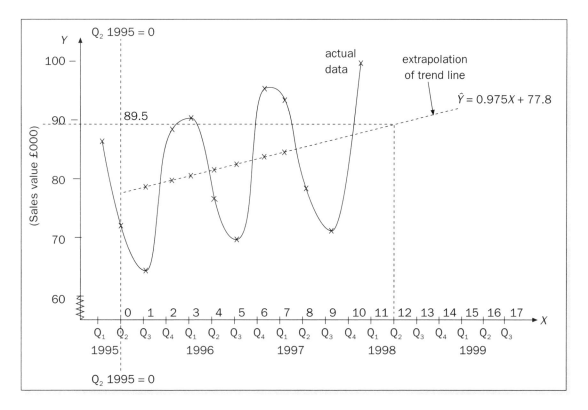

figure 4.4

Using the regression analysis to find the trend line and using that line for forecasting

Of course, the better the fit of our regression line to the existing trend data, the more confident we can be in extrapolating the line to make forecasts in the future.

This brings us back to the coefficients of determination and correlation (Chapter 3, pp. 58–68). In this particular case there is an extremely good fit for our trend regression line.

Using original data

$$R^2 = \left[\frac{n\sum XY - \sum X \sum Y}{\sqrt{\left[n\sum X^2 - \left(\sum X\right)^2 \right] \times \left[n\sum Y^2 - \left(\sum Y\right)^2 \right]}} \right]^2$$

i.e. $R^2 = \left[\dfrac{8(3{,}000.6) - (36)(657.7)}{\sqrt{\left[8(204) - (36)^2\right] \times \left[8(54{,}111.5) - (657.7)^2\right]}} \right]^2$

i.e. $R^2 = \left[\dfrac{24{,}004.8 - 23{,}677.2}{\sqrt{\left[1{,}632 - 1{,}296\right] \times \left[432{,}892.0 - 432{,}569.3\right]}} \right]^2$

$R^2 = \left[\dfrac{327.6}{\sqrt{336 \times 322.7}} \right]^2 = \left[\dfrac{327.6}{329.3} \right]^2 = \left[0.995\right]$

$\underline{R^2 = \text{coefficient of determination} = 0.995}$

$\underline{R \ = \text{coefficient of correlation} = 0.997}$

With over 99 per cent of the total variation 'explained' or 'accounted for' by our regression line (see p. 60), we can have considerable confidence in forecasting into the future by extrapolating from our regression line.

Forecasting: trend and seasonal factors

Of course any forecast for the sales in a particular quarter will be more accurate if it takes into account the *seasonal variation*, *S*, components already identified as well as the trend. The adjusted values for *S* were as follows (£000):

Q1 (+9.84)   Q2 (−6.21)   Q3 (−13.76)   Q4 (+10.14)

We must add or subtract these seasonal variation values to our trend forecast if we are to be more realistic about the likely future sales in a particular quarter.

For example, we can forecast the trend using the equation

$$\hat{Y}_T = 0.975X + 77.8$$

where $X = 0$ for Q2,1995.

This gives the *trend* forecast for Q2, 1998 as follows:

▶   when $X = 12$ (i.e. Q2, 1998)

$$\hat{Y}_T = 0.975 \, (12) + 77.8$$

$$\underline{\hat{Y}_T = 89.5}$$

However Q2 also has a *seasonal* component

$$\underline{S = -6.21}$$

So our forecast for $\hat{Y}_{T+S}$ with *both* *T* and *S* included is:

$$\hat{Y}_{T+S} = 89.5 - 6.21$$

$$\underline{\hat{Y}_{T+S} = 83.29 \, (\pounds000)}$$

Table 4.5 shows the forecast ($\hat{Y}$) for sales value (£000) over the period 1998–2000 inclusive.

table 4.5

Forecasts of $\hat{Y}_{T+S}$ including trend (*T*) and seasonal variation (*S*) components.

Additive model with least squares line $\hat{Y}_T = 0.975X + 77.8$ for trend forecast (Q2, 1995 = 0).

Year and quarter		X*	($\hat{Y}_T$) Trend forecast	(S) Seasonal variation	$\hat{Y}_{T+S}$ Total forecast
1998	Q1	11	88.5	+9.84	98.34
	Q2	12	89.5	−6.21	83.29
	Q3	13	90.5	−13.76	76.74
	Q4	14	91.5	+10.14	101.64
1999	Q1	15	92.4	+9.84	102.24
	Q2	16	93.4	−6.21	87.19
	Q3	17	94.4	−13.76	80.64
	Q4	18	95.4	+10.14	105.54
2000	Q1	19	96.4	+9.84	106.24
	Q2	20	97.3	−6.21	91.09
	Q3	21	98.3	−13.76	84.54
	Q4 etc.	22	99.3	+10.14	109.44

Note: * Quarter 2 1995 = 0

4.2 The data below show UK sales of a particular model of car over three years (figures in 100,000 units).

Quarter	1	2	3	4
1995	66	106	140	82
1996	73	119	165	91
1997	85	130	205	100

(a) **Use the technique of moving averages to find values for the trend component (T).**

(b) **Plot the original data and your trend values on a scatter diagram.**

(c) **Find a 'least squares line' to best fit your trend values.**

(d) **Estimate the season variation component (S).**

(e) **Forecast future sales, taking both trend and seasonal variation into account in:**

    (i) **Quarter 1, year 2000**

    (ii) **Quarter 3, year 2000**

(f) **How confident can you be in these forecasts?**

Note: **An answer can be found on p. 335.**

4.6 Forecasting: exponential smoothing

A widely used technique in business forecasting is that of **exponential smoothing**. The idea here is that the forecast at time t for the next time period $(t + 1)$ should take into account the *observed error* in the forecast made for t in the previous time period $(t - 1)$.

Clearly such 'exponential smoothing' implies a learning process, whereby future forecasts are continually revised (smoothed) in the light of previous experience. Strictly speaking, this approach is most appropriate when there is little or no trend (T) in the data and little or no seasonal variation (S). It is best used for short-term forecasting, for example forecasting the outcome of the next time period.

We can express this approach as follows:

Next forecast = Previous forecast + Some proportion of the previous forecasting error

$$\hat{Y}_{t+1} = \hat{Y}_t + \alpha(Y_t - \hat{Y}_t)$$

where Y_t = actual data (observed outcome) in time period t.

$\hat{Y}_t, \hat{Y}_{t+1}$ = forecast data for next time period (t or $t + 1$) made in previous time period (t – 1 or t respectively)

α = smoothing constant

Put another way

$$\hat{Y}_{t+1} = \hat{Y}_t + \alpha(E_t)$$

where E_t = error term = $Y_t - \hat{Y}_t$

The value assigned to α, the **smoothing constant**, can vary between zero and one

i.e. $0 \leq \alpha \leq 1$

We can usefully consider the extreme values of α by way of illustration.

▶ When $\alpha = 0$, no adjustment is made for the previous forecasting error. The next forecast is then assumed to be the same as the previous forecast.
▶ When $\alpha = 1$, full adjustment is made for the previous forecasting error. The next forecast is then the previous forecast ± the entire amount of any previous forecasting error.

In practice α can be derived *experimentally*, based on the average size of the error term in previous forecasts. Values of between 0.1 and 0.3 are typically assigned to α.

In the Table 4.6 below we continue this exponential forecast into other quarters, based on the actual values of Y (quarterly sales) shown (000 units)

table 4.6
Exponential forecast of future demand (000 units), $\alpha = 0.2$

Quarter	Y_t (actual sales)	$\hat{Y}_t$ (forecast sales)	E_t $(Y_t - \hat{Y}_t)$
1	96		
2	102	84	18
3	104	87.6	16.4
4	100	90.9	9.1
5	88	92.7	−4.7
6	92	91.8	0.2
7	96	91.8	4.2
8	94	92.6	1.4
9	90	92.9	−2.9
10	96	92.3	3.7

WORKED
EXAMPLE **4.3**
••••••••••••

A firm is at the end of quarter 2. At the end of quarter 1 it had forecast that demand for its product in quarter 2 would be 84,000 units, only to find that actual demand turned out to be higher at 102,000 units. Provide an exponential forecast for demand in quarter 3, using $\alpha = 0.2$.

Solution

Y_2 = 102,000 (actual demand Q2)

$\hat{Y}_2$ = 84,000 (forecast demand Q2)

Here t, the current time period, is quarter 2 and α is 0.2.

$$\hat{Y}_{t+1} = \hat{Y}_t + \alpha(Y_t - \hat{Y}_t)$$

i.e. $\hat{Y}_{2+1} = \hat{Y}_2 + 0.2(Y_2 - \hat{Y}_2)$

$\hat{Y}_3 = 84,000 + 0.2\ (102,000 - 84,000)$

$\hat{Y}_3 = 84,000 + 0.2\ (18,000)$

$\hat{Y}_3 = 84,000 + 3,600$

$\underline{\hat{Y}_3 = 87,600}$

The impact of this exponential smoothing with $\alpha = 0.2$ on forecast sales is shown in Figure 4.5.

figure 4.5
Forecasting future sales using exponential smoothing and different values for α

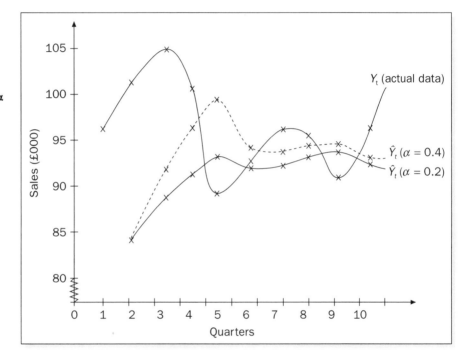

Different values of α

In Table 4.8 we assumed the 'smoothing constant', α, to be 0.2. We have already looked at the impact of extreme values ($\alpha = 0$, $\alpha = 1$) of α on exponential smoothing. In general we can say the following.

▶ When α is close to 0, only a small proportion of the latest error (E_t) will be included in the next forecast ($\hat{Y}_{t+1}$). Clearly that next forecast will not differ greatly from the previous forecast.

▶ When α is close to 1, a large proportion of the latest error (E_t) will be included in the next forecast ($\hat{Y}_{t+1}$). Clearly that next forecast will differ greatly from the previous forecast.

As we can see from Figure 4.5, using $\alpha = 0.2$ gives a smoother sequence of forecasts than would occur using $\alpha = 0.4$. This is because the $\alpha = 0.2$ sequence of forecasts for $\hat{Y}_{t+1}$ is less influenced by any actual observation (Y_t) and its divergence from its forecast value ($\hat{Y}_t$).

Choosing a value for α

It would seem reasonable to choose a value of α which, on previous experience, would have produced the 'best' forecast using exponential smoothing. 'Best' in this context would arguably be the value of α which gave a smaller sequence of errors (E_t), where $E_t = Y_t - \hat{Y}_t$.

Two possible ways of evaluating previous forecasts suggest themselves.

Mean absolute error (MAE)

Here we select that value of α which, on previous experience, minimises the average of the *absolute errors* (ignoring sign) of deviations between actual (Y_t) and forecast ($\hat{Y}_t$) values:

$$\text{MAE} = \frac{\sum\limits_{i=1}^{n} |E_t|}{n}$$

where $|\ \ |$ is modulus, i.e. ignore signs
n is number of error terms ($Y_t - \hat{Y}_t$)

Notice that n, the number of error terms, will be one less than the number of items of data since we do not have a forecast and therefore error term for the first item of data.

Mean squared error (MSE)

Here we select that value of α which, on previous experience, minimises the average of the *squares* of the errors. We have no sign problem here, as all squared values are positive:

$$\text{MSE} = \frac{\sum\limits_{i=1}^{n} E_t^2}{n}$$

where n is number of error terms ($Y_t - \hat{Y}_t$)

WORKED
EXAMPLE **4.4**
••••••••••••••

Use the data of Table 4.6 to provide forecasts using $\alpha = 0.2$, 0.3 and 0.4 respectively. Which value of α would you select for future forecasts?

Solution

We have already plotted the data for $\alpha = 0.2$ and 0.4 on Figure 4.5. Here we formally work out MAE and MSE for the nine error terms (E_t) based on these ten items of data.

	α = 0.2		α = 0.3		α = 0.4	
Quarter Y_t	E_t	E_t^2	E_t	E_t^2	E_t	E_t^2
1 96						
2 102	18.0	324.0	18.0	324.0	18.0	324.0
3 104	16.4	269.0	14.6	213.2	12.8	163.8
4 100	9.1	82.8	6.2	38.4	3.7	13.7
5 88	−4.7	22.1	−7.6	57.8	−9.8	96.0
6 92	0.2	0.0	−1.4	2.0	−1.9	3.6
7 96	4.2	17.6	3.1	9.6	2.9	8.4
8 94	1.4	2.0	0.1	0.0	−0.3	0.1
9 90	−2.9	8.4	−3.9	15.2	−4.2	17.6
10 96	3.7	13.7	3.3	10.9	3.5	12.3
	$\Sigma|E_t| = 60.6$	$\Sigma E_t^2 = 739.6$	$\Sigma|E_t| = 58.2$	$\Sigma E_t^2 = 671.1$	$\Sigma|E_t| = 57.1$	$\Sigma E_t^2 = 639.5$

Note: Although there are ten items of data there are only nine error terms, hence $n = 9$.

$$\text{MAE} = \frac{\Sigma|E|_t}{n}$$

(a) $\alpha = 0.2 = \dfrac{60.6}{9} = 6.73$

(b) $\alpha = 0.3 = \dfrac{58.2}{9} = 6.47$

(c) $\alpha = 0.4 = \dfrac{57.1}{9} = 6.34$

$$\text{MSE} = \frac{\Sigma E_t^2}{n}$$

(a) $\alpha = 0.2 = \dfrac{739.6}{9} = 82.18$

(b) $\alpha = 0.3 = \dfrac{671.1}{9} = 74.57$

(c) $\alpha = 0.4 = \dfrac{639.5}{9} = 71.06$

In this particular example the value $\alpha = 0.4$ will give the minimum value for *both* mean absolute error (MAE) and mean square error (MSE). It follows that our previous experiences of forecasting would arguably lead to the choice of $\alpha = 0.4$ for future forecasts when choosing between the possible values of $\alpha = 0.2$, 0.3 or 0.4.

REVIEW QUESTIONS

4.1 As a result of local government cutbacks some branch libraries are threatened with closure. A newly appointed chief librarian claims that a certain branch library has a declining patronage, based on his observations of the last three months. The head librarian of the branch disagrees with the analysis and quotes quarterly data recorded over the past three years for book issues to support his case. That data are as follows:

Year	Q1	Q2	Q3	Q4
1995	2,542	2,826	2,991	2,644
1996	2,766	2,905	3,048	3,137
1997	2,944	3,140	3,333	3,125

(a) Calculate the trend line using the moving average method.
(b) Plot the original data and the trend values on a scatter diagram.
(c) Calculate the seasonal variation factors.

4.2 The manufacturer of snow chains is considering building a new production plant to cope with growing demand. A tyre firm is interested in investing in the company and has been provided with the following quarterly sales figures:

Unit sales 1994–1997 (000s)

Year	Q1	Q2	Q3	Q4
1	441.1	397.7	396.1	472.8
2	476.4	454.4	450.8	553.5
3	580.7	573.2	571.6	703.6
4	692.0	676.5	659.9	752.8

(a) Calculate the trend line using the moving average method.
(b) Plot the original data and the trend values on a scatter diagram.
(c) Estimate and then eliminate the season variation component. In other words find the de-seasonalised data.

4.3 A company producing torches is negotiating with a company for the supply of torch bulbs. The bulb company therefore needs to plan its production to meet the needs of the torch company and thus uses that company's quarterly sales figures over the past three years to forecast future demand. The sales figures are as follows:

Quarterly sales Figures 1995–1997 (000s)

Year	Q1	Q2	Q3	Q4
1	349.4	295.5	196.9	389.3
2	447.5	418	324.1	456.4
3	550.6	528.6	415.2	615.3

Using the moving average technique find the trend observations and the seasonal variation factors. Fit a least squares regression line to the trend observations. Use this trend regression line and your estimates of the seasonal variation factors to forecast future demand for the four quarters of year 4 for torches.

4.4 The area sales manager of a company is responsible for providing a forecast for the value of sales. However, she has been taken ill and the deputy has now to make the forecast for the next month. The exponential smoothing method, favoured by the company, uses an α of 0.2. However, the deputy believes that an α of 0.3 is a more realistic smoothing constant. Using the data provided, forecast for the next month using each smoothing constant.

t	Y
1	3.85
2	3.22
3	3.18
4	3.61
5	3.62
6	3.48
7	3.53
8	3.62
9	3.36
10	3.58
11	3.62
12	3.24

Calculate the mean absolute error and the mean square error for each smoothing constant (assume an initial forecast for t=1 of 3.49). Which smoothing constant should be recommended based on the criterion of minimising the mean square error?

Note: Answers can be found on pp. 402–415.

Further study and data

Texts

Bancroft, G. and O'Sullivan, G. (1993), *Quantitative methods for accounting and business studies*, 3rd edn, McGraw Hill, chapter 10.

Curwin, J. and Slater, R. (1996), *Quantitative methods for business decisions*, 4th edn, Chapman and Hall, chapter 20.

Lawson, M., Hubbard, S. and Pugh, P. (1995), *Maths and statistics for business*, Addison Wesley Longman, chapter 11.

Morris, C. (1996), *Quantitative approaches in business studies*, 4th edn, Pitman, chapter 15.

Oakshott, L. (1996), *Essential elements of quantitative methods*, BPP, chapter 3.

Swift, L. (1997), *Mathematics and statistics for business, management and finance*, Macmillan, part C9.

Thomas, R. (1997), *Quantitative methods for business studies*, Prentice Hall, chapter 6.

Waters, D. (1997), *Quantitative methods*, 2nd edn, Addison Wesley Longman, chapter 9.

Wisniewski, M. with Stead, R. (1996), *Foundation quantitative methods for business*, Pitman, chapter 13.

Sources of information and data

See the list at the end of Chapter 1 (p. 25).

CHAPTER 5

Probability

Objectives
....

When you have read this chapter you should be able to:

▶ distinguish between *experimental* and *theoretical* probability;

▶ apply the 'AND' rule to *independent events* but the 'OR' rule to *mutually exclusive* events;

▶ use *Venn diagrams* to solve problems where events are not mutually exclusive;

▶ solve problems involving *conditional probability*, including those where *Bayes theorem* can be used;

▶ use *decision tree* analysis to show all the probabilities in complex situations, often involving conditional probabilities;

▶ identify situations in which probability calculations can aid the decision-making process, as in the case of *expected values*;

▶ calculate probabilities involving *permutations* or *combinations* of events.

Introduction
....

In this chapter we look at the basis for calculating the **probabilities** with which particular events, or combinations of events, might be expected to occur. In fact probabilities, together with the probability distributions we consider in Chapters 6 and 7, are the basis for many economic and business decisions. For example *insurance* against all kinds of possible future events is only possible because actuaries have worked out, often using past data, the probabilities of those events occurring. These probabilities then determine the *insurance premiums* to be charged for cover against such events. Of course if circumstances change, and with them the associated probabilities of such events occurring, then insurance premiums will have to rise or fall. The greater likelihood of burglary has, for instance, caused a rise in premiums for insuring house contents against theft.

In this chapter we consider the basis for probability calculations involving both **mutually exclusive** ('OR' rule) and **independent** ('AND' rule) events. In fact some events are neither mutually exclusive nor independent, in which case the **Venn** diagram can help us solve probability problems. We then move on to consider **conditional probabilities**, as in the case of Bayes' theorem. Decision tree analysis is seen as being particularly helpful in showing *all* the probabilities. The idea of **expected value** is also explored and applied to practical decision-making situations, using decision tree analysis in some cases. The chapter concludes by looking at **permutations** and **combinations** of events, which is the background to work on the Binomial and Poisson distributions in Chapter 6.

Answers to the 'Self-check questions', responses to each 'Pause for thought', and answers to the 'Review questions' can be found at the end of the book.

5.1 Probability calculations

Experimental probability

This can be found by performing an *experiment* many times and keeping an accurate record of the results. The *experimental probability* of a particular event happening can then be worked out as follows:

$$\text{Experimental probability} = \frac{\text{number of times the event has happened}}{\text{total number of possible occurrences}}$$

Example

When a normal dice was rolled 100 times, the number five was actually rolled 19 times. This gives an *experimental probability* ratio of $\dfrac{19}{100} = 0.19$.

Theoretical probability

This is found by considering *equally likely* events. The theoretical probability is found by using the following ratio.

Theoretical probability

$$= \frac{\text{number of ways an event can occur}}{\text{total number of different equally likely events that can occur}}$$

Examples

1   Rolling a dice and getting an even number has theoretical probability $\dfrac{3}{6} = \dfrac{1}{2}$

2   Rolling a dice and getting a number 5 has theoretical probability $\dfrac{1}{6} = 0.17$ (2 d.p)

Of course if an event is *impossible*, then its theoretical probability is 0. On the other hand, if the event is *certain*, then its theoretical probability is 1.

Notice that if we know the theoretical probability of an event occurring, then we also know the theoretical probability of it *not* occurring.

If the probability of an event occurring is, say, p then the probability of the event *not* occurring is $1 - p$.

Example

The theoretical probability of rolling a 5 on a dice $= \dfrac{1}{6}$

The theoretical probability of *not* rolling a 5 on a dice $= 1 - \dfrac{1}{6} = \dfrac{5}{6}$

PAUSE FOR THOUGHT 5.1 *Can you work out the theoretical probabilities for three different events?*

SELF-CHECK QUESTIONS

5.1 Write down the theoretical probability of the following events:

(a) rolling a dice and getting a 2
(b) rolling a dice and not getting a 3
(c) rolling a dice and getting an odd number
(d) rolling a dice and getting a 2 or a 3
(e) drawing an ace from a pack of cards
(f) drawing a card from a pack of cards and not getting a diamond
(g) being born on 31 April
(h) rolling a dice and getting a number less than 7
(i) buying a box of matches with an even number of matches in it
    (no quality control)
(j) picking a blue ball from a bag containing two blue and seven white balls
(k) picking a ball that is not blue from the above bag
(l) meeting someone whose birthday is not on a Saturday.

5.2 A bag contains 20 marbles, all the same size. Ten are blue, five are white, three are yellow and two are black. What is the theoretical probability of choosing at random

(a) a blue marble   (b) a black marble
(c) a white marble   (d) a marble that is yellow or black
(e) a marble that is not white

5.3 Two unbiased dice are thrown. Their scores are added to make a total between 2 and 12.

(a) There are 36 possible totals as indicated in Figure 5.1
    Copy and complete the table.

figure 5.1

one dice						
6	(1,6)					
5	(1,5)					
4	(1,4)					
3	(1,3)					
2	(1,2)	(2,2)	(3,2)			
1	(1,1)	(2,1)	(3,1)	(4,1)	(5,1)	(6,1)
	1	2	3	4	5	6

other dice

(b) **Write down the theoretical probability of throwing a total of**

(i)   2   (ii)   3   (iii) 4
(iv) 6   (v)   7   (vi) 8
(vii) 10   (viii) 12

(c) **What is the theoretical probability of not getting a total of 7?**

Note: **Answers can be found on p. 338.**

5.2 Mutually exclusive events: OR rule

If one event excludes the possibility of another event happening, then we say that the two events are **mutually exclusive**

Example (i) tossing a coin and getting a head and a tail;
        (ii) rolling a dice once and getting a 2 and a 3.

Events that are mutually exclusive can have their probabilities *added* to find the probability of one **OR** the other happening.

> **OR rule: Mutually Exclusive Events**
> For two mutually exclusive events A and B, the probability of A OR B occurring can be written as:
>
> P(A) OR P(B) = P(A) + P(B)

Example

If I roll a dice what is the probability that I roll a three or four?

Probability of rolling a three $= \dfrac{1}{6}$

Probability of rolling a four $= \dfrac{1}{6}$

The probability of rolling a three OR a four $= \dfrac{1}{6} + \dfrac{1}{6} = \dfrac{2}{6} = \dfrac{1}{3}$

WORKED
EXAMPLE **5.1**

A stockbroker uses past experience to work out the probabilities of a particular share changing in price over the year. His findings for 'events' A to E and associated experimental probabilities, are as follows:

A   Share price rises by 15% or more: P(A) = 0.2
B   Share price rises *less than* 15%: P(B) = 0.3
C   Share price remains unchanged: P(C) = 0.1
D   Share price falls *less than* 15%: P(D) = 0.25
E   Share price falls by 15% or more: P(E) = 0.15

Find:

(i)   the probability that the share price will rise
(ii) the probability that the share price will not rise
(iii) the probability that the share price will fall

Solution

The events A to E are mutually exclusive, if one happens the others do not:

(i)   P(A or B) = P(A) + P(B) = 0.2 + 0.3 = 0.5
(ii) 1 − P(A or B) = 1 − 0.5 = 0.5
(iii) P(D or E) = P(D) + P(E) = 0.25 + 0.15 = 0.40

PAUSE FOR THOUGHT 5.2   *Can you identify three different situations involving mutually exclusive events and calculate the probability using the OR rule?*

5.3 Venn diagrams: events not mutually exclusive

Sometimes events can occur at the same time, so that they are *not* mutually exclusive. In solving this type of problem it can help to make use of a **Venn diagram**.

Suppose, for example, that we have a pack of 52 cards and that event A is drawing a club and event B drawing a picture card. We now want to work out the probability of a card drawn at random being either a club or a picture card, i.e. P(A OR B). A pack of 52 cards will have 13 clubs and 12 picture cards.

In this case we *cannot* use the OR rule for mutually exclusive events since here a club could itself be a picture card, i.e. events A and B are *not* mutually exclusive. Of the 13 club cards in the pack, the Jack, Queen and King of clubs are picture cards. There is therefore a danger of double counting if we use the conventional OR rule for mutually exclusive events. The correct answer here is:

$$P\,(A\ OR\ B) = \frac{13}{52} + \frac{12}{52} - \frac{3}{52} = \frac{22}{52}$$

OR rule: Non-Mutually Exclusive Events

P(A OR B) = P(A) + P(B) − P(AB)

The Venn diagram (Figure 5.2) can be useful in solving problems involving events that are *not* mutually exclusive, i.e. which 'overlap' in some way.

figure 5.2
Venn diagram for pack of cards, where A = club card and B = picture card

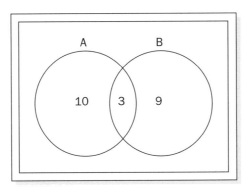

We can note the following from Figure 5.2.

▶ The area of the rectangle corresponds to *all* the possible events in the sample, here the 52 different cards which could be drawn from the pack.
▶ The circle A corresponds to the 13 club cards.
▶ The circle B corresponds to the 12 picture cards.
▶ The *overlap* between the two circles corresponds to the fact that three of the club cards can themselves be picture cards.

When completing a Venn diagram it is essential that you first consider the *area of overlap* before going any further. Therefore enter the 3 in the area of overlap in Figure 5.2, then 10 in the remainder of the circle A representing club cards and 9 in the remainder of the circle B representing picture cards. The required probability that a card drawn at random from the pack is a club OR a picture is obtained by adding up these numbers, namely 10 + 3 + 9 = 22, and then dividing by the total sample of 52 to obtain the result (22/52) already outlined.

SELF-CHECK QUESTIONS

5.4 A company puts in two separate bids, A and B, for a particular contract. The probability that it will obtain the contract by bid A is 0.3, but 0.5 that it will obtain the contract by bid B. What is the probability that it will obtain the contract by bid A or bid B?

5.5 A company usually recruits 25 management trainees per annum. In 1997, 140 applications were received and of these:

78 had previous work experience
43 had passed a vocational exam
21 had both work experience and had passed a vocational exam (and had been included in the above figures)

(a) Use a Venn diagram to illustrate this situation.
(b) What is the probability that an applicant selected at random had previous work experience or had passed a vocational exam?

Note: **Answers can be found on pp. 338–339.**

5.4 Independent events: AND rule

If *one* event has no effect on another event then we say that the events are **independent**. To find the probability of BOTH events happening (one event **AND** then the other) we *multiply* their probabilities.

Example
From a normal pack of cards, what is the probability of drawing an Ace, putting it back and then drawing a King?

Probability of drawing an ace $\dfrac{4}{52} = \dfrac{1}{13}$

Probability of drawing a King $\dfrac{4}{52} = \dfrac{1}{13}$

Since we have independent events, we multiply their individual probabilities,

i.e. $\dfrac{1}{13} \times \dfrac{1}{13} = \dfrac{1}{169}$

Events that are independent can have their probabilities *multiplied* to find the probability of one AND the other happening.

AND rule

For two independent events A and B, the probability of A AND B occurring can be written as:

P(A) AND P(B) = P(A) × P(B)

WORKED
EXAMPLE **5.2**
· · · · · · · · · · · · · ·

Each one of three separate boxes has 100 electrical components in it. The first box has six faulty items, the second 8 and the third 5. One component is taken from each box. What is the probability that:

(a) all three components are faulty
(b) all three components are good?

Solution

Selecting a component from each box is an independent event. Let us call selecting a component from the respective boxes as events A, B and C.

(a) Here we let P represent the probability of selecting a *faulty* component.

P(A AND B AND C) = P(A) × P(B) × P(C)
                           = 0.06 × 0.08 × 0.05
P(A AND B AND C) = 0.000240

In other words the probability of selecting three faulty components is 0.024 per cent or 0.000240 as a decimal.

(b) Here we let P represent the probability of selecting a *good* component

P(A AND B AND C) = P(A) × P(B) × P(C)
                           = 0.94 × 0.92 × 0.95
P(A AND B AND C) = 0.82156

In other words the probability of selecting three good components is 82.156 per cent or 0.82156 as a decimal.

SELF-CHECK
QUESTIONS

5.6 A product is made up of five independently produced components. The probability of any one component being defective is 0.03. What is the probability of all five components being 'good' (i.e. of none being defective)?

5.7 In a given batch of seeds, the probability of a seed germinating is 0.95. The probability of a blue flower coming from any one of the germinating seeds is 0.4. What is the probability that any one seed will result in a blue flower?

5.8 Two school friends always do their best at homework, but at mathematics the probability that Lee gets problems right is 3/4, while the probability that Conrad gets the problems right is 9/10. What is the probability that

(a) both get a problem correct
(b) both get a problem wrong
(c) neither gets a problem wrong?

Note: Answers can be found on p. 339.

5.5 Conditional probability

Here we look at situations where the probability of an event occurring depends in part on whether or not other events have already occurred. We call this **conditional probability**.

Some events are neither mutually exclusive nor independent. However, if they do happen, they influence the probability of other, subsequent, events happening. For example, if we purchase a cheaper, lower quality machine tool, then the probability of its requiring repair over the next year will be higher than if we had selected a more expensive, higher quality machine tool. In other words we are looking at *dependent* events involving situations of conditional probability.

It will help to become familiar with some terminology:

$P(A)$ = Probability of event A
$P(B|A)$ = Probability of event B, given that event A has already occurred.
$P(C|AB)$ = Probability of event C, given that events A and B have already occurred, etc.

The contrast between *independent* events (AND rule) and *dependent* events (conditional probability) can be illustrated in the following example involving drawing coloured balls from a bag. When we *replace* the ball selected on the first draw before we draw the second ball, then the second draw is *independent* of the first. However when we *do not replace* the first ball before we draw the second ball, then the second draw is *dependent* on the first.

WORKED
EXAMPLE **5.3**

A bag contains 40 balls, of which 16 are red and 24 are blue. Three balls are drawn separately from the bag. What is the probability of drawing three red balls:

(a) when each ball drawn is *replaced* before the next draw?
(b) when each ball drawn is *not replaced* before the next draw?

Solution

(a) Here we have replacement so that we can treat the events as being independent. It follows that the AND rule applies. Because of replacement the probabilities of selecting a particular colour of ball on each draw remain the same.

Let A = getting a red ball on first draw
Let B = getting a red ball on second draw
Let C = getting a red ball on third draw

$$P(ABC) = P(A) \times P(B) \times P(C)$$

where $P(A) = P(B) = P(C) = \dfrac{16}{40} = 0.4$

So $P(ABC) = 0.4 \times 0.4 \times 0.4 = 0.064$

In other words, with replacement, there is a 6.4 per cent or 0.064 probability of selecting three successive red balls from the bag.

(b) Here we do *not* have replacement, so the probabilities of selecting subsequent red balls are *dependent* on whether a previous red ball has been selected.

$$P(ABC) = \dfrac{16}{40} \times \dfrac{15}{39} \times \dfrac{14}{38} = \dfrac{3,360}{59,280} = 0.057 \text{ (to 3 d.p.)}$$

In other words, without replacement, there is a 5.7 per cent or 0.057 probability of selecting three successive red balls from the bag.

Bayes' theorem

The idea of conditional probability can be expressed more formally using *Bayes' theorem*. This states that the probability of two *dependent events* occurring can be expressed as the probability of the first event occurring multiplied by the conditional probability of the second event occurring given that the first has already occurred (and so on for more than two events).

Where A and B are *dependent events*
$$P(A \text{ AND } B) = P(A) \times (P(B|A)$$
but $P(B \text{ AND } A) = P(B) \times P(A|B)$
i.e. $P(A) \times P(B|A) = P(B) \times P(A|B)$

We can express this result as follows:

Formulae for Bayes theorem

$$P(B|A) = \dfrac{P(B) \times P(A|B)}{P(A)}$$

i.e. $P(B \text{ given } A) = \dfrac{P(B \text{ AND } A)}{P(A)}$

Alternatively we can express the above as:

$$P(A|B) = \dfrac{P(A) \times P(B|A)}{P(B)}$$

i.e. $P(A \text{ given } B) = \dfrac{P(A \text{ AND } B)}{P(B)}$

This result is often referred to as *Bayes' theorem* and is widely used in calculations for problems involving conditional probabilities.

WORKED
EXAMPLE **5.4**
....

40 workers in a large office can be classified as follows:

	Clerical grade	Administrative grade
Male	4	6
Female	22	8

(a) If a worker is selected at random from the office, what is the probability that the worker will be in the administrative grade?

(b) If the worker selected is female, what is the probability that she will be in the administrative grade?

(c) If the worker selected is male, what is the probability that he will be in the administrative grade?

(d) If the worker selected is in the administrative grade, what is the probability of the worker being male?

Solution

(a) P(admin. grade) $= \dfrac{14}{40} = 0.35$

(b) We can work this out as $\dfrac{8}{30} = 0.267$ (to 3 d.p.) since of the 30 female workers only eight are in the administrative grade.

However we can also work this out more formally using Bayes' theorem.

Via Bayes' theorem

$$(\text{admin. grade} | \text{female}) = \frac{P(\text{admin. grade AND female})}{P(\text{female})}$$

where:

$$P(\text{admin. grade AND female}) = \frac{8}{40} = 0.2$$

$$P(\text{female}) = \frac{30}{40} = 0.75$$

$$\text{So } P(\text{admin. grade} | \text{female}) = \frac{0.2}{0.75} = 0.267 \text{ (to 3 d.p.)}$$

(c) We can work this out as $\dfrac{6}{10} = 0.6$ since of the ten male workers six are in the administrative grade.

Via Bayes' theorem

$$P(\text{admin. grade}|\text{male}) = \frac{P(\text{admin. grade AND male})}{P(\text{male})}$$

where:

$$P(\text{admin. grade AND male}) = \frac{6}{40} = 0.15$$

$$P(\text{male}) = \frac{10}{40} = 0.25$$

$$\text{So } P(\text{admin. grade}|\text{male}) = \frac{0.15}{0.25} = 0.6$$

(d) We can work this out as $\dfrac{6}{14} = 0.429$ (to 3 d.p.) since of the 14 administrative grade workers six are male.

Via Bayes' theorem

$$P(\text{male}|\text{admin. grade}) = \frac{P(\text{male AND admin. grade})}{P(\text{admin. grade})}$$

where

$$P(\text{male AND admin. grade}) = \frac{6}{40} = 0.15$$

$$P(\text{admin. grade}) = \frac{14}{40} = 0.35$$

$$\text{So } P(\text{male}|\text{admin. grade}) = \frac{0.15}{0.35} = 0.429 \text{ (to 3 d.p.)}$$

5.6 Decision trees

It is often helpful to visualise a problem involving probability on a **decision tree**. When we can clearly see *all* the possibilities in a given situation it makes it much easier to calculate the relevant probabilities. Although decision trees can be used in any situation, they are particularly helpful when solving problems involving conditional probability.

WORKED
EXAMPLE **5.5**

A bag contains five blue marbles, three yellow marbles and two white marbles. Two marbles are then drawn from the bag, the first marble *not* being replaced before the second marble is drawn.

What is the probability that:

(a) both marbles are the same colour

(b) both marbles are a different colour

(c) at least one marble is blue?

The decision tree (Figure 5.3) helps us see all the possibilities involved in this problem.

figure 5.3
Using a decision tree

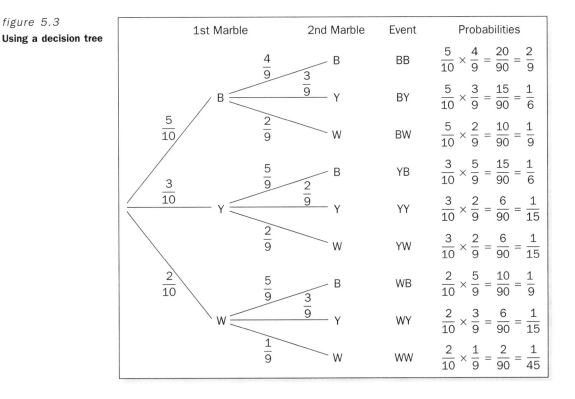

Notice that to find the probability of an event involving any two outcomes occurring (e.g. blue marble AND blue marble, BB) we *multiply* the probabilities.

So $P(BB) = P(B) \times P(B|B)$

The probability of two blues is the probability of the first marble being blue x the probability of the second marble being blue given that the first is blue:

i.e. $P(BB) = \dfrac{5}{10} \times \dfrac{4}{9} = \dfrac{20}{90} = \dfrac{2}{9}$

However when we calculate solutions to (a), (b) or (c) below which involve either one OR more events occurring, we *add* the probabilities.

Solution

(a) Both marbles having the same colour can be achieved in three different ways, either two blues OR two yellows OR two whites.

   i.e.   P(both marbles same colour) = P(BB) + P(YY) + P(WW)

$$= \dfrac{2}{9} + \dfrac{1}{15} + \dfrac{1}{45} = \dfrac{14}{45}$$

(b) Both marbles having a different colour will have the probability of 1 *minus* the probability they both have the same colour.

    i.e. P(both marbles different colour) = 1 − P(both marbles same colour)

$$= 1 - \frac{14}{45} = \frac{31}{45}$$

(c) The probability of at least one marble being blue can be achieved in five possible ways:

P(BB) OR P(BY) OR P(BW) OR P(YB) OR P(WB)

$$\frac{2}{9} \quad + \quad \frac{1}{6} \quad + \quad \frac{1}{9} \quad + \quad \frac{1}{6} \quad + \quad \frac{1}{9}$$

    i.e. P(at least one marble blue) $= \dfrac{20 + 15 + 10 + 15 + 10}{90} = \dfrac{70}{90} = \dfrac{7}{9}$

Clearly the decision tree is a useful visual aid, helping us see more clearly how we can apply the various probability rules already learned, especially in situations involving conditional probability. As we shall see in the next section, the decision tree is also helpful in applying the idea of *expected value* to business decision making.

SELF-CHECK QUESTIONS

5.9 **A box of 20 components contains six defective components. If three components are drawn consecutively from the box, what is the probability of all three components being good (non-defective):**

    (a) if there is replacement
    (b) if there is no replacement

    Use a decision tree to help solve the next problem.

5.10 **Two cards are dealt out to a player from a full pack (without replacement). What is the probability of:**

    (a) both being a diamond
    (b) one of them being a diamond
    (c) neither of them being a diamond?

Note: **Answers can be found on p. 339.**

DID YOU KNOW?

The expected value of the benefits from reducing the lead content in petrol by 1 gram per gallon in the USA has been estimated at over $1 billion per annum. This calculation involved estimating the probabilities of certain health and economic benefits occurring (e.g. reduced adult blood pressure, raised children's IQs, greater fuel economy, etc.) and then placing a monetary value on each of these benefits.

5.7 Expected value

The expected value (EV) of a particular event which has different possible outcomes is a weighted average of the values (pay-offs) associated with each possible outcome. The probabilities of each outcome are used as the weights and these are *multiplied* by the respective pay-offs of each outcome.

Take, for example a situation in which there are two possible outcomes having pay-offs X_1 and X_2 with the probabilities of each outcome p_1 and p_2 respectively, then the expected value EV(X) is:

$$EV(X) = p_1 X_1 + p_2 X_2$$

For example, if there is a 60 per cent chance of earning £1,000 and a 40 per cent chance of earning £5,000 from an investment, then:

$$E(X) = 0.60(£1,000) + 0.40(£5,000)$$
i.e. $$E(X) = £600 + £2,000 = £2,600$$

More generally, using the short-hand notation of Chapter 2, the expected value (EV) of a particular course of action over n possible outcomes can be defined as:

Formulae for expected value

$$EV = \sum_{i=1}^{n} p_i \cdot X_i$$

where p_i = probability of ith outcome
X_i = value of ith outcome

and $\sum_{i=1}^{n} p_i = 1$

This last condition merely states that we have covered all possible outcomes, so the sum of their probabilities must be 1.

WORKED
EXAMPLE **5.6**
· · · · · · · · · · · · · ·

A fair coin is tossed and, for a £1 stake, the gambler is promised £1.80 if the result is a head, but only £0.10 if the result is a tail. What is the expected value to the gambler of each throw?

Let p_1 = the probability of head (0.5)
p_2 = the probability of tail (0.5)
X_1 = the 'pay-off' of a head (£1.80)
X_2 = the 'pay-off' of a tail (£0.10)

Solution

$$EV = \sum_{i=1}^{2} p_i \cdot X_i$$

i.e. EV = $p_1 X_1 + p_2 X_2$
EV = $0.5 \times £1.80 + 0.5 \times £0.10$
EV = £0.90 + £0.05
EV = £0.95

The gambler can therefore 'expect' to lose 5 pence on each throw of the dice, though he/she might be lucky and get more heads than tails on the early throws of the dice, and thereby win by 'quitting while they are ahead'.

On the other hand, the individual *offering* the gamble can 'expect' to make a profit (revenue – cost) of £0.05 on each throw (£1.00 – £0.95).

Clearly the greater the number of 'trials', e.g. throws of the dice in our example, the more likely it will be that the *theoretical probabilities* (see p. 99) will apply rather than the *experimental probabilities* (see p. 99) of a 'lucky' or 'unlucky' run.

Expected value and decision trees

We can relate this idea of expected value (EV) to the decision tree analysis already presented (p. 108). As we have seen, a decision tree is a diagram which can usefully represent a series of choices and their possible outcomes. Where the outcome is *pure chance*, then the overall probability of 1 will be divided *equally* between all the possible outcomes (e.g. 0.5 for each of two pure chance outcomes). Where the outcome is *uncertain* but where some outcomes are more likely than others, then the decision maker may assign *probabilities* to each possible outcome. The sum of these probabilities over all possible outcomes must, of course, be equal to 1.

The sequence of decisions and outcomes is represented graphically as the branches of the 'tree' (see Figure 5.4). At every point (node) that a decision must be made or an outcome must occur, the tree branches out further until all the possible outcomes have been displayed.

figure 5.4
Decision tree

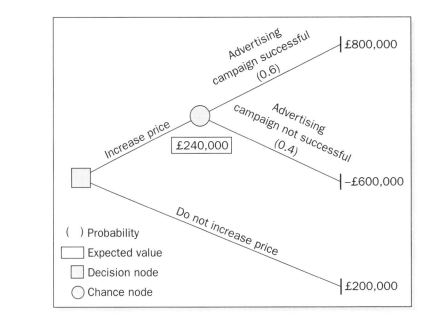

► **Boxes (decision nodes)** are usually used to indicate situations where the decision maker consciously selects a particular course of action (strategy) and where the outcome of that action is 'certain'. Branches coming out of these boxes simply indicate the alternative decisions or strategies which might be taken, each of which has a probability of 1 once selected.

► **Circles (chance nodes)** are usually used to indicate situations reflecting a 'state of nature', i.e. situations whose outcomes are *not* entirely under the conscious control of the decision maker. Branches coming out of such circles show the various possibilities which might occur, together with estimates of their probability of occurrence.

► **Pay-offs** are the valuations placed at the end of particular branches emanating from chance nodes. They are the values which management allocates to that event or outcome should it actually occur, and are often denoted by a straight (vertical) line at the end of the branch.

In Figure 5.4, at the *decision node* box, the decision maker must decide between a strategy of increasing price or keeping price unchanged. If this latter strategy is pursued, only one profit outcome is possible which is evaluated at £200,000. If the former strategy (increasing price) is pursued, then the decision maker intends to support the policy change by an active advertising campaign. However the outcome of such an advertising campaign is not entirely under the control of the decision maker. He estimates that there is a 60 per cent (0.60) chance of the campaign being a success and a 40 per cent (0.40) chance of it being a failure. These two branches are therefore shown as emanating from a *chance node*, indicated by a circle. The firm estimates profits of £800,000 should the advertising campaign (allied to a price increase) be successful, but losses of £600,000 should it fail.

Backward induction

Which branch the firm should choose in order to maximise the expected profit can easily be determined. The process of solving this problem is called *backward induction*. This requires us to begin at the right-hand side of the decision tree, where the profit figures are located. The first step is to calculate the *expected profit* when the firm is situated at the chance node immediately to the left of these pay-off figures.

Because there is a 0.60 probability that the branch culminating in a profit of £800,000 will occur, and a 0.40 probability that the branch culminating in a loss of £600,000 will occur, the expected value (EV) of profit when situated at this chance node is:

EV (profit) = 0.60 (£800,000) + 0.40 (−£600,000) = £240,000

This number is written below the chance node in question to show that this is the expected profit when located at that node.

Moving further to the left along the decision tree, it is clear that the firm has a choice of two branches, one of which leads to an expected profit of £240,000, the other of which leads to an expected profit of £200,000. If the firm wants to maximise expected profit, it should choose the former branch. In other words, it should increase its price and accompany this with an advertising campaign.

WORKED
EXAMPLE **5.7**
••••••••••••••

Firm A faces a choice between two policy options. One is to make a certain annual profit of £100,000 from interest on a sum of money left on deposit in a bank. The second is to invest that same sum of money in new product development (perfume).

If Firm A introduces the perfume, there is a 70 per cent probability that a major competitor, Firm B, will react by introducing a similar product and a 30 per cent probability that it will not.

Should it decide to introduce the new perfume product, Firm A can choose a high price (HP), a medium price (MP) or a low price (LP) for its new perfume product.

How much profit Firm A *estimates* that it will make depends on a number of factors.

(i)   Whether or not Firm B reacts with a similar product
(ii) What strategy on price Firm A selects.
(iii) What counter strategy on price Firm B selects.

Firm A calculates the following table to represent the estimated profits (in present value terms) from the different possible outcomes. Firm A has assigned various probabilities to each possible outcome.

Competition	Firm A's price strategy	Firm B's price response	Probability	Firm A's profit £s
Yes	HP	HP	0.6	150,000
Yes	HP	MP	0.3	100,000
Yes	HP	LP	0.1	90,000
Yes	MP	HP	0.3	120,000
Yes	MP	MP	0.5	100,000
Yes	MP	LP	0.2	60,000
Yes	LP	HP	0.0	250,000
Yes	LP	MP	0.4	150,000
Yes	LP	LP	0.6	100,000
No	HP		–	600,000
No	MP		–	300,000
No	LP		–	200,000

Construct a decision tree and use it to suggest whether Firm A should invest in the new perfume or leave its funds to earn interest in the bank.

Solution

Figure 5.5 presents the decision tree for this problem.

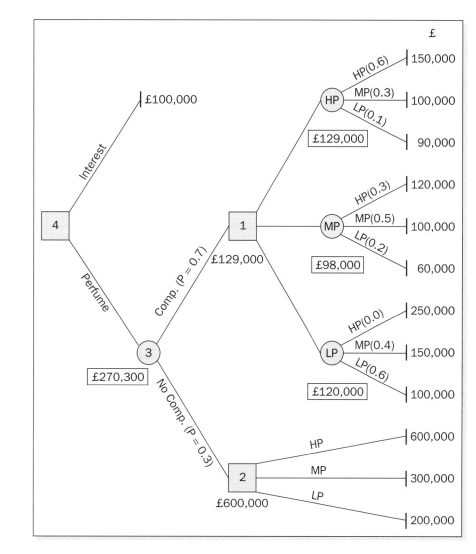

figure 5.5
Decision tree:
perfume problem

Using the technique of *backward induction* we begin our solutions at the right-hand side and work leftwards, back to the initial decision node (Box 4). However we can see that there are two 'earlier' decision nodes (Boxes 1 and 2) and four chance nodes (Circles HP, MP, LP and (3). The pay-offs are listed at the end of the branches furthest to the right.

At decision box 1, Firm A must choose between a high price (HP), medium price (MP) and low price (LP) strategy. Its choice will depend on the expected value (shown underneath each chance node) of each pricing strategy, which in turn depends on the probabilities of the price responses of Firm B and the pay-offs estimated for each response.

Using our earlier expected value (EV) formula:

$$EV = \sum_{i=1}^{n} p_i X_i$$

with all values in £000s we can say:

EV(Firm A, HP strategy) = 0.6(150) + 0.3(100) + 0.1(90)

= 90 + 30 + 9

i.e. <u>EV (HP) = £129(000)</u>

EV (Firm A, MP strategy) = 0.3(120) + 0.5(100) + 0.2(60)

= 36 + 50 + 12

i.e. <u>EV (MP) = £98(000)</u>

EV (Firm A, LP strategy) = 0.0(250) + 0.4(150) + 0.6(100)

= 0 + 60 + 60

i.e. <u>EV (LP) = £120(000)</u>

At decision node 1, Firm A will select the strategy with the highest expected profit pay-off, i.e. a higher price (HP) strategy (in the event of competition from Firm B), yielding £129,000 in expected profit.

At decision node 2, Firm A has no probabilities to contend with since the pay-offs listed are *not* associated with the possible reactions of Firm B. Here it can select the higher price (HP) strategy (in the event of no competition from Firm B) yielding £600,000 in expected profit.

However there are probabilities associated with whether or not Firm B will react with a new product of its own. Therefore we must take these into account in working out the expected value at chance node 3.

EV (perfume product) = 0.7(129) + 0.3(600)

= 90.3 + 180

i.e. <u>EV (perfume product) = £270.3(000) = £270,300</u>

At the initial decision box (4) we can see that, based on our expectations, there will be greater profit from investing the available money in the new perfume product than from leaving the money earning interest in the bank.

An approach such as that in worked example 5.7 is often said to be using different *scenarios,* i.e. the evaluation of different possible outcomes for various policy initiatives. Of course if the *probabilities* were to change, for any reasons, or the expected pay-offs were to change, then any initial decision must be reevaluated in the light of these new circumstances.

There is also the issue of the *risk* associated with any decision. For example the £100,000 earned via bank interest is likely to be much less risky than the higher expected value of £270,300 earned via new product development. We return to the ideas of investment appraisal and risk analysis in Chapter 9, p. 209.

SELF-CHECK QUESTIONS

5.11 A machine produces 35 defective items per 2,000 items produced.

(a) What is the probability of an item selected at random being defective?

(b) If 4,500 items are produced per day, how many defective items would you expect?

5.12 A company is considering introducing a new computer system for one of its northern branch offices. The company can lease a small, medium or large

computer system. The firm estimates that if the economy continues to expand over the next year the extra profits from each system will be £100,000, £150,000 and £200,000 respectively. If the economy slows down the extra profits generated will be £60,000, £20,000 and a loss of £20,000 respectively. It is estimated that the probability of continued expansion is 0.4 and of slowdown is 0.6. Construct a decision tree diagram to represent this problem and use the expected value approach to recommend one of the computer systems.

5.13 Clover design have developed a new product and are considering either test marketing it at a cost of £65,000 or abandoning it. If the project is abandoned (at any stage) the firm can recoup £20,000 from the sale of specialist equipment. The probability of a favourable result from the test market is estimated as 0.65 and an unfavourable result as 0.35. If the test market is unfavourable the project will be abandoned. A favourable test market could be followed either by abandonment of the project or by development. It is estimated that the extra profits generated will depend on the response of rival firms: if there is no response then profits will be £250,000 on the other hand, if rivals do respond and develop a similar product, then losses of £90,000 will be incurred. The probability of rivals responding is 0.3 and of not responding is 0.7. Illustrate this problem with a decision tree diagram and advise the company.

Note: Answers can be found on p. 340.

5.8 Permutations and combinations

The ideas of permutations and combinations will, as we shall see, play an important role in the *probability distributions* considered in chapter 6. It will be useful, at the outset, to become familiar with a certain type of notation often used in these types of problems.

Factorial notation

The exclamation mark of English language means something rather different here. For example 6! is the mathematical symbol for 6 factorial which means $6 \times 5 \times 4 \times 3 \times 2 \times 1 = 720$. Some calculators have a key marked $x!$, and if you enter 6 and press this key you obtain 720.

Use your calculator to show that $7! = 5,040$.

Note: $1! = 1$ and $0! = 1$.

Permutations

Suppose you are given ten desirable qualities for a new product and are asked to place 4 of these in order of merit, i.e. first, second, third, fourth, in how many different ways can this be done?

Clearly the ordering of the four qualities selected *does* matter here. We are therefore seeking the number of possible *permutations*. The first place can in fact be chosen in ten different ways; having chosen the first place, there are nine possible places left, so that the second place can be chosen in nine different ways. Similarly, the third place can be chosen in eight different ways and the fourth place in seven different ways. The total number of ways is $10 \times 9 \times 8 \times 7 = 5{,}040$.

This may be written using factorial notation

$$10 \times 9 \times 8 \times 7 = \frac{10 \times 9 \times 8 \times 7 \times 6 \times 5 \times 4 \times 3 \times 2 \times 1}{6 \times 5 \times 4 \times 3 \times 2 \times 1} = \frac{10!}{6!} = 5{,}040$$

Formula for permutations

In general, if there are *n* items and *r* are to be placed *in order*, the number of different ways (*permutations*) in which this can be done is:

$$_nP_r = \frac{n!}{(n-r)!}$$

The example above would be written

$$_{10}P_4 \text{ i.e. } \frac{10!}{(10-4)!} = \frac{10!}{6!} = 5{,}040$$

In other words 5,040 different permutations are possible when choosing four out of ten items and then ordering them accordingly.

Combinations

Here we are *not* interested in the ordering of the items selected.

Consider again the example used for permutations. Suppose we wish to select four desirable qualities of a new product out of the ten desirable qualities given (*irrespective of the order of merit*). The number of ways of doing this is equal to the number of permutations, 5,040, *divided* by the number of ways of placing the four selected items in order of merit. In fact we can arrange the four selected items in $4 \times 3 \times 2 \times 1 = 4! = 24$ different ways. The result of 5,040 divided by 24 is 210, and this is called the number of *combinations*.

Using factorial notation, the number of combinations is equal to:

$$\frac{10!}{6! \times 4!} = \frac{10 \times 9 \times 8 \times 7 \times 6 \times 5 \times 4 \times 3 \times 2 \times 1}{(6 \times 5 \times 4 \times 3 \times 2 \times 1) \times (4 \times 3 \times 2 \times 1)} = \frac{3{,}628{,}800}{720 \times 24} = 210$$

Formula for combinations

In general, if there are *n* items and *r* are to be selected irrespective of order, the number of ways (*combinations*) in which this can be done is:

$$_nC_r = \frac{n!}{(n-r)! \times r!}$$

It is useful to find $_nC_r$ for $r = 0, 1, 2, 3 \ldots$

$$r = 0: {_nC_0} = \frac{n!}{n! \times 0!} = 1$$

$$r = 1: {_nC_1} = \frac{n!}{(n-1)! \times 1!} = n$$

$$r = 2: {_nC_2} = \frac{n!}{(n-2)! \times 1!} = \frac{n(n-1)}{2 \times 1}$$

$$r = 3: {_nC_3} = \frac{n!}{(n-3)! \times 3!} = \frac{n(n-1)(n-2)}{3 \times 2 \times 1}$$

The values

$$1, n, \frac{n(n-1)}{2 \times 1}, \frac{n(n-1)(n-2)}{3 \times 2 \times 1}, \frac{n(n-1)(n-2)(n-3)}{4 \times 3 \times 2 \times 1}, \ldots$$

are called *binomial coefficients*. We need these in the next chapter when we consider Binomial and Poisson probability distributions.

SELF-CHECK QUESTIONS

5.14 How many ways can we select three elements from a set of eight elements:

(a) where the selected elements are ranked in order?
(b) where the selected elements are not ranked in order?

5.15 A batch of 20 video recorders contains four defectives. A sample of five videos is to be selected from the batch.

(a) How many possible samples are there?
(b) If all the samples were to contain only non-defective videos, how many ways can this occur?

5.16 Five students (A, B, C, D and E) have been elected to the student union.

(a) If three students are to be selected for a committee, how many different committees are possible?
(b) If the three members are to become chairperson, treasurer and secretary, how many different line ups from the five students are possible?

Note: Answers can be found on p. 341.

REVIEW QUESTIONS

5.1 An insurance company estimates that, in a large city, one home in every 50 is broken into each year. The company has recently sold 1,600 home insurance policies in the city.

(a) How many claims can the company expect in a one year period?
(b) If the typical claim is for £750 what is the minimum (ignore all other costs) the company must charge for each policy in order to break even?

5.2 The probability that a record shop will sell at most eight copies of a particular CD each day is 0.60 and the probability that it will sell from nine to 12 copies of the CD each day is 0.35. What is the probability of:

(a) at least nine sales;
(b) at most 12 sales;
(c) more than 12 sales?

5.3 A sample of four items is selected from a batch that contains eight defective items and 24 without defects. What is the probability that:

(a) all four items selected will be defective (assume replacement);
(b) all four items are not defective (again assume replacement)?
(c) How would your answers to (a) and (b) alter if there was no replacement?

5.4 Two hundred first year business studies students enrol at a university. Seventy are male and choose the marketing stream, 16 are male and do not choose marketing, 90 are female and choose marketing, 24 are female and do not choose marketing. If a student is selected at random what is the probability that the student will:

(a) be male;
(b) be female;
(c) be in the marketing stream;
(d) be male and study marketing?
(e) If a student is female, find the probability that she is not studying marketing.

5.5 Records show that for every 100 items produced in a factory during the day shift, two are defective, and for every 100 produced during the night shift, four are defective. If, during a 24 hour period, 2,000 items are produced during the day and 800 during the night, what is the probability that an item picked at random from the 2,800 produced during the 24 hour period:

(a) was produced in the day shift and was defective;
(b) was produced in the night shift and was defective;
(c) is defective irrespective of the shift?
(d) If a selected item is defective, what is the probability that it came from the day shift?
(e) If a selected item is defective, what is the probability that it came from the night shift?

5.6 A market research company has studied the quality of after-sales service provided by 100 electrical retailers in a region. The findings are summarised below:

	Good service	Poor service
High street chain	40	24
Independent retailer	26	10

(a) If a retailer is selected at random, what is the probability that the retailer gives good service?

(b) If a retailer is selected at random, what is the probability that the one selected is independent and gives good service?

(c) What is the probability that a retailer that is part of a high street chain will give poor service?

5.7 A sales representative finds that the probability of making a sale on the first visit to a new client is 0.5. On the second visit the probability of making a sale is 0.6 if a sale was made on the first visit and 0.4 if no sale was made on the first visit. Use a tree diagram to work out the probability of just one sale resulting from the two visits.

5.8 An employer is attempting to estimate the proportion of employees who drink alcohol regularly during their lunch break. In an attempt to ensure honest answers the employer asks each employee to secretly toss a coin.

If a head is obtained then the employee answers the question, 'were you born in an odd numbered year?'

If a tail is obtained then the employee answers the question, 'do you drink regularly at lunch time?'

The percentage of employees answering yes to either question was 37 per cent. Use a tree diagram to estimate the percentage of regular lunch time drinkers.

(N.B. let the probability of a lunch time drinker be p)

5.9 A company is contracted to finish a £100,000 project by 31 December. If it does not complete on time a penalty of £8,000 per month or part of a month is incurred. The company estimates that if it continues alone there is only a 40 per cent chance of completing on time and that the project might be one, two, three or even four months late with equal probability.

Sub-contractors can be hired by the firm at a cost of £18,000. If the sub-contractors are hired then the probability that the company completes on time is doubled. If the project is still late it will only now be one or two month late with equal probability.

Draw a decision tree to represent the problem of whether the company should continue alone or use subcontractors and analyse using the expected value technique.

5.10 In a lottery, a player wins first prize by selecting the correct six number combination from a selection of six different numbers drawn from the range 1 to 49. How many different possible combinations are there?

5.11 An office safe has buttons numbered 0–9 inclusive. In order to open the safe three different numbers have to be pressed in sequence. What is the probability that someone randomly pressing three buttons will open the safe?

5.12 Liker Airways has 15 video programmes available to show during its trans-atlantic flights. If six videos are to be shown during the flights:

(a) If the order is unimportant, how many different combinations are there?

(b) If 900 of the combinations of six programmes are thought to be incompatible, what is the probability that a selection of six taken at random will be compatible?

5.13 A textile designer has chosen to use eight different colours in this year's fabric designs. Production constraints mean that only five different colours can be used in each design.

How many different colour groupings can be advertised? (Assume all fabrics have five different colours.)

Answers to Review questions are to be found on pp. 415–419 at the back of the book.

Further study and data
....

Texts

Bancroft, G. and O'Sullivan, G. (1993), *Quantitative methods for accounting and business studies*, 3rd edn, McGraw Hill, chapters 12 and 13.

Curwin, J. and Slater, R. (1996), *Quantitative methods for business decisions*, 4th edn, Chapman and Hall, chapter 10.

Lawson, M., Hubbard, S. and Pugh, P. (1995), *Maths and statistics for business*, Addison Wesley Longman, chapter 4.

Morris, C. (1996), *Quantitative approaches in business studies*, 4th edn, Pitman, chapter 8.

Oakshott, L. (1996), *Essential elements of business statistics*, BPP, chapter 4.

Swift, L. (1997), *Mathematics and statistics for business, management and finance*, Macmillan, part C2.

Thomas, R. (1997), *Quantitative methods for business studies*, Prentice Hall, chapter 2.

Waters, D. (1997), *Quantitative methods*, 2nd edn, Addison Wesley Longman, chapter 13.

Wisniewski, M. with Stead, R. (1996), *Foundation quantitative methods for business*, Pitman, chapter 8.

Sources of information and data

See the list the end of Chapter 1 (p. 25).

CHAPTER 6

Probability distributions

Objectives
....

When you have read this chapter you should be able to:

▶ understand the main properties of a Normal distribution;

▶ work out the probabilities of particular events occurring when these follow a *Normal* distribution;

▶ know that a 'confidence' interval is a range of values within which a particular value might lie;

▶ use and interpret the probability (*Z*) tables associated with the *Normal* distribution;

▶ be familiar with the *Binomial* and *Poisson* distributions, and be able to work out the probabilities of events occurring when these follow such distributions;

▶ be able to identify when and how to use the *Normal approximation* to the Binomial and Poisson distributions.

Introduction
....

Chapter 5 looked at the idea of probabilities and their application to business situations. In this chapter we look at the idea of a **probability distribution**. One of the most important probability distributions you will encounter in any quantitative methods course is the **Normal distribution** and its associated table of probabilities. We considered some of the properties of the Normal distribution in Chapter 2. Here we note how these properties can be used to develop the so called **Z-tables**, from which we can derive estimates of probability. The **Binomial** and **Poisson** probability distributions are also introduced and related to the work on probability in Chapter 5. Other probability distributions, such as the **Student-t** and **Chi-squared** distributions, are considered in Chapter 7.

Answers to 'Self-check questions', responses to each 'Pause for thought' answers to the 'Review questions' can be found at the end of the book.

6.1 Normal distribution
....

We noted in Chapter 2 (p. 35) that the **Normal distribution** is perfectly symmetrical ('bell' shaped), with all three measures of central location, namely arithmetic mean, median and mode, being the same value for some variable X_i. If we call this arithmetic mean value the Greek letter μ ('mew'), then we know that since this is also the median value, then 50 per cent of the distribution will lie either side of μ. We can of course express such percentages as *decimals*, with the whole distribution underneath the Normal curve expressed as 1 and with 0.5 of the distribution then lying either side of μ.

Indeed the symmetry of any Normal distribution around μ will allow us to calculate probabilities involving the distribution of the variable X_i around μ. We can do this by calculating the **standard deviation** (σ) for the variable X_i.

figure 6.1
Areas and probabilities under the Normal distribution

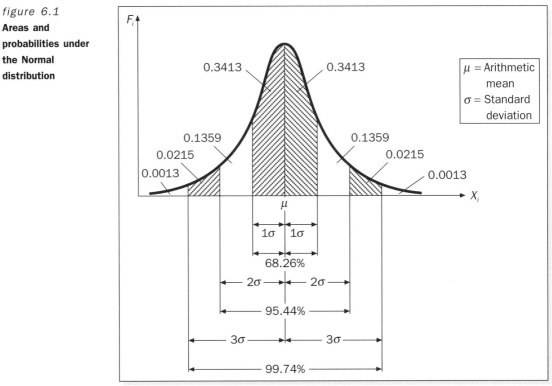

This measure of dispersion (see Chapter 2) can then be used to calculate probabilities for any Normal distribution. For example, as shown in Figure 6.1, we know that 68.26 per cent of all the observations will lie within one standard deviation of the mean; 95.44 per cent of the observations will lie within two standard deviations of the mean; and 99.74 per cent of the observations will lie within three standard deviations of the mean; etc.

PAUSE FOR THOUGHT 6.1   *Can you suggest three different types of distribution you might expect to be Normal or close to Normal?*

Confidence interval

We use the term **confidence intervals** to refer to those ranges of values from the arithmetic mean (μ) expressed in terms of the standard deviation (σ), within which we can expect a particular value of the variable X_i to lie. We return to consider confidence intervals further in Chapter 7 (p. 152).

6.2 Standard normal distribution
....

The calculation of probabilities under any Normal distribution can be taken a step further by transforming the values of the variable X_i into the numbers of

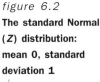

figure 6.2

The standard Normal (Z) distribution: mean 0, standard deviation 1

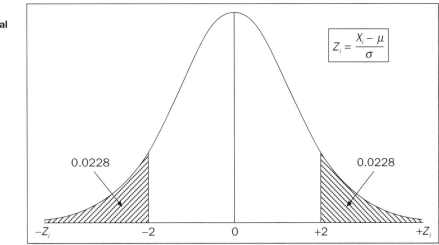

standard deviations (σ) from the mean (μ). The resulting distribution is often referred to as the **standard Normal distribution** and the transformation which brings it about is often called the **Z score** or **Z statistic**:

$$Z_i = \frac{X_i - \mu}{\sigma} = \frac{\text{Value of variable} - \text{Arithmetic mean}}{\text{Standard deviation}}$$

In other words the Z statistic simply calculates the number of standard deviations from the arithmetic mean. If the distribution of the variable X_i is Normal, then the distribution of the Z statistic will also be Normal, as shown in Figure 6.2.

A table giving the area shaded in Figure 6.2 for any value of the Z statistic is presented in full in Appendix 2 (p. 314). For example, for a Z score of +2.0 we will have 0.0228 (2.28 per cent) of the distribution to the *right* of that Z score.

Of course, since the Z statistic is normally distributed, a Z score of –2.0 will give us an equivalent area, but this time to the *left* of that Z score.

In other words, if the particular value for X_i is two standard deviations above (or below) the mean for a normally distributed variable, then we can expect 0.0228 (2.28 per cent) of the distribution to be above (or below) that value.

If $Z = +$, then area in right-hand tail
If $Z = -$, then area in left-hand tail

Note that the mean of the standard Normal (Z) distribution is a Z score of 0. In other words when the value of X_i is the mean (μ) itself, then we are zero standard deviations from the mean, so the Z score is 0. It therefore follows that for $Z = 0$, 0.5 (50 per cent) of the distribution will lie to the right, and 0.5 (50 per cent) to the left.

To help you become familiar with using the full Z table (p. 314), a small section of that table is shown below:

Z	0.00	0.01	0.02	0.03	0.04	0.05	0.06	0.07	0.08	0.09
1.0	0.1587	0.1562	0.1539	0.1515	0.1492	0.1469	0.1446	0.1423	0.1401	0.1379
1.1	0.1357	0.1335	0.1314	0.1292	0.1271	0.1251	0.1230	0.1210	0.1190	0.1170
1.2	0.1151	0.1131	0.1112	0.1093	0.1075	0.1056	0.1038	0.1020	0.1003	0.0985
1.3	0.0968	0.0951	0.0934	0.0918	0.0901	0.0885	0.0869	0.0853	0.0838	0.0823
1.4	0.0808	0.0793	0.0778	0.0764	0.0749	0.0735	0.0721	0.0708	0.0694	0.0681

For example, if the Z score is found to be +1.15, then go *down* the Z column to the 1.1 row and *across* the 1.1 row to the position underneath the 0.05 column. We read off the value 0.1251, which tells us that 0.1251 or 12.51 per cent of the distribution is in the *right-hand tail*. Of course had the Z score been –1.15, then 0.1251 or 12.51 per cent of the distribution would have been in the *left-hand tail*.

Check that for Z = +1.38 you would read 0.0838 (8.38 per cent) in the right-hand tail, and for Z = –1.42 you would read 0.0778 (7.78 per cent) in the left-hand tail.

WORKED
EXAMPLE **6.1**
••••••••••••••••

Suppose a variable X_i has a Normal distribution with a mean of 100 and a standard deviation of 10. Suppose that we want to find the probability of X_i being:

(a) 115 or more
(b) 75 or less
(c) between 75 and 115

Solution

We can use Figure 6.3 to help solve this problem. Note that we show both the variable X_i and its associated Z scores, Z_i on the same diagram.

figure 6.3

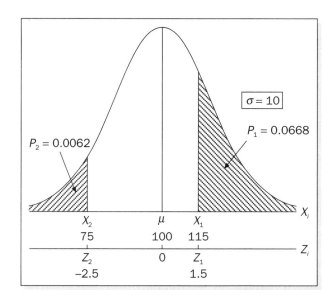

(a) For $X_1 = 115$, $Z_1 = \dfrac{X_1 - \mu}{\sigma} = \dfrac{115 - 100}{10} = +1.5$

From the Z tables (p. 314), we find that $Z_1 = +1.5$ gives 0.0668 as the area in the right-hand tail.

i.e. $Z_1 = +1.5$
$P_1 = 0.0668$
$P_1 = 6.68\%$

There is a 6.68 per cent chance of X_i being 115 or more.

(b) For $X_2 = 75$, $Z_2 = \dfrac{X_2 - \mu}{\sigma} = \dfrac{75 - 100}{10} = -2.5$

From the Z tables (p. 314), we find that $Z_2 = -2.5$ gives 0.0062 as the area in the left-hand tail.

i.e. $Z_2 = -2.5$
$P_2 = 0.0062$
$P_2 = 0.62\%$

There is a 0.62 per cent (i.e. less than 1 per cent chance) of X_i being 75 or less.

(c) The whole area beneath the Z curve is 1.00, so the area between $X_2 = 75$ and $X_1 = 115$ is $1.00 - (0.0062 + 0.0668) = 1 - 0.0730 = 0.9270$.

In other words there is a 92.7 per cent chance of X_i being between 75 and 115.

In solving problems of this kind it is always helpful to draw a sketch diagram to indicate what has been given in the question and what needs to be found, as in Figure 6.3 above. Sometimes we will need to make use of the fact that the area to each side of the mean under the normal curve is 0.50 (50 per cent). You will see in Worked example 6.2 that sometimes we must subtract the area in the respective tails of the distribution from 0.50 in order to obtain the area required. Note also that whenever we seek to find an area which extends across the mean (μ), then it is usually helpful to solve for each side of the mean separately before combining the result.

WORKED
EXAMPLE **6.2**
• • • • • • • • • • • • • • • •

The attendance at a night club is thought to be normally distributed, with a mean of 80 persons and a standard deviation of 12 persons. What is the probability that on any given night the attendance is:

(a) 74 persons or more
(b) 83 persons or less
(c) between 70 and 85 persons?

Solution

Figure 6.4 represents the areas we require in each case.

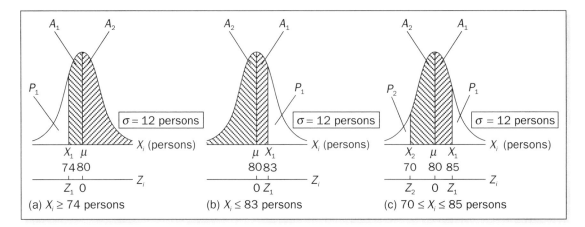

figure 6.4

The areas required are shaded (A_1 and A_2): the areas given in the Z tables are unshaded (P_1 and P_2)

Remember that when we calculate the Z score, the Z tables (p. 314) give us the area in the *tails* of the distribution.

(a) To find $X_i \geq 74$ means we require the shaded areas A_1 and A_2 in Figure 6.4(a).

$$\text{For } X_1 = 74, \ Z_1 = \frac{X_1 - \mu}{\sigma} = \frac{74 - 80}{12} = -0.5$$

$$Z_1 = -0.5$$
$$P_1 = 0.3085$$
$$A_1 = 0.5000 - 0.3085 = 0.1915$$
$$A_2 = 0.5000$$
$$\underline{A_1 + A_2 = 0.6915}$$

There is a 0.6915 (69.15 per cent) probability that the attendance will be 74 persons or more.

(b) To find $X_i \leq 83$ means we require the shaded areas A_1 and A_2 in Figure 6.4(b).

$$\text{For } X_1 = 83, \ Z_1 = \frac{X_1 - \mu}{\sigma} = \frac{83 - 80}{12} = +0.25$$

$$Z_1 = +0.25$$
$$P_1 = 0.4013$$
$$A_1 = 0.5000 - 0.4013 = 0.0987$$
$$A_2 = 0.5000$$
$$\underline{A_1 + A_2 = 0.5987}$$

There is a 0.5987 (59.87 per cent) probability that the attendance will be 83 persons or less.

(c) To find $70 \leq X_i \leq 85$ persons we required the shaded areas A_1 and A_2 in Figure 6.4(c).

$$\text{For } X_1 = 85, \ Z_1 = \frac{X_1 - \mu}{\sigma} = \frac{85 - 80}{12} = \frac{+5}{12} = +0.42 \text{ (rounded)}$$

$$Z_1 = +0.42$$
$$P_1 = 0.3372$$
$$A_1 = 0.5000 - 0.3372 = 0.1628$$
$$\underline{A_1 = 0.1628}$$

For $X_2 = 70$, $Z_2 = \dfrac{X_2 - \mu}{\sigma} = \dfrac{70 - 80}{12} = \dfrac{-10}{12} = -0.83$

$Z_2 = -0.83$
$P_2 = 0.2033$
$A_2 = 0.5000 - 0.2033$
$A_2 = 0.2967$

$\underline{A_1 + A_2 = 0.4595}$

There is a 0.4595 (45.95 per cent) probability that the attendance will be between 70 and 85 persons.

Finding the variable value when probability known

So far we have known the *specific values* of the variable X_i and found the probabilities with which these values might occur. Here we reverse the process. Suppose we know the *probabilities* with which specific values of the variable X_i might occur, how can we then find these values of X_i? Worked example 6.3 shows how we go about solving such problems.

WORKED
EXAMPLE **6.3**
··················

The life of a machine component is normally distributed with mean 60 hours and standard deviation 30 minutes. If 2.5 per cent (0.025) of components last more than X_1 hours, find the value of X_1.

Solution

In a question like this, do make sure that you express all values in the *same unit*, here hours or minutes. If we use hours, then the standard deviation is 0.5 hours, as shown in Figure 6.5.

figure 6.5
**Probability known,
value of variable
unknown**

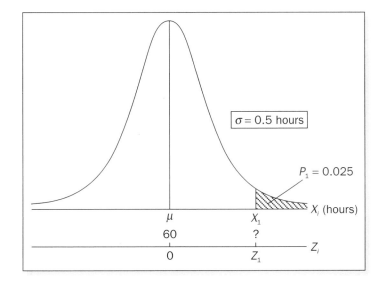

$P_1 = 0.025$

We can therefore look in the *body* of the Z tables (p. 314), to find the Z value (Z_1) which would give us the probability in the right-hand tail of 0.025.

$Z_1 = +1.96$

We know that

$$Z_1 = \frac{X_1 - \mu}{\sigma}$$

i.e. $+1.96 = \dfrac{X_1 - 60}{0.5}$

$+1.96(0.5) + 60 = X_1$

$\underline{60.98 = X_1}$

In other words we would expect 2.5 per cent (0.025) of the machine components to last more than 60.98 hours.

Note: if the left-hand tail had been involved then the calculations would have used a *negative* value for Z. You can check this yourself by finding the number of hours (X_2) for which 2.5 per cent (0.025) of the components last *less than* X_2 hours. Check that your answer is 59.02 hours and that –1.96 was used in your calculation.

SELF-CHECK QUESTIONS

6.1 Find the area beneath the (Normal) curve over the following values for the Z score. Draw diagrams in each case and use the Z tables (p. 314).

(a) $Z_1 = 0$ and $Z_2 = 0.2$
(b) $Z_1 = 0.5$ and $Z_2 = 1.0$
(c) $Z_1 = 0.95$ and $Z_2 = 2.55$
(d) $Z_1 = 1.55$ and $Z_2 = (+)$ infinity
(e) $Z_1 = -1.5$ and $Z_2 = 0$
(f) $Z_1 = -1.85$ and $Z_2 = -1.05$
(g) $Z_1 = -1.55$ and $Z_2 = (-)$ infinity

6.2 Attendants at rock concerts in a stadium are normally distributed with mean 20,000 persons and standard deviation 4,000 persons. For a future event, what is the probability:

(a) more than 28,000 persons will attend
(b) less than 14,000 persons will attend
(c) between 17,000 and 25,000 persons will attend.

6.3 Use the same data as in question 6.2.

(a) If you know that there is a 5 per cent (0.05) probability that more than a certain number of people (X_1) will attend, what is the value of X_1?
(b) If there is a 1 per cent (0.01) probability that less than X_2 people will attend, what is the value of X_2?

Note: Answers can be found on pp. 342–344.

6.3 Binomial distribution

The **Binomial distribution** can be used to describe the likely outcome of events for discrete variables which:

(a) have only two possible outcomes

and

(b) are independent.

Suppose we are conducting a questionnaire. The *Binomial distribution* might be used to analyse the results if the only two responses to a question are 'yes' or 'no' *and* if the response to one question (e.g. 'yes') does not influence the likely response to any other question (i.e. 'yes' or 'no').

> Put rather more formally, the *Binomial distribution* occurs when there are *n* independent trials (or tests) with the probability of 'success' or 'failure' in each trial (or test) being constant.

Let p = the probability of 'success'.

Let q = the probability of 'failure'.

then $q = 1 - p$

For example, if we toss an unbiased coin ten times, we might wish to find the probability of getting four heads! Here $n = 10$, p (head) = 0.5, q (tail) = 0.5 and $q = 1 - p$

The probability of obtaining r 'successes' in 'n' trials (tests) is given by a formula which incorporates our work on combinations in Chapter 5, namely:

$$P(r) = {}_nC_r p^r q^{n-r}$$

$$\text{where } r = 0, 1, 2, 3 \ldots n$$

In Chapter 5 we saw that:

$$_nC_r = \frac{n!}{(n - r)! \, r!}$$

The probability of getting exactly four heads out of ten tosses of an unbiased coin, can therefore be solved as:

$$P(4) = {}_{10}C_4 0.5^4 0.5^6$$

$$\text{now } _{10}C_4 = \frac{10!}{(10 - 4)! \, 4!} = \frac{10 \times 9 \times 8 \times 7}{4 \times 3 \times 2 \times 1} = 210$$

So $P(4) = 210 \times (0.5)^4 \times (0.5)^6$
$P(4) = 210 \times 0.0625 \times 0.015625$
$\underline{P(4) = 0.2051}$

In other words the probability of getting exactly four heads out of ten tosses of an unbiased coin is 0.2051 or 20.51 per cent.

It may be useful to state the formulae for finding *all* the possible probabilities of obtaining *r* successes in *n* trials.

Where $P(r) = {_nC_r}p^r q^{n-r}$

and $r = 0, 1, 2, 3, \ldots n$

then, from our knowledge of combinations (see p. 119):

$P(0) = q^n$

$P(1) = npq^{n-1}$

$P(2) = \dfrac{n(n-1)}{2 \times 1}p^2 q^{n-2}$

$P(3) = \dfrac{n(n-1)(n-2)}{3 \times 2 \times 1}p^3 q^{n-3}$

$P(4) = \dfrac{n(n-1)(n-2)(n-3)}{4 \times 3 \times 2 \times 1}p^4 q^{n-4}$

....

$P(n-2) = \dfrac{n(n-1)}{2 \times 1}p^{n-2}q^2$

$P(n-1) = np^{n-1}q$

$P(n) = p^n$

PAUSE FOR THOUGHT 6.2 *Can you think of three different types of problem which might be solved using the Binomial distribution?*

We can, of course, use this approach to answer questions which ask for the probability of an *exact* number of 'successes' occurring, such as P(4). We can also use this approach to answer broader questions such as the probability of 'less than 4' successes occurring, which would be P(0) + P(1) + P(2) + P(3), and so on.

Cumulative Binomial distribution

An alternative to such calculations would be to use tables of the **cumulative Binomial distribution** presented in Appendix 3 (p. 315). These tables are *cumulative* in that they give the probabilities of *r or more* 'successes'. For example, if we require the probability of six or more items in a sample of ten being defective, when $p = 0.20$, then from the table we find that P(6 or more) = 0.0064. It therefore follows that for the same sample, P(5 or less) = 1 − 0.0064 = 0.9936.

WORKED EXAMPLE **6.4**

A firm produces a product and finds that 10 per cent of its output is defective. A small sample of five items is taken from the production line. Find the probability of getting each of the following numbers of defective items in the sample: 0, 1, 2, 3, 4 and 5 defective items respectively.

Solution

Here $n = 5$, $p = 0.1$, $q = 0.9$. Using the formulae listed above (p. 132), we can calculate the probabilities as being:

$P(0) = q^5 = (0.9)^5 = 0.5905$

$P(1) = npq^4 = 5 \times 0.1 \times (0.9)^4 = 0.3281$

$P(2) = \dfrac{n(n-1)}{2 \times 1} p^2 q^3 = \dfrac{5 \times 4}{2 \times 1} \times (0.1)^2 \times (0.9)^3 = 0.0729$

$P(3) = \dfrac{n(n-1)(n-2)}{3 \times 2 \times 1} p^3 q^2 = \dfrac{5 \times 4 \times 3}{3 \times 2 \times 1} \times (0.1)^3 \times (0.9)^2 = 0.0081$

$P(4) = np^4 q = 5 \times (0.1)^4 \times 0.9 = 0.00045$

$P(5) = p^5 = (0.1)^5 = 0.00001$

So, for example, the probability of exactly two out of our five items being defective is 0.0729 or 7.29 per cent.

SELF-CHECK QUESTIONS

6.4 Evaluate the following expression using your knowledge of combinations.

    (a) $_3C_2$ **(b)** $_{10}C_3$

    (c) $_{12}C_5$ **(d)** $_{14}C_8$

6.5 If 10 per cent of the items produced by a manufacturer are defective, find the probability that for a sample of six items: (a) two items will be defective (b) three items will be defective.

6.6 The probability that an invoice contains an error is 5 per cent (0.05). If an audit of ten invoices is taken, what is the probability of finding less than three incorrect invoices. Solve using the cumulative Binomial probabilities table (p. 315).

Note: **Answers can be found on pp. 344–345.**

Normal approximation to the Binomial

Using the formula on p. 131 to calculate the probabilities for given numbers of successes to occur is obviously time consuming. It is therefore useful to note that if n is large and $p > 0.1$ then we can solve calculations such as those in Worked example 6.4 using the *Normal distribution* considered at the start of this chapter. The Z statistic is calculated as before:

$$Z = \frac{X_i - \mu}{\sigma}$$

However when we are using the Normal distribution to solve, as an *approximation*, Binomial-type problems, we must express μ and σ in particular ways.

figure 6.6

Normal approximation to the Binomial distribution

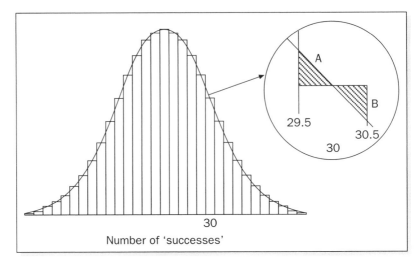

For a Binomial distribution

$\mu = np$

$\sigma = \sqrt{npq}$

where p = probability of 'success'

q = probability of 'failure'

n = number of trials

Generally speaking, as a 'rule of thumb' we can use the **Normal approximation to the Binomial distribution** when $np > 5$, and $p > 0.1$

Continuity correction

Whereas the Binomial distribution represents *discrete* data, the Normal distribution represents *continuous* data. Strictly speaking, whenever we are approximating a discrete variable with a continuous one we should use a **continuity correction**.

The idea behind the continuity correction is illustrated in Figure 6.6. The curve, representing the continuous distribution, cuts through the blocks of the histogram, representing the discrete distribution.

Clearly some areas, such as A are *included* under the continuous distribution, while other areas, such as B, are *excluded* under the continuous distribution. Overall these areas will tend to cancel each other out. However, since each block of the discrete (Binomial) distribution represents a whole number, such as the number of 'successes', it can be regarded as extending from 0.5 below and above that whole number.

Thus, in Figure 6.6, the block representing 30 'successes' extends from 29.5 to 30.5. It follows that to find the area, and therefore the probability, for a series of outcomes, it will be necessary to go from 0.5 below the lowest whole number (integer) to 0.5 above the highest whole number (integer).

In Figure 6.6, to find the probability of between, say, 26 and 30 'successes', we must find the area under the normal curve from 25.5 to 30.5.

P(26 to 30) = P(25.5 to 30.5)

In Figure 6.6, to find the probability of, say, 30 or more 'successes', we must find the area under the normal curve to the right of 29.5

P(30 or more) = P(29.5 or more)

Continuity correction

To adjust *discrete* data to *continuous* data, find the probability from 0.5 below the lowest whole number (integer) to 0.5 above the highest whole number (integer).

WORKED
EXAMPLE **6.5**
••••••••••••••••

Past data suggest that for every 100 telephone enquiries at the reception desk of a hotel, only some 20 bookings are made. Find the probability that from the next 100 enquiries received, the hotel will receive 30 or more bookings.

Solution

This is a Binomial situation as each enquiry leads to only one of two outcomes, booking (success) or non-booking (failure). There is an established or fixed probability ($p = 0.2$) of any enquiry leading to a booking, based on past experience.

However because n is large ($n = 100$) and p is > 0.1 ($p = 0.2$), then we can use the Normal approximation to the Binomial theorem. Note that with the continuity correction, X_1 will be 29.5 rather than 30.

$p = 0.2$

$q = 0.8$

$\mu = np = 100(0.2) = 20$

$\sigma = \sqrt{npq} = \sqrt{100(0.2)(0.8)} = 4$

$Z_1 = \dfrac{X_1 - np}{\sqrt{npq}} = \dfrac{29.5 - 20}{4} = +2.38$

$Z_1 = +2.38$

Using the Z tables (p. 314)

$P_1 = 0.0087$

There is a 0.0087 (0.87 per cent) probability of the next 100 hotel enquiries yielding 30 or more bookings.

figure 6.7

**Normal approximation
to the Binomial
distribution**

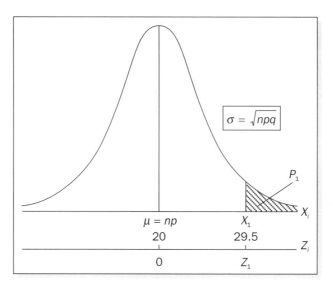

Clearly this is a much quicker method than finding P(30), P(31) . . . P(100) using
the conventional formula for the Binomial distribution presented on p. 136.

**SELF-CHECK
QUESTIONS**

**6.7 From the previous hotel booking problem calculate the probability that the
next 100 enquiries will yield:**

(a) **25 or more bookings**   (b) **16 or more bookings**
(c) **less than 14 bookings**

**6.8 Suppose that 10 per cent of all houses in a district have burglar alarms. A
random sample of 121 houses is selected; use the Normal approximation to
find the probability that:**

(a) **Exactly 14 of the houses have alarms?**
(b) **Fewer than ten houses have alarms?**
(c) **From seven to 11 inclusive of the selected houses have alarms?**
(d) **From nine to 13 inclusive of the selected houses have alarms?**

Note: **Answers can be found on pp. 345–346.**

6.4 *Poisson distribution*
. . . .

The **Poisson distribution** may be regarded as a special case of the Binomial
distribution. As with the Binomial distribution, the Poisson distribution can be
used where there are only two possible outcomes, 'success' (p) or 'failure' (q),
and these events are independent. The Poisson distribution is usually used
where n is very large but p is very small, and where the mean np is constant and
typically < 5. As p is very small ($p < 0.1$ and often much less), then the chance
of the event occurring is extremely low. The Poisson distribution is therefore
typically used for unlikely events such as accidents, strikes, etc.

The Poisson distribution is also used to solve problems where events tend to occur at random, such as incoming phone calls, passenger arrivals at a terminal, etc.

Whereas the formula for solving Binomial problems uses the probabilities, for both 'success' (p) and 'failure' (q), the formula for solving Poisson problems only uses the probabilities for 'success' (p).

If μ is the mean, it is possible to show that the probability of r successes is given by the formula:

$$P(r) = \frac{e^{-\mu}\mu^r}{r!}$$

where e = exponential constant = 2.7183
μ = mean number of successes = np
n = number of trials
p = probability of 'success'
r = number of successes

If we substitute $r = 0, 1, 2, 3, 4, 5 \ldots$ in this formula we obtain the following expressions:

$$P(0) = e^{-\mu} \qquad P(1) = \mu e^{-\mu} \qquad P(2) = \frac{\mu^2 e^{-\mu}}{2 \times 1}$$

$$P(3) = \frac{\mu^3 e^{-\mu}}{3 \times 2 \times 1} \qquad P(4) = \frac{\mu^4 e^{-\mu}}{4 \times 3 \times 2 \times 1} \qquad P(5) = \frac{\mu^5 e^{-\mu}}{5 \times 4 \times 3 \times 2 \times 1}$$

In questions you are either given the mean μ or you have to find μ from the information given, which is usually data for n and p; μ is then obtained from the relationship $\mu = np$.

You have to be able to work out e raised to a negative power. Remember from your work on powers (p. 293) that e^{-3} is the same as $\frac{1}{e^3}$ so you can simply work this out using $\frac{1}{2.7183^3}$.

Alternatively, many calculators have a key marked e^x. The easiest way to find (say) e^{-3} on your calculator is to enter 3, press +/– key, press e key, and you should obtain 0.049787. If your calculator does not have an e key but has an x^y key, enter 2.7813, press x^y key, enter 3, press +/– key, then press = key; you should obtain 0.049786.

WORKED
EXAMPLE **6.6**
....

(a) In a large company with many employees, accidents occur at random at the mean rate of 3 per day. Calculate the probability that four accidents occur on a single day.

(b) There is a 0.001 probability of a faulty call on a telephone line and 2,000 calls are made each day. What is the probability of there being less than three faulty calls on that line in a day?

Both (a) and (b) can be answered using the Poisson distribution.

Solution

(a) Here accidents occur at random, and relatively few accidents occur. Although p (accidents) is unknown, $\mu = np = 3$ is known. The occurrence of non-accidents (q) is irrelevant here. We can therefore use the Poisson distribution to solve the problem.

$$P(r) = \frac{e^{-\mu}\mu^r}{r!}$$

$$P(4) = \frac{e^{-3}3^4}{4 \times 3 \times 2 \times 1}$$

$$P(4) = \frac{0.0498 \times 81}{24} = 0.1681$$

$$\underline{P(4) = 0.1681}$$

In other words there is a 0.1681 (16.81 per cent) probability of four accidents occurring on a single day.

(b) Here the probability p is very low ($p = 0.001$) and the number of trials, n, is very large ($n = 2,000$). The mean (μ) $= np = 2,000\ (0.001) = 2$ faulty calls per day. Since it is also true that $\mu = np < 5$ the Poisson distribution would again seem appropriate.

To get less than three faulty calls means $P(0) + P(1) + P(2)$

Using $P(r) = \dfrac{e^{-\mu}\mu^r}{r!}$

We get $P(0) = \dfrac{e^{-2}2^0}{0!} = \dfrac{e^{-2}1}{1} = e^{-2} = 0.1353$

$P(1) = \dfrac{e^{-2}2^1}{1} = 0.2706$

$P(2) = \dfrac{e^{-2}2^2}{2 \times 1} = 0.2706$

So the probability of getting less than three faulty calls is $0.1353 + 0.2706 + 0.2706 = 0.6765$ or 67.65 per cent.

Cumulative Poisson distribution

An alternative to such lengthy calculations would be to use tables of the **cumulative Poisson distribution** presented in Appendix 4 (p. 316). These tables are *cumulative* in that they give the probabilities of *r or more* 'successes'.

For example, if we require the probability of less than three faulty calls occurring in a single day when they typically occur at random at the mean rate of two per day on a telephone line (see Worked example 6.6(b) above), then we *adapt r* to be *three or more* for purposes of the cumulative tables. So for $\mu = 2$, $r = 3$ we read off the value 0.3233 from the cumulative tables. The probability of *less than three* faulty calls is, of course, 1 – probability of *three or more* faulty calls, i.e. $1 - 0.3233 = 0.6767$. This is close to the probability found by using the lengthier method $P(0) + P(1) + P(2)$ for the Poisson distribution in the answer to Worked example 6.6(b) above.

Normal approximation to the Poisson distribution

If the Poisson distribution is appropriate *except* that μ $(= np) > 30$ (instead of $\mu = < 5$) then the **Normal approximation to the Poisson distribution** can be used. The Z statistic is calculated as before and the Z tables of Appendix 2 (p. 314) can be used to find probabilities in the respective tails of this distribution.

$$Z = \frac{X_i - \mu}{\sigma}$$

where $\mu = np$

$$\sigma = \sqrt{np(1 - p)}$$

i.e. $\quad Z = \dfrac{X_i - np}{\sqrt{np(1 - p)}}$

Note: the continuity correction when adjusting discrete data to continuous data (see p. 135) will also apply here.

The following flow chart will give you some guidance on when to use the Binomial or Poisson distributions, or the Normal approximations to these distributions.

Of course the flow chart only applies to variables which are discrete (take on fixed values), which can take one of two possible outcomes (p,q) and which occur independently.

figure 6.8
Selecting the distribution to use (discrete variable, two outcomes, each independent)

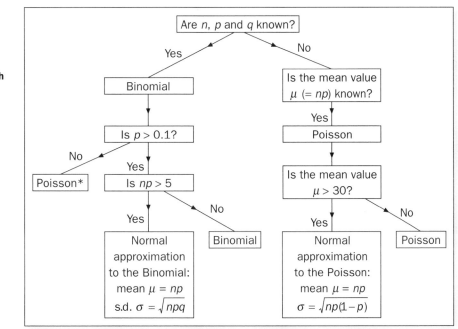

Note: *Poisson is used here as an approximation to the Binomial.

**SELF-CHECK
QUESTIONS**

6.9 Suppose $n = 1,000$ and $p = 0.0002$ use the Poisson distribution to find:

(a) $P(X = 0)$ (b) $P(X = 4)$
(c) $P(X > 1)$ (d) $P(X \leq 4)$
mean value $\mu = np = 1,000 \times 0.0002 = 0.2$

6.10 The average number of trips per family to amusement parks in the UK is Poisson distributed with a mean of 0.7 trips per year. What is the probability of randomly selecting a family and finding that:

(a) The family did not make a trip to an amusement park last year?
(b) The family took two or more trips last year?
(c) The family took three or fewer trips over a three year period?
(d) Took exactly four trips over a six year period?

Note: **Answers can be found on p. 347.**

**REVIEW
QUESTIONS**

6.1 If the variable X_i follows a Normal distribution with mean = 100 and standard deviation = 5, find the probability that:

(a) $P(X_i > 107)$ (d) $P(101 < X_i < 109)$
(b) $P(X_i > 98)$ (e) $P(91 < X_i < 94)$
(c) $P(X_i < 95)$ (f) $P(93 < X_i < 106)$

6.2 Find, using the standard Normal tables (Z tables, p. 314), the value of Z_1 for each of the following:

(a) $P(Z > Z_1) = 0.3300$
(b) $P(0 < Z < Z_1) = 0.4732$
(c) $P(Z < Z_1) = 0.8212$
(d) $P(Z < Z_1) = 0.5478$

figure 6.9

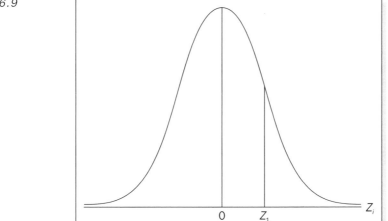

6.3 The mean height of 4,000 children in a town is 130 cm with a standard deviation of 7 cm. Assuming the heights to be normally distributed, find how many children are of:

(a) height over 144 cm
(b) height less than 123 cm
(c) between 126.5 cm and 137 cm
(d) determine the upper and lower quartile heights.

6.4 The daily delivery of mail at a large city firm follows a time pattern conforming to the Normal distribution, with a mean time of arrival of 9.40 am and with a standard deviation of 20 minutes.

Estimate the number of occasions during the 250 working days in the year when the mail arrives

(a) before the main gates open at 9 a.m.
(b) after the arrival of the office staff at 9.20 a.m.
(c) between 10 a.m. and 10.20 a.m.

6.5 The life of a certain type of machine component is known to be approximately normally distributed with mean 25 hours and standard deviation 30 minutes. Calculate the probability that a randomly selected component lasts for:

(a) between 24 and 24.5 hours
(b) between 24.25 and 24.75 hours
(c) more than 24.5 hours
(d) less that 24 hours 15 minutes
(e) If 28.1 per cent of the components last less than 'K' hours, find the value of K.

6.6 An engineer designs a car seat to comfortably fit women above the height of 157.5 cm. The mean height of women in the UK is 160.9 cm with a standard deviation of 6.0 cm. What proportion of women will be excluded from buying this car? (Assume the height of women is normally distributed)

6.7 A tyre company has invented a revolutionary new product. In order to overcome consumer resistance a mileage guarantee is offered with the tyre. Road tests suggest that the mean life of the tyre is 42,000 miles, with a standard deviation of 4,000 miles. The tests suggest that tyre life is normally distributed.

(a) What percentage of tyres will last for more than 45,000 miles?
(b) What should the guaranteed mileage be if the firm wishes to replace no more than 4 per cent of tyres?

6.8 The amount of coffee that an automatic filling machine puts into nominal 100 g jars, is normally distributed and varies from jar to jar. The machine fills 50,000 jars per week and is currently set to a mean fill of 100.50 g. All jars below the nominal weight are rejected. The current reject rate is 1,500 jars per week and each reject costs the firm 80p.

(a) Find the standard deviation of the jar weights
(b) If the reliability (standard deviation) of the machine cannot be changed and the firm wishes to save £400 per week on reject costs, to what mean fill should the machine be set?

6.9 Air Inexcel has a policy of booking as many as 16 persons for an aeroplane that seats only 14. Records show that only 85 per cent of booked passengers actually arrive for the flight. Find the probability that if Inexcel books 16 people on a flight, enough seats will not be available.

6.10 A firm has agreed to accept delivery of a component shipped in batches of 1,000 if, in a random sample of ten, no more than one component is defective. What is the probability that this acceptance sampling rule would lead to a batch with 20 per cent defective items being accepted?

6.11 Suppose that 40 per cent of all students have their own personal computer. If 24 students are selected at random, find:

(a) the probability that eight will have computers;
(b) the probability that eight will have computers (using the Normal approximation to the Binomial). Compare the results with part (a).

6.12 An airline offers all 180 passengers on the London/Madrid flight a lunch choice of chicken kiev or beef in beer. As passengers choose once the flight is in progress, there is no way of knowing in advance how many will choose beef on any particular flight. The airline does not want to disappoint customers but at the same time, wants to avoid the food waste and cost of carrying excessive meals. Historical evidence suggests that 65 per cent of passengers choose chicken when offered the choice. What is the probability that, on any particular flight, the number of passengers choosing chicken will be more than 125? (use the Normal approximation to the Binomial to evaluate)

6.13 The reception desk in a hotel usually receives four guests per five minute period. Assuming that the conditions for a Poisson distribution hold, find:

(a) the probability that over a five minute period exactly four guests will arrive?
(b) the probability that two or more people will arrive?
(c) the probability that exactly six people will arrive over a ten minute period?

6.14 A certain process produces 100 m long rolls of high quality silk. In order to assess quality a 10 m sample is taken from the end of each roll and inspected for blemishes. The number of blemishes in each sample is thought to follow a Poisson distribution with an average of two blemishes per 10 m sample. Determine the probability that:

(a) there will be no blemishes observed in a 10 m sample
(b) there will be more than seven blemishes observed if a 30 m sample is taken.

6.15 The proportion of defective components produced by a firm is 0.6 per cent. The components are sold in boxes of 250 and the company guarantees to replace any box containing more than three defectives. The cost of each replacement box is £4. The company is thinking about introducing a more comprehensive inspection scheme that would cost 10p per box but would eliminate all defectives. Use the Poisson approximation to the Binomial to decide whether this inspection scheme is worthwhile.

Further study and data
••••••••••••••••••••••••••

Texts

Bancroft, G and O'Sullivan, G. (1993), *Quantitative methods for accounting and business studies*, 3rd edn, McGraw Hill, chapter 14.

Curwin, J. and Slater, R. (1996), *Quantitative methods for business decisions*, 4th edn, Chapman and Hall, chapters 11 and 12.

Lawson, M., Hubbard, S. and Pugh, P. (1995), *Maths and statistics for business*, Addison Wesley Longman, chapters 5 and 6.

Morris, C. (1996), *Quantitative approaches in business studies*, 4th edn, Pitman, chapter 9.

Oakshott, L. (1996), *Essential elements of business statistics*, BPP, chapters 5 and 6.

Swift, L. (1997), *Mathematics and statistics for business, management and finance*, Macmillan, parts C3 and C5.

Thomas, R. (1997), *Quantitative methods for business studies*, Prentice Hall, chapter 2.

Waters, D. (1997), *Quantitative methods*, 2nd edn, Addison Wesley Longman, chapter 14.

Wisniewski, M. with Stead, R. (1996), *Foundation quantitative methods for business*, Pitman, chapter 8.

Sources of information and data

See the list at the end of Chapter 1 (p. 25).

CHAPTER 7

Sampling and tests of hypotheses

Objectives

When you have read this chapter you should be able to:

▶ appreciate the key features of the different types of sample;

▶ be aware of the properties of the distribution of sample means, e.g. the *standard error*;

▶ apply the '*Z*' score and tables to the distribution of sample means drawn from a *Normal population*;

▶ understand the Central Limit Theorem;

▶ apply the '*Z*' score and tables to the distribution of sample means drawn from a *skewed population*;

▶ understand and calculate *confidence intervals* for either the population mean or the sample mean;

▶ know when and how to use the *Student t distribution*;

▶ know when and how to use the *Chi-squared distribution*.

Introduction

Chapter 6 introduced the Normal distribution and the *Z* statistic. In this chapter we continue to apply these ideas, but in the context of **sampling**. Most firms would find it either impractical or too expensive to survey *all* their customers or to carefully examine every item that flows from their production line. Instead they usually resort to selecting a *sample* from the whole group or, as it is often called, the *population*. Of course here the term 'population' can refer to all the items under consideration as much as to all the people.

We briefly consider the *types* of sample that might be selected, and when each type might be most appropriate. We then go on to consider the **distribution of sample means** which, as we shall see, can under certain conditions be regarded as being normally distributed, thereby allowing us to use the *Z* table probabilities of Chapter 6. The **Central Limit Theorem** is suggesting that even when the 'population' is skewed, a random sampling procedure using large samples can still result in a Normal distribution for the sample means.

We move on to explore **confidence limits**, i.e. the ranges of values within which we can, with varying degrees of confidence, expect an observation to lie. This is used as the basis for testing various theories or **hypotheses**. When we use *large samples* ($n \geq 32$) for such tests, then the *Z* tables are still appropriate. However when we use *small samples* ($n < 32$), then we must use the **student t distribution**. Finally a number of other distributions used to test hypotheses are introduced such as the **Chi-squared distribution**.

The term *statistical inference* is often used to refer to the many procedures discussed in this chapter whereby attributes are ascribed to the 'population' based on the results of our sample investigations.

Answers to 'Self-check questions', responses to each 'Pause for thought' and answers to 'Review questions' can be found at the end of the book.

7.1 Types of sample
....

Different **types** of sample may be used, depending in part on the characteristics or attributes of the 'populations' to be sampled and on the objectives of those undertaking the sample. Here we briefly review some of the key features of the various types of sample.

Random sampling

A **random sample** is used when the intention is to give each item in the 'population' as much chance of being selected in the sample as every other item. A common way to conduct random sampling is to list all the 'members' or items in the population and then to use **random number tables** (merely a collection of random digits) or computer generated random numbers to help select the sample. Such procedures avoid various types of 'bias' which might creep into the selection of items to be included in the sample when undertaken by humans. Even the selection of numbers by individuals might be influenced by unconscious preferences for odd, even numbers, etc.

The key objective of random sampling is to obtain a sample that fairly reflects the population as a whole. Random sampling is more likely to be used when the population itself is relatively homogeneous, i.e. is composed of items of broadly the same type. Of course there may be considerable practical difficulties in actually locating and interviewing each 'member' of the population that has been randomly selected. For example, if the chosen adult is not at home or otherwise available a researcher may have to return or seek to contact that individual on another occasion – another member of the household, etc. will not be acceptable.

Suppose the random number table (see Appendix 5, p. 317) is used in seeking a random sample of, say, 40 items. This might involve linking together two columns of the five digits displayed in the table. These might begin 83635 . . . , suggesting we choose the first listed item in the first column, then 66791, and so on.

Random sampling

- ▶ each item selected has an equal chance of being drawn;
- ▶ usually adopted when the population is largely homogeneous, i.e. when it is difficult to distinguish between items;
- ▶ implementation often involves the use of computer-generated random numbers;
- ▶ selection is unbiased;
- ▶ a major drawback is that a population listing is required and the chosen items need to be located, then questioned or measured.

PAUSE FOR THOUGHT 7.1 *Can you identity three well-known products for which a random sampling procedure might be considered appropriate for testing customer response?*

The random sampling procedure will also be important should we wish to apply the **Central Limit Theorem** (see pp. 150–152).

Stratified sampling

Of course there will be times when we might prefer a *non-random* sampling procedure. Such a non-random procedure might, for example, be preferred when the population is *segmented* or *heterogeneous*, i.e. when it contains very different sub-sets of items or subjects. If, say, 40 per cent of all adults have incomes over £x and 15 per cent have incomes below £y, then we might wish our sample of adults to exactly mirror such proportions, rather than give every adult an equal chance of selection. This is the basis of **stratified sampling**. Note that the intention here is still to obtain a representative sample, but one which 'fairly' reflects a population which itself is heterogeneous. We might say that such a sample is free from 'selective bias', since the proportion of any identified attribute in the sample is merely a reflection of its contribution to the population as a whole.

Stratified sampling

► used when the population has a number of identifiable attributes;
► populations stratified in this way are known as heterogeneous;
► the composition of the sample must reflect the attributes present in the population, e.g. the proportion of low-, middle- and high-income earners;
► individuals or items *within* each stratum may still be selected randomly;
► a stratified sample is free from selective bias, since it reflects the proportions of any given attribute present in the population as a whole.

DID YOU KNOW?
It costs five times as much to recruit a new customer via marketing strategies (e.g. sample surveys of new products/designs, etc.) as it does to service and retain an existing customer.

DID YOU KNOW?
By the year 2011 it is estimated that 17 per cent of the UK population will be aged over 65 years. This 'ageing' population will mean an increased demand for those products targeted toward the elderly.

Quota sampling

The use of **quota sampling** is widespread in market research. Here the intention is often to deliberately introduce selective bias into the samples, in the sense that attributes of the members or items selected will represent the choice of the samples rather than the attributes of the population as a whole. In this sense there is no attempt to seek a representative or unbiased sample from the population. For example, if a firm sells most of its product to those with incomes over £x, then the sample may contain 80 per cent of such adults even if they only comprise, say, 40 per cent of the population. Nor is there usually any attempt to use random sampling *within* the quotas selected, as often happens within the different strata in stratified sampling. It is often left to the discretion of interviewers, etc. to include specified numbers (quotas) of subjects possessing given attributes within the sample. To do so accurately may be costly, requiring highly trained interviewers.

Quota sampling

▶ widely used in market research;

▶ sample includes a specified number or quota of subjects with given attributes;

▶ interviewers must be highly trained as they are often responsible for identification and selection of respondents;

▶ a 'biased' sample therefore results, but one which may be useful in representing the customers seen as most likely to purchase the firms products.

PAUSE FOR THOUGHT 7.2 *Can you identify three well-known products for which a quota sampling procedure might be considered appropriate for testing consumer response?*

Multi-stage and cluster sampling

Other types of non-random sampling include **multi-stage** and **cluster** sampling.

Multi-stage sampling

▶ usually involves sampling of subjects with a given attribute;

▶ often occurs where there is a wide geographical spread of such subjects which makes sampling expensive;

▶ whole geographical area is therefore divided into regions;

▶ a small number of such regions is then selected randomly;

▶ regions selected are further broken down into *sub-regions* (e.g. North West England into parliamentary constituencies), from which a random sample is selected;

▶ sub-regions selected are further broken down into *units* (e.g. towns or streets), from which a random sample is again selected;

▶ eventually individual households or persons with a given attribute are identified in specific towns or streets;

▶ costs of interviewing is then much reduced, though some risks of bias in procedure especially if only small numbers of regions, sub-regions, etc. are selected.

Cluster sampling

▶ items chosen in *clusters* rather than individually;

▶ example, cluster might be *all* residents in a particular road or group of roads;

▶ useful method where the population is widely spread geographically but where the various clusters are broadly representative of that population;

▶ similar to above sampling method, except that the cluster itself is the *single-stage* involved.

7.2 Distribution of sample means

If the distribution of the population (X_i) is Normal then the distribution of the arithmetic means ($\overline{X}_i$) of *samples* of size n taken from that population will be Normal (see Figure 7.1). The new distribution will have the same arithmetic mean μ but a different standard deviation. We call this the *standard error* (SE) and it can be found by dividing the standard deviation of the population (σ) by the square root of the sample size (i.e. $\sqrt{n}$).

Standard error (SE) = standard deviation of distribution of sample means

$$\text{SE} = \frac{\sigma}{\sqrt{n}} \text{ or SE} = \frac{s}{\sqrt{n}}$$

Note: where the *population* standard deviation (σ) is not available, the *sample* standard deviation (s) is often used as an approximation:

figure 7.1
Distribution of population for variable X_i and for the means $\overline{X}_i$ of samples of size n drawn from that population

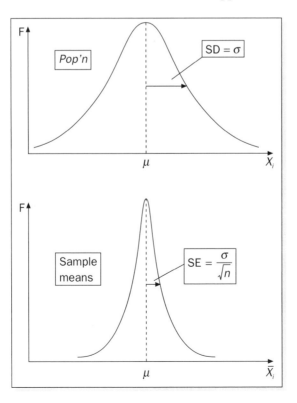

Of course if the sample were, say, of size 1 then we would be back to individual members of the population X_i and there would be no difference between SD and SE (SD = SE = $\sigma/\sqrt{1}$ = σ). However if the samples were of a size greater than 1, then the samples themselves would tend to *average out* any extreme values of X_i, so that the distribution of sample means ($\bar{X}_i$) could be expected to have a smaller dispersion around the population mean (μ) than would the distribution of each item of the population. The *larger* the sample size n, the smaller this dispersion of $\bar{X}_i$ around μ is likely to be. For example, samples of size 36 taken from the population (X_i) give an SE for the distribution of sample means ($\bar{X}_i$) of $\sigma/\sqrt{36}$ which is *smaller* than the SE had the samples taken from the population only been of size 4, giving SE = $\sigma/\sqrt{4}$.

Using the Z statistic

Because the distribution of sample means is *Normal*, we can still use the *Z* statistic. However note that we now calculate the *Z* statistic as:

$$Z = \frac{\bar{X}_i - \mu}{\dfrac{\sigma}{\sqrt{n}}}$$

WORKED
EXAMPLE **7.1**
....

A production line makes units which are normally distributed with a mean weight of 200 grams and a standard deviation (σ) of 9 grams. What is the probability of a sample of 36 units having a (sample) mean weight of 203 grams or more?

Solution

figure 7.2

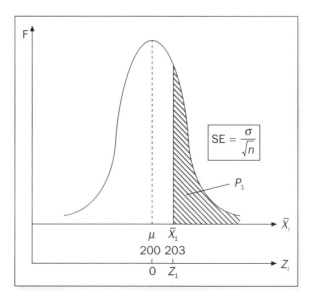

$\mu = 200$ grams

$\sigma = 9$ grams

$n = $ sample size $= 36$

$$SE = \frac{\sigma}{\sqrt{n}} = \frac{9}{\sqrt{36}} = 1.5$$

$$Z_1 = \frac{\bar{X}_1 - \mu}{\sigma / \sqrt{n}} = \frac{203 - 200}{1.5} = +2$$

Using the Z tables (Appendix 2, p. 314)

$\underline{P_1 = 0.0228}$

7.3 Central Limit Theorem

Even if the population is *not* normally distributed, the **Central Limit Theorem** tells us that if sampling is random and the sample size (n) is ≥ 32, then the distribution of the sample means can be regarded as approximately normally distributed, with mean μ and standard error $\sigma/\sqrt{n}$, as shown in Figure 7.3.

We can therefore still use our Z statistic for calculating probabilities for the distribution of sample means even when the population is not itself normally distributed. All we need do is use a random sampling procedure and make sure that our sample size is large enough (at least 32).

figure 7.3
Central Limit Theorem: population skewed, but distribution of sample means ($\bar{X}_i$) Normal, with same mean (μ) and

$$SE = \frac{\sigma}{\sqrt{n}}$$

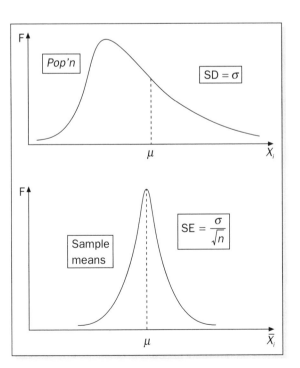

WORKED EXAMPLE **7.2**
....

The output of glass panels has a mean thickness of 4 cm and a standard deviation of 1 cm. If a random sample of 100 glass panels is taken, what is the probability of the sample mean having a thickness of between 3.9 cm and 4.2 cm?

Solution

The Central Limit Theorem applies as random sampling has been adopted and $n \geq 32$. The distribution of sample means ($\bar{X}_i$) is therefore Normal with mean (μ) = 4 cm and standard error $\sigma/\sqrt{n} = 1/\sqrt{100} = 0.1$ cm.

figure 7.4

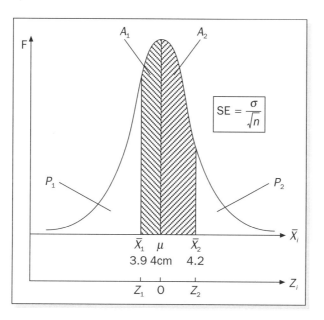

$$Z_1 = \frac{\bar{X}_1 - \mu}{\sigma / \sqrt{n}} = \frac{3.9 - 4.0}{0.1} = -1$$

$P_1 = 0.1587$

$A_1 = 0.5000 - 0.1587$

$\underline{A_1 = 0.3413}$

$$Z_2 = \frac{\bar{X}_2 - \mu}{\sigma / \sqrt{n}} = \frac{4.2 - 4.0}{0.1} = +2$$

$P_2 = 0.0228$

$A_2 = 0.5000 - 0.0228$

$\underline{A_2 = 0.4772}$

$\underline{A_1 + A_2 = 0.8185}$

i.e. there is an 81.85 per cent chance of the sample mean of 100 glass panels having a thickness of between 3.9 cm and 4.2 cm.

7.1 It is thought that the annual cost of transport to and from work for employees of a company is normally distributed with mean £100 a year and standard deviation £10. What is the probability that a *sample* of 100 employees will give a sample mean of:

(a) less than £98 a year
(b) more than £103 a year?

7.2 A departmental manager believes that the average value of a large population of invoices is £10 with a standard deviation of £2. What is the probability that a *sample* of 36 invoices selected at random will give a sample mean:

(a) below £9.50
(b) above £10.75
(c) above £11?

7.3 An automatic machine fills jars of jam with a mean net weight of 340 grams and a standard deviation of 8 grams. What is the probability that a *sample* of 64 jars selected at random will have a sample mean:

(a) above 340.75 grams
(b) below 338.5 grams
(c) between 339 grams and 342 grams?

Note: Answers can be found on pp. 347–348.

7.4 Confidence intervals

. . . .

A **confidence interval** is a range of values within which we can have a certain level of confidence (usually 95 per cent or 99 per cent) that a particular value of a variable will lie. In the context of sampling, we are usually interested in one of two possible *types* of confidence interval.

Confidence interval for the sample mean

This is the range of values around the *population mean* (μ) within which we can be 95 per cent or 99 per cent confident that a particular *sample mean* ($\bar{X}_i$) will lie.

95 per cent confidence interval

In terms of Figure 7.5, we wish to find the values for $\bar{X}_1$ and $\bar{X}_2$, which are 47.5 per cent (0.475) either side of the population mean μ.

Of course this will imply 2.5 per cent (0.025) in each tail of the distribution for $\bar{X}_i$.

We have already seen (p. 130) how we calculate the Z_1 and Z_2 scores (+1.96 and –1.96 respectively) which will give us 0.025 in each tail. We can then use our formula for the Z statistic (as applied to the distribution of sample means) to calculate $\bar{X}_1$ and $\bar{X}_2$:

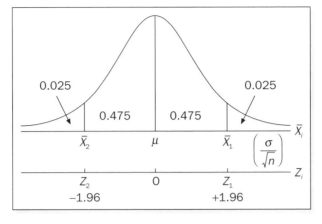

$$Z_1 = \frac{\bar{X}_1 - \mu}{\sigma/\sqrt{n}}$$

i.e. $\qquad 1.96 = \dfrac{\bar{X}_1 - \mu}{\sigma/\sqrt{n}}$

$$+1.96\left(\sigma/\sqrt{n}\right) = \bar{X}_1 - \mu$$

$$\mu + 1.96\left(\sigma/\sqrt{n}\right) = \bar{X}_1$$

We can use the same procedure for finding Z_2, except that we insert −1.96 for the Z_2 score. You should then be able to show that:

$$\mu - 1.96\left(\sigma/\sqrt{n}\right) = \bar{X}_2$$

The end values of the confidence interval are called the *confidence limits*. Here $\bar{X}_1$ and $\bar{X}_2$ are the confidence limits for the 95 per cent confidence interval.

> In general, the **95 per cent *confidence interval* for the sample mean** can be written as follows:
>
> $\qquad \bar{X}_i = \mu \pm 1.96\,(\sigma/\sqrt{n})$
>
> i.e. $\quad \bar{X}_i = \mu \pm 1.96$ SE

In other words we can be 95 per cent confident that a single sample mean ($\bar{X}_i$) will lie within 1.96 standard errors (SE) of the population mean μ.

99 per cent confidence interval

The approach here is exactly the same as above *except* that we wish to find the values for the distribution of sample means, namely $\bar{X}_1$ and $\bar{X}_2$, which are 49.5 per cent (0.495) either side of the population mean μ. Of course this will imply 0.5 per cent (0.005) in each tail of the distribution for $\bar{X}_i$.

As we shall see in Figure 7.6(b) below, the only difference will be that our Z_1 and Z_2 scores respectively will be +2.58 and –2.58 in order to give 0.005 in each tail.

In general the **99 per cent *confidence interval for the sample mean*** can be written as follows:

$$\bar{X_i} = \mu \pm 2.58(\sigma/\sqrt{n})$$

i.e. $\bar{X_i} = \mu \pm 2.58$ SE

In other words we can be 99 per cent confident that a single sample mean ($\bar{X_i}$) will lie within 2.58 standard errors (SE) of the population mean (μ).

The end values of this 99 per cent confidence interval, $\bar{X_1}$ and $\bar{X_2}$, will be the 99 per cent *confidence limits*.

WORKED
EXAMPLE **7.3**

A large number of random samples of size 100 are taken from the production line for glass panels which is thought to produce panels with mean thickness 4 cm and standard deviation 1 cm.

Find (a) the 95 per cent and (b) the 99 per cent confidence intervals and associated confidence limits for the sample mean.

Solution

figure 7.6

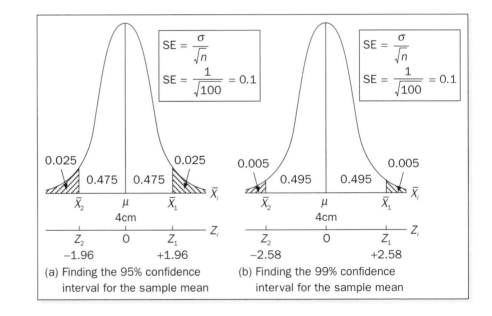

(a) Finding the 95% confidence interval for the sample mean

(b) Finding the 99% confidence interval for the sample mean

(a) $\bar{X_i} = \mu \pm 1.96(\sigma/\sqrt{n})$

$\bar{X_i} = 4 \pm 1.96(1/\sqrt{100})$

$\bar{X_i} = 4 \pm 1.96(0.1)$

$\bar{X_i} = 4 \pm 0.196$

$\underline{\bar{X_i} = 4.196 \quad \text{and} \quad 3.804}$

The 95 per cent *confidence interval* is 3.804 cm to 4.196 cm

In terms of Figure 7.6 (a) the *confidence limits* are:

$\bar{X}_1 = 4.196$ cm

$\bar{X}_2 = 3.804$ cm

(b) $\bar{X}_i = \mu \pm 2.58(\sigma/\sqrt{n})$

Note: if you check the Z tables in Appendix 2 (p. 314) you will see that 2.575 is strictly the Z score giving 0.005 in each tail. Rounding up the 5 in the third decimal place gives 2.58.

$\bar{X}_i = 4 \pm 2.58 \, (1/\sqrt{100})$

$\bar{X}_i = 4 \pm 2.58 \, (0.1)$

$\underline{\bar{X}_i = 4 \pm 0.258}$

The 99 per cent *confidence interval* is 3.742 cm to 4.258 cm.

In terms of Figure 7.6(b) the *confidence limits* are:

$\bar{X}_1 = 4.258$ cm

$\bar{X}_2 = 3.742$ cm

Confidence interval for the population mean

This is the range of values around the *sample mean* ($\bar{X}_i$) within which we can be 95 per cent or 99 per cent certain that the *population mean* (μ) will lie.

The previous analysis applies here except that in this case we are likely to be given information about a particular *sample* and asked to find the ranges of values within which we might expect to find the population mean μ.

It may be that instead of being given information about the *population standard deviation* (σ) we are only given information about the *sample standard deviation* (s). However we have already noted (p. 148) that we can use s as an approximation to σ in calculating the standard error for the distribution of sample means:

i.e. $\text{SE} = \dfrac{\sigma}{\sqrt{n}} = \dfrac{s}{\sqrt{n}}$

We have seen that the Z statistic for the distribution of sample means is:

$$\pm Z = \frac{\bar{X}_i - \mu}{s / \sqrt{n}}$$

i.e. $\pm Z \left(s / \sqrt{n} \right) = \quad - \mu$

$\mu = \quad \pm \quad \left(\dfrac{s}{\sqrt{n}} \right)$

All we have done is re-arrange the terms to have μ on the left-hand side this time instead of $\bar{X}_i$. As before the **confidence intervals for population mean** can be written as follows:

$$\mu = \bar{X}_i \pm 1.96 \left(\frac{s}{\sqrt{n}} \right) \text{ for a 95\% confidence interval}$$

$$\mu = \bar{X}_i \pm 2.58 \left(\frac{s}{\sqrt{n}} \right) \text{ for a 99\% confidence interval}$$

WORKED
EXAMPLE **7.4**
••••••••••••

Estimate (a) the 95 per cent and (b) the 99 per cent confidence intervals and associated confidence limits for the *population mean* when we are given the following *sample data*:

sample mean $(\bar{X}_i)$ = 950 kg
sample standard deviation (s) = 15 kg
sample size (n) = 36

Solution

(a) *95 per cent confidence interval and confidence limits for μ*

$\mu = \bar{X}_i \pm 1.96(s/\sqrt{n})$

$\mu = 950 \pm 1.96(15/\sqrt{36})$

$\mu = 950 \pm 1.96(2.5)$

$\mu = 950 \pm 4.9$

$\underline{\mu = 945.1 \text{ kg to } 954.9 \text{ kg}}$

In other words we can be 95 per cent confident that the population mean μ will lie in the interval between 945.1 kg and 954.9 kg, given the sample data provided. These values are the 95 per cent *confidence limits* for the population mean.

(b) *99 per cent confidence interval and confidence limits for μ*

$\mu = \bar{X}_i \pm 2.58(s/\sqrt{n})$

$\mu = 950 \pm 2.58(15/\sqrt{36})$

$\mu = 950 \pm 2.58(2.5)$

$\mu = 950 \pm 6.45$

$\underline{\mu = 943.55 \text{ kg to } 956.45 \text{ kg}}$

We can be 99 per cent confident that the population mean μ will lie in the interval between 943.55 kg and 956.45 kg, given the sample data. These values are the 99 per cent *confidence limits* for the population mean.

**SELF-CHECK
QUESTIONS**

7.4 The management of a company claim that the average weekly earnings of their employees is £550 with a standard deviation of £120. A random sample of 144 employees is taken. Calculate (a) the 95 per cent and (b) the 99 per cent confidence intervals for the *sample* mean.

7.5 A random sample of 64 households was selected in a town and the average expenditure per week on a certain product was found to be £6.15 with a (sample) standard deviation of £1.30. Calculate (a) the 95 per cent and (b) the 99 per cent confidence intervals for the *population* mean.

Note: Answers can be found on p. 349.

ACTIVITY **5**
•••••••••••••

Confidence interval for μ when s is unknown

Two random samples of components were selected from a production process with the intention of estimating their life expectancy in hours. The first random sample contained 60 components, the second random sample contained 120 components. Estimate the 90 per cent, 95 per cent and 99 per cent confidence intervals for the population mean from each sample.

The data from the samples were as follows:

Sample 1

286.5	304.5	301.3	313.9	309.7	287.4
310	310	306.4	288.4	310.4	285.7
300.6	296.5	304.6	291.5	299.2	296.7
314.4	307.2	299.8	316.1	287	307.9
293.7	302.4	312.4	302.1	296.4	292.7
287.5	310.1	305.5	295.6	291	301.2
298.5	299.7	307.7	304.3	292.6	296.2
304.6	302	290.8	314	298.5	291.6
301.9	297.2	298.2	302.1	295.2	299.7
292.9	294.6	296.2	306.5	284.2	304.6

Sample 2

297	311.9	301.4	305	305.1	309.7	295.1	319.4
310.5	301.2	313.4	288.4	301.8	295.2	305.8	289.2
309.8	295	301.3	303.7	304.3	290.2	298.3	304.7
298.6	294.9	292.2	301.6	309.2	305.7	312.8	301.2
291.9	305.8	290	300	298.5	302.1	301.8	299.1
295.2	321.6	297.9	303.9	293.9	300.6	301.5	311.3
291.5	301.2	310.4	299.4	308.9	299.6	291.1	287.7
286.6	290.1	305.7	306.2	304.8	301.6	299.3	307.9
297.4	297.4	317.2	302.4	305.5	290	313.6	292.1
309.6	295.4	309.8	299.4	289.5	307.8	299.1	296.1
291.4	298.1	292.7	292.6	277	301.8	291.5	308.6
297.7	302.3	293.2	289	300.1	303.8	297.2	276.4
304.8	296.7	297.4	290.2	299.7	303.1	288.6	293.9
304.4	304.8	303.2	299.1	290.8	304	286	308.2
306.2	304.4	297.2	296.6	315.7	302.6	297.9	288.3

1   Enter all the data from Sample 1 into column **A** and the data from Sample 2 into column **B**.

2 Analyse the two samples by setting out a table of results as follows:

		D	E	F
2	**SAMPLE**	1	2	
3	Size			
4	Median			
5	Mean			
6	Std Dev			
7	Std Error			
8	Variance			
9	Min			
10	Max			
11	Range			

3 Comment on your table of results.

4 Calculate the standard error by using: $SE = \dfrac{s}{\sqrt{n}}$

5 Applying the Central Limit Theorem we can say that for 95 per cent:

$$\mu = \bar{X} \pm 1.96 \frac{s}{\sqrt{n}}$$

For 90 per cent and 99 per cent:

$$\mu = \bar{X} \pm 1.645 \frac{s}{\sqrt{n}} \text{ and } \mu = \bar{X} \pm 2.575 \frac{s}{\sqrt{n}} \text{ respectively.}$$

6 Use the above formulæ to find the respective confidence intervals. It is suggested that another table, such as the one below, will produce a clear layout for your solutions.

Conf level %	Z	Z*E	Lower	Upper	Interval
Sample 1					
90	1.645				
95	1.96				
99	2.575				
Sample 2					
90	1.645				
95	1.96				
99	2.575				

Comment on your results. Check with the responses on pp. 466–467.

7.5 Tests of hypotheses: principles

We can use our work on the distribution of sample means and the Central Limit Theorem for testing **hypotheses** (theories). A hypothesis is an assumption about a situation. We usually want to *test* this assumption against one or more alternative assumptions.

It will be useful at this stage to become familiar with the terminology widely used in this topic area. For simplicity we assume that we are testing a main hypothesis (*Null* hypothesis, H_0) against one other hypothesis (*Alternative* hypothesis, H_1).

Null hypothesis (H_0): the hypothesis to be tested.

For example that the mean thickness of glass panels is 4 cm:

$H_0 : \mu = 4$ cm

Alternative hypothesis (H_1): the hypothesis we wish to accept if we reject the null hypothesis.

For example that the mean thickness of glass panels is *not* equal to 4 cm.

$H_1 : \mu \neq 4$ cm

In testing our null hypothesis, there are essentially two *types of error* we might wish to avoid.

▶ **Type 1 error:** rejecting the null hypothesis when it is, in fact, true.
▶ **Type 2 error:** accepting the null hypothesis when it is, in fact, false.

Avoiding a Type 1 error is usually the main concern of problems in this topic area. When testing the null hypothesis we usually state the *maximum risk* we are willing to take of committing a Type 1 error, i.e. of rejecting the null hypothesis when it is, in fact, true. This is called the *level of significance* and is typically either 5 per cent (0.05) or 1 per cent (0.01)

Levels of significance

The maximum risk we are willing to take of making a Type 1 error, i.e. of rejecting the null hypothesis when it is, in fact, true.

Confidence limits and critical values

If we look back to Figure 7.6 (p. 154) we can usefully illustrate the idea of the level of significance. It is clear that there is a 95 per cent (0.95) chance of any sample mean ($\overline{X}_i$) lying within 1.96 standard errors (SE) of the true population mean μ. However there is still a 5 per cent (0.05) chance of a single sample mean lying *outside* this 95 per cent *confidence interval* even though the population mean really is μ.

Here this 5 per cent (0.05) chance is split evenly to be 2.5 per cent (0.025) in each tail. If the sample mean lies outside the *confidence limits* $\overline{X}_1$ or $\overline{X}_2$ then our decision will be to reject H_0 even though we might be wrong in rejecting H_0. However the chance of our being wrong is *less than 5 per cent*, since there was a less than 5 per cent chance of actually getting a sample mean $\overline{X}_i$ outside $\overline{X}_1$ and $\overline{X}_2$ when μ really is the population mean.

These *confidence limits* for the population mean, μ, can therefore be regarded as the *critical values* for tests of hypotheses. In other words they are the values of $\overline{X}_i$ (or their Z_i equivalents) *outside of which* we are willing to reject the null hypothesis (H_0). In that sense they are the values 'critical' to the decision we are about to take in our test of the null hypothesis (H_0).

> **Critical values**
>
> These are the values of X_i or Z_i for the sample *outside* of which we are willing to reject the null hypothesis (H_0) at a particular level of significance.

Two- and one-tailed tests

Two-tailed tests

The approach so far has involved a **two-tailed test**, i.e. where we split the risk of being wrong in rejecting the null hypothesis *equally* between each tail of the distribution.

Let us formally set out the null (H_0) and alternative (H_1) hypotheses for a *two-tailed* test. We use our earlier example of thickness of glass panels by way of illustration.

$$H_0 : \mu = 4 \text{ cm}$$

$$H_1 : \mu \neq 4 \text{ cm}$$

Since the alternative hypothesis (H_1) says $\mu \neq 4$ cm it is clear that we are just as interested in situations where $\mu > 4$ cm as we are in situations where $\mu < 4$ cm.

> **Two-tailed test**
>
> We divide the risk we are willing to take in making a Type 1 error equally between each tail of the distribution

If we test the null hypothesis at a 5 per cent (0.05) level of significance, we place 2.5 per cent (0.025) in each tail. Here we will reject H_0 if we think that $\mu > 4$ cm or if we think that $\mu < 4$ cm.

Acceptance and rejection regions

▶ The region *within which* we are willing to accept the null hypothesis (H_0) we call the *acceptance region*.
▶ The region *outside which* we are willing to reject the null hypothesis (H_0) we call the *rejection region*.

figure 7.7

Acceptance and rejection regions for the null hypothesis (H_0): two tailed tests at (a) 5% (0.05) (b) 1% (0.01) levels of significance

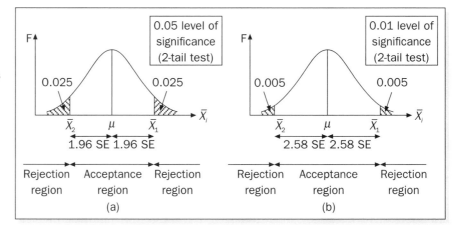

$\bar{X}_1$ and $\bar{X}_2$ correspond to the **critical values**, i.e. the sample means at the boundary between the acceptance and rejection regions for the null hypothesis (H_0).

WORKED
EXAMPLE **7.5**
....

Find the critical values for a two-tailed test at the 5 per cent (0.05) level of significance for the earlier example of glass panels, mean (μ) = 4 cm, standard error ($\sigma/\sqrt{n}$) = 0.1 cm.

Solution

$\mu \pm 1.96$ SE = critical values

$4 \pm 1.96(0.1)$ = critical values

3.804 cm = $\bar{X}_2$; 4.196 cm = $\bar{X}_1$

We can be 95 per cent certain of getting a sample mean in the *acceptance region* 3.804 cm to 4.196 cm if the true (population) mean is 4 cm.

If, however, we get a sample measurement *outside* these critical values (i.e. in the *rejection region*), then we can reject $H_0 : \mu = 4$ cm with less than a 5 per cent (0.05) chance of being wrong. This is because there is a less than 5 per cent (0.05) chance of $\bar{X}_i$ being outside these critical values if $H_0 : \mu = 4$ cm is true.

WORKED
EXAMPLE **7.6**
....

Find the critical values for a two-tailed test at the 1 per cent (0.01) level of significance for the earlier example of glass panels, mean (μ) = 4 cm, standard error ($\sigma/\sqrt{n}$) = 0.1 cm.

Solution

This time we place half of 1 per cent (0.005) in each tail, giving a Z score of ±2.58.

$\mu \pm 2.58$ SE = critical values

$4 \pm 2.58(0.1)$ = critical values

3.742 cm = $\bar{X}_2$; 4.258 cm = $\bar{X}_1$

We can be 99 per cent certain of getting a sample mean in the *acceptance region* 3.742 cm to 4.258 cm if the true (population) mean is 4 cm.

If however, we get a sample measurement *outside* these critical values (i.e. in the *rejection region*), then we can reject $H_0 : \mu = 4$ cm with less than a 1 per cent (0.01) chance of being wrong. This is because there is a less than 1 per cent chance of $\bar{X}_i$ being outside these critical values if $H_0 : \mu = 4$ cm is true.

One-tailed test

Here we do *not* split the risk of being wrong in rejecting the null hypothesis equally between each tail of the distribution. Here we are only concerned with *one side* (and therefore *one tail*) of the distribution when testing our null hypothesis (H_0) against an alternative hypothesis (H_1). We therefore place *all* the risk of making a Type 1 error in one tail.

One-tailed test

We place the risk we are willing to take in making a Type 1 error in one tail of the distribution

---

Let us formally set out the null (H_0) and alternative (H_1) hypotheses for a **one-tailed** test. We again use our earlier example of thickness of glass panels by way of illustration.

EITHER

$H_0 : \mu = 4$ cm

$H_1 : \mu > 4$ cm

In testing H_0 against H_1 we are only interested in rejecting H_0 (i.e. accepting H_1) if the sample means suggest a true (population) mean *greater than* 4 cm.

OR

$H_0 : \mu = 4$ cm

$H_1 : \mu < 4$ cm

In testing H_0 against H_1 we are only interested in rejecting H_0 (i.e. accepting H_1) if the sample mean suggests a true (population) mean *less than* 4 cm.

Acceptance and rejection regions

Figure 7.8 indicates the relevant acceptance and rejection regions for a one-tail test at 5 per cent (0.05) and 1 per cent (0.01) levels of significance. Remember the Z scores are calculated using the Z tables (Appendix 2, p. 314) and are used to give the area in the respective tails.

WORKED
EXAMPLE **7.7**
••••••••••••••

Look again at Figure 7.8(a), p. 163. Find the critical values for a one-tailed test at the 5 per cent (0.05) level of significance for the earlier example of glass panels, mean (μ) = 4 cm, standard error ($\sigma/\sqrt{n}$) = 0.1 cm.

Solution

$\bar{X}_1 = \mu + 1.65$ SE
$\bar{X}_1 = 4 + 1.65(0.1)$
$\bar{X}_1 = 4.165$ cm

$\bar{X}_2 = \mu - 1.65$ SE
$\bar{X}_2 = 4 - 1.65(0.1)$
$\bar{X}_2 = 3.835$ cm

figure 7.8
Acceptance and rejection regions for the null hypotheses (H₀): one-tailed tests at (a) 5% (0.05) (b) 1% (0.01) levels of significance

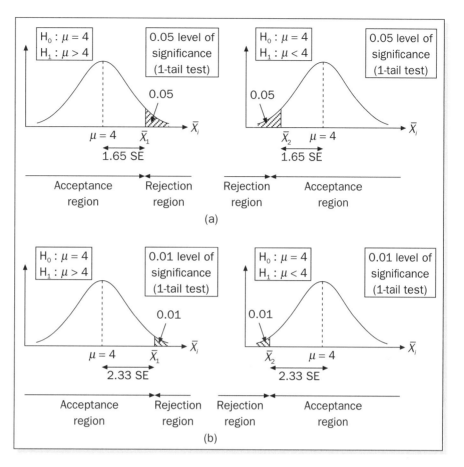

If the sample mean $\bar{X}_i$ lies *outside* these critical values then we would be outside the *acceptance region* and in the *rejection region*.

▶ For $H_0 : \mu = 4$ cm
$\quad\quad H_1 : \mu > 4$ cm

Reject H_0 if $\bar{X}_i > 4.165$ cm

▶ For $H_0 : \mu = 4$ cm
$\quad\quad H_1 : \mu < 4$ cm

Reject H_0 if $\bar{X}_i < 3.835$ cm

7.6 Tests of hypotheses: practice
....

In this section we develop a simple seven-step plan for tackling all problems involving tests of hypotheses. This seven-step plan draws on the ideas presented in the previous section.

However before we outline these steps let us select *one* of two alternative approaches to finding critical values.

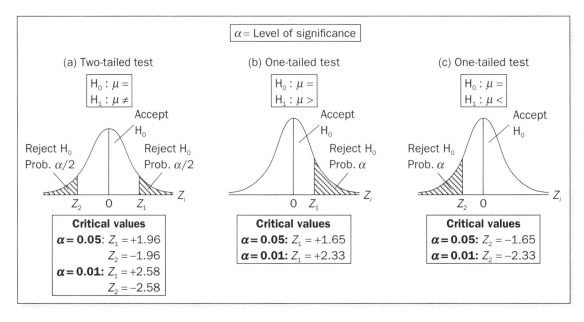

figure 7.9

Using the Z scores for the critical values

(a) Two-tailed test

(b) One-tailed test

(c) One-tailed test

Critical values: Z scores or sample mean values

As we saw in Figure 7.8 (p. 163), the critical values can be expressed in terms of the *sample means*, $\bar{X}_1$ and $\bar{X}_2$ respectively. However they can just as easily be expressed in terms of the *Z scores*, i.e. the number of standard errors from μ, the population mean.

In Figure 7.9, α (alpha) is the *level of significance* at which the test is conducted. The *Z scores* are shown for the respective *critical values*. These *Z scores* can be said to depend on both the level of significance and on whether the test is one- or two-tailed.

In this approach we calculate the *Z-score* using the *sample data* provided. If the *Z* score for the sample data lies *outside* the relevant *Z* critical values, then the decision rule will be to *reject* the null hypothesis (H_0).

It will be useful at this stage to go through a worked example before using this to illustrate our seven-step plan for testing hypotheses.

WORKED EXAMPLE **7.8**
••••••••••••••

It is thought that the average wage for a large company is £130 a week with a standard deviation of £30. A sample of 100 employees finds the sample average to be £123.

Solution

Test $H_0 : \mu = £130$

$H_1 : \mu \neq £130$

using a 5 per cent level of significance.

This is a two-tailed test since the alternative hypothesis (H_1) has been expressed as ≠.

If the Z score if calculated for the sample data and found to be outside the Z critical value, then reject H_0.

figure 7.10

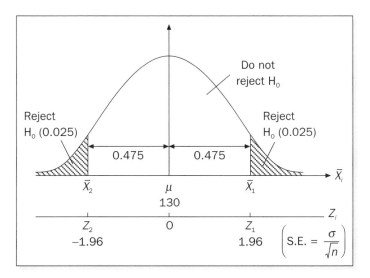

Here $\bar{X} = 123$,

gives $Z = \dfrac{\bar{X} - \mu}{\sigma / \sqrt{n}}$

$Z = \dfrac{123 - 130}{30/\sqrt{100}}$

i.e. $Z = \dfrac{123 - 130}{3}$

$Z = -\dfrac{7}{3}$

$\underline{Z = -2.33}$

Our Z score is *outside* the Z critical value of –1.96, so we reject H_0.

We can now formally set out our *seven-step plan* for testing a hypothesis, using this example to illustrate each step.

Step		Example
1	State hypotheses	$H_0 : \mu = £130$
		$H_1 : \mu \neq £130$
2	State significance level	5% (0.05)
3	State critical values	$Z_1 = +1.96$
		$Z_2 = -1.96$
4	Calculate the Z score for the sample	$Z = -2.33$
5	Compare this Z sample score with the Z critical values	Here $Z = -2.33$ is *outside* $Z_2 = -1.96$
6	Come to a conclusion	Reject H_0
7	Put your conclusion in words	The sample evidence does *not* support the null hypothesis at a 5 per cent level of significance

Note: A sketch diagram will usually help in Step 3 (e.g. Figure 7.9(a) for $\alpha = 0.05$)

It will be useful for you to see this seven-step plan applied to a couple of examples, before trying it out yourself.

WORKED
EXAMPLE **7.9**
•••••••••••••

A manager of a health store believes the average amount spent per week on vitamin C supplements to be £2.50. A random sample of 100 shoppers found an average expenditure on such supplements of £2.40 with a standard deviation of £0.40. Test the manager's belief at a 5 per cent level of significance.

Solution

Note: We shall use a *two-tailed* test here, since any divergence from £2.50 (above or below) would invalidate the manager's belief. Since only the sample mean (*s*) is available, we use this instead of the population mean (σ) in calculating the standard error.

Step 1 $H_0 : \mu = £2.50$
       $H_1 : \mu \neq £2.50$
Step 2 5 per cent (0.05) level of significance
Step 3 Critical values for Z: ±1.96

figure 7.11

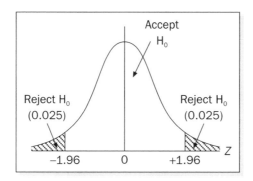

Step 4 For sample data

$$Z = \frac{\bar{X} - \mu}{s / \sqrt{n}} = \frac{2.40 - 2.50}{0.40 / \sqrt{100}}$$

$$Z = \frac{-0.10}{0.40 / 10} = \frac{-0.10}{0.04} = -2.50$$

Step 5 −2.50 is *outside* −1.96

Step 6 Reject null hypothesis (H_0)

Step 7 Evidence does not support the health store manager's belief that average spending on Vitamin C supplement is £2.50 per week.

WORKED EXAMPLE **7.10**

The expected mean diameter of a batch of cables is 2 cm. A quality control inspector takes a sample of 64 cables and finds that the sample has a mean diameter of 1.94 cm and a standard deviation of 0.4 cm. Test whether the manufacturing process is now producing cables with a smaller diameter than previously at a 1 per cent level of significance.

Solution

Note: We shall use a *one-tailed* test here, since our concern is that the manufacturing process is producing *smaller* diameter cables than claimed. Again we use sample standard deviation (s) as an approximation for the population standard deviation (σ). Our test is at the 1 per cent level of significance this time; i.e. we are less willing than in the previous worked example to take the risk of rejecting the null hypothesis (H_0) when it is in fact true.

Step 1 $H_0 : \mu = 2.00$ cm
$\quad\quad\quad H_1 : \mu < 2.00$ cm

Step 2 1 per cent (0.01) level of significance

Step 3 Critical value for Z: −2.33

figure 7.12

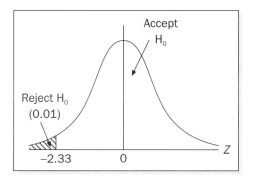

Step 4 For sample data

$$Z = \frac{\bar{X} - \mu}{s/\sqrt{n}} = \frac{1.94 - 2.00}{0.4/\sqrt{64}}$$

$$Z = \frac{-0.06}{0.4/8} = \frac{-0.06}{0.05} = -1.2$$

Step 5 -1.2 is *inside* -2.33

Step 6 Accept null hypothesis (H_0)

Step 7 There is insufficient evidence from the sample data to reject the initial hypothesis that the manufacturing process is still producing cables of diameter of 2 cm. We would be taking more risk than we are willing to take if we were to accept the alternative hypothesis that the cables are now being produced with a diameter of less than 2 cm.

You can now test your familiarity with this *seven-step* approach with the following Self-check questions. There are also more questions for practice (Review questions) at the end of this chapter.

SELF-CHECK QUESTIONS

7.6 A firm manufactures light bulbs and the sales manager claims that tests have proved that the average life of these bulbs is 1,000 hours. We wish to buy some of these light bulbs but before doing so we wish to check the claim that their average life is correct. We therefore take a sample of 36 bulbs and test them; we find that the average life of the bulbs in the sample is 940 hours with a standard deviation of 126 hours. Is the manufacture's claim justified? Test at both (a) 5 per cent (0.05) and (b) 1 per cent (0.01) levels of significance.

7.7 A factory manager asserts that the mean running time of machines is 14 hours a day. A random sample of 64 machines shows that their mean running time was only 13 hours 20 minutes, with a standard deviation of 3 hours. Test the manager's assertion at the 5 per cent significance level.

***Note:* Keep the units the same throughout (i.e. hours or minutes).**

7.8 A machine produces electronic components whose lifetimes have a mean of 100 hours and a standard deviation of 14 hours. A new technique is now introduced into their production. A *sample* of 49 components gives a mean of 104 hours. Has the new technique produced longer lasting components? Test at a 5 per cent level of significance.

***Note:* Answers can be found on p. 349.**

ACTIVITY 6

Hypothesis testing or significance testing

A company believes that the average amount spent by customers has changed from its original value. The accounting department, however, disputes this claim and maintains that sales remain at £1.48 per customer. To support their view the accounting department quote the following random sample of spending (£) by 75 customers.

1.61	1.16	1.72	1.11	1.58	1.44	1.37	1.60	1.71	1.10
1.50	1.87	1.54	1.09	1.41	1.52	1.59	1.10	1.40	1.60
1.68	1.30	1.69	1.55	1.59	1.54	1.80	1.55	1.52	1.37
1.15	1.44	1.43	1.81	1.53	1.03	1.61	1.72	1.29	1.35
1.09	0.88	0.90	1.06	1.83	1.80	1.33	1.91	1.31	1.42
1.86	1.62	1.71	0.95	1.58	1.45	1.59	1.79	1.01	1.13
1.53	1.46	1.67	1.67	1.53	1.75	0.94	1.01	1.42	2.07
1.23	1.23	1.41	1.46	1.19					

Use a spreadsheet with which you are familiar to conduct the following tests.

1 Test, at the 5 per cent significance level, the hypothesis that the average amount spent by each customer remains at £1.48.
2 Test the same hypothesis at the 1 per cent significance level.

Conduct the hypothesis test:

Step 1 State the hypothesis: $H_0 : \mu = £1.48$: $H_1 : \mu \neq £1.48$

	F	**G**	**H**	**I**
2	**H$_0$:**	Average equals		1.48
3	**H$_1$:**	Average is not equal		1.48

Step 2 State the significance level: 0.01, 0.05 or 0.1 (1%, 5% or 10%) – for this example use 0.05

	F	**G**
5	**Sig level**	0.05

Step 3 State the critical values

	F	**G**	**H**
7	**Critical values**	**Lower**	**Upper**
8		=NORMSINV($G$5/2)	=1–NORMSINV($G$5/2)

Step 4 Calculate the Z statistic using the formula:

$$Z = \frac{\bar{X} - \mu}{\dfrac{s}{\sqrt{n}}}$$

$$= \frac{sample\ mean - hypothesized\ mean}{standard\ error}$$

	F	**G**
10	**Z statistic**	=(D4–I2)/D6

Step 5 Compare the Z value to the critical values.
Step 6 Come to a conclusion. If the Z value falls between the critical values then ***accept*** the null hypothesis that μ = £1.48.

The decision on whether to accept or reject the null hypothesis can also be made by the computer using the logical operators **IF()**, and **OR()**.

The **IF** function returns one value if the logical_value evaluates to **TRUE** and another value if it evaluates to **FALSE** i.e.:

$$=IF(logical\_test, \textit{value\_if\_true}, \textit{value\_if\_false}) \text{ or}$$
$$=IF(True, \textit{Then return this, Else return this})$$

The **OR** function returns **TRUE** if one or more of the arguments is true and returns **FALSE** if all the arguments are false.

$$=OR(logical\ 1, logical\ 2)$$

These two functions can be combined to make the decision – thus:

	F	G
12	**Compare**	=IF(OR(G10<G8, G10>H8), 'REJECT','ACCEPT')

This can be translated as:
If the value in cell G10 is less than that of G8 OR greater than that of cell H8 then return REJECT else return ACCEPT.

Now try changing the value in cell **G5** to 0.1.

This construction can only be used for two-tailed tests although combinations of the logical operators can be used to develop both one-tailed tests and two-tailed tests. A response to this activity can be found on p. 467.

7.7 Student *t* distribution

For repeated *small* samples ($n < 32$) it is no longer accurate to assume that the distribution of sample means follows a *Normal* distribution. As a result we can no longer use the Z tables to work out the probabilities. Instead, we assume that the distribution of sample means follows the *Student t* distribution (called '*t*' distribution for simplicity). This distribution actually changes as the sample size changes. We must therefore apply different probabilities to samples taken with different sizes. The concept of *degrees of freedom* (v) captures this idea, where the number of degrees of freedom is expressed as $v = n - 1$, where n is sample size (see Figure 7.13).

We can illustrate this idea using $2\frac{1}{2}$ per cent (0.025) in the tail of the t distribution:

v (n – 1)	0.025
1	12.706
2	4.303
5	2.571
10	2.228
30	2.042

figure 7.13
Showing how the distribution of sample means ($\bar{X}_i$) expressed in terms of standard errors (*t*), takes different shapes depending on the number of degrees of freedom v (= *n* − 1)

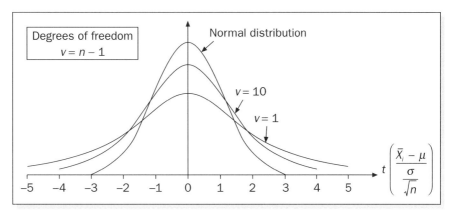

figure 7.14
Showing how the *t* score for $2\frac{1}{2}$% (0.025) in the right-hand tail will vary depending on the number of degrees of freedom v (= *n* − 1)

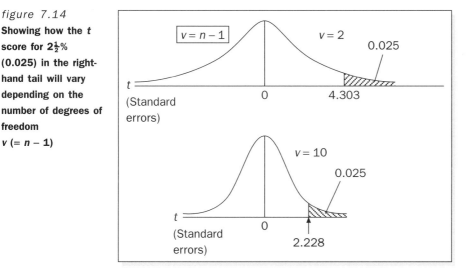

Notice that the *critical values* (i.e. number of *standard errors* from the mean) vary depending on the value of v (= *n* − 1). So with a sample size (*n*) of 3 and v (= *n* − 1) of 2, we must be 4.303 standard error from the mean to get $2\frac{1}{2}$ per cent (0.025) in either tail. However with a sample size (*n*) of 11 and v (= *n* − 1) of 10, we need only be 2.228 standard errors from the mean to get $2\frac{1}{2}$ per cent (0.025) in either tail.

Critical values

We express the **critical values** for the *t* distribution as

$$t_{\alpha,v}$$

where α = level of significance shown in the tables
$\quad\quad\quad v$ = number of degrees of freedom

So for $\alpha = 0.025$, and $v = 2$ in the table above, we can write.

$$t_{\alpha,v} = t_{0.025,2} = 4.303$$

and when $v = 10$

$$t_{\alpha,v} = t_{0.025,10} = 2.228$$

t statistic

We calculate the ***t* statistic** or ***t* score** exactly as we did for Z, i.e. we use the *sample* data to find the number of *standard errors* from the mean:

$$t = \frac{\bar{X}_i - \mu}{\sigma / \sqrt{n}}$$

$$\text{or} \quad t = \frac{\bar{X}_i - \mu}{s / \sqrt{n}}$$

As before we use the *population* standard deviation (σ) or the *sample* standard deviation (s) for calculating t, depending on the information we are given in the question.

t tables

The full ***t* tables** to be used in finding the appropriate critical values can be found in Appendix 6, p. 318.

It will be useful to go through our seven-step plan for a problem involving *small samples* and therefore the t distribution. Our steps are exactly as before, except in the way we calculate the critical values.

WORKED
EXAMPLE **7.11**
· · · · · · · · · · · · · · · ·

A company requires batteries for its transport vehicles that last on average 20,000 kilometres before replacement. A battery company claims that it can supply batteries that meet this requirement. The buying company decides to test that claim and buys 16 batteries and finds that they last an average of 19,500 kilometres with a standard deviation of 1,200 kilometres. Test the suppliers claim against the buyers concern that batteries last less than 20,000 kilometres, at a 5 per cent level of significance.

Solution

Note: This is arguably a *one-tail* test because the buyer is only worried if the batteries fall *below* the claim of 20,000 kilometres. The sample size is less than 32, so it is a t test example. We use s rather than σ in calculating standard errors.

Step 1 $H_0 : \mu = 20,000$ km

$\quad\quad\quad H_1 : \mu < 20,000$ km

Step 2 $\alpha = 0.05$

Step 3 $\quad v = n - 1$

$\quad\quad\quad\quad = 16 - 1$

$\quad\quad\quad\quad = 15$

$\quad\quad t_{0.05,15} = -1.753$

figure 7.15

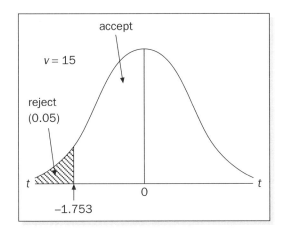

Step 4 $t = \dfrac{\bar{X}_i - \mu}{\sigma/\sqrt{n}}$ (here s for σ)

$$= \dfrac{19{,}500 - 20{,}000}{1{,}200/\sqrt{16}}$$

$$= \dfrac{-500}{300} = -1.667$$

Step 5 $-1.667 > -1.753$

Step 6 Accept H_0

$\mu = 20{,}000$ km

Step 7 There is insufficient evidence for us to conclude that the batteries perform less well than is claimed.

SELF-CHECK QUESTIONS

7.9 It is believed that the mean time that third year students spend in the library per week is 18 hours. Assume that the time spent in the library is normally distributed. A random sample of 25 students gives a mean time of 18.6 hours with a standard deviation of 1.02 hours. Test the view that the mean time spent in the library is greater than 18 hours at the 5 per cent significance level.

7.10 Suppose we want to test, on the basis of a random sample of eight cartons, whether the average fat content of a certain make of ice cream is less than 15 per cent. The sample mean for fat content is found to be 14.3 per cent with a sample standard deviation of 0.96 per cent. What conclusion would you come to at the 1 per cent significance level?

7.11 Workers on a production line produce an average of 154 faulty items per shift. A training package has been developed and tested on a random sample of 20 workers. The twenty workers in the sample produce an

average of 141 faulty items with a standard deviation of 12 items. The training package will be applied to all workers only if it can be shown that it improves worker performance. Based on the sample should the firm proceed with the programme? Test at the 1 per cent level of significance.

Note: Answers can be found on p. 351.

Chi-squared test

The **Chi-squared (χ^2)** test looks not at an *individual* item of data (i.e. a single parameter) but at the *whole* distribution. As a result it is known as a *non-parametric* test, unlike the Z and t tests which are known as parametric tests with their focus on a single parameter such as a sample mean which is then compared with an allegedly known value of a parameter from the population.

For non-parametric tests, such as the Chi-squared test, the null hypothesis (H_0) and alternative hypothesis (H_1) are defined in terms of the distribution as a whole. Usually we test:

H_0 : the distribution as a whole is evenly (equally) spread.
H_1 : the distribution as a whole is *not* evenly (equally) spread.

χ^2 statistic

The **χ^2 statistic** or score makes use of actually *observed values* (O) which are then contrasted with the *expected values* (E) we should anticipate if the null hypothesis (H_0) is in fact true. It is defined as:

$$\chi^2 = \sum_{i=1}^{n} \left[\frac{(O - E)^2}{E} \right]$$

where O = observed values
$\quad\quad E$ = expected values (if null hypothesis, H_0, is true)
$\quad\quad n$ = number of observations in the sample

The χ^2 distribution follows the pattern shown in Figure 7.16.

Note that, as with the t distribution, the χ^2 distribution actually changes as the sample size (n) changes. We therefore again make use of the idea of *degrees of freedom* (v) (see p. 170), with the number of degrees of freedom expressed as $v = n - 1$, where n corresponds to the number of observations in the sample.

Of course if the distribution as a whole *is* evenly spread throughout, as our null hypothesis H_0 suggests, then the *observed values* (O) would exactly equal the *expected values* (E). It follows that ($O - E$) in the numerator of the χ^2 statistic will equal zero for every one of the n observations in the sample, and summing the squares of zero will still give us zero for χ^2. In other words χ^2 = zero will correspond to a *perfectly evenly spread* distribution. The less evenly spread the distribution, the greater the discrepancy between any observation (O) and its expected value (E), when the latter is calculated on the assumption that the distribution *is* evenly spread (i.e. H_0 is true).

figure 7.16
χ^2 **varies with** v,
where v **is the**
number of degrees of
freedom

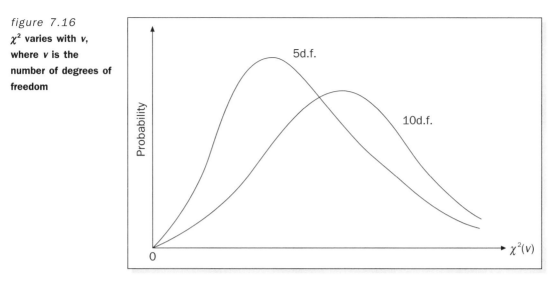

Critical values

The **critical values** are those values for χ^2 outside of which we are willing to *reject* the null hypothesis (H_0) that the distribution is evenly spread. In this case we reject H_0, where the observations (O) are sufficiently different from the expected values (E) we should anticipate if the distribution really is evenly spread.

▶ As we have already noted the χ^2 distribution will vary with the *number of degrees of freedom* (v), where $v = n - 1$. It follows that the critical values will therefore vary with v.
▶ The *level of significance* (α), as before, represents the maximum risk we are willing to take in rejecting the null hypothesis (H_0) when it is in fact true.

The critical values for the χ^2 distribution can therefore be expressed as:

$$\chi^2_{\alpha,v}$$

where α = level of significance
$\quad\quad v$ = number of degrees of freedom ($n - 1$)

All tests involving the χ^2 distribution are *one-tailed* tests.

Appendix 7 (p. 319) gives a full table of critical values for a given level of significance (α) and a given number of degrees of freedom (v). For example, as shown in Figure 7.17, for a 5 per cent level of significance ($\alpha = 0.05$) and 10 degrees of freedom ($v = 10$), we have a critical value of 18.3 for χ^2. In other words if, from our sample data, we calculate the χ^2 statistic as over 18.3, then we will reject the null hypothesis H_0 that the data is evenly spread. There will then be less than a 5 per cent chance of being wrong in deciding to reject the null hypothesis.

figure 7.17
finding the critical value of χ^2

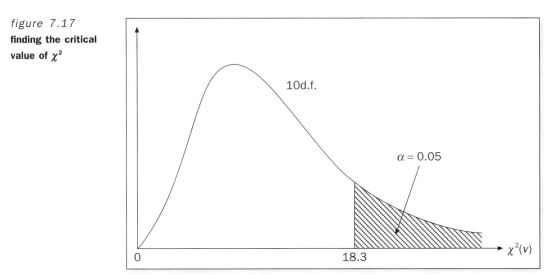

WORKED EXAMPLE **7.12**
....

Over a year a large company experiences 100 computer breakdowns. These are classified into the four time-period slots indicated below.

Time of computer breakdowns	Number of breakdowns
9.00 a.m.–11.00 a.m.	22
11.00 a.m.–1.00 p.m.	18
1.00 p.m.–3.00 p.m.	26
3.00 p.m.–5.00 p.m.	34

Test the hypothesis that computer breakdowns are spread evenly through the working day, using a 5 per cent (0.05) level of significance.

Solution

We can follow the same seven steps in testing a hypothesis as for the Z and t distributions.

Step 1 H_0: Breakdowns evenly spread

H_1: Breakdowns not evenly spread

Step 2 $\alpha = 0.05$

Step 3 $\quad v = n - 1$

$= 4 - 1$

$= 3$

$\chi^2_{0.05,3} = 7.81$

Step 4 Calculate the χ^2 statistic from the sample data

$$\chi^2 = \sum_{i=1}^{4} \frac{(O - E)^2}{E}$$

O	E	(O − E)	(O − E)^2	$\dfrac{(O - E)^2}{E}$
22	25	−3	9	0.36
18	25	−7	49	1.96
26	25	+1	1	0.04
34	25	+9	81	3.24
				5.60

Note: If H_0 is true, then we expect 25 breakdowns to occur in each of the four time-periods of two hours.

$$\chi^2 = 5.60$$

Step 5 5.60 < 7.81

Step 6 Accept H_0

Step 7 Cannot reject H_0 that computer breakdowns are evenly spread over time. In other words there is not enough evidence to conclude that the computer breakdowns that occur at different times are due to anything other than chance.

Data shown in table or matrix form

Often the data are shown, or can be represented, in table or matrix form. As we shall see from Worked example 7.13 we follow exactly the same procedures as above, with one difference which relates to calculating the *number of degrees of freedom (v)*:

$$v = (r - 1) \times (c - 1)$$

where v = number of degrees of freedom
r = number of rows in table
c = number of columns in table.

As we shall also see in Worked example 7.13, we can devise a useful formula for calculating the *expected values (E)* when data are presented in tabular form:

$$E = \text{row total} \times \frac{\text{column total}}{\text{grand total}}$$

where E = expected value

WORKED
EXAMPLE **7.13**
················

A survey of job satisfaction was undertaken for systems analysts and computer programmers employed by a large firm. A questionnaire asked 100 workers of each type whether or not they were satisfied with their job. The results are shown below:

Type of employee	Satisfied	Not satisfied	Totals
Systems analysts	63	37	100
Computer programmers	53	47	100
Totals	116	84	200

Is there a significant relationship between the type of employee and job satisfaction? Test at a 5 per cent level of significance.

Solution

This is a χ^2 test since we are testing the null hypothesis (H_0) of no association between type of employee and job satisfaction against the alternative hypothesis (H_1) that there is such an association. We are using *observations* from sample data (200 employees) to help test H_0.

If 'everything is in proportion' and there is no association, then H_0 is true. We should then *expect* that the *overall proportion* of satisfied employees should be reflected in the totals for each type of employee claiming to be satisfied. We return to this idea below when working out the 'expected' values (E).

Sometimes tabular data are given with row and column totals provided. If not, it will help if you insert such row and column totals. Note also that the sum of the respective row and column totals is referred to as the 'grand total', here the 200 employees involved in the survey.

We can follow our usual seven steps, but remembering to apply the procedures already mentioned for data in tabular form:

Step 1 H_0: no association between type of employees and job satisfaction
(i.e. responses are in proportion).
H_1: association between type of employee and job satisfaction
(i.e. responses are not in proportion).

Step 2 $\alpha = 0.05$

Step 3 $v = (r - 1) \times (c - 1)$
$v = (2 - 1) \times (2 - 1)$
$v = 1$

(*Note:* when using tabular data, do *not* count the row total or column total when calculating v)

$$\chi^2_{\alpha,v} = \chi^2_{0.05,1} = 3.84$$

Step 4 Calculate the χ^2 statistic from the sample data.

$$\chi^2 = \sum_{i=1}^{4} \frac{(O - E)^2}{E}$$

where O = observations
E = expected values if H_0
(no association) is true.

Here we can apply our formula to work out expected values.

$$E = \text{row total} \times \frac{\text{column total}}{\text{grand total}}$$

E (Systems analysts satisfied) $= 100 \times \dfrac{116}{200} = 58$

E (Systems analysts not satisfied) $= 100 \times \dfrac{84}{200} = 42$

E (Computer programmers satisfied) $= 100 \times \dfrac{116}{200} = 58$

E (Computer programmers not satisfied) $= 100 \times \dfrac{84}{200} = 42$

The formula simply helps us impose the *overall proportions* of satisfied/not satisfied on the totals for systems analysts and computer programmers respectively. The resulting values tell us what to expect if the null hypothesis H_0 (no association) is true.

We can express our table of expected values (E) as:

Expected values		
	Satisfied	Not satisfied
Systems analysts	58	42
Computer programmers	58	42

We can now calculate χ^2, as follows:

O	E	$(O - E)$	$(O - E)^2$	$\dfrac{(O - E)^2}{E}$
63	58	+5	25	25/58 = 0.431
37	42	−5	25	25/42 = 0.596
53	58	−5	25	25/58 = 0.431
47	42	+5	25	25/42 = 0.596
				2.054

$\underline{\chi^2 = 2.054}$

Step 5 2.054 < 3.84

Step 6 Accept H_0

Step 7 No association between type of employee and job satisfaction. There is not enough evidence to conclude that these different types of employees have different views as to job satisfaction.

Note: Review question 7.15 is a χ^2 question.

REVIEW QUESTIONS

7.1 The manageress of a restaurant claims that her weekly turnover is £3,130 with a standard deviation of £115 per week. If the turnover is normally distributed and a random sample of 25 weekly turnover figures is recorded, what is the probability that the sample mean will be:

(a) less than £3,100?   (b) greater than £3,190?   (c) between £3,110 and £3,180?

7.2 The mean salary of business studies graduates, one year after graduating, is £12,500 with a standard deviation of £1,300. What is the probability that a random sample of 49 of these had a mean salary of at least £13,000?

7.3 A sample of 49 observations is taken from a normal population. The sample mean is 58, and the standard deviation of the sample is 10. Determine the 95 per cent and the 99 per cent confidence intervals for the population mean.

7.4 A wine shop owner wishes to estimate the mean number of bottles sold to account-holders per month. A sample of 60 accounts gives a mean of 8.6 bottles per month with a standard deviation of 2.3. Develop a 99 per cent confidence interval for the population mean.

7.5 The Durable Construction Company produces frames for solar panels. The frames need to withstand certain pressures. A sample of 45 frames is taken from the production line and tested for the weight they can support before they distort. The test results from the sample of 45 frames suggest an average weight of 39.8 kilos before distortion with a standard deviation of 6 kilos.

(a) Construct a 99 per cent confidence interval for the population mean.
(b) Construct a 90 per cent confidence interval for the population mean.
(c) How large should the sample be if we want a 99 per cent confidence interval for the population mean with a margin of error of 2 kilos?

7.6 Transport economist, Sisson, wishes to estimate how often residents of Cambridge use the city bus system per month.

(a) How many residents must be surveyed if he wants to develop a 95 per cent confidence interval with a margin of error of three trips per month? A previous pilot study gave the standard deviation as 14 trips.
(b) If Sisson randomly selects 160 residents and obtains a mean of 22.4 trips with a standard deviation of 15, construct a 95 per cent confidence interval for the population mean.

7.7 The owner of a restaurant believes that the average amount spent on a meal per couple is £50.00. She takes a random sample of 40 couples and finds that the mean expenditure is £53.70 with a standard deviation of £7.80. Test the owner's claim at the 5 per cent level of significance.

7.8 A car manufacturer states that its new model does 32.5 mpg. A recent independent study of 50 of the new cars selected randomly showed a mean mpg of only 30.4 with a standard deviation of 5.3 mpg. Test the view that the manufacturer's claim is too high using a 1 per cent level of significance.

7.9 The expected life of a car engine is 90,000 miles. A random sample of 190 cars gives a mean life of 96,700 miles with a standard deviation of 37,500 miles. Test whether the cars are lasting longer than expected at the 1 per cent level of significance.

7.10 An estate agent advertises that it can sell houses in 40 days or less. A random sample of 64 recently sold homes shows a sample mean selling time of 45 days with a standard deviation of 20 days. Using the 5 per cent level of significance, test the validity of the agent's claim against a rival's claim that this is untrue.

7.11 A poll of 121 randomly selected students reveals that the mean number of CDs they buy a year is 7.01 with a standard deviation of 3.74. Test the claim that the mean for all students is less than 7.5 CDs at the 1 per cent level of significance.

7.12 A machine is set to cut metal rods to a length of 8.75 cms. It is felt by the operator that the rods are too short. The hypothesis is to be tested at the 1 per cent significance level from the following sample of rods: 9.0, 8.5, 8.7, 8.4, 8.6, 8.3, 8.5 and 8.8. What conclusion can be drawn on the basis of the sample?

7.13 A mail order firm claims that new procedures enable it to dispatch orders more quickly than previously. Records show that the previous average delay was 20 days. A random sample of 17 orders using the new procedure showed a delay time of 18 days with a sample standard deviation of 2.5 days. Is the claim made for the new procedures supported at the 5 per cent level?

7.14 A recruitment agency claims that four bedroom detached houses near the Cambridge Science Park can be rented for £900 per month on average. A random sample of 20 houses gave a mean rental of £1,050 per month for this type of property with a sample standard deviation of £290 per month Test the agency's claim against the claim that rentals are higher at the 10 per cent significance level.

7.15 Using the following observations recorded by a researcher, check if the assumption of no relation between lung cancer and smoking can be accepted at the 5 per cent level of significance.

Observation table

	Smokers	Non-smokers	Totals
Cancer sufferers	200	200	400
Non sufferers	150	450	600
Totals	350	650	1,000

Answers to Review questions can be found on p. 425.

Further study and data
....

Texts

Bancroft, G. and O'Sullivan, G. (1993), *Quantitative methods for accounting and business studies*, 3rd edn, McGraw Hill, chapters 15–18.

Curwin, J. and Slater, R. (1996), *Quantitative methods for business decisions*, 4th edn, Chapman and Hall, chapters 13–16.

Lawson, M., Hubbard, S. and Pugh, P. (1995), *Maths and statistics for business*, Addison Wesley Longman, chapters 7–9.

Morris, C. (1996), *Quantitative approaches in business studies*, 4th edn, Pitman, chapters 10–12.

Oakshott, L. (1996), *Essential elements of business statistics*, BPP, chapter 7.

Swift, L. (1997), *Mathematics and statistics for business, management and finance*, Macmillan, parts C6 and C7.

Thomas, R. (1997), *Quantitative methods for business studies*, Prentice Hall, chapter 2.

Waters, D. (1997), *Quantitative methods*, 2nd edn, Addison Wesley Longman, chapters 15–16.

Wisniewski, M. with Stead, R. (1996), *Foundation quantitative methods for business*, Pitman, chapter 9.

Sources of information and data

See the list at the end of Chapter 1, p. 25.

CHAPTER 8

Index numbers

Objectives

· · · · · · · · · · · ·

By the end of this chapter you should be able to:

▶ appreciate the use of index numbers in a range of practical situations;

▶ construct an index number for changes in the value of a variable;

▶ understand the idea of *weighting* in the calculation of index numbers;

▶ calculate index numbers using *base period weightings*, i.e. the Laspeyres index;

▶ calculate index numbers using *current period weightings*, i.e. the Paasche index;

▶ calculate index numbers for *price movements*, with quantities as weights;

▶ calculate index numbers for *quantity movements*, with prices as weights;

▶ change the base of an index number;

▶ know when and how price and quantity *relative* index numbers might be used;

▶ understand the construction and importance of the Retail Price Index (RPI).

Introduction

· · · · · · · · · · · · · ·

An **index number** is a useful way of measuring the change in the value of a variable over time, as compared with its value at some fixed point in time. We call that fixed point in time the *base value* of the variable and give it an index of 100.

If we express data for *different* variables in terms of index numbers, then this will often make it much easier to compare their respective rates of change. Look for example at Table 8.1.

The table presents two alternative index numbers for measuring changes in retail prices; one which includes mortgage interest payments and one which excludes such payments. We can immediately see that over the period 1990–1996 retail prices have risen much more slowly from the base year of 1990 when we *include* mortgage payments (100–120.8) than when we *exclude* mortgage payments (100–124.5). This is because mortgage interest payments were very high in 1990 and have fallen since then, acting as a counterweight to other items of retail expenditure which have risen since 1990.

We return to a more detailed analysis of the Retail Price Index (RPI) later in the chapter. However before leaving Table 8.1 we can usefully note how to calculate the *percentage change* from one index number to another:

$$\% \text{ change} = \frac{\text{new index} - \text{old index}}{\text{old index}} \times 100$$

Take, for example, the annual percentage change for the Retail Price Index including mortgage payments from 1995 to 1996.

$$\% \text{ change} = \frac{120.8 - 118.2}{118.2} \times 100 = 2.2\%$$

table 8.1

**Using index numbers
to compare different
variables, here
different measures of
the RPI.**

Year	Retail Price Index including mortgage interest	Annual % change	Retail Price Index excluding mortgage interest	Annual % change
1990	100.0		100.0	
1991	105.9	5.9	106.7	6.7
1992	109.8	3.7	111.7	4.7
1993	111.5	1.6	115.1	3.0
1994	114.3	2.5	117.8	2.3
1995	118.2	3.4	121.1	2.9
1996	120.8	2.2	124.5	2.8

Of course index numbers can be used to measure changes in a wide variety of variables other than price, such as revenue, cost, profit, output, employment, etc.

Answers to the 'Self-check questions', responses to each 'Pause for thought' and answers to the 'Review questions' can be found at the end of the book.

8.1 Constructing an index number

Index numbers can, as we have noted, be used to measure changes in both *prices* and *quantities*. Although we shall return to quantities later, it will simplify matters to illustrate the construction of an index number in terms of prices only.

Simple price index

Table 8.2 shows the price (pence per 10 grams) of three different types of drink in each of three separate years.

To construct a **simple price index** we calculate the ratio of the new price to the base year price for each type of drink, and then multiply by 100. The ratio of new price to base year price is called the **price relative**.

$$\text{Simple price index} = \frac{P_n}{P_0} \times 100$$

where P_n = new price (year n)
P_0 = base year price (year 0)

table 8.2

Drink	Price (pence per 10 grams)		
	Year 0	Year 1	Year 2
Tea	6	8	10
Coffee	12	14	15
Chocolate	18	18	20

table 8.3
**Calculating the
simple price index**

Year	Tea			Coffee			Chocolate		
	Price	P_n/P_0	Simple price index	Price	P_n/P_0	Simple price index	Price	P_n/P_0	Simple price index
0	6	1.00	100	12	1.00	100	18	1.00	100
1	8	1.33	133	14	1.16	116	18	1.00	100
2	10	1.66	166	15	1.25	125	20	1.11	111

Table 8.3 constructs the **simple price index** for each type of drink from the data in Table 8.2.

As we can see, taking year 0 as the base year, the price of tea has risen by 66 per cent over the whole time period, the price of coffee by 25 per cent and the price of chocolate by 11 per cent.

PAUSE FOR THOUGHT 8.1 *Can you identify three products (goods or services) whose price is now cheaper in real terms than 20 years ago and three products whose price is now dearer?*

Simple aggregate price index

If we want to derive an index for the overall change in price of all three types of drink, then we need a **simple aggregate price index**.

To include all three types of drink we could sum their respective prices in each of the three years. We could then construct an index from these sums. Remembering the use of the sigma notation from Chapter 2, we could represent the sum of the respective prices of tea, coffee and chocolate in the base year as ΣP_0 and in year n as ΣP_n.

$$\text{Simple aggregate price index} = \frac{\Sigma P_n}{\Sigma P_0} \times 100$$

where P_n = new prices (year n)
P_0 = base year prices (year 0)

The calculations are shown in Table 8.4.

This price index tells us that, taking year 0 as the base year, the combined or aggregate prices of the three drinks has risen by 25 per cent.

table 8.4
**Calculating the
simple aggregate
price index**

Price in given year (pence per 10 grams)	Tea	Coffee	Chocolate	$\Sigma P_n/\Sigma P_0$	Simple aggregate price index
P_0	6	12	18	36/36 = 1.00	100
P_1	8	14	18	40/36 = 1.11	111
P_2	10	15	20	45/36 = 1.25	125

Of course this simple aggregate price index has ignored the relative *quantities* consumed of tea, coffee and chocolate in each of the three years. If an individual consumed more tea per week than, say, coffee or chocolate, then the fact that tea experienced the greatest percentage increase in price over the period (see Table 8.3 above) should be taken into account by calculating a *weighted* aggregate price index.

8.2 Weighted aggregate index numbers

Suppose we have information on both the prices and quantities consumed of tea, coffee and chocolate by an individual in a typical week for each of the three years. Table 8.5 presents the data available.

We can see from Table 8.5 that this individual consumes greater quantities of tea than either of the other two drinks. To get a true picture of the change in the combined or aggregate *price* of these three drinks over the period we should take these respective *quantities* into account. We would then be treating these quantities as the weights for our (weighted) **aggregate price index**.

DID YOU KNOW?

In 1947, more than one-third of a household's weekly budget was spent on food, but this has now fallen to only 14 per cent. Some items have disappeared altogether over time; for example in the 1950s table mangles, gramophone records and home perm kits appeared in the weights for the Retail Price Index (p. 194). On the other hand, new items such as satellite dishes and Internet subscriptions have entered the weights of the RPI in the 1990s.

Note however that the quantities used as weights *change* over the time period. We must therefore make a decision as to whether to use the *base year* quantities as weights or the *current year* quantities as weights. This clearly matters since tea is 50 per cent ($10/20 \times 100$) of the total quantity of all three drinks consumed in the base year (year 0) but only 46.6 per cent ($14/30 \times 100$) of the total quantity of all three drinks consumed in the current year (year 2).

We must therefore decide at the outset whether to use *base year* quantities (or prices) as weights, as in the **Laspeyres index**, or *current year* quantities (or prices) as weights, as in the **Paasche index**.

table 8.5

Prices (pence per 10 grams) and quantities (multiples of 10 grams) of drinks purchased by an individual in a typical week

Drinks	Year 0		Year 1		Year 2	
	Price	Quantity	Price	Quantity	Price	Quantity
Tea	6	10	8	12	10	14
Coffee	12	6	14	6	15	8
Chocolate	18	4	18	7	20	8

8.3 The Laspeyres (base weighted) price index

To derive a representative *price* index we need to control the quantities purchased. Otherwise the observed change in *value* (price × quantity) could reflect in part a change in price and in part a change in quantity. We therefore consider a *typical basket* of items purchased by the consumer in which the quantity of items of each kind is fixed. In the **Laspeyres price index** we regard the *base year* quantities as fixed.

> Laspeyres price index $= \dfrac{\sum P_n Q_0}{\sum P_0 Q_0} \times 100$
>
> where $\sum P_n Q_0$ = value of base year basket of items in year n
> $\sum P_0 Q_0$ = value of base year basket of items in base year (year 0)

WORKED EXAMPLE **8.1**
••••••••••••••••

We now calculate the Laspeyres price index for the data presented in Table 8.5.

Solution

table 8.6
Calculating the Laspeyres (base-weighted) price index

Drinks	Year 0						Year 1			Year 2		
	P_0	Q_0		$P_0 Q_0$	P_1	Q_0		$P_1 Q_0$	P_2	Q_0		$P_2 Q_0$
Tea	6	10		60	8	10		80	10	10		100
Coffee	12	6		72	14	6		84	15	6		90
Chocolate	18	4		72	18	4		72	20	4		80
			$\sum P_0 Q_0 = 204$				$\sum P_1 Q_0 = 236$				$\sum P_2 Q_0 = 270$	

Year	$\dfrac{\sum P_n Q_0}{\sum P_0 Q_0}$	Laspeyres price index
0	$\dfrac{204}{204} = 1.00$	100
1	$\dfrac{236}{204} = 1.16$	116
2	$\dfrac{270}{204} = 1.32$	132

As we can see from Table 8.6, using *base year* quantities as representing our typical basket of items, the combined price of the three drinks has risen by 32 per cent over the period.

Typically the Laspeyres price index tends to *overstate* the true increase in the cost of living. This is because using the *base year* quantities as weights rules out any possibility of substitution by consumers. We might expect, in practice, consumers to buy rather less of any item that has experienced relatively rapid increases in prices. Had *current year* quantities been used instead, then the weighting given to items experiencing relatively rapid price increases is likely to have diminished.

8.4 The Paasche (current-weighted) price index
•••

The **Paasche price index** uses the *current year* quantities as representing our typical basket of items. It compares what a basket of items costs now (in the current year) as compared to what the same basket of items would have cost in the base year.

Paasche price index = $\dfrac{\sum P_n Q_n}{\sum P_0 Q_n} \times 100$

where $\sum P_n Q_n$ = value of the basket of items bought in year n at year n prices
$\sum P_0 Q_n$ = value of the basket of items bought in year n at year 0 prices

---

WORKED
EXAMPLE **8.2**
················

We now calculate the Paasche price index for the data presented in Table 8.5 (p. 186).

Solution

table 8.7
Calculating the Paasche (current-weighted) price index

Drinks	Year 0			Year 1				Year 2			
	P_0	Q_0	P_0Q_0	P_1	Q_1	P_1Q_1	P_0Q_1	P_2	Q_2	P_2Q_2	P_0Q_2
Tea	6	10	60	8	12	96	72	10	14	140	84
Coffee	12	6	72	14	6	84	72	15	8	120	96
Chocolate	18	4	72	18	7	126	126	20	8	160	144
			$\sum P_0Q_0$ = 204			$\sum P_1Q_1$ = 306	$\sum P_0Q_1$ = 270			$\sum P_2Q_2$ = 420	$\sum P_0Q_2$ = 324

Year	$\dfrac{\sum P_n Q_n}{\sum P_0 Q_n}$	Paasche price index
0	$\dfrac{204}{204} = 1.00$	100
1	$\dfrac{306}{270} = 1.13$	113
2	$\dfrac{420}{324} = 1.30$	130

As we can see from Table 8.7, using current year quantities as representing our typical basket of items, the combined price of the three drinks has risen by 30 per cent over the period. This is *below* the 32 per cent recorded for the Laspeyres price index.

Note that, strictly speaking, the Paasche price index involves changes in *both* prices and quantities, since the quantities are also allowed to change year-by-year. Therefore it cannot be regarded as a 'pure' price index. Further, the Paasche price index tends to *understate* the true increase in the cost of living because we have used the *current year* quantities as weights.

For example, suppose consumers may well have purchased greater current quantities of an item because it is now cheaper than in the base year, i.e. the 'substitution principle'. However when we multiply those greater current quantities by the (artificially high) base year prices then prevailing, the denominator is inflated and the Paasche price index thereby understated.

Note also that actually constructing a Paasche price index will require more accurate (and therefore more costly) information than the Laspeyres price index, since we must continually obtain data for *current* quantities of each item.

PAUSE FOR THOUGHT 8.2   *Whichever price index is used, what problems might you encounter when interpreting changes in the index over a considerable period of time?*

8.5 The Laspeyres (base-weighted) quantity index

The idea of a Laspeyres or base-weighted index (see Section 8.3 above) is used here to measure changes in *quantity* or *volume,* rather than changes in prices. This time the weights are the *base-year prices* rather than the base-year quantities as before.

$$\text{Laspeyres quantity index} = \frac{\sum P_0 Q_n}{\sum P_0 Q_0} \times 100$$

where $\sum P_0 Q_n$ = value of year n basket of items at prices in base year (year 0)
$\sum P_0 Q_0$ = value of base year basket of items at prices in base year (year 0)

WORKED
EXAMPLE **8.3**

We now calculate the **Laspeyres quantity index** for the data presented in Table 8.5 (p. 186).

Solution

table 8.8
Calculating the Laspeyres (base-weighted) quantity index

Drinks	Year 0			Year 1			Year 2		
	P_0	Q_0	$P_0 Q_0$	P_0	Q_1	$P_0 Q_1$	P_0	Q_2	$P_0 Q_2$
Tea	6	10	60	6	12	72	6	14	84
Coffee	12	6	72	12	6	72	12	8	96
Chocolate	18	4	72	18	7	126	18	8	144
			$\sum P_0 Q_0 = 204$			$\sum P_0 Q_1 = 270$			$\sum P_0 Q_2 = 324$

Year	$\dfrac{\sum P_0 Q_n}{\sum P_0 Q_0}$	Laspeyres quantity index
0	$\dfrac{204}{204} = 1.00$	100
1	$\dfrac{270}{204} = 1.32$	132
2	$\dfrac{324}{204} = 1.59$	159

As we can see from Table 8.8, using base year prices as weights, there has been a 59 per cent rise in quantity (volume) consumed of the three drinks over the period.

8.6 The Paasche (current-weighted) quantity index

The idea of a Paasche or current-weighted index (see Section 8.4 above) is used here to measure changes in *quantity* or *volume,* rather than changes in prices. This time the weights are the *current year prices* rather than the current year quantities as before.

Paasche quantity index $= \dfrac{\sum P_n Q_n}{\sum P_n Q_0} \times 100$

where $\sum P_n Q_n$ = value of year n basket of items at prices in year n

$\sum P_n Q_0$ = value of base year basket of items at prices in year n.

WORKED EXAMPLE 8.4

We now calculate the **Paasche quantity index** for the data presented in Table 8.5 (p. 186).

Solution

table 8.9
Calculating the Paasche (current-weighted) quantity index.

Drinks	P_0	Q_0	P_0Q_0	P_1	Q_1	P_1Q_1	P_1Q_0	P_2	Q_2	P_2Q_2	P_2Q_0
					Year 1				Year 2		
Tea	6	10	60	8	12	96	80	10	14	140	100
Coffee	12	6	72	14	6	84	84	15	8	120	90
Chocolate	18	4	72	18	7	126	72	20	8	160	80
			$\sum P_0Q_0$ = 204			$\sum P_1Q_1$ = 306	$\sum P_1Q_0$ = 236			$\sum P_2Q_2$ = 420	$\sum P_2Q_0$ = 270

Year	$\dfrac{\sum P_nQ_n}{\sum P_nQ_0}$	Paasche quantity index
0	$\dfrac{204}{204} = 1.00$	100
1	$\dfrac{306}{236} = 1.30$	130
2	$\dfrac{420}{270} = 1.56$	156

As we can see from Table 8.9, using current-year prices as weights, there has been a 56 per cent rise in quantity (volume) of the three drinks over the period.

Again, note that the Paasche quantity index involves changes in *both* quantities and prices, therefore is a less 'pure' quantity index than the Laspeyres version.

SELF-CHECK QUESTION

8.1 A company making components for the motor industry uses three main materials – plastic, steel tubing and cloth. The table below shows the price (in £) and the quantity used in each of the years 1995 and 1997.

	Plastic		Steel tubing		Cloth	
	Price(£)	Quantity	Price(£)	Quantity	Price(£)	Quantity
1995	1.20	4,000	5.30	1,000	2.30	2,000
1997	2.50	2,000	5.80	800	2.70	4,000

(a) Calculate Laspeyres and Paasche *price* index numbers for 1997 with 1995 as base.

(b) Calculate Laspeyres and Paasche *quantity* index numbers for 1997 with 1995 as base.

(c) Comment on your results.

Note: Answers can be found on p. 352.

8.7 Changing the base year

Sometimes the **base year** of an index may be changed to a later date. This may reflect the fact that, say, the pattern of expenditure (and therefore the quantity weights in a price index) or the prices (and therefore the price weights in a quantity index) may have changed substantially over time, so that the original base year becomes less and less representative of the true situation. This is especially problematic when calculating a Laspeyres (base-weighted) price or quantity index which places special emphasis on the base year situation.

To change the base year (i.e. move the 100) we simply use a *scaling factor* to move the existing index up or down. Look, for example, at the price index numbers we previously calculated from the data in Table 8.5 (p. 186). These are shown in Table 8.10 below.

Suppose we now wish to make *year 1* the base year for the Laspeyres price index! We simply multiply the existing index number by the scaling factor $\frac{100}{116}$, giving the solution shown in Table 8.11. This table also shows the Paasche price index with the new base year as Year 1, this time multiplying the existing index numbers by the scaling factor $\frac{100}{113}$.

In general terms, we can use the following expression to convert an existing series of index numbers to a new series with a new base year:

table 8.10
Laspeyres and Paasche price index numbers

Year	Laspeyres (base-weighted)	Paasche (current-weighted)
0	100	100
1	116	113
2	132	130

table 8.11
Changing the base of the index numbers in Table 8.10 from Year 0 to Year 1

Year	Laspeyres (base-weighted)	Paasche (current-weighted)
0	86	88
1	100	100
2	114	115

> New index = old index × scaling factor
>
> New index = old index × $\dfrac{\text{value in period } T_1}{\text{value in period } T_2}$
>
> where T_1 = value of old index in original base year (100)
> $\qquad T_2$ = value of old index in new base year

SELF-CHECK QUESTIONS

8.2 Look back to the Laspeyres *quantity* index of Table 8.8 (p. 189). Recalculate the index with Year 1 as base.

8.3 Look back to the Paasche *quantity* index of Table 8.9 (p. 190). Recalculate the index with Year 1 as base.

Note: **Answers can be found on p. 354.**

8.8 Price and quantity relative index numbers

So far we have assumed that there is an easily identified unit of quantity for our Laspeyres and Paasche index numbers. In our example of three types of drink, the common unit of quantity involved 10 gram weights of the respective drinks. Although many categories of product do indeed have an easily identified unit of quantity in terms of weight, area, volume, etc. others do not. For example, it is difficult to find a unit of quantity which adequately represents different types of house; area of floor space might be used, but houses with similar floor spaces might have many other features which are quite different, such as number of rooms, floor space at ground or higher levels, etc.

This problem of lacking an easily identified unit of measurement for quantities is compounded when we seek to devise aggregate index numbers which cover a *wide variety* of different product categories. This is certainly the case for the Retail Price Index which seeks to cover the 14 *broad product categories* shown in Table 8.13 (p. 195), each of which in turn contains many individual products.

When we face the problem of aggregating units which have no easily identified and common unit of measurement, the usual practice is to calculate a 'weight' for each item which corresponds to the proportion of some total value which corresponds to that item, for example, the proportion of total consumer expenditure on that item in the base year (when calculating a price index) or the proportion of the total value of output contributed by that item in the base year (when calculating a quantity index).

The procedure for deriving such a **weighted index number** when units are diverse, is to use price or quantity 'relatives':

> Price relative = $R = \dfrac{P_n}{P_0}$
>
> Quantity relative = $R = \dfrac{Q_n}{Q_0}$
>
> where n = current year price or quantity
> $\qquad 0$ = base year price or quantity

The formula for deriving a weighted index number for prices or quantities when units are diverse, is as follows:

Weighted index number $= \dfrac{\Sigma WR}{\Sigma W}$

where R = price or quantity relative for each item

W = weight for each item (corresponding to the proportion of the total value of expenditure or output related to that item)

WORKED
EXAMPLE **8.5**
················

Table 8.12 shows the weights and price relatives for 11 very different food items purchased over time in a particular market. The *weights* correspond to the share of total expenditure on the 11 items attributed to each item. The *price relatives* show the present price in relation to the base year price (January 1980 = 100).

table 8.12

Finding a weighted index for different food items

Food item	Weight	Price relative (Jan. 1980 = 100)
Bread	203	313.0
Sugar	78	371.8
Salt	39	443.5
Meat	137	376.7
Butter	69	466.0
Fish	64	251.6
Cooking oil	74	215.8
Fruit	159	373.1
Margarine	75	348.6
Soup	63	344.7
Pepper	39	368.9

Calculate a weighted price index for these foodstuffs, with January 1980 as base.

Solution

W	R	WR
203	313.0	63,539.0
78	371.8	29,000.4
39	443.5	17,296.5
137	376.7	51,607.9
69	466.0	32,154.0
64	251.6	16,102.4
74	215.8	15,969.2
159	373.1	59,322.9
75	348.6	26,145.0
63	344.7	21,716.1
39	368.9	14,387.1
1,000		347,240.5

where W = weight

R = price relative

$$\text{Weighted index of food prices} = \frac{\Sigma WR}{\Sigma W} = \frac{347{,}240.5}{1{,}000} = 347.2$$

In other words, the average price of this group of 11 food items has risen by 247.2 per cent since January 1980; put another way, the average price has risen by almost 3.5 times the average price prevailing in January 1980.

We now consider in some detail the use of this weighted index approach involving price relatives in the calculation of the Retail Price Index.

SELF-CHECK QUESTIONS

8.4 The output of a major multinational in terms of various products is shown below. The weights correspond to the proportion of the total value of output derived from each product. The *quantity relatives* show the value of current output of each product compared to the value in 1990.

Product category	Weight	Quantity relative (1990 = 100)
Energy	264	101
Metals	25	82
Mineral products	41	88
Chemicals	68	95
Engineering	325	84
Foodstuffs	99	92
Textiles	52	82
Other	126	83
	1,000	

Calculate a weighted quantity index for these products, with 1990 as base.

***Note:* Answers can be found on p. 354.**

8.9 The Retail Price Index (RPI)

The RPI, which was formerly compiled by the Department of Employment, is now the responsibility of the Office for National Statistics. It measures the change from month to month in the cost of a representative 'basket' of goods and services of the type bought by a typical household.

A number of stages are involved in the calculation of the RPI. The first stage is to select the items to be included in the index (currently around 600) and to weight these items according to their relative importance in the average family budget. Obviously items on which a family spends a large proportion of its income are given heavier weights than those items on which

DID YOU KNOW?

Since the RPI was set up in 1947, prices have risen by over 20 times but wages have risen by almost 60 times reflecting the major increase in living standards over the past 50 years or so.

table 8.13

General index of retail prices: group weights

	1987	1997
Food	167	136
Catering	46	49
Alcoholic drink	76	80
Tobacco	38	34
Housing	157	186
Fuel and light	61	41
Household goods	73	72
Household services	44	52
Clothing and footwear	74	56
Personal goods and services	38	40
Motoring expenditure	127	128
Fares and other travel costs	22	20
Leisure goods	47	47
Leisure services	30	59
	1,000	1,000

the family spends relatively little. For example, in 1997 the weight given to tea in the index was 2, whereas that for electricity was 23 (out of a total 'all items weight' of 1,000). The weights used are changed annually to reflect the changes in the composition of family expenditure. The new weights are derived from the Family Expenditure Survey in which about 7,000 households, carefully chosen to represent all regions and types of household, take part each year. Each member of the household aged over 16 years records his or her day-to-day expenditure on items over a two-week period, together with any longer-term payments, such as telephone bills, season tickets, etc. It is from these records that the weights for the RPI are based. The new weights, which begin in January each year, are largely based on the pattern of expenditure shown in the survey over the year to the previous June. For some items, however, such as selected consumer durables (e.g. furniture and carpets), where sales fluctuate widely from year to year, expenditure is averaged over a three-year period.

The weights for this 'general RPI' are obtained by excluding those pensioner households who derive 75 per cent or more of their income from state benefits and any households who are in the top 4 per cent of income earners (these categories together accounting for 16 per cent of all households). These two groups are excluded because the pattern of their expenditure differs markedly from that of the great majority of households.

The weights used for groups of items are shown in Table 8.13. It can be seen that food has been replaced as the largest item by housing (rent, mortgage interest rates and council tax, water charges, repairs and dwelling insurance). This is part of a longer-run trend associated with differing income elasticities of demand for the items in the 'basket'.

The second stage of deriving the RPI involves collecting the price data. For most items, prices are collected on a specific day each month, usually the Tuesday nearest the middle of the month. Prices are obtained from a sample of retail outlets in some 180 different areas. Care is taken to make sure a representative range of retail outlets, small retailers, supermarkets, department stores, etc. are surveyed. In all around 150,000 price quotations are collected each month. An average price is then calculated for each item in the index. For example on 15 July 1997, 611 price quotations were taken for tomatoes; the prices ranged from 45p to 79p per pound, with an average of 58p.

The final stage is to calculate the RPI from all these data. All index numbers must relate to some base period or reference data. In the case of the RPI the base period is January 1987 = 100. The index is calculated each month through a weighted price relative method. Since the weights are revised each year to keep the index up to date, the index is calculated afresh each year by means of a chain base method. In July 1997 the RPI stood at 157.5, which means the average prices have risen by 57.5 per cent between January 1987 and July 1997. As the index is an average, this figure conceals the fact that some prices have increased more rapidly (rent 117 per cent, water 158 per cent and beer 86 per cent), whilst other prices have fallen (audio-visual equipment by around 35 per cent).

A separate index is calculated for one-pensioner and two-pensioner households. These have weights which differ from the general RPI because of the different pattern of expenditure of these households. For example, pensioners spend a higher proportion of their income on housing, fuel and food, and a smaller proportion on clothing, alcoholic drink, durable goods and transport. Despite this, 'pensioner' price indices have moved fairly closely in line with the general RPI for several years.

Once the RPI has been constructed, the rate of inflation can then be calculated, with the most usual measure being the 12-monthly change in the RPI. For example, the RPI stood at 152.4 in July 1996. In July 1997 it stood at 157.5 and therefore the annual rate of inflation over that period was:

$$\frac{157.5 - 152.4}{152.4} \times 100\% = 3.3\%$$

Inflation as measured by the RPI is shown in Figure 8.1.

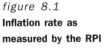

figure 8.1

Inflation rate as measured by the RPI

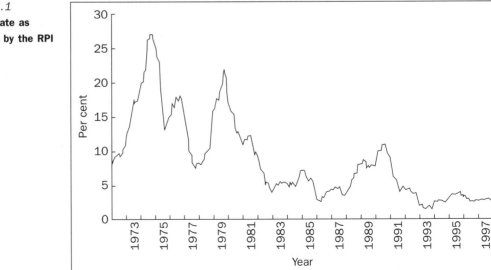

8.1 Compute a simple price index for the following years using 1992 as the base year.

Year	1992	1993	1994	1995	1996	1997
Price(£)	66.90	69.20	71.30	72.70	78.40	81.60

8.2 Rebase your answer to the above problem, making 1995 the base year.

8.3 Suppose the Government wishes to compare the cost of family food buying over the years. A basket of five items is used: bacon, eggs, coffee, beer and cheese. Use the data in the following table to construct an unweighted aggregate price index for the years 1995, 1996 and 1997 using 1995 as the base year:

	Year		
Item	*1995*	*1996*	*1997*
Bacon (kilo)	304	327	452
Eggs (doz)	135	146	154
Coffee (227 g)	205	197	221
Beer (pint)	147	155	164
Cheese (kilo)	458	455	532

Source: Labour Market Trends (August each year).

8.4 In order to improve its information as to the impact of food price increases on families the government has estimated the relative importance of the various items in the family budget. The weights are given below:

	Year (weights)		
Item	*1995*	*1996*	*1997*
Bacon (kilo)	15	18	12
Eggs (doz)	30	24	35
Coffee (227 g)	12	18	10
Beer (pint)	24	20	22
Cheese (kilo)	19	20	21

Using 1995 as the base year, construct
(a) a Laspeyres *price* index for the data
(b) a Paasche *price* index for the data.

8.5 A firm produces three items of pine furniture: tables, chairs and beds. Output and prices are given below:

	1995		*1996*		*1997*	
Product	Q_0	P_0	Q_1	P_1	Q_2	P_2
Tables	200	50	300	60	300	80
Chairs	100	80	200	100	300	120
Beds	300	100	400	120	500	150

Construct (a) a Laspeyres and (b) a Paasche *quantity* index for the firm, using 1995 as the base year.

8.6 The following data are taken from Labour Market Trends:

General index of retail prices 1987 = 100

1990	1993	1994	1995	1996	1997
126.1	140.7	144.1	149.1	152.7	157.5

Average earnings in UK (all workers) 1990 = 100

1990	1993	1994	1995	1996	1997
100.0	116.1	120.3	124.8	128.9	137.0

Rebase the the Retail Price Index to enable comments to be made about the development of real earnings since 1990.

8.7 Given the data in the following table, find the weighted price relative index for 1997. Use the values of expenditure in 1995 as the weights.

	$1995(Q_0)$	$1995(P_0)$	$1997(P_1)$
Soya	40 Kilo	30p	45
Flour	80 Kilo	40p	50
Milk	50 Litres	20p	25

8.8 The following information on the Retail Price Index is taken from Labour Market Trends, August 1997.

Item	Food	Catering	Alcohol	Tobacco	Housing	Fuel and light	Household goods
Weight	136	49	80	34	186	41	72
Index Jan. 1997	141.0	179.2	171.1	200.1	172.1	133.2	135.6
Index July 1997	142.2	182.7	175.0	205.2	180.9	131.2	137.3

Item	Household services	Clothing and footwear	Personal goods	Motoring	Fares and other travel	Leisure goods	Leisure services
Weight	52	56	40	128	20	47	59
Index Jan. 1997	142.7	116.3	166.7	162.9	166.6	123.7	177.8
Index July 1997	143.8	115.9	169.8	165.9	170.9	123.9	182.5

Note: January 1987 = 100.

If, in January 1997, the index stood at 154.4, what level was it in July 1997? (Hint: calculate the price relatives for each category and then calculate the weighted mean of the price relatives)

Note: Answers to Review questions can be found on pp. 429–432.

Further study and data
••••••••••••••••••••••••••••

Texts

Bancroft, G. and O'Sullivan, G. (1993), *Quantitative methods for accounting and business studies*, 3rd edn, McGraw Hill, chapter 11.

Curwin, J. and Slater, R. (1996), *Quantitative methods for business decisions*, 4th edn, Chapman and Hall, chapter 5.

Lawson, M., Hubbard, S. and Pugh, P. (1995), *Maths and statistics for business*, Addison Wesley Longman, chapter 12.

Morris, C. (1996), *Quantitative approaches in business studies*, 4th edn, Pitman, chapter 7.

Oakshott, L. (1996), *Essential elements of quantitative methods*, BPP, chapter 1.

Thomas, R. (1997), *Quantitative methods for business studies*, Prentice Hall, chapter 5.

Waters, D. (1997), *Quantitative methods*, 2nd edn, Addison Wesley Longman, chapter 6.

Wisniewski, M. with Stead, R. (1996), *Foundation quantitative methods for business*, Pitman, chapter 7.

Sources of information and data

Business Monitor MM23 has detailed information on price indices. However, you may not find this in the library you are using. *Economic Trends* contains most of the information you need on prices.

See also the list at the end of Chapter 1 (p. 25).

CHAPTER 9

Time value of money

Objectives

By the end of this chapter you should be able to:

▶ distinguish between simple and compound interest and undertake appropriate calculations;

▶ use the discounting process to find the present value of future streams of income and expenditure;

▶ use various techniques such as net present value (NPV) and internal rate of return (IRR) to compare alternative investment projects;

▶ use various techniques such as straight line and reducing balance to estimate rates of depreciation on capital assets;

▶ solve other problems involving monetary returns, such as the present value of annuities and other financial instruments.

Introduction

When we compare different types of investment, whether personal or corporate, we must be careful to consider the *time profile* of any returns on these investments. Otherwise we could easily make an unwise decision as to which, if any, investments to pursue.

This idea can easily be illustrated in terms of the fact that, say, £100 today is certainly *not* the same as £100 in one year's time. Suppose the interest I could receive on £100 placed in my bank account was 10 per cent per annum. Then in one year's time my £100 would be worth £100 + £100 (0.10) = £110, since I can get my £100 back and earn 10 per cent interest (0.10 as a decimal) on the £100 held by the bank for that year. I might therefore regard £100 now as equivalent to £110 in 12 months time rather than £100 in 12 months time.

When different projects yield different monetary returns over a succession of time periods (i.e. have different time profiles) it is even more important that we have a clear framework by which the time factor can be taken into account. Only then can we be sure that we are comparing 'like with like' in terms of the different monetary values which flow from different projects.

Just as the monetary *returns* on a project can vary over time, so too can the monetary *costs* of investing in the project. If, say, the total costs for two alternative projects are identical, but one requires a higher proportion of these costs to be incurred *later* than the other, then for the reasons already mentioned we could regard this as the less costly project. For example, £110 of costs incurred next year could be paid for by putting aside £100 now at 10 per cent interest, but £110 of costs incurred in two year's time could be paid for by putting aside *less than* £100 now at 10 per cent interest.

Clearly the time profile of both monetary returns and monetary costs must explicitly be taken into account if we are to take appropriate business decisions.

Answers to the 'Self-check questions', responses to each 'Pause for thought' and answers to the 'Review questions' can be found at the end of the book.

9.1 Simple and compound interest

An **interest rate** is usually quoted as a *percentage*, and indicates the amount received (or paid) for each £1 saved (or borrowed). For example an interest rate (i) of 10 per cent indicates the receipt of 10 pence on each £1 saved.

If we know the amount received (or paid) over some time period and the initial amount saved (or borrowed) at the start of that period, then we can calculate the rate of interest (i):

$$i = \frac{\text{interest received (or paid) for the period}}{\text{initial amount saved (or borrowed) at start of period}}$$

So if £20 is received on £200 saved in a bank account over 1 year, then:

$$i = \frac{20}{200} = \frac{10}{100} = 0.10 \text{ per annum}$$

To convert this decimal to a *percentage*, multiply by 100, to get

$$i = 0.10 \times 100 = 10\% \text{ per annum}$$

The amount of interest received (or paid) each year will depend not only on the value of i, but also on whether the calculation involves simple interest or compound interest.

Simple interest (SI)

If any money saved receives an interest payment at the end of each period which is *not re-invested*, then the savings scheme offers **simple interest (SI)**.

The simple interest (SI) earned over a number of time periods is calculated as follows:

Formula for simple interest

$$SI = P \times \frac{i}{100} \times T$$

where SI = Simple interest earned
  P = Principal, i.e. initial amount at start of period
  i = Rate of interest as a *percentage*
  T = Number of time periods

WORKED
EXAMPLE **9.1**
••••••••••••••

Calculate the simple interest earned over five years if £1,640 is invested at a rate of interest of 9 per cent per annum.

Solution

$$SI = P \times \frac{i}{100} \times T$$

$$SI = 1,640 \times \frac{9}{100} \times 5$$

$$\underline{SI = £738}$$

Compound interest (CI)

Most types of account receive (or pay) **compound interest** (CI). For example, if any money saved receives an interest payment which *is then reinvested*, the savings scheme offers compound interest.

In terms of this chapter we shall assume that any interest received or paid is compound interest, unless told otherwise.

Table 9.1 shows the payment of compound interest on an initial amount of £100 (Principal) invested at a 10 per cent per annum compound interest rate.

table 9.1

Compound interest

Principal	After 1 year	After 2 years	After 3 years
£100	$100 + 100(0.10)$ $= 100(1 + 0.10)^1$ $= £110$	$110 + 110(0.10)$ $= 110(1 + 0.10)$ $= 100(1 + 0.10)^2$ $= £121$	$121 + 121(0.10)$ $= 121(1 + 0.10)$ $= 100(1 + 0.10)^3$ $= £133.10$

Note: For all compound interest rate problems we express *i*, the rate of interest, as a *decimal*.

PAUSE FOR THOUGHT 9.1   *Can you extend Table 9.1 so that it covers the situation after four years? Can you see a pattern emerging?*

Finding end value (A_t) after period t

We can easily derive a formula from Table 9.1 for finding A_t the value of the initial amount of £100 at the end of any time period (t) when it grows at a compound rate of i (as a decimal).

Formula for compound interest

$A_t = P(1 + i)^t$

where A_t = value at end of time period t

P = principal, i.e. initial amount at start of period

i = compound interest rate, as a *decimal*

t = end of time period in question

Thus, from Table 9.1

▶ **At end of $t = 1$**

$$A_1 = 100(1 + 0.10)^1 = £110$$

▶ **At end of $t = 2$**

$$A_2 = 100(1 + 0.10)^2 = £121$$

▶ **At end of $t = 3$**

$$A_3 = 100(1 + 0.10)^3 = £133.10$$

WORKED
EXAMPLE **9.2**
••••••••••••••

£1,000 is invested at a compound interest rate of 15 per cent per annum. What is the value of this initial investment at the end of ten years?

Solution

$A_t = P(1 + i)^t$

i.e. $A_{10} = 1,000(1 + 0.15)^{10}$

$A_{10} = 1,000(4.0456)$

$\underline{A_{10} = £4,045.6}$

Finding total compound interest (CI_t) after period t

Here we merely take the end value after period t (A_t) and subtract the initial amount P to find the total compound interest paid over this time period:

> **Formula for total compound interest paid**
>
> $$CI_t = A_t - P$$
>
> i.e. $CI_t = P(1 + i)^t - P$
>
> where CI_t = compound interest paid up to end of period t
> A_t = value at end of period t
> P = principal, i.e. initial amount at start of period
> i = compound interest rate, as a decimal
> t = end of time period in question

WORKED
EXAMPLE **9.3**
••••••••••••••

Find the total compound interest paid in the previous worked example up to the end of the 10th year.

Solution

$A_{10} = 1,000(1 + 0.15)^{10} - 1,000$
$A_{10} = £4,045.6 - £1,000$
$\underline{A_{10} = £3,045.6}$

Finding the annual percentage rate (APR)

We can use the above approach to find the annual percentage rate (APR) for situations in which the interest rate is expressed monthly, quarterly, etc. For example in the case of a monthly interest rate, we can find the total compound interest paid on £1 after 12 successive monthly time periods, and then express this value as a percentage of the initial £1.

Formula for annual percentage rate (APR)

$APR = [1(1 + i)^t - 1] \times 100$

when APR = annual percentage rate
$\quad\quad\quad i$ = compound (monthly, quarterly, etc.) interest
$\quad\quad\quad t$ = number of time periods (months, quarters, etc.) in year

---

In terms of the previous formula for total compound interest paid, we simply regard P as £1 and express the result as a percentage by multiplying by 100.

WORKED
EXAMPLE **9.4**
....

Find the APR on a 1 year loan at 2 per cent per month.

Solution

$APR = [1(1 + 0.02)^{12} - 1] \times 100$

$\quad\quad\quad = [1(1.2682) - 1] \times 100$

$\quad\quad\quad = [0.2682] \times 100$

$\underline{APR = 26.82\%}$

Compound factors

Tables of **compound factors** can simplify many of the calculations considered so far. These compound factors tell us the number of times by which an initial amount will have grown, for any compound interest rate (i) and any time period (t). In Worked example 9.2, we noted that £1,000 invested at 15 per cent (0.15) per annum will have grown by the *compound factor* 4.0456 by the end of period (year) 10.

We can use Table 9.2 (or similar tables) to solve many relevant calculations:

table 9.2
Compound factors at various interest rates (*i*) as decimals and at end of various time periods (*t*).

Time (t) years	Interest rate (i) as decimal					
	0.05	*0.10*	*0.15*	*0.20*	*0.25*	*0.30*
1	1.05	1.1	1.15	1.2	1.25	1.3
5	1.2763	1.6105	2.0114	2.4883	3.0518	3.7129
10	1.6289	2.5937	4.0456	6.1917	9.3132	13.7859
15	2.0789	4.1772	8.1371	15.4070	28.4217	51.1859
20	2.65353	6.7275	16.3665	38.3376	86.7362	190.0497
25	3.3864	10.8347	32.9190	95.3692	264.6978	705.6412
30	4.3219	17.4494	66.2118	237.3763	807.7936	2,619.9963

▶ £1,000 invested at a compound interest rate of 15 per cent (0.15) will, by the end of period (year) 20, have grown by a *compound factor* of 16.3665, being worth £16,366.5.

▶ £1,000 invested at a compound interest rate of 20 per cent (0.20) will, by the end of period (year) 20, have grown by a *compound factor* of 38.3376, being worth £38,337.6.

etc.

If we go *down any of the columns* in Table 9.2, we can see the significance of growth taking place at a given compound interest rate. For example, at a given compound interest rate of, say, 0.10 (10 per cent) the compound factors get progressively larger for each five year increase in time. Between five and ten years the compound factor grows from 1.61 to 2.59, but between ten and fifteen years the compound factor grows much more rapidly from 2.59 to 4.17 and so on.

Similarly, if we go *across any of the rows* in Table 9.2, we can see that for any given time period, the compound factors get progressively larger for each 0.05 (5 per cent) increase in interest rate. For example, at the ten year time period, between 0.15 (15 per cent) and 0.20 (20 per cent) interest rates the compound factor grows from 4.04 to 6.19, but grows much more rapidly from 6.19 to 9.31 for the next 0.05 per cent (5 per cent) increase in interest rates from 0.20 (20 per cent) to 0.25 (25 per cent).

SELF-CHECK QUESTION

9.1 Use Table 9.2 (p. 204) to calculate the value of an initial amount of £1,000 growing at a compound rate in each of the following circumstances.

(a) compound interest rate 0.05 (5%) after 15 years
(b) compound interest rate 0.10 (10%) after 25 years
(c) compound interest rate 0.15 (15%) after 20 years
(d) compound interest rate 0.20 (20%) after 30 years
(e) compound interest rate 0.25 (25%) after 10 years
(f) compound interest rate 0.30 (30%) after 30 years

Note: **Answers can be found on p. 355.**

9.2 Discounting and present value

We have already noted that £100 invested at an interest rate of 10 per cent per annum will give a return of £110 in one year's time. Put another way, at an interest rate of 10 per cent per annum we can expect an investor to regard £110 in one year's time as being equivalent to £100 now (since he/ she can readily convert the one into the other). This process of converting a future money value into a **present value equivalent** is referred to as **discounting**.

Discounting

The **discounting** process essentially involves *reversing* the growth process involving compound interest rates already discussed. Looking back at Table 9.1

(p. 202) we can see that £100 invested at an interest rate of 10 per cent per annum would be worth £133.10 after three years; reversing the process we can say that £133.10 after three years would only be worth £100 now if we **discount** at an interest rate of 10 per cent.

We have already derived an equation (p. 202)

$$A_t = P(1 + i)^t$$

where A_t is the value of some initial amount, P (the principal) at the end of period t when it grows at a compound interest rate i (as a decimal).

So, from Table 9.1, for $P = £100$, $t = 3$ years, and $i = 0.10$

$$A_3 = £100 \, (1 + 0.10)^3 = £133.10$$

Re-arranging gives us:

$$£100 = £133.10 \times \frac{1}{(1 + 0.10)^3}$$

More generally:

Present value = future amount × discount factor

In other words £133.10 received after 3 years at a 10 per cent (0.10) interest rate, is *equivalent* to £100 received now.

▶ We call the £100 the **present value** equivalent of the £133.10 in three years' time.
▶ We call the £133.10 the future amount to be **discounted**.
▶ We call the factor $\dfrac{1}{(1 + 0.10)^3}$ by which we multiply the future amount (£133.10) to get the present value equivalent, the **discount factor**.
▶ We call the process of reducing any future amount to its present value equivalent, **discounting**.
▶ We call the rate of interest (i) we apply in the discounting process, the **discount rate**.

In general, we can express the discount factor as follows:

Formula for the discount factor

Discount factor $= \dfrac{1}{(1 + i)^t}$

where i = discount rate (interest rate) as a decimal
t = time period in question

Notice that:

▶ the higher the rate (i) at which we discount, the bigger the denominator and the *smaller the discount factor.*
▶ the higher the number of time periods (t) over which the discounting takes place, the bigger the denominator and the *smaller the discount factor.*

table 9.3
Discount factors at various interest (discount) rates as decimals and at end of various time periods

Time (t) years	Interest rate			(Discount rate)		
	0.05	0.10	0.15	0.20	0.25	0.30
1	0.9524	0.9091	0.8696	0.8333	0.8000	0.7692
5	0.7835	0.6209	0.4972	0.4019	0.3277	0.2693
10	0.6139	0.3855	0.2472	0.1615	0.1074	0.0725
15	0.4810	0.2394	0.1299	0.0649	0.0352	0.0195
20	0.3769	0.1486	0.0611	0.0261	0.0115	0.0053
25	0.2953	0.0923	0.0304	0.0105	0.0038	0.0014
30	0.2314	0.0573	0.0151	0.0042	0.0012	0.0004

DID YOU KNOW?

Discounting can be used as an 'excuse' for shifting environmental costs on to future generations. For example if the impact of nuclear waste is valued at £1,000m damage in 100 years time, then the present value of that damage at, say, a discount rate of 8 per cent (0.08) would only be £450,000. Such a small present value figure might lead decision makers to ignore this future cost and, by doing nothing now, pass these environmental costs on to future generations.

Remember the discount factor is the number (or factor) by which we multiply the future amount to find its present value equivalent. The *smaller the discount factor*, the smaller will be the present value equivalent for any future amount.

It is often helpful to refer to a **Table of discount factors**, as in Table 9.3.

The *compound* nature of the discounting process can be seen from Table 9.3.

▶ For any given interest rate (discount rate), the discount factor falls progressively more rapidly as time increases. Here we are *moving down the columns*. Thus at a 0.10 (10 per cent) interest (discount) rate, an estimated amount in five years time will be worth (today) 0.6209 or 62.09 per cent of its nominal value; but an estimated amount in 20 years time will be worth (today) only 0.1486 or 14.86 per cent of its nominal value at that time.

▶ For any given time period, the discount factor falls progressively more rapidly as the interest (discount) rate increases. Here we are *moving across the rows*. Thus if we discount an estimated amount in ten years time at a discount rate of 0.05 (5 per cent), it will be worth (today) 0.6139 or 61.39 per cent of its nominal value; but if we discount that same amount in 10 years time at a discount rate of 0.20 (20 per cent), it will be worth (today) only 0.1615 or 16.15 per cent of its value at that time.

SELF-CHECK QUESTIONS

9.2 Use Table 9.3 above to estimate the value of £100,000 received in the future with the characteristics outlined below.

(a) **in 1 years time at a discount rate of 0.25 (25 per cent)**
(b) **in 5 years time at a discount rate of 0.10 (10 per cent)**
(c) **in 10 years time at a discount rate of 0.30 (30 per cent)**
(d) **in 15 years time at a discount rate of 0.05 (5 per cent)**
(e) **in 20 years time at a discount rate of 0.15 (15 per cent)**
(f) **in 25 years time at a discount rate of 0.20 (20 per cent)**

Note: **Answer can be found on p. 355.**

Present value

From this analysis we can derive a simple formula for the **present value** (PV) of an amount £A received at end of time period t.

Formula for present value

Present value (*PV*) of £A received at end of time period t:

$$PV = £A_t \times \frac{1}{(1 + i)^t}$$

where A_t = expected amount received at end of time period t
$\quad\quad i$ = rate of discount (as a decimal)
$\quad\quad t$ = end of time period in question

$\dfrac{1}{(1 + i)^t}$ = discount factor

WORKED
EXAMPLE **9.5**
· · · · · · · · · · · · · ·

Use Table 9.3 (p. 207) to find the present value of £1,000 received at the end of five years time when discounted at an annual rate of 10 per cent.

Solution

$$PV = £1,000 \times \frac{1}{(1 + 0.10)^5}$$

$$PV = £1,000 \times 0.6209$$

$$\underline{PV = £620.9}$$

In other words, under these conditions you would be indifferent between a sum of £1,000 at the end of five years time and a sum of £620.9 today.

9.3 Investment appraisal
· ·

The analysis of discounting and present value is highly relevant to attempts by business to appraise or rank different investment projects. As we shall see, discounting and present value underpin the techniques of net present value (NPV) and internal rate of return (IRR) for **investment appraisal**. Here we briefly consider these and other techniques widely used by business.

Non-discounting techniques

Payback period

This is a crude but widely used method of investment appraisal which does *not* rely on the discounting process. In its simplest form, the firm will select that project with the shortest **payback period** – i.e. which requires the shortest time to payback (in nominal terms) any initial capital outlay.

Suppose we have the following information on the expected cash flows (£m) for two projects, A and B over the eight time periods (t = 0 being today) regarded as the 'life' of each project.

table 9.4

Expected cash flows (£m) of two investment projects over 8 time periods

	$t = 0$	$t = 1$	$t = 2$	$t = 3$	$t = 4$	$t = 5$	$t = 6$	$t = 7$	$t = 8$
Project A	−18	0	0	5	6	7	8	9	10
Project B	−6	2	2	2	2	2	0	0	0

The cash flows are expressed in *nominal terms*, i.e. in the money values expected to be received in future. These values correspond to *net revenues* (i.e. revenue-cost) or *profits* expected in future time periods.

Project A is a capital intensive project with £18 millions expected to be spent on capital outlay this year ($t = 0$), but no net revenues are received until $t = 3$, though net revenues rise steadily thereafter.

Project B, in contrast, is a less capital intensive project, but also a less 'productive' project. Only £6 million is expected to be spent on capital outlay this year ($t = 0$) and net revenues are expected from next year onwards. However the net revenues remain static in value from $t = 1$ to $t = 5$ and are expected to cease altogether by $t = 6$.

▶ Project A is expected to pay back the initial capital outlay of £18 million by time period $t = 5$.

▶ Project B is expected to pay back the initial capital outlay of £6 million by time period $t = 3$.

On the strict application of the payback criterion, Project B is preferred to Project A as it is expected to repay the initial capital outlay the quickest.

Of course this investment decision can be criticised. While project B may be 'less risky' in terms of a more rapid payback, it would also seem 'less productive' in that little subsequent net revenue is generated after payback by project B as compared to project A. Further, all future values are expressed in nominal terms whereas the present value equivalent of those future values would be a more realistic basis for comparing the two projects.

Average rate of return (ARR)

The **average rate of return** is the average percentage return per time period on the initial capital outlay over the expected life of a project. The ARR is calculated as follows:

Formula for average rate of return

$$ARR = \frac{\text{total return} - \text{initial capital outlay}}{\text{initial capital outlay}} \times 100 \div \text{time period of project}$$

WORKED EXAMPLE **9.6**
••••••••••••••

Work out the average rate of return on projects A and B in Table 9.4 above.

Solution

▶ Project A: $ARR = \dfrac{45 - 18}{18} \times 100 \div 8$

$\underline{ARR = 18.75\% \text{ per annum}}$

▶ Project B: ARR $= \dfrac{10 - 6}{6} \times 100 \div 8$

ARR $= 8.33\%$ per annum

Notice that whereas the payback criterion results in project B being preferred to project A, the ARR criterion results in project A being preferred to project B. Again, however, we could criticise the approach for expressing future values only in nominal terms.

We now consider rather more sophisticated methods of investment appraisal which look beyond the payback period and which consider 'real' rather than nominal values for expected future returns.

Discounting techniques

Net present value (NPV)

The idea here is to first find the *present value* (PV) of all the expected future net revenues expressed in nominal terms. In other words we use the *discounting process* to find the present value (p. 208) of the future cash flows.

From this present value (PV) we then subtract any initial capital outlay in the current time period ($t = 0$). (Of course if the capital outlay extends beyond the current time period, then we will have to discount this also.)

NPV $=$ PV $-$ K

where NPV $=$ net present value

PV $=$ present value of future net revenues

K $=$ initial capital outlay

Let us consider in more detail how we find the present value (PV) of a stream of expected net revenues (i.e. profits). We use our formula for present value (PV) on p. 208, but apply this to *each* time period, we then have:

$$PV = £A_t \times \frac{1}{(1 + i)^t}$$

where $£A_t =$ expected return in time t

$i =$ rate of discount (as a decimal)

$t =$ time period in question

$\dfrac{1}{(1 + i)^t} =$ discount factor

Suppose we use a discount rate of 0.10 (10 per cent) and apply this formula to the net revenues for Project B in Table 9.4 (p. 209). We have:

▶ **$t = 1$** PV $= £2(m) \times \dfrac{1}{(1 + 0.10)^1} = £2(m) \times 0.909 = 1.818$

▶ **$t = 2$** PV $= £2(m) \times \dfrac{1}{(1 + 0.10)^2} = £2(m) \times 0.826 = 1.652$

▶ $t = 3$ PV = £2(m) $\times \dfrac{1}{(1 + 0.10)^3}$ = £2(m) $\times$ 0.751 = 1.502

▶ $t = 4$ PV = £2(m) $\times \dfrac{1}{(1 + 0.10)^4}$ = £2(m) $\times$ 0.683 = 1.366

▶ $t = 5$ PV = £2(m) $\times \dfrac{1}{(1 + 0.10)^5}$ = £2(m) $\times$ 0.621 = 1.242

There are no net revenues after $t = 5$. We must then *sum* these present values calculated for each future time period to get the total present value of expected net revenues for Project B. In this case the sum of these present values over the 5 time periods is £7.58m.

NPV = PV − K

NPV = £7.58m − £6m

<u>NPV = £1.58m for Project B</u>

Using our sigma notation from chapter 2 (p. 28), we can write a general formula for NPV:

Formula for net present value

$$\text{NPV} = \sum_{t=0}^{n}\left[A_t \times \frac{1}{(1 + i)^t} \right] - K$$

where n = number of time periods

A_t = net revenue in time period t

i = rate of discount (as a decimal)

t = end of time period in question

K = initial capital outlay

Note: when $t = 0$, the discount factor for net revenue is:

$$\frac{1}{(1 + i)^0} = \frac{1}{1} = 1$$

This is because anything raised to the power 0 is 1 (see Appendix 1, p. 293).

Discounted cash flow

In fact we can set down these calculations for NPV using tables. These are often called **discounted cash flow** tables. Instead of subtracting the initial capital outlay at the end, a *negative* figure is recorded for time period 0, i.e. the start of the project.

DID YOU KNOW?

When managers are comparing projects which have different degrees of 'risk', then a higher rate of discount is often applied to the more risky project(s). This means a lower discount factor, and therefore a smaller present value for any future returns expected from that more risky project.

We illustrate this using our data for investment Projects A and B from Table 9.4 (p. 209). Note that Nominal Cash Flow (NCF) are the original data, whereas Discounted Cash Flow (DCF) are the original data discounted, here using a discount rate of 0.10 (10%).

As we can see, the NPV for project A (sum of the discounted cash flows) is

table 9.5

Discounted Cash
Flows for Projects
A and B (£m) with
0.10 (10%) discount
rate

	Nominal cash flow (NCF)			Discounted cash flow (DCF)	
Time (year)	NCF (Project A)	NCF (Project B)	Discount factor	DCF (Project A)	DCF (Project B)
0	−18	−6	1.000	−18.000	−6.000
1	0	2	0.909	0.000	1.818
2	0	2	0.826	0.000	1.652
3	5	2	0.751	3.755	1.502
4	6	2	0.683	4.098	1.366
5	7	2	0.621	4.347	1.242
6	8	0	0.564	4.512	0.000
7	9	0	0.513	4.617	0.000
8	10	0	0.466	4.660	0.000
Sum	27	4		7.989	1.580
			NPV	7.989	1.580

£7.989m. This is higher than the NPV for project B of only £1.580m. The usual 'decision rule' would be that if a scarcity of financial resources means choosing between these projects, then choose the project with the higher NPV, namely project A.

SELF-CHECK
QUESTIONS

9.3 Two major investment projects each have the same initial capital outlay of £1,000 million. The expected net revenues on the respective projects over the next 4 years are outlined below (£m):

	Project A	Project B
Year 0	−1,000	−1,000
Year 1	400	400
Year 2	500	400
Year 3	350	400
Year 4	300	400

Calculate the NPV for the respective projects using a 0.10 (10 per cent) rate of discount. Set out your answer in the form of a discounted cash flow table.
    Comment on your results.

Note: Answers can be found on p. 355.

Internal rate of return (IRR)

In finding the net present value (NPV) for projects A and B in Table 9.5 we used a *discount rate* of 0.10 (10 per cent). Of course we could have used lower or higher rates of discount to find the NPV of each project.

Figure 9.1 below shows an inverse relationship between the NPV for a project and the rate of discount; in other words the higher the rate of discount we use in calculating NPV, the lower the value of NPV.

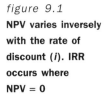

figure 9.1
NPV varies inversely with the rate of discount (*i*). IRR occurs where NPV = 0

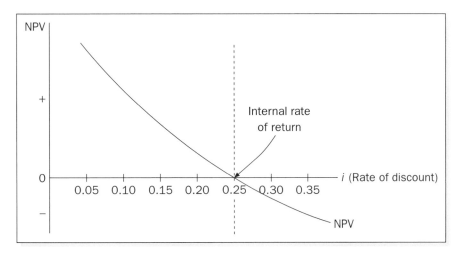

In Figure 9.1 we can see that the NPV falls as the rate of discount, *i*, rises. At some rate of discount, here *i* = 0.25 (25 per cent), the value of NPV is zero. We call this rate of discount which makes NPV = zero, the **internal rate of return (IRR)**.

> **Internal rate of return (IRR)** is that rate of discount which makes NPV = 0 for any project.

WORKED EXAMPLE **9.7**
....

Find the internal rate of return for project A and for project B in Table 9.4 (p. 209).

Solution

We apply the procedure for calculating the NPV of each project at a 0.10 (10 per cent) rate of discount shown in Table 9.5. However we repeat this procedure for a *range* of possible discount rates.

In Table 9.6 below we work out the *discount factors* for each of the eight time periods (years) using discount rates of 0.05 (5 per cent), 0.10 (10 per cent), 0.15 (15 per cent) and 0.20 (20 per cent) respectively.

table 9.6
Discount factors for each time period at various discount rates

Time	0.05 (5%)	0.10 (10%)	0.15 (15%)	0.20 (20%)
0	1.000	1.000	1.000	1.000
1	0.952	0.909	0.870	0.833
2	0.907	0.826	0.757	0.694
3	0.863	0.751	0.658	0.578
4	0.822	0.683	0.573	0.482
5	0.784	0.621	0.497	0.402
6	0.745	0.564	0.433	0.334
7	0.709	0.513	0.377	0.278
8	0.675	0.466	0.328	0.232

Applying these discount factors to the respective nominal cash flows for each project shown in Tables 9.4 and 9.5 gives the following results for NPV.

Rate of discount	NPV Project A	NPV Project B
0.05 (5%)	15.812	2.652
0.10 (10%)	7.989	1.580
0.15 (15%)	2.344	0.710
0.20% (20%)	−1.910	−0.022

We can usefully plot the NPV curve for Project A on a diagram, as in Fig. 9.2.

figure 9.2
Finding IRR for Project A

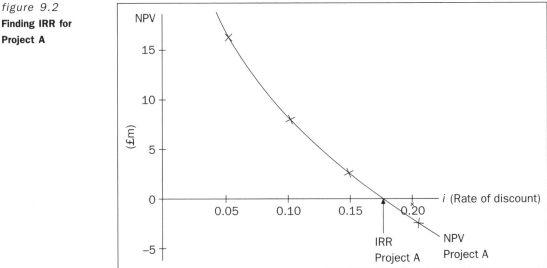

As we can see, the NPV curve for project A intersects the zero axis in between the 0.15 (15 per cent) and 0.20 (20 per cent) discount rates. This intersection point of the NPV curve with the horizontal axis is the Internal rate of return (IRR) for project A.

PAUSE FOR THOUGHT 9.2 *Plot the NPV curve for project B on this same diagram. What do you notice?*

To find the exact rate of discount at which the intersection takes place we would need to use discount rates which vary by, say, 0.01 (1 per cent) instead of 0.05 (5 per cent) as here. This is an iterative (step by step) process which is easily solved by statistical packages on a computer.

Using NPV and IRR criteria
To *use* the investment criteria we have discussed, the *decision rules* are as follows.

figure 9.3
Potential for conflict between NPV and IRR investment criteria for Projects I and II respectively

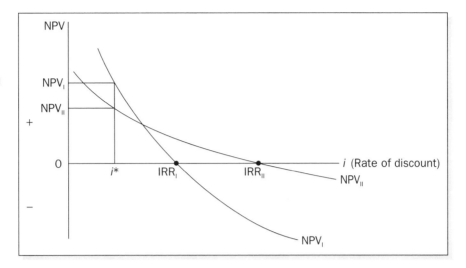

If selecting between alternative projects:

▶ Choose that project which has the *highest NPV* at the rate of discount applied.
▶ Choose that project which has the *highest IRR*.

Often these decision rules will give the same result, but not always.

In the case of our two projects A and B, using the NPV criterion at a discount rate of 0.10 (10 per cent) clearly favours project A; NPV of £7.989 m for project A as compared to only £1.580m for project B.

However the decision is much closer in terms of the IRR criterion with both projects having NPV = 0 at rather similar rates of discount. It is when the respective NPV curves intersect *above* the horizontal axis that the two types of decision rule may give conflicting advice (see Figure 9.3).

In Figure 9.3, at a rate of discount i^*, project I has the highest NPV. However because the respective NPV curves intersect above the horizontal axis, project II has the highest IRR.

PAUSE FOR THOUGHT 9.3   *Can you suggest how a manager might measure risk? In other words, can you think of any statistical measures which might give a manager some idea of the different levels of risk between two investment projects with similar net present values?*

SELF-CHECK QUESTIONS

9.4 Use *all* the methods of investment appraisal to consider the relative merits of the two investment projects outlined below. Each investment project has the same initial capital outlay (£100,000) but different flows of net revenue thereafter.

	Nominal Cash Flow	
Year	Project I	Project II
0	–£100,000	–£100,000
1	£38,000	£5,000
2	£30,000	£57,000
3	£23,000	£60,000
4	£22,500	£12,000
5	£22,500	£1,000

Comment on your results.

Note: **Answer can be found on p. 355.**

9.4 Depreciation

Just as some investments might *grow* at a simple or compound rate through the impact of interest rates on an initial amount, other investments might *decline* as a result of **depreciation**. This is particularly true in the case of the book value of capital equipment and other assets. The impact of 'wear and tear' and technical obsolescence (more advanced equipment becoming available) means that businesses must often reduce the initial value of these capital assets over time.

There are in fact a number of ways in which such depreciation can be handled by businesses.

Straight line method

The **straight line** method reduces the value of capital by the same *absolute amount* each year.

Formula for straight line depreciation

$$\text{Annual depreciation} = \frac{\text{initial value of capital} - \text{scrap value}}{\text{estimated life of capital}}$$

WORKED EXAMPLE **9.8**

Take, for example, an item of capital costing £40,000 with an estimated scrap value of £10,000 and useful 'life' of ten years. Use the straight line method to estimate annual depreciation.

Solution

$$\text{Annual depreciation} = \frac{£40,000 - £10,000}{10}$$

Annual depreciation = £3,000 per annum

Although straight-line depreciation is simple to calculate, in fact most capital items do not lose value in a linear way. Rather they lose more absolute value in the early years and less absolute value in the later years.

Reducing-balance method

The above aspect is reflected in part by the **reducing-balance** method of calculating depreciation. Here a *fixed percentage* of the initial capital value of the equipment is written off each year. This results in more absolute depreciation being accounted for in the early years of an asset and less in the later years.

The formula for calculating the reducing-balance method of depreciation can be derived from our earlier work on compound interest.

We noted (p. 202) that an initial amount P which *increases* at a fixed percentage, i, has a value after t periods of:

$$A_t = P \times (1 + i)^t$$

However if that initial amount P *decreases* at a fixed percentage, i, we now subtract i instead of adding it. So an item with an initial valuation of P which depreciates at a rate i per time period, has a **depreciated value** after t periods as shown.

Formula for reducing balance depreciation

$A_t = P \times (1 - i)^t$
A_t = depreciated value after t periods
P = initial value
i = rate of depreciation (as a decimal)
t = time period in question

Of course if we knew any three of the four variables in the equation above, we can solve for the other. So, for example, if we knew the depreciated value (A_t) of an asset purchased for an initial value (P) after t periods, we could calculate i, the rate of depreciation required to give this result. We solve such a problem in the worked example below.

WORKED
EXAMPLE **9.9**
. . . .

A company purchases a capital item for £50,000.

(a) Use the straight-line method to find annual depreciation if the item is expected to last five years and have a scrap value of £10,000.
(b) Use the reducing-balance method of depreciation to find the value of the item after five years with a depreciation rate of 20 per cent per annum.
(c) Use the reducing-balance method of depreciation to find the rate of depreciation, i, required to give a depreciated value of £20,000 after five years.

Solutions

(a) Annual depreciation $= \dfrac{£50,000 - £10,000}{5} = £8,000$ per annum

(b) $A_t = P \times (1 - i)^t$
$A_5 = £50,000 \times (1 - 0.20)^5$
$A_5 = £50,000 \times (0.8)^5$
$A_5 = £50,000 \times 0.32768$
$\underline{A_5 = £16,384}$

(c) $20,000 = 50,000 \times (1 - i)^5$

$$0.4 = (1 - i)^5$$
$$\sqrt[5]{0.4} = (1 - i)$$
$$0.83 = 1 - i$$
$$i = 1 - 0.83$$
$$\underline{i = 0.17}$$

A depreciation rate of 17 per cent per annum

9.5 Annuities and other financial instruments

Here we apply some of the methods discussed in this chapter to problems involving a range of financial instruments. We also make use of the idea of *geometric progressions* and the formula for summing such progressions (see box, p. 310).

Annuities

In an **annuity** the investor pays a lump sum and in return receives regular payments of a fixed amount over a specified time period. Annuities are usually offered by insurance companies and can be quite attractive, especially to retired people to supplement any pension provision.

The lump sum to be paid for a particular annuity is the *present value* of that annuity. We can therefore use our earlier analysis of discounting (p. 206), as in the worked example below.

WORKED
EXAMPLE **9.10**

How much should I pay as a lump sum for an annual annuity of £5,000, starting at end of year 1 and continuing for 12 years altogether. Assume that the annual rate of discount is 0.10 (10 per cent).

Solution

$$PV = 5,000 \times \frac{1}{(1 + 0.10)^1} + 5,000 \times \frac{1}{(1 + 0.10)^2} + \ldots 5,000 \times \frac{1}{(1 + 0.10)^{12}}$$

$$PV = \frac{5,000}{(1.1)^1} + \frac{5,000}{(1.1)^2} + \ldots + \frac{5,000}{(1.1)^{12}}$$

We can, of course, work this out term by term to give

$$\underline{PV = £34,062.5}$$

However we might note that the expression for *PV* is a *geometric progression* (see p. 309) of the form: $a, ar^1, ar^2 \ldots ar^{n-1}$

where $a = \dfrac{5,000}{(1.1)^1}$, $r = \dfrac{1}{1.1}$ and $n = 12$

Using our formula for the sum $(S_n = a \times \dfrac{1 - r^n}{1 - r})$

we have $S_{12} = \dfrac{5{,}000}{1.1} \times \dfrac{1 - \left(\dfrac{1}{1.1}\right)^{12}}{1 - \dfrac{1}{1.1}}$

i.e. $\qquad S_{12} = £4{,}545 \times \dfrac{1 - 0.318}{1 - 0.909}$

$\qquad\quad S_{12} = £4{,}545 \times \dfrac{0.682}{0.091}$

$\qquad\quad S_{12} = £4{,}545 \times 7.49$

$\qquad\quad \underline{S_{12} = £34{,}062.5}$

We can therefore express a formula for finding the present value of an annuity (i.e. the value to be paid for that annuity) as follows:

Present value of an annuity

$PV = a \times \dfrac{1 - r^n}{1 - r}$

where a = regular sum received multiplied by the discount factor

$\qquad r$ = common ratio (discount factor) = $\dfrac{1}{(1 + i)}$

$\qquad i$ = rate of discount (as a decimal)

$\qquad n$ = number of time periods for annuity

Mortgages and other payments by instalments

When a **mortgage** is taken on a property, for example, it is normally repaid by a series of regular equal instalments. To pay off the mortgage the present value of that series of payment instalments must be equal to the initial amount borrowed.

▶ The previous formula for PV of an annuity can therefore be applied to problems involving mortgages.

Note: When a series of payments occurs more frequently than once a year, as is often the case with mortgages, we can still use geometric progressions to calculate present value provided that the interest is calculated at the same frequency as the payments.

WORKED
EXAMPLE **9.11**

Suppose I estimate that I can afford to repay £400 a month for 20 years. Interest is calculated at 12 per cent per annum, payable monthly. How large a mortgage can I afford?

Solution

Altogether there will be $20 \times 12 = 240$ monthly repayments of £400. The interest rate is 1 per cent per month. The present value of the repayments and therefore the mortgage I can afford is:

$$\text{Mortgage} = PV = \frac{400}{1.01^1} + \frac{400}{1.01^2} + \frac{400}{1.01^3} + \ldots \frac{400}{1.01^{240}}$$

Using our earlier formula for PV

$$PV = a \times \frac{1 - r^n}{1 - r}$$

i.e. $\quad PV = \dfrac{£400}{1.01} \times \dfrac{1 - \left(\dfrac{1}{1.01}\right)^{240}}{1 - \left(\dfrac{1}{1.01}\right)}$

$$PV = £396.04 \times \frac{1 - 0.0918}{1 - 0.9901}$$

$$PV = £396.04 \times \frac{0.9082}{0.0099}$$

$$PV = £396.04 \times 91.7374$$

$$\underline{PV = £36{,}331.6}$$

I can therefore afford a mortgage of £36,331.6

REVIEW QUESTIONS

9.1 A company is required by the terms of a contract to signal its ability to pay by depositing a sum of £20,500 in a bank for the duration of a contract lasting 3 years, which it can reclaim, with interest, at the end of the contract period. What will be the sum available to the company on completion of the contract if the compound interest rate is fixed at 12 per cent per annum?

9.2 The interest quoted to a small business for a short-term loan of 1 year is 2.5 per cent per month. What is the annual percentage rate (APR)?

9.3 A sole trader wishes to purchase a vehicle for the business and is quoted an annual percentage rate of interest of 22.9 per cent on a loan of £12,000 over 3 years. Calculate:

(a) the interest paid on the loan.
(b) the total cost of the loan if repayment is made over $2\frac{1}{2}$ years at the monthly equivalent interest rate of 1.73 per cent (= 22.9 per cent APR).
(c) the difference in the amount of interest paid between (a) and (b).

9.4 A manager of a graphics company has to decide whether to accept an offer of a final cash payment, in respect of copyright, of £96,600 in 4 years from Waffle plc or one from Blarney plc offering £105,000 after 5 years. Calculate the present value of each option if the interest rate is fixed at 8.5 per cent over the lifetime of the agreement. Which option should be accepted?

9.5 A company has just purchased a new machine as part of its plastic moulding production line for £147,000. This particular part of the process is expected to have a productive life of 8 years and yield a scrap value of £20,000.

(a) Use the straight line method to find the annual depreciation.
(b) What would the annual depreciation be if the asset had a scrap value of £40,000?
(c) Using the reducing balance method, what is the book value of the asset after 8 years if the rate of depreciation is estimated at 18 per cent?
(d) Using the reducing balance method, what rate of depreciation is required to give a depreciated value of £40,000?

9.6 After conducting a preliminary analysis a large company has identified three investment opportunities. The initial capital outlay and revenue flows from each project (in £m) were:

Year	Project A	Project B	Project C
0	−24.00	−20.00	−15.50
1	0.02	0.09	1.29
2	3.38	3.86	4.76
3	5.98	6.81	7.21
4	7.82	8.94	8.64
5	8.90	10.25	9.05
6	9.22	10.74	8.44
7	8.78	10.41	6.81
8	7.58	9.26	4.16
9	5.62	7.29	0.49

The financial director's team considered that an interest rate of 8.25 per cent would be a prudent figure on which to appraise the three investment opportunities.

(a) Which project would be chosen using the pay-back method?
(b) What is the average rate of return on each of the projects?
(c) Which project would be chosen using net present value (discounted cash flow)?
(d) Calculate the internal rate of return for each project.
(e) Plot the respective NPV curves on a diagram. Is there any conflict between the NPV and IRR criteria? Explain your answer.

9.7 A company is considering investing in a new production line at a cost of £450,000. The projected end of year profits from installing the new line are as follows:

Year	Profit (£000)
1	−15
2	105
3	105
4	105
5	105
6	105
7	105
8	105
9	105
10	105

Calculate the NPV of the project if the discount rate is 13.5 per cent. If the discount rate increased to 14 per cent what effect would it have on the project?

Note: Answers can be found on pp. 432–44.

Further study and data

Texts

Bancroft, G. and O'Sullivan, G. (1993), *Quantitative methods for accounting and business studies*, 3rd edn, McGraw Hill, chapter 3.

Curwin, J. and Slater, R. (1996), *Quantitative methods for business decisions*, 4th edn, Chapman and Hall, chapter 9.

Lawson, M., Hubbard, S. and Pugh, P. (1995), *Maths and statistics for business*, Addison Wesley Longman, chapter 14.

Morris, C. (1996), *Quantitative approaches in business studies*, 4th edn, Pitman, chapter 16.

Oakshott, L. (1996), *Essential elements of quantitative methods*, BPP, chapter 2.

Swift, L. (1997), *Mathematics and statistics for business*, Management and Finance, part B3.

Thomas, R. (1997), *Quantitative methods for business studies*, Prentice Hall, chapter 4.

Waters, D. (1997), *Quantitative methods*, 2nd edn, Addison Wesley Longman, chapter 7.

Wisniewski, M. with Stead, R. (1996), *Foundation quantitative methods for business*, Pitman, chapter 14.

Sources of information and data

The Reports and Accounts of individual companies may be useful here. See also the list at the end of Chapter 1 (p. 25).

CHAPTER 10

Linear programming and break – even analysis

Objectives

By the end of this chapter you should be able to:

▶ appreciate how **linear relationships** can be used to solve various business-related problems;

▶ express certain problems in terms of a **linear objective function** to be maximised or minimised;

▶ identify a set of **linear constraints** which will influence maximisation or minimisation outcomes;

▶ solve such **linear programming** problems using both graphical and mathematical techniques;

▶ use linear analysis to identify that level of output and sales which the firm must reach if it is to cover all costs;

▶ solve such **break-even** problems using both graphical and mathematical techniques.

Introduction

In this chapter we concentrate on straight line (*linear*) relationships and their application to resolve various business-related problems. In the next chapter we move on to *non-linear* relationships and their applications.

We have already noted some of the characteristics of linear relationships involving intercept and gradient in Chapters 3 and 4 when we calculated the simple linear least squares line and used it for forecasting. You can also consider the characteristics of linear relationships in more detail in Appendix 1 (p. 306). In the first part of this chapter we seek to maximise or minimise some expression (or function) which is subject to a set of constraints, on the assumption that the key relationships can, for all practical purposes, be regarded as linear. For example, we might seek to find the output which maximises profit for the firm, subject to a set of constraints involving the resources available to the firm (e.g. land, labour and capital) and the processes of production in which they are combined.

When we assume relationships to be linear we are, in effect, assuming that everything is *proportional*. For example, in terms of factor input this means that we assume *constant returns* (double input, double output), and so on. Of course in reality most relationships turn out to be non-linear or non-proportional. Nevertheless there is much empirical evidence to suggest that for relatively small changes in output or input, the assumption of a linear or proportional relationship is a close approximation to reality. It is in this sense that the techniques considered in this chapter can be of practical use to business.

The first part of the chapter looks at **linear programming**, the second part looks at **break-even analysis**.

Answers to the 'Self-check questions', responses to each 'Pause for thought' and answers to the 'Review questions' can be found at the end of the book.

10.1 Linear programming

·····························

As we have noted, **linear programming** involves the use of straight line relationships to maximise or minimise some function, usually called the 'object-ive function'.

Deriving the objective function

We shall use the letter Z to relate to the **objective function**. Suppose we are faced with the following problem:

> A firm can produce two types of a certain product, namely *basic* (B) and *de-luxe* (D). The estimated profit per unit is £10 Basic, and £15 De luxe. How much of each type of product should the firm produce in order to maximise total profit?

The objective function (Z) is here a total profit function, and the intention is to maximise that function. We can express this as:

maximise $Z = 10B + 15D$
    where Z = total profit in £s

Every unit of the basic product (B) adds £10 to total profit (Z); every unit of the de-luxe product (D) adds £15 to total profit (Z).

We can graph this objective function, Z, as shown in Figure 10.1.

The objective function in this example is a *line of constant profit*, sometimes called an *isoprofit line* (iso = constant). It shows the different combinations of output of the two products, B and D, which yield a particular level of profit.

In Figure 10.1 we can note the following:

▶ Z_1 shows the different combinations of output of B and D yielding £150 profit; for example £150 profit could be obtained from 10D and zero B, or 15B and zero D, or any combination of outputs shown on the Z_1 line (e.g. 7.5B and 5D).

▶ Z_2 shows the different combinations of output of B and D yielding £300 profit; for example £300 profit could be obtained from 20D and zero B, or 30B and zero D, or any combination of outputs shown on the Z_2 line (e.g. 15B and 10D).

▶ Z_3 shows the different combinations of output of B and D yielding £450 profit; for example £450 profit could be obtained from 30D and zero B, or 45B and zero D, or any combination of outputs shown on the Z_3 line (e.g. 22.5B and 15D).

We can note the following properties from graphing the objective function, Z.

▶ The *slope* of the objective function, Z, is given by the relative profitability of the two products.

$$\text{Slope of Z} = \frac{\text{profitability of D}}{\text{profitability of B}} = \frac{P_D}{P_B} = \frac{15}{10} = \frac{3}{2}$$

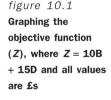

figure 10.1
**Graphing the
objective function
(*Z*), where *Z* = 10B
+ 15D and all values
are £s**

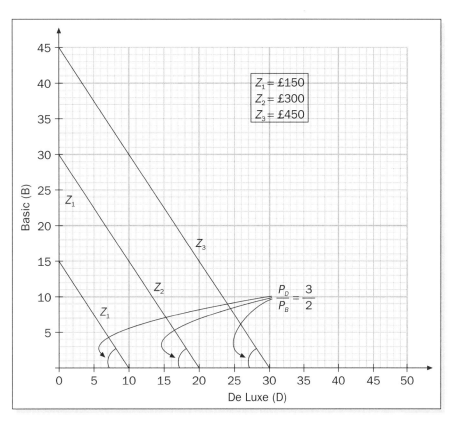

▶ The *position* of the objective function, *Z*, is given by the total profitability from producing the two products.

Notice from Figure 10.1 that successively higher values for *Z*, the objective function, are obtained by shifting the *Z* line outwards from the origin and parallel to itself.

> The further from the origin is the *Z* line representing the objective function, the greater is its value.

Deriving the structural constraints

Of course a firm will only be interested in combinations of output which are *feasible*, i.e. which can actually be produced given the limited resources available to the firm. For example, the firm is only likely to have limited amounts of, say, land, labour and capital equipment available for the production process. In other words, the firm must seek to maximise (or minimise) its objective function (here profit) subject to a set of constraints which reflect both the limited resources available and the production processes which determine the amounts in which those resources must be combined.

figure 10.2
Graphing the constraints as equalities

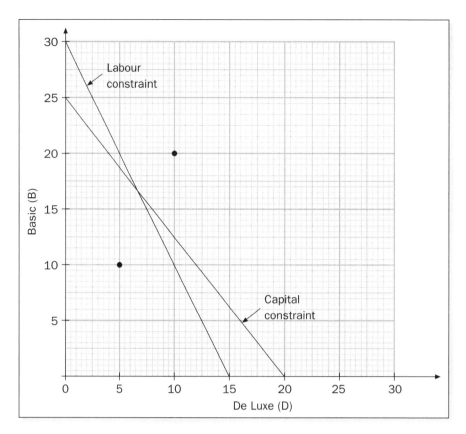

Suppose our firm must allocate a certain amount of labour and capital between the basic (B) and de-luxe (D) products. If it uses more resources for one type of product, then less are available for the other type of product. Suppose the situation facing the firm is as follows.

> The firm has 60 hours of labour available per day and 100 units of capital. Each unit of basic product (B) requires two hours of labour and four units of capital. Each unit of de-luxe product (D) requires four hours of labour and five units of capital.

We can summarise the **structural constraints** facing the firm by using inequalities.

$2B + 4D \leq 60$ . . . **labour constraint**

$4B + 5D \leq 100$ . . . **capital constraint**

In other words the *feasible* combinations of products B and D must involve using less than or equal to the 60 hours of labour actually available in total. Similarly, the *feasible* combinations of products B and D must involve using less than or equal to the 100 units of capital actually available in total.

We can graph these *inequalities*, as in Figure 10.2. The constraint lines we draw for labour and capital correspond to the equals sign in each inequality.

The labour constraint line

For example, if we use *all* our 60 hours of labour available per day on the Basic product (B) we can produce 30 units of B, but zero D ($30 \times 2 + 0 \times 4 = 60$). At the other extreme, if we use *all* our 60 hours of labour available per day on the De-luxe product (D), we can produce 15 units of D, but zero of B ($15 \times 4 + 0 \times 2 = 60$). The labour constraint line between these two extremes represents all other combinations of B and D which use *all* our labour resources when we produce some of each product, e.g. 20B, 5D ($20 \times 2 + 5 \times 4 = 60$) or 10B, 10D ($10 \times 2 + 10 \times 4 = 60$), etc.

Notice that it is feasible to produce any combination *on or inside* the labour constraint line. A point inside the line such as 10B and 5D is certainly feasible, but will only use up 40 hours of labour ($10 \times 2 + 5 \times 4$), which is less than the 60 hours available. Any point inside the labour constraint line corresponds to using less than the total labour available.

Notice also that it is not feasible to produce any combination *outside* the labour constraint line. A point outside the line such as 20B, 10D would use up 80 hours of labour ($20 \times 2 + 10 \times 4$), which is more than the 60 hours available.

In summary, as regards the labour constraint line, we can say:

▶ combinations of products *on* the constraint line use up *all* the resources available and are feasible;
▶ combinations of products *inside* the constraint line use up *less than* the total resources available and are feasible;
▶ combinations of products *outside* the constraint line use up *more than* the total resources available and are not feasible.

The capital constraint line

We can repeat this reasoning and draw the capital constraint line, as in Figure 10.2. This shows that if our firm uses *all* its 100 units of capital per day it can produce the combinations of products B and D *on* the capital constraint line. For example 25B, 0D ($25 \times 4 + 0 \times 5 = 100$), or 12.5B, 10D ($12.5 \times 4 + 10 \times 5 = 100$), or 0B, 20D ($0 \times 4 + 20 \times 5 = 100$).

PAUSE FOR THOUGHT 10.1   *Use Figure 10.2 to check that combinations of B and D inside the capital constraint line are feasible, but use up less than the 100 units of capital available (e.g. check B = 10, D = 5).*

Use Figure 10.2 to check that combinations of B and D outside the capital constraint line are not feasible, as they use up more than the 100 units of capital available (e.g. check B = 20, D = 10)

Feasible region

The **feasible region** of production for the firm corresponds to those combinations of products B and D which meet *all* the production constraints faced by the firm, in this case both labour and capital constraints.

In Figure 10.3, the feasible region is shaded and corresponds to area OVWX. All combination of product on or inside this area are feasible.

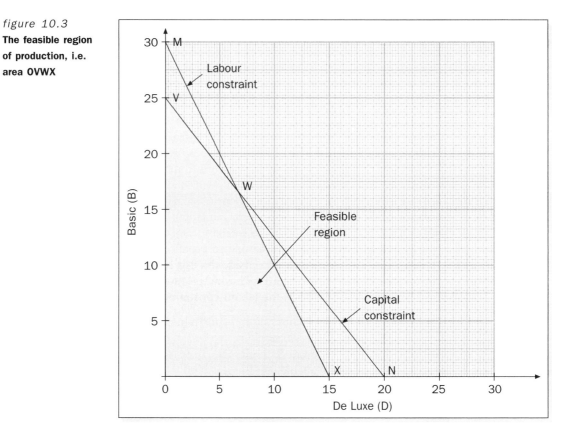

figure 10.3

**The feasible region
of production, i.e.
area OVWX**

Can you see why the following combinations of product are not *feasible?*

▶ Combinations *inside* MVW
▶ Combinations *inside* WXN
▶ Combinations to the right of segment MWN

Non-negative constraints

In linear programming it is usual to limit the analysis to zero or positive outputs (here of B and D) only. These **non-negative constraints** are expressed as:

$B \geq 0, D \geq 0$

If we put all the parts of the linear programme involving basic (B) and de-luxe (D) products together, we have the following problem.

Maximise $Z = 10B + 15D$ . . . objective function

Subject to:
$2B + 4D \leq 60$ . . . labour constraint
$4B + 5D \leq 100$ . . . capital constraint
$B \geq 0, D \geq 0$ non-negative constraints

10.2 Solving the linear programme: maximisation

A solution to a linear programme involving *maximisation*, is to find the value of the straight line representing Z (the objective function) which is furthest from the origin but still feasible. We have noted (p. 225) that as the objective function moves further from the origin it increases in value. However only combinations of product which can actually be produced (i.e. which are *feasible*) are of interest to the firm. The maximisation solution must therefore involve a *tangency* (just touching) between the objective function of Figure 10.1 and the feasible region of Figure 10.3.

Corner point solutions

Because all relationships are *linear*, any tangency between the objective function and the feasible region must occur at one (or more) of the corner points. In terms of Figure 10.3, the tangency solution must occur at one of the corner points V, W or X or along segment VW or segment WX (i.e. involving two corner points in each of these cases). In any event, if we find the value of the objective function at each and every corner point in the feasible region, we must have found the maximum value for Z.

Let us illustrate this idea by solving for Z at each of the corner points in Figure 10.3.

Value of Z at corner point V
We know, from Figure 10.3, that the co-ordinates of corner point V are zero D and 25B. We can find the value of Z at this corner point by substituting these co-ordinates directly into the Z function.

$Z_v = 10B + 15D$

$Z_v = 10(25) + 15(0)$

$Z_v = £250$

Value of Z at corner point X
Similarly, we know from Figure 10.3 that the co-ordinates of corner point X are 15D and 0B. We can therefore find the value of Z at this corner point by substituting these co-ordinates directly into the Z function.

$Z_x = 10B + 15D$

$Z_x = 10(0) + 15(15)$

$Z_x = £225$

Value of Z at corner point W
The value of Z at corner point W requires a little more effort to solve! We have two options:

(i) Draw a **precise graph** so that we can read off the co-ordinates at which the two constraints (labour and capital) intersect.

(ii) Use simple **simultaneous equations** (see Appendix 1, p. 300) to solve for the co-ordinates at W. This can easily be done since two constraint lines, each represented by an equation, have the *same value* in B and D at the point of intersection.

If we use approach (ii), we can say that these two equations must solve simultaneously.

(1) . . . $2B + 4D = 60$ . . . labour constraint

(2) . . . $4B + 5D = 100$ . . . capital constraint

Here we can multiply equation (1) by 2 and then subtract the two equations, thereby eliminating B.

(1) $\times$ 2 . . . $4B + 8D = 120$

(2) $\quad$ . . . $\underline{4B + 5D = 100}$

Subtracting $\quad 3D = 20$

$$D = \frac{20}{3} = 6\frac{2}{3}$$

We can now substitute this value for D into either equation, and solve for B.

From (1) $2B + 4(6\frac{2}{3}) = 60$

$$2B + 26\frac{2}{3} = 60$$

$$2B = 60 - 26\frac{2}{3}$$

$$2B = 33\frac{1}{3}$$

$$B = 16\frac{2}{3}$$

The co-ordinates at corner point W are therefore $D = 6\frac{2}{3}$, $B = 16\frac{2}{3}$.

We can now solve for Z at W.

$Z_w = 10B + 15D$

$Z_w = 10(16\frac{2}{3}) + 15(6\frac{2}{3})$

$Z_w = 166\frac{2}{3} + 100$

$Z_w = £266\frac{2}{3}$

Clearly, the objective function, Z, reaches its maximum value at corner point W. This implies that the profit-maximising firm should produce a daily output of $16\frac{2}{3}$ basic items (B) and $6\frac{2}{3}$ de-luxe items (D). If only whole units are possible in terms of production, then this will round downwards to 16B and 6D.

Figure 10.4 summarises the previous analysis graphically. The Z function reaches its maximum value (i.e. is furthest from the origin) at the combination of products given by corner point W. The value of the Z function in this case is £266$\frac{2}{3}$.

Using the simultaneous equation method will usually provide a more accurate solution for the co-ordinates of a corner point which cannot be observed directly from a sketch diagram.

figure 10.4
Finding a corner point to maximise Z

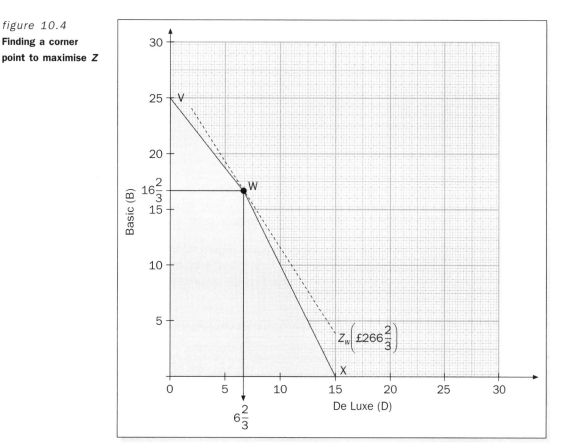

Worked Example 1 uses the above approach for solving a linear programming problem. This problem again involves maximisation, but this time with *three* structural constraints.

Any solution always involves the following four stages.

▶ Identifying the relevant variables in the problem.
▶ Expressing the objective function.
▶ Stating the structural and non-negative constraints.
▶ Solving the problem.

WORKED
EXAMPLE **10.1**
••••••••••••••••

A firm uses three types of factor input, namely labour, capital and raw material in producing two products, *X* and *Y*. Each unit of *X* contributes £20 to profit, each unit of *Y* contributes £30 to profit. To produce one unit of *X* requires one unit of labour, one unit of capital and two units of raw material. To produce one unit of *Y* requires one unit of labour, two units of capital, and one unit of raw material. The firm has 50 units of labour, 80 units of capital and 80 units of raw material available.

Use a linear programming approach to find the feasible output combination of products *X* and *Y* which will maximise profit for the producer. What is the value of total profit at this combination?

Solution

Set out as a linear programming problem

Maximise $Z = 20X + 30Y$ objective function

Subject to:

$1X + 1Y \leq 50$ . . . labour constraint

$1X + 2Y \leq 80$ . . . capital constraint

$2X + 1Y \leq 80$ . . . raw material constraint

$X \geq 0,\ Y \geq 0$ . . . non-negative constraints

It is always useful to draw a diagram (Figure 10.5) to represent the feasible region. Using graph paper will help this drawing to be more accurate even if we subsequently use algebra (simultaneous equations) to solve for the co-ordinates of some of the corner points.

figure 10.5
Graphing the constraints as equalities to find the feasible region

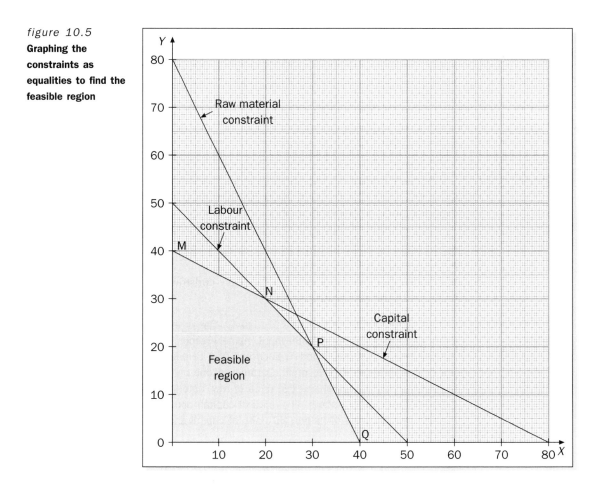

As we can see, the *feasible region* which meets all the constraints is given by area OMNPQ in Figure 10.5.

We now solve for Z, the objective function, at each of the *corner points* of the feasible region.

The value of Z is easiest to solve at corner points M and Q, since the co-ordinates are known for these corner points.

Value of *Z* at M ($X = 0$, $Y = 40$)

$Z_m = 20(0) + 30(40)$

$\underline{Z_m = £1{,}200}$

Value of *Z* at Q ($X = 40$, $Y = 0$)

$Z_Q = 20(40) + 30(0)$

$\underline{Z_Q = £800}$

Value of *Z* at N

We can find the co-ordinates at N *either* by a precise graph or by using simultaneous equations. Here we use the latter approach.

Two lines intersect at N, i.e. have the same (simultaneous) values in terms of X and Y at N. These intersecting lines are the equalities for the labour and capital constraints.

$(1) \ldots 1X + 1Y = 50$ labour constraint

$(2) \ldots \underline{1X + 2Y = 80}$ capital constraint

subtracting $-Y = -30$ so $\underline{Y = 30}$

substituting $Y = 30$ in equation (1)

$\qquad 1X + 30 = 50$

$\qquad\qquad \underline{X = 20}$

$\qquad\qquad Z_N = 20(20) + 30(30)$

$\qquad\qquad \underline{Z_N = £1{,}300}$

Value of *Z* at P

Here the two lines which intersect are the equalities for the labour and raw material constraints.

$\qquad (1) \ldots 1X + 1Y = 50 \ldots$ labour constraint

$\qquad (2) \ldots 2X + 1Y = 80 \ldots$ raw material constraint

$(1) \times 2 \qquad (3) \ldots 2X + 2Y = 100$

$(2) - (3) \qquad\qquad -1Y = -20$

$\qquad\qquad\qquad \underline{Y = 20}$

substituting $Y = 20$ in equation (1)

$$1X + 20 = 50$$

$$\underline{X = 30}$$

$$Z_p = 20(30) + 30(20)$$

$$Z_p = 600 + 600$$

$$\underline{Z_p = £1,200}$$

Clearly the objective function Z is a maximum at £1,300 at corner point N, when the firm produces 20 units of product X and 30 units of product Y.

ACTIVITY **7**
••••••••••••

Many of the linear programming problems are relatively simple to solve graphically and algebraically. Larger problems with many constraints, however, are time consuming to solve but can be handled with relative ease using *Excel*. The example below provides a good basis to explore the procedure.

A firm makes two models: basic and deluxe. Both pass through three production processes which take the following times to complete:

	Process I	*Process II*	*Process III*
Basic (b)	12 mins	10 mins	10 mins
DeLuxe (d)	16 mins	10 mins	20 mins

Both **Processes I and III** are available for eight hours per day (480 minutes) but **Process II** is available for ten hours per day (600 minutes). The contribution to profit of each model is £5.50 for the basic model and £9.50 for the deluxe model.

If the firm's objective is to maximise profit find out how many of each model should be produced each day.

Let b = *basic and* d = *deluxe then:*

Maximise

$z = 5.5b + 9.5d$ . . . **the linear objective function**

Subject to:

Process I $12b + 16d \leq 480$
Process II $10b + 10d \leq 600$ **the linear structural constraints**
Process III $10b + 20d \leq 480$

and

$b \geq 0, d \geq 0$ . . . **the non-negativity constraints**

The following solution is illustrated using the 'Solver' tool in *Excel*.

The first stage is to prepare for the optimisation process as follows:

1   Set up the maximising table:

Label three cells: **Model   Contribution   Quantity**.

Place the coefficients of the objective function into the **Contribution** column, i.e. 5.5 and 9.5.

Set any value in the **Quantities** column (they will change), 0 is the simplest option for the initial entry.

For ease of reading, label the corresponding rows with the terms from the objective function, i.e. **b (basic)** and **d (deluxe)**

2　Translate the objective function into a spreadsheet formula:

From $z = 5.5b + 9.5d$

to　　=**(B4*C4)+(B5*C5)**

if　　**A3 to C5** contains the maximising table.

3　Construct a table of linear structural constraints − for this you need three columns:

Label cells in the last two rows of the constraints table:　**Constraints Quantities**.

The next three rows calculate the constraints, i.e. $12b + 16d$ etc.

Use the cells that contains the quantities of b and d in your *Excel* formula − even though they still contain zero at this point. Therefore if **A3 to C5** contains the maximising table then the next row should contain three cells as follows:

Process 1　=(12*\$C\$4)+(16*\$C\$5)　480

Enter the respective formulae for the remaining two processes.

4　Your spreadsheet should now resemble:

	A	B	C
3	**Model**	**Contribution**	**Quantities**
4	b	5.5	0
5	d	9.5	0
6			
7			
8	**Objective Function**	0	
9			
10		**Constraints**	**Quantities**
11	Process 1	0	480
12	Process 2	0	600
13	Process 3	0	480

5　From the **Tools** on menu bar select **Solver**.

6　Complete the entry boxes:

Set target cell to:　　　. . . the cell that contains the objective function (B8 in the above)

Equal to:　　　　　　　. . . as the aim is to maximise the objective function select **Max**

By changing cells:　　　. . . The values that can be changed are the quantities of b and d, i.e. the values in cells **C4** & **C5**.

Subject to the constraints: . . . Click the Add icon and enter all the constraints including the non-negativity constraints, e.g. **\$B\$11 <= \$C\$11**, etc.

When you have finished entering all five constraints (three process and two non-negativity) enter **OK**.

Finally, click on the **Options** icon and ensure that the **Assume linear model** is selected – leave the other options in their default setting.

The Solver dialogue box should now resemble:

Select **Solve**

7 A menu box entitled **Solver Results** will appear and as we are at this level not carrying out any sensitivity analysis select **Keep Solver** Solution and press the **OK** icon

8 You should find the optimal solution as:

Profit maximise when we produce 12 *deluxe* and 24 *basic* units

Profit will be £246.

10.3 Solving the linear programme: minimisation
••

The procedure for solving a **minimisation** problem by linear programming is essentially the same as that for a maximisation problem. The solution will involve a tangency between an objective function, Z, and one or more corner points of a feasible region.

However a number of differences can usefully be noted.

▶ The minimum value for the objective function will involve a line which is feasible but *nearest to the origin* and therefore of lowest value.
▶ The feasible region will reflect inequalities of the *greater than or equal to* variety; in other words the feasible region will include combinations on or to the right of the structural constraints.

A worked example will help illustrate these points.

WORKED
EXAMPLE **10.2**
••••••••••••••••

A travel company operates two types of vehicle, A and B. Vehicle A can carry 40 passengers and 30 tons of baggage; vehicle B can carry 60 passengers but only 15 tons of baggage. The travel company is contracted to carry at least 960 passengers and 360 tons of baggage per journey. If vehicle A costs £1,000 to operate per journey and vehicle B costs £1,200 to operate per journey, what choice of vehicles will minimise the total cost per journey?

Solution

We can set out the problem as a linear programme.

Minimise $Z = 1{,}000A + 1{,}200B$

where Z = total cost (£'s)

subject to:

$40A + 60B \geq 960$ . . . passenger constraint

$30A + 15B \geq 360$ . . . baggage constraint

$A \geq 0,\ B \geq 0$ . . . non-negative constraints

figure 10.6
**Solving a
minimisation problem**

We can graph the *objective function* as in Figure 10.6(a) and the *feasible region* as in Figure 10.6(b).

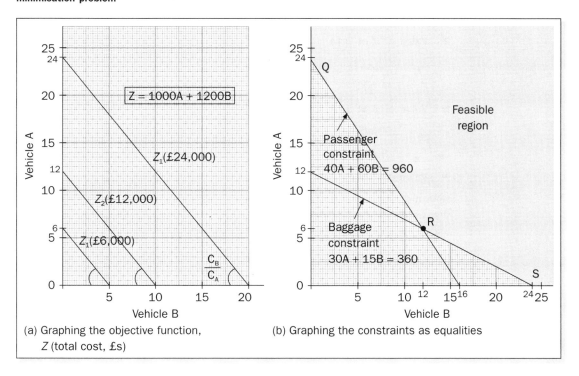

(a) Graphing the objective function, Z (total cost, £s)

(b) Graphing the constraints as equalities

As before, Figure 10.6(a) indicates that the *position* of the objective function Z (total cost in £s) depends on its value, and the *slope* of the objective function depends on the relative costs (profits in the previous example) of the two products $\left(\dfrac{C_B}{C_A} = \dfrac{1{,}200}{1{,}000} = \dfrac{6}{5} \right).$

We can see that the nearer to the origin is the line representing the Z function, the lower is its value. So, for example, total cost (Z) is £6,000 when the firm uses 6 vehicles of type A and zero vehicles of type B, or 5 vehicles of type B and zero vehicles of type A, or any combination of vehicles given by points along the Z_1 line.

Of course the solution to the minimisation linear programme will involve the corner point (or points) which gives the lowest value for Z, total cost, but which is *feasible* in terms of meeting the various constraints. In this problem, the solution will be that combination of vehicle inputs which can meet the passenger and baggage constraints at lowest total cost to the travel company.

Figure 10.6(b) graphs these passenger and baggage constraints as equalities. The company must *meet or better* these constraints ($\geq$) giving the shaded area to the right of the constraint lines as the *feasible region* of combinations of vehicle inputs.

PAUSE FOR THOUGHT 10.3   *Check that any combination of vehicle inputs below and to the left of the segment QRS fails to meet one or both constraints.*

The value of the objective function, Z, will be at a minimum at one or more of the corner points, i.e. at Q, R or S respectively.

▶ **Value of Z at Q (A = 24, B = 0)**

$Z_Q = 1,000(24) + 1,200(0)$

$\underline{Z_Q = £24,000}$

▶ **Value of Z at S (A = 0, B = 24)**

$Z_S = 1,000(0) + 1,200(24)$

$\underline{Z_S = £28,800}$

▶ **Value of Z at R**

Here the coordinates are, as yet, unknown unless our graph is drawn precisely so that we can read off the coordinates directly from the graph. Even then, we can use simultaneous equations to solve the coordinates at R.

We have two lines which intersect at point R, i.e. which have the same (simultaneous) values of A and B at point R.

(1) . . . $40A + 60B = 960$ . . . passenger constraint

(2) . . . $30A + 15B = 360$ . . . baggage constraint

Multiplying equation (2) by 4 gives equation (3).

(3) $120A + 60B = 1,440$

(1) − (3) $-80A = -480$

$$A = \frac{-480}{-80} = 6$$

$$\underline{A = 6}$$

Subtracting equation (3) from equation (1) eliminates B and gives the solution A = 6.

Substituting A = 6 in equation (1)

$$40(6) + 60B = 960$$

$$60B = 960 - 240$$

$$60B = 720$$

$$\underline{B = 12}$$

So the co-ordinates of corner point R, are A = 6, B = 12.

The value of Z at point R is:

$$Z_R = 1,000(6) + 1,200(12)$$

$$\underline{Z_R = £20,400}$$

Clearly the company can minimise its total cost by providing six vehicles of type A and 12 vehicles of type B per journey. This will cost the company £20,400, which is the lowest feasible total cost given that 960 passengers and 360 tons of baggage must be carried per journey.

SELF-CHECK QUESTIONS

10.1 (i) From the following information construct a linear programme to maximise profit and interpret the results:

A company manufactures two products, A and B.
Profits per unit are: A £4 and B £3.
Total labour hours available are 110 hours.
Labour required per unit is: A, 1 hour and B, 2 hours.
Production capacity limitations are: 70 units of A, 150 units of B (i.e. output of the respective products cannot exceed these levels given restrictions on production capacity).

(ii) Owing to uncertainty about aspects of the information in (i) above, you are required to carry out a simple sensitivity test of the results obtained in (i) and to state your findings in each of the following cases:

(a) A £1 decrease in profits per unit for B.
(b) A ten hour increase in total labour hours available.
(c) A 10 per cent increase in labour hours required per unit of A.

Treat each case separately in relation to the solution you obtained in (i).

10.2 A firm manufacturing a particular foodstuff uses two inputs, *X* and *Y*, in producing each unit of output. Each unit of input *X* costs £2, each unit of input *Y* costs £3.

Each unit of input *X* provides 1 gram of protein and 1 gram of vitamins, whereas each unit of input *Y* provides 1 gram of protein and 2 grams of vitamins. Each unit of output must contain at least 10 grams of protein and at least 14 grams of vitamins.

What combination of these inputs, *X* and *Y*, will minimise the firm's total costs of production while still meeting the protein and vitamin requirements?

Note: Answers can be found on p. 356.

10.4 Break-even Analysis

A further application of the linear principle involves **break-even analysis**. The idea here is to find that level of output which the firm must achieve if it is to 'break-even', i.e. to cover all its costs.

Check that you are familiar with the following definitions of revenue, cost and profit from your studies in business economics or related modules. As we shall see, these definitions are widely used in break-even analysis:

▶ **Total revenue** = price × quantity sold

$$\text{i.e.} \quad \text{TR} = \text{P} \times \text{Q}$$

▶ **Average revenue** = revenue per unit sold

$$\text{i.e.} \quad \text{AR} = \frac{\text{TR}}{\text{Q}} = \text{P}$$

▶ **Total cost** = total fixed cost + total variable cost

$$\text{i.e.} \quad \text{TC} = \text{TFC} + \text{TVC}$$

▶ **Total profit** = total revenue − total cost

$$\text{i.e.} \quad \text{TP} = \text{TR} - \text{TC}$$

We also use these definitions further in chapter 11. Here, however, we should notice that at the break-even level of output, total revenue exactly equals total cost so that total profit is zero.

At break-even output

$$\text{TR} = \text{TC}$$

$$\text{i.e.} \quad \text{TR} = \text{TFC} + \text{TVC}$$

$$\text{and} \quad \text{TP} = \text{TR} - \text{TC} = 0$$

Types of cost

▶ **Fixed costs** These are costs that *do not* vary with output, and are sometimes called 'overheads'. Costs such as business rates, lighting, heating are often regarded as fixed costs. Fixed costs are incurred before production begins and are unchanged thereafter.

▶ **Variable costs** These are costs that *do* vary with output, and are sometimes called 'running costs'. Costs such as wages, raw materials, energy are often regarded as variable costs.

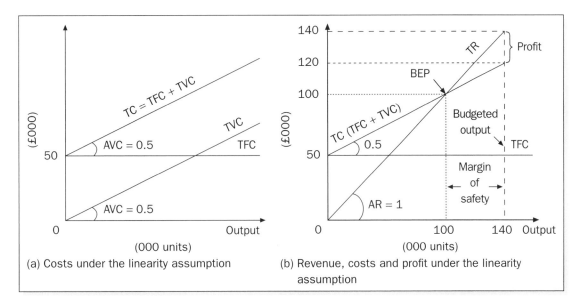

(a) Costs under the linearity assumption

(b) Revenue, costs and profit under the linearity assumption

figure 10.7

Aspects of
break-even analysis

Costs and linearity

The linearity assumption underlying break-even analysis is reflected in the cost lines of Figure 10.7a)

In this example the firm has:

Total fixed costs (TFC)   = £50,000
Average variable costs (AVC) = £0.50 per unit

Notice that both TFC and TVC are represented by straight lines with *constant* slopes or gradients.

▶   slope of TFC = zero
▶   slope of TVC = AVC = 0.50

You should be familiar with the fact that we obtain the TC line by summing vertically the TFC and TVC lines. The slope of TC will be the same as that for TVC, i.e. 0.5.

Note: Since AVC is constant at £0.5 per unit, *marginal cost* (MC) = AVC in this case. In other words each extra (marginal) unit adds £0.5 to Total Cost, which is the same as the £0.5 AVC per unit.

Revenue and linearity

Figure 10.7(b) reproduces the cost lines of Figure 10.7(a), together with a total revenue (TR) line drawn on the assumption that the firm can sell each unit at a price (AR) of £1.

Of course the TR then has a slope (= AR) of 1 and an intercept of zero (since zero output means zero revenue).

NB. Since price (AR) is constant at £1 per unit, *marginal revenue* (MR) = AR in this case. In other words each extra (marginal) unit adds £1 to Total Revenue, which is the same as the £1 AR per unit.

Break-even point (BEP)

The **break-even point** (BEP) is often defined as that level of output for which all costs are covered;

i.e. where TR = TC so that TP = zero.

In Figure 10.7(b) we can see that BEP occurs at an output of 100,000 units.

Check

▶   TR = P × Q = £1 × 100,000 = £100,000

▶   TC = TFC + TVC

TFC = £50,000

TVC = AVC × Q

TVC = £0.5 × 100,000

TVC = £50,000

i.e. TC = £50,000 + £50,000 = £100,000

▶   TP = TR − TC

i.e. TP = £100,000 − £100,000

TP = £0

Clearly we can solve for BEP either:

(a) using graphical analysis
(b) using simple algebra

Even if we use graphical analysis, simple algebra can be a useful check on our solution.

The following expressions will help our calculations of BEP.

Contribution per unit
This tells the firm what each unit of output is contributing (over and above the variable costs of its production) to the fixed costs already incurred.

$$\text{Contribution per unit (C/U)} = \text{Price (AR)} - \text{AVC}$$

We can now express the Break Even Point (BEP) as:

$$\text{BEP} = \frac{\text{Total Fixed Costs}}{\text{Contribution per unit}}$$

In our example:

C/U = £1 − £0.5

C/U = £0.5

$$\text{BEP} = \frac{\text{TFC}}{\text{C/U}} = \frac{£50,000}{£0.5} = 100,000 \text{ units}$$

In other words the firm must produce 100,000 units if it is to earn sufficient revenue over and above its variable costs to cover the £50,000 of fixed costs already incurred.

Budgeted output

Budgeted output is the level of output the firm intends (budgets) to produce. One would normally expect the budgeted output to be *greater than* the BEP.

Suppose the budgeted output in Figure 10.7(b) is 140,000 units. At this budgeted output:

$TR = P \times Q = £1 \times 140,000 = £140,000$

$TC = TFC + TVC$

$\quad = £50,000 + (140,000 \times £0.5)$

$\quad = £50,000 + £70,000 = £120,000$

$TP = TR - TC$

$TP = £140,000 - £120,000$

$\underline{TP = £20,000 \text{ at budgeted output}}$

In other words at a budgeted output of 140,000 units, the firm can expect to earn a total profit (TP) of £20,000, as can be seen on Figure 10.7(b) (p. 241).

Margin of safety

The firm will usually seek to operate with some **margin of safety**, here defined as the difference between budgeted (intended) output and the break-even output.

> Margin of safety = budgeted output – break-even output

In Figure 10.7(b)

Margin of safety = 140,000 – 100,000

$\underline{\text{Margin of safety} = 40,000 \text{ units}}$

The margin of safety is often expressed as a *percentage of the budgeted output*.

> $\text{Margin of safety (\%)} = \dfrac{\text{budgeted output} - \text{BEP}}{\text{budgeted output}} \times 100$

i.e. margin of safety $= \dfrac{40,000}{140,000} \times 100$

$\underline{\text{Margin of safety} = 28.6\%}$

This tells us that the output of the firm can fall by as much as 28.6 per cent *below* its budgeted output and still break even or better.

In other words the margin of safety is a useful measure of *risk*. The larger the margin of safety, the lower the risk of indebtedness should unexpected events cause the firm to fall short of the budgeted output.

Break-even analysis can be used to compare different situations ('scenarios') facing the firm, as in the worked example below.

WORKED
EXAMPLE **10.3**
••••••••••••••

A company sells a product which has a variable cost of £3 a unit. Fixed costs are £10,000. It has been estimated that if the price is set at £5 a unit, the sales volume will be 10,000 units; whereas if the price is reduced to £4 a unit, the sales volume will rise to 15,000.

(a) Draw a break-even chart covering each of the possible sales prices, and state the budgeted profits, the break-even points and the margins of safety.
(b) Compare the two possible situations. Consider the assumptions and limitations of your analysis.

Solution

Figure 10.8 presents a break-even chart with the total revenue line and budgeted output varying depending on the price set.

figure 10.8
**Break-even analysis
under different price
scenarios**

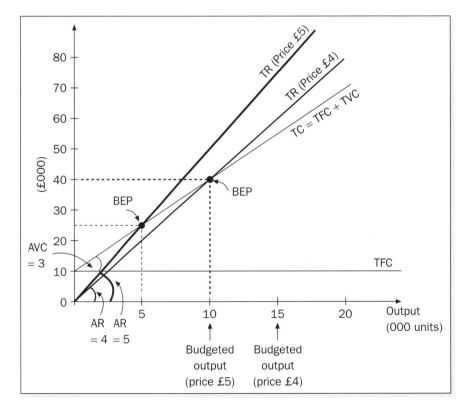

▶ **Price = £5**

Budgeted Profit (at 10,000 units) = TR − TC

$$TR = £5 \times 10,000 = £50,000$$

$$TC = TFC + TVC = £10,000 + (£3 \times 10,000)$$

$$= £40,000$$

i.e. budgeted profit = £50,000 − £40,000 = £10,000

Contribution per unit (C/U) = price − AVC

$$= £5 − £3$$

$$\underline{C/U = £2}$$

$$BEP = \frac{\text{total fixed cost}}{\text{contribution per unit}}$$

$$BEP = \frac{£10,000}{£2}$$

$$\underline{BEP = 5,000 \text{ units}}$$

Margin of safety = budgeted output − BEP

$$= 10,000 − 5,000$$

$$\underline{\text{Margin of safety} = 5,000 \text{ units}}$$

As a percentage:

$$\text{Margin of safety} = \frac{\text{budgeted output} − BEP}{\text{budgeted output}} \times 100$$

$$= \frac{10,000 − 5,000}{10,000} \times 100$$

$$\underline{\text{Margin of safety} = 50\%}$$

In summary, for £5 price scenario

Budgeted profit = £10,000
BEP = 5,000 units
Margin of safety (%) = 50%

▶ **Price = £4**

Budgeted profit (at 15,000 units) = TR − TC

$$TR = £4 \times 15,000 = £60,000$$

$$TC = TFC + TVC = £10,000 + (£3 \times 15,000)$$

$$= £55,000$$

Budgeted profit = £60,000 − £55,000

$$\underline{\text{Budgeted profit} = £5,000}$$

$$\text{Contribution per unit (C/U)} = \text{Price} - \text{AVC}$$

$$= \pounds4 - \pounds3$$

$$\underline{\text{C/U} = \pounds1}$$

$$\text{BEP} = \frac{\text{TFC}}{\text{C/U}}$$

$$\text{BEP} = \frac{\pounds10{,}000}{\pounds1}$$

$$\underline{\text{BEP} = 10{,}000 \text{ units}}$$

$$\text{Margin of safety} = \text{budgeted output} - \text{BEP}$$

$$= 15{,}000 - 10{,}000$$

$$\underline{\text{Margin of safety} = 5{,}000 \text{ units}}$$

As a percentage:

$$\text{Margin of safety} = \frac{\text{budgeted output} - \text{BEP}}{\text{budgeted output}} \times 100$$

$$= \frac{15{,}000 - 10{,}000}{15{,}000} \times 100$$

$$\underline{\text{Margin of safety} = 33.3\%}$$

In summary for £4 price scenario

Budgeted profit = £5,000
BEP = 10,000 units
Margin of safety = 33.3%

The £5 price scenario would appear to be the most attractive for the firm. Setting a price of £5 would give it a higher budgeted profit, a lower break-even point and a higher margin of safety, than would setting a price of £4. The £5 price would seem to be both more profitable and less risky for the firm than the £4 price. As well as an *extra* £5,000 in expected profit, the firm need produce and sell 5,000 *less* units in order to break even. The margin of safety reinforces this aspect of reduced risk, in that at a price of £5 it can experience a fall in its sales of up to 50 per cent below its budgeted (expected) output before losses are actually incurred. In contrast, at a £4 price the firm can only see sales fall 33.3 per cent below expectation before losses are actually incurred.

Of course all this break-even analysis is based on the linearity assumption. This may *not* actually be valid in practice. For example the assumption that variable cost per unit (AVC) is constant at all levels of output may be unrealistic. If various economies of scale occur, then AVC might *fall* as output increases, raising the contribution per unit (price – AVC) at the £4 price scenario with its higher budgeted output. In this case the TVC and TC curves would cease to be straight lines (linear).

Further, the TR curves may not be linear in practice! In order to sell more output it may be that the firm may have to *reduce price*. It may therefore make little sense to draw a TR curve as a straight line with a constant slope representing a given and unchanged price as output varies.

For these and other reasons the break-even analysis may be oversimple. Nevertheless the linearity assumption may have some validity for *relatively small changes in output*, which is often the most likely result of policy changes by a firm.

In this worked example we compared two different *price scenarios*. Of course we could equally compare two different *cost scenarios*, as in Self-check question 10.3 below.

<table>
<tr><td>

**SELF-CHECK
QUESTION**

</td><td>

10.3 A company expects to sell 8,000 units of its product each year at a price of £4 a unit, a variable cost of £2 a unit and fixed costs of £15,000. New technology reduces variable costs to £1.50 a unit but raises fixed costs to £20,000. Budgeted output remains unchanged at 8,000 units per year and price unchanged at £4 a unit.

(a) Draw a break-even chart to compare the situation before and after technical change. Which break-even solution might the company prefer? Explain your reasoning.

(b) Consider the assumptions and limitations of your analysis.

Note: **Answers can be found on p. 359.**

</td></tr>
<tr><td>

**REVIEW
QUESTIONS**

</td><td>

10.1 A farmer can produce potatoes (X) or barley (Y) with his resources. He makes a net profit of £70 per acre of potatoes (X) and £100 per acre of barley (Y). He draws up the following summary statement of his resources and input requirements.

Requirements per acre

Resources	X (potatoes)	Y (barley)	Amount available
Labour	12 man days	3 man days	1,080 man days
Equipment	3 machine days	5 machine days	450 machine days
Land	1 acre	1 acre	100 acres

Find the number of acres he should devote to each product in order to maximise total net profit. What is his net profit in this situation?

10.2 A confectionery company makes among other products, two similar brands of sweet marketed as Rockets (R) and Starships (S). Both contain a colouring agent, E132 and an anti-oxidant, E320.

Each Rocket contains 2.5 grams of E132 and 5.0 grams of E320, whereas each Starship contains 5.0 grams of E132 and 2.5 grams of E320. Each Rocket generates a profit of 5.0 pence and each Starship 2.0 pence.

</td></tr>
</table>

For a particular production run, 80 kilograms of E132 and 70 kilograms of E320 are available. Marketing considerations restrict the number of Rockets produced to no more than 10,000 but there is no such restriction on Starships.

How many of each brand would you advise the firm to make in order to maximise its profits on this production run? What will be the level of profit?

10.3 A specialist producer of motorcycles manufactures a 1,500 cc and 2,000 cc version. Each 1,500 cc motorcycle makes a net profit of £3,700 and each 2,000 cc motorcycle makes a net profit of £3,600. Manufacture of these motorcycles involves three key processes. The hours required for each process and the hours available per month are shown below.

Process	Hours required per motorcycle		Hours available per month
	1,500 cc	2,000 cc	
Motorcycle assembly	600	1,200	9,000
Component manufacture	300	300	3,000
Engine shop	900	0	6,300

Use a linear programming approach to find the output mix of the two types of motorcycle which will maximise total net profit. Comment on your results.

10.4 A farmer mixes two foodstuffs, X and Y, to produce his cattle feed. The following table indicates the presence of three types of nutrient in each ton of foodstuff, X and Y.

Units of nutrient per ton of foodstuff

Nutrient	X	Y	Total requirement
vitamin	3	10	9 units
protein	3	3	6 units
starch	8	3	12 units

The farmer has received advice as to the total requirement of each type of nutrient he must feed his cattle. This is shown in the last column of the table. He must not fall below these requirements. If each ton of foodstuff X costs £120 and each ton of foodstuff Y costs £110, what combination of X and Y will minimise the total cost of his cattle-feed while meeting his total nutrient requirements?

10.5 A company makes kitchen units with a projected selling price of £600. The variable costs per unit are estimated at £200. The fixed costs are £12,000 for the time period in question.

(a) Find the break-even output.
    If Budgeted Output is 60 units over the time period, estimate the profit earned and the margin of safety.

(b) Suppose a new, more capital intensive manufacturing process is introduced, with a higher fixed cost of £25,000 but a lower variable cost of £100 per unit. Would you recommend adopting the new process if your budgeted output remains at 60 units? Explain your reasoning.

10.6 The costs of producing and selling a particular brand of bicycle are as follows:

Material per unit	£100
Labour per unit	£ 70
Other variable costs per unit	£ 30

The fixed overhead cost is £40,000 for the time period in question. The firm estimates it can sell 500 bicycles per week at a price of £300 each.

(a) Calculate the budgeted profit; break even point and margin of safety.
(b) If the firm estimates it could raise price to £400 and sell 300 bicycles, what would you recommend? Explain your reasoning.
(c) If the firm remains with the pricing strategy in (a) but finds a new, more capital intensive process which raises fixed costs to £60,000 per time period but reduces variable costs to £150 per unit, what would you recommend? Explain your reasoning.

Note: Answers to Review questions can be found on p. 442.

Further study and data
....

Texts

Bancroft, G. and O'Sullivan, G. (1993), *Quantitative methods for accounting and business studies*, 3rd edn, McGraw Hill, chapter 19.
Curwin, J. and Slater, R. (1996), *Quantitative methods for business decisions*, 4th edn, Chapman and Hall, chapter 21.
Lawson, M., Hubbard, S. and Pugh, P. (1995), *Maths and statistics for business*, Addison Wesley Longman, chapter 13.
Morris, C. (1996), *Quantitative approaches in business studies*, 4th edn, Pitman, chapter 18.
Oakshott, L. (1996), *Essential elements of quantitative methods*, BPP, chapter 4.
Swift, L. (1997), *Mathematics and statistics for business, management and finance*, part A5.
Thomas, R. (1997), *Quantitative methods for business studies*, Prentice Hall, chapter 8.
Waters, D. (1997), *Quantitative methods*, 2nd edn, Addison Wesley Longman, chapters 7 and 11.
Wisniewski, M. with Stead, R. (1996), *Foundation quantitative methods for business,* Pitman, chapter 10.

CHAPTER 11

Calculus and business applications

Objectives
· · · · · · · · · · · ·

When you have read this chapter you should be able to:

▶ use the process of *differentiation* to calculate turning points, both maximum and minimum;

▶ apply differentiation to situations involving two variables *and* to situations involving more than two variables (*partial differentiation*);

▶ solve a variety of business related problems using the process of differentiation, such as the output/ price the business must set if it seeks the maximisation of revenue or profit, or the minimisation of cost, etc.;

▶ use the process of *integration* to calculate areas under a curve;

▶ solve a variety of business related problems using the process of integration, such as the total revenue, profit or cost of producing various levels of output, etc.

Introduction
· · · · · · · · · · · · · ·

In this chapter we look at the idea of **calculus** and its application to the solution of a number of business related problems. We have already seen (Chapter 10) how we can find maximum or minimum solutions involving *linear* relationships between variables. Here we see how calculus helps us find maximum or minimum solutions involving *non-linear* relationships between variables.

Calculus can, for our purposes, be regarded as involving two key processes, namely **differentiation** and **integration**. We consider each of these processes separately, beginning with differentiation.

Some basic mathematical techniques are reviewed in Appendix 1 (p. 284) and may help you with this chapter.

Answers to the 'Self-check questions', responses to each 'Pause for thought' and answers to the 'Review questions' can be found at the end of the book.

11.1 Differentiation
· ·

Differentiation refers to the process whereby we calculate the gradient to a curve at any point. Clearly for a *linear function* or equation $y = mx + c$, the gradient, m, is a constant at every point. In Figure A.5 (p. 304) the gradient of the curve $y = 3x + 2$ is clearly $+ 3$ at all points along that curve.

However to find the gradient to a *non-linear function*. We would need to draw a straight line touching the curve at each particular point (the *tangent* to that point) and then find the slope (*gradient*) of that tangent. Clearly in Figure A.6 (a and b, p. 304) gradients to these non-linear (quadratic) functions will be changing at each and every point (i.e. for different values of *x*). It would be extremely tedious to draw and measure the gradients to a large number of points along non-linear functions.

We can short-circuit this whole process by using the technique of *differentiation*. We can then establish a formula which will give the value of the

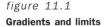

figure 11.1

Gradients and limits

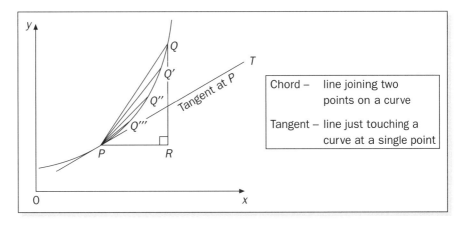

Chord –	line joining two points on a curve
Tangent –	line just touching a curve at a single point

tangent drawn at any point on the curve. This formula is often referred to as the *first derivative* of the curve. So important is this technique to understanding much of the analysis underpinning the solution of business related problems that we shall consider it in some detail.

Gradients and limits

The idea of **limits** is central to understanding the process of differentiation. In fact we shall see that the slope of a *tangent* just touching a curve is in fact the limit of the slope of a *chord* joining two points along that curve. In Figure 11.1 we can connect two separate points on the curve, namely *P* and *Q*, by drawing the straight line *PQ*. This chord can easily be depicted as the hypotenuse of the right-angled triangle *PQR*, and from trigonometry we know that the tan. of angle *QPR* will give us the slope of the chord.

Slope of chord *PQ* = tan. *QPR*

$$= \frac{\text{side opposite}}{\text{side adjacent}}$$

$$= \frac{QR}{PR}$$

PAUSE FOR THOUGHT 11.1   *Can you suggest three other examples illustrating the idea of a limit?*

We can always calculate the slope of a chord since we can find the actual values for *QR* and *PR*. However we cannot actually calculate the slope of a tangent. But what we can do is take the *limit* of the slope of a chord as a close approximation to the slope of a tangent to that point on the curve. It will be useful to use Figure 11.1 to explain this.

As *Q* approaches (gets nearer to) *P* along the curve, the slope of the chord *PQ* gets closer and closer to the slope of the *tangent* at *P*, namely *PT*. Of course another way of expressing the idea of *Q* approaching *P* is to say that *PR* (the base of the triangle) tends to zero, i.e. *PR* → 0. As long as *P* and *Q* are separate

figure 11.2
Process of
differentiation

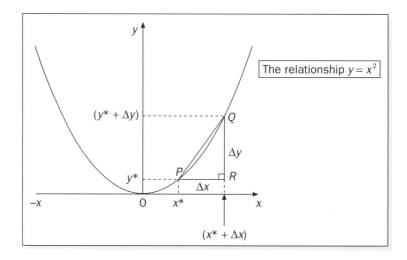

points along the curve, the slope of *PQ* will never actually equal the slope of *PT*, but it will become so close to the value of *PT* that for all intents and purposes it can be regarded as identical. We can use the following shorthand to express this idea (using Figure 11.1 on page 251).

Slope of tangent *PT* = limit to the slope of the chord *PQ*, as *Q* approaches *P*

i.e. Slope of tangent $PT = \lim_{PR \to 0} \left(\dfrac{QR}{PR} \right)$

We now apply these ideas to curves involving the dependent variable *y* and the independent variable *x*. For purposes of illustration we shall use the simple *quadratic* relationship $y = x^2$ as in Figure 11.2. The symbol Δ refers to a *change* in any variable.

We construct a chord *PQ* connecting point *P* (with co-ordinates *x**, *y**) and point *Q* (with co-ordinates $x^* + \Delta x$, $y^* + \Delta y$).

Following our earlier reasoning we can state the following:

$$\text{Slope of tangent to curve at } P = \lim_{PR \to 0} \left(\frac{QR}{PR} \right)$$

$$\text{Slope of tangent to curve at } P = \lim_{\Delta x \to 0} \left(\frac{\Delta y}{\Delta x} \right)$$

$$\text{Slope of tangent to curve at } P = \frac{dy}{dx}$$

The expression $\dfrac{dy}{dx}$ is merely shorthand for the expression directly above it, and is termed the *first derivative*. Put another way we have *differentiated* the variable *y* with respect to *x*. Of course what we have done is to find an expression for the slope of the *tangent* to any point on the curve as being the limit of a known expression for the slope of the *chord* to that curve.

From Figure 11.2 we can show that for the curve $y = x^2$, the first derivative will always be $\dfrac{dy}{dx} = 2x$ at each and every point on that curve. The workings behind this solution are indicated in Box 1 at the end of this chapter (p. 252).

This extremely powerful result tells us that for any given value of x we can find the slope of the tangent to the curve at that point.

Thus for $x = 1$, the slope of the tangent to the curve at $x = 1$ is

$$\frac{dy}{dx} = 2x = 2(1) = 2;$$

for $x = 2$, the slope of the tangent to the curve at $x = 2$ is

$$\frac{dy}{dx} = 2x = 2(2) = 4; \text{ and so on.}$$

If we repeat this process for other curves then we shall see that a *pattern* emerges which forms the basis for an important formula used in differentiation.

Suppose we differentiate (find $\dfrac{dy}{dx}$ for) the curve $y = 3x^2$ using our earlier approach. As we can see from Box 2 at the end of this chapter (p. 252), the solution will be that $\dfrac{dy}{dx} = 6x$.

Thus for $x = 1$, the slope of the tangent to the curve $y = 3x^2$ at $x = 1$ is

$$\frac{dy}{dx} = 6x = 6(1) = 6;$$

for $x = 2$, the slope of the tangent to the curve at $x = 2$ is

$$\frac{dy}{dx} = 6x = 6(2) = 12;$$

and so on.

General Formula for Differentiation

In fact the pattern which will always result from such differentiation will give us the following general formula.

If $y = ax^n$

when a = any constant

x = any variable

n = any power

then $\dfrac{dy}{dx} = nax^{n-1}$

Thus if $y = 1x^2$

$$\frac{dy}{dx} = 2 \cdot 1x^{2-1} = 2x$$

and if $y = 3x^2$

$$\frac{dy}{dx} = 2 \cdot 3x^{2-1} = 6x$$

and so on.

This extremely powerful result will allow us to find (in the limit) the slope of the tangent drawn to any point on a particular curve.

PAUSE FOR THOUGHT 11.2 *Can you suggest what we get if we differentiate, respectively, the equations for the following curves:*

(a) Total cost

(b) Total revenue

(c) Total profit?

SELF-CHECK QUESTIONS

11.1 Use the 'rule' for differentiation to find the gradient ($\frac{dy}{dx}$) to each of the following expressions

(a) $y = 9x$ (b) $y = 4x^2$ (c) $y = 3x^3$ (d) $y = 5x^4$

(e) $y = \dfrac{x^3}{3}$ (i.e. $y = \dfrac{1}{3}x^3$)   (f) $y = \dfrac{x^4}{4}$ (i.e. $y = \dfrac{1}{4}x^4$)

(g) $y = \sqrt{x}$ (i.e. $y = x^{\frac{1}{2}}$)   (h) $y = \sqrt[3]{x}$ (i.e. $y = x^{\frac{1}{3}}$)

(i) $y = \sqrt[3]{x^2}$ (i.e. $y = x^{\frac{2}{3}}$)   (j) $y = 10$ (i.e. $y = 10x^0$)

Note: **question (g) to (h) make use of your knowledge of powers/ indices – see Appendix 1, p. 293).**

11.2 For each of the curves or lines given by the expressions in Question 11.1 above, find the value of the gradient at:

(i) $x = 1$

(ii) $x = 2$

Note: **Answers can be found on p. 360.**

11.2 Turning points
• •

Clearly the ideas of *maxima* and *minima* (i.e. **turning points**) are vital to many business related problems. As we can see from Figure 11.3(a) the value of the first derivative (the gradient) $\frac{dy}{dx}$ will be zero for any turning point, whether maximum or minimum. In other words we can differentiate the equation of the curve $y = x^3$ by finding $\frac{dy}{dx}$. If we plot $\frac{dy}{dx}$ (= $3x^2$) against x, as in Figure 11.3(b), set $\frac{dy}{dx} = 0$ and solve for x, then for a quadratic equation we can expect two solutions for the turning points x_1 and x_2.

Unfortunately we will not, at this stage, be able to distinguish between the maximum and minimum solutions. However by taking second derivatives (i.e. finding the gradient of the gradient), we can distinguish between the different turning points.

figure 11.3
Using differentiation to identify turning points

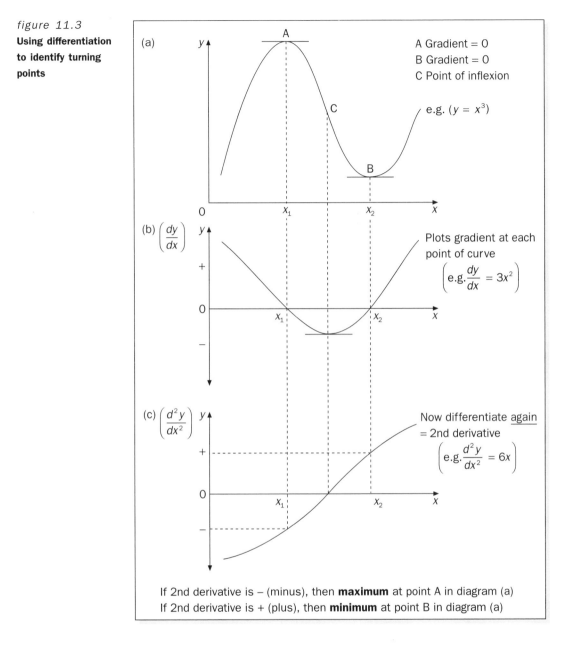

(a)

A Gradient = 0
B Gradient = 0
C Point of inflexion

e.g. $(y = x^3)$

(b) $\left(\dfrac{dy}{dx}\right)$

Plots gradient at each point of curve

$\left(\text{e.g.} \dfrac{dy}{dx} = 3x^2\right)$

(c) $\left(\dfrac{d^2y}{dx^2}\right)$

Now differentiate <u>again</u> = 2nd derivative

$\left(\text{e.g.} \dfrac{d^2y}{dx^2} = 6x\right)$

If 2nd derivative is – (minus), then **maximum** at point A in diagram (a)
If 2nd derivative is + (plus), then **minimum** at point B in diagram (a)

Figure 11.3(c) shows the gradient $\left(\dfrac{dy}{dx}\right)$ of the gradient $\left(\dfrac{dy}{dx}\right)$ already displayed in Figure 11.3(b). This is known as finding the *second derivative* and is expressed as $\dfrac{d^2y}{dx^2}\left(\dfrac{dy}{dx}\text{ of }\dfrac{dy}{dx}\right)$.

▶ Where we have the **maximum** at x_1, the value of the first derivative is zero, and the value of the second derivative (at x_1) is *negative*.

▶ Where we have the **minimum** at x_2, the value of the first derivative is zero, and the value of the second derivative (at x_2) is *positive*.

The following worked example illustrates this approach.

WORKED
EXAMPLE **11.1**
·················

$y = x^3 - 27x + 3$

Find the turning points for this equation.
Distinguish between maximum and minimum turning points.

Solution

$$\frac{dy}{dx} = 0 \text{ at a turning point}$$

i.e. $\dfrac{dy}{dx} = 3x^2 - 27 = 0$ (applying our general formula for differentiation to each term separately)

$$3x^2 = 27$$

$$x^2 = 9$$

$$\underline{x = +3 \text{ or } -3 \text{ are the turning points}}$$

$\dfrac{d^2y}{dx^2} = 6x$ (second derivative, applying $\dfrac{dy}{dx}$ to the previous $\dfrac{dy}{dx}$)

At $x = +3$, second derivative $= +18$

$$\underline{x = +3 \text{ is a minimum}}$$

At $x = -3$, second derivative $= -18$

$$\underline{x = -3 \text{ is a maximum}}$$

PAUSE FOR THOUGHT 11.3 *Can you suggest how this idea of finding turning points might be helpful to managers in achieving their objectives, given that statisticians have worked out equations showing how revenue and cost vary with output?*

SELF-CHECK
QUESTIONS

11.3 Find the maximum and/or minimum turning points for the following curves.

(a) $y = x^2 - 10x + 16$ (b) $y = 9 - 6x + x^2$

(c) $y = 12 + 4x - x^2$ (d) $y = x^3 - 27x + 6$

(e) $y = x^3 - 3x^2$ (f) $y = \dfrac{x^3}{3} - \dfrac{7}{2}x^2 + 12x$

(*Note:* **use your 'rule' to differentiate each term separately, not forgetting the sign in front of each term**).

Note: **Answers can be found on p. 360.**

11.3 Rules for differentiation
· ·

We can set out our earlier 'rule' for differentiating an expression more formally. In all the examples above we were differentiating an expression involving sums (plus signs) or differences (minus signs). However there are other types of expression to which our rule could apply, such as those involving multiplication (product) or division (quotient).

In all the following 'rules' we use the letters u and v to stand for parts of the expression we are differentiating, with each of these parts involving the variable x in some way (i.e. u and v are functions of x).

The derivative of a sum or difference

If $y = u + v$ or $y = u - v$ (where u and v are functions of x)

$$\frac{dy}{dx} = \frac{du}{dx} + \frac{dv}{dx} \text{ or } \frac{dy}{dx} = \frac{du}{dx} - \frac{dv}{dx}$$

WORKED
EXAMPLE **11.2**
· · · · · · · · · · · · · · ·

$y = 2x^4 - 4x^2$

Solution

$$\frac{dy}{dx} = 8x^3 - 8x$$

The derivative of a product

If $y = uv$ (where u and v are functions of x)

$$\frac{dy}{dx} = u\frac{dv}{dx} + v\frac{du}{dx}$$

WORKED
EXAMPLE **11.3**
· · · · · · · · · · · · · · ·

$y = (3x + 1)(3x^2)$ $(u = 3x + 1, \dfrac{du}{dx} = 3$

$v = 3x^2, \dfrac{dv}{dx} = 6x)$

Solution

$$\frac{dy}{dx} = (3x + 1) \cdot (6x) + (3x^2) \cdot (3)$$

$$\frac{dy}{dx} = 18x^2 + 6x + 9x^2$$

$$\frac{dy}{dx} = 27x^2 + 6x$$

The derivative of a quotient

$y = \dfrac{u}{v}$ (where u and v are functions of x)

$$\frac{dy}{dx} = \frac{u\dfrac{dv}{dx} - v\dfrac{du}{dx}}{v^2}$$

WORKED
EXAMPLE **11.4**
················

$y = \dfrac{3x - 2}{5x + 3}$ $[u = 3x - 2, \dfrac{du}{dx} = 3$

$v = 5x + 3, \dfrac{dv}{dx} = 5]$

Solution

$$\frac{dy}{dx} = \frac{(3x - 2) \cdot (5) - (5x + 3) \cdot (3)}{(5x + 3)^2}$$

$$\frac{dy}{dx} = \frac{15x - 10 - 15x - 9}{25x^2 + 30x + 9}$$

$$\frac{dy}{dx} = \frac{-19}{25x^2 + 30x + 9}$$

The derivative of a function of a function

If $y = f(u)$ where $u = f(x)$

$$\frac{dy}{dx} = \frac{dy}{du} \cdot \frac{du}{dx}$$

WORKED
EXAMPLE **11.5**
················

$y = (3x^2 + 2)^4$ $[y = u^4, \dfrac{dy}{du} = 4u^3$

$u = 3x^2 + 2, \dfrac{du}{dx} = 6x]$

Solution

$$\frac{dy}{dx} = 4u^3 \cdot 6x$$

$$= 24x \cdot u^3$$

$$= 24x \cdot (3x^2 + 2)^3$$

11.4 Differentiate each of the following expressions using an appropriate rule

(a) $y = 7x^5 + 3x^2$ (b) $y = 4x^5 - 4x^3$

(c) $y = (2x + 3)(2x^3)$ (d) $y = (3x + 4)(3x^4)$

(e) $y = \dfrac{(2x + 3)}{2x^2}$ (f) $y = \dfrac{4x^2 - 2}{2x^2 + 4}$

(g) $y = (2x^2 + 3)^2$ (h) $y = (3x^3 + 4)^3$

Note: **Answers can be found on p. 362.**

11.4 Applications of differentiation

Revenue, cost and profit

Obviously turning points, involving maximum or minimum outcomes, are likely to have widespread applications in economics or business. These applications make use of some introductory ideas involving revenue, cost or profit.

▶   Total revenue (TR)   = price (average revenue) × quantity

     Average revenue (AR)   = price = $\dfrac{\text{TR}}{\text{quantity}}$

▶   Total cost (TC)   = total fixed cost (TFC) + total variable cost (TVC)

     Average total cost (ATC) = $\dfrac{\text{TC}}{\text{quantity}}$

▶   Total profit (TP)   = total revenue − total cost

Suppose that statisticians employed by a large firm have estimated the demand (average revenue) curve and average total cost curve for the firm as follows

$$D = AR = 21 - x$$

$$ATC = \frac{x^2}{3} - 3x + 9$$

where x = output in units

       AR = average revenue (£)

       ATC = average total cost (£)

The firm can use *differentiation* to find, for example, the output which maximises either total revenue or total profit.

Maximum total revenue

Total Revenue = average revenue (price) × quantity (output)

$$TR = AR \times x$$

$$TR = (21 - x) \times x$$

$$TR = 21x - x^2$$

If we let $y = TR$

then $\dfrac{dy}{dx} = 0$ for a turning point

i.e. $21 - 2x = 0$

$21 = 2x$

$\underline{10.5 = x}$

2nd derivative $= \dfrac{d^2y}{dx^2} = -2$

So the turning point is a maximum since the 2nd derivative is negative.

<u>An output of 10.5 units will maximise total revenue</u>

Maximum total profit

Remember total profit (TP) = total revenue – total cost

Total revenue (TR) = average revenue × quantity (output)

Total cost (TC) = average total cost × quantity (output)

So TR $= (21 - x) \cdot x = 21x - x^2$

$$TC = \left(\dfrac{x^2}{3} - 3x + 9\right) \cdot x = \dfrac{x^3}{3} - 3x^2 + 9x$$

TP = TR – TC

$$TP = [21x - x_2] - \left[\dfrac{x^3}{3} - 3x^2 + 9x\right]$$

$$TP = -\dfrac{x^3}{3} + 2x^2 + 12x$$

If we let y = TP

then $\dfrac{dy}{dx} = 0$ for a turning point

i.e. $-x^2 + 4x + 12 = 0$

$(-x + 6)(x + 2) = 0$ (factorising)

<u>i.e. $x = 6$ and $x = -2$ are the solutions.</u>

Taking the 2nd derivative

$\dfrac{d^2y}{dx^2} = -2x + 4$

▶ when $x = +6$, 2nd derivative is negative (-8)
so $x = +6$ is a maximum
▶ when $x = -2$, 2nd derivative is positive $(+8)$
so $x = -2$ is a minimum.

<u>An output of six units will maximise total profit</u>

The (maximum) Total Profit earned at an output of 6 units is:

$$TP = -\frac{6^3}{3} + 2(6)^2 + 12(6)$$

i.e. $\quad$ TP = −72 + 72 + 72

$\quad$ TP = £72

Price

We can, of course, easily find the *price* at which the above outputs must be sold. Remember price = average revenue.

Price = AR = 21 − x

▶ $\quad$ when x = 10.5 (maximum total revenue), price = 21 − 10.5 = £10.5
▶ $\quad$ when x = 6 (maximum total profit), price = 21 − 6 = £15

Minimum cost

The firm in our previous example has estimated that its average total cost (ATC) is given by the expression

$$ATC = \frac{x^2}{3} - 3x + 9$$

where ATC = average total cost (£)
$\qquad$ x = output in units

We may now wish to find the 'technical optimum' output, i.e. that level of output for which ATC is a minimum. Again we can use our rules of differentiation to solve such a problem.

$\quad$ Let y = ATC

$$\frac{dy}{dx} = 0 \text{ for a turning point}$$

$$\frac{2}{3}x - 3 = 0$$

$$\frac{2}{3}x = 3$$

$$x = 4.5$$

To check that this turning point is a minimum, we find the 2nd derivative.

$$\frac{d^2y}{dx^2} = +\frac{2}{3}$$

The sign of the 2nd derivative is positive, so the turning point is a minimum.

An output of 4.5 units will minimise average total cost, i.e. be a technically efficient output.

Figure 11.4 presents a visual overview of these solutions involving revenue, profit, price and cost.

figure 11.4
**Finding turning
points: revenue, cost
and profit**

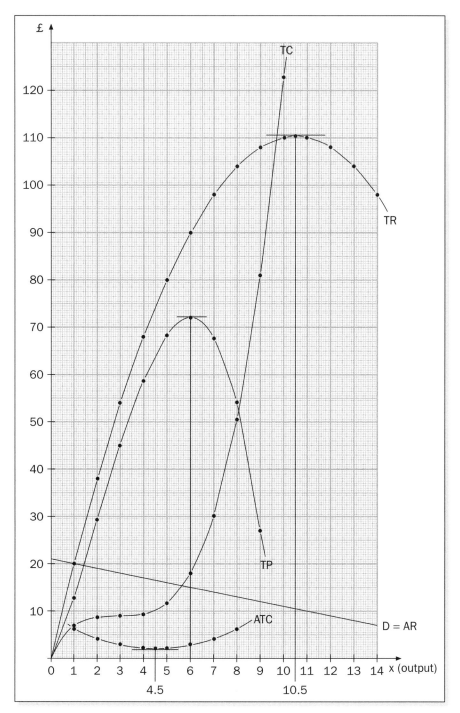

11.5 Average revenue (£) = $32 - \frac{2}{3}x^2$

Average cost (£) = $\frac{1}{3}x^2 - x + 11$

where x = output in units

(a) Find an expression for (i) total revenue
(ii) total cost
(iii) total profit

(b) At what output is total profit a maximum?
How much profit is earned at this output?
What price is charged for this output?

11.6 For a firm, total revenue and total cost are indicated below:

TR = $40x - 8x^2$

TC = $8 + 16x - x^2$

where TR = Total Revenue (£)
TC = Total Cost (£)
x = output (in 1,000 units)

(a) Find the level of output at which total profit (y) is a maximum. What price will be charged for this output? How much profit will be earned?

(b) If the firm were to seek to maximise Total Revenue rather than profit, how would your output target differ from (a) above? What profit would be earned at this new output level?

11.7 Suppose the total cost function is as follows:

$$TC = \frac{x^3}{3} - x^2 + 11x$$

where TC = total cost (£)
x = output (in 1,000 units)

What output would make average total cost a minimum?

Note: Answers can be found on p. 363.

Marginal analysis

In some of the solutions to problems involving revenue, cost and profit we needed to differentiate (find the gradient to) the total revenue, total cost and total profit curves respectively. When we did this we were in fact finding the expressions for *marginal* revenue, *marginal* cost and *marginal* profit respectively.

We can usefully illustrate this idea in terms of marginal revenue (MR). Remember that marginal revenue is the addition to total revenue (TR) from selling the last unit of output. We can therefore say that MR is, in the *limit*, the rate of change of total revenue with regard to output. In other words MR is the slope of the tangent to any particular point on the total revenue curve. We have already noted that the slope of that tangent is *zero* (i.e. MR = 0) when total revenue is a maximum.

If we differentiate (find the gradient to) the total revenue, total cost and total profit curves respectively, then we will find marginal revenue, marginal cost and marginal profit curves.

▶ If total revenue (TR) $= y$

then marginal revenue (MR) $= \dfrac{dy}{dx}$

▶ If total cost (TC) $= y$

then marginal cost (MC) $= \dfrac{dy}{dx}$

▶ If total profit (TP) $= y$

then marginal profit (MP) $= \dfrac{dy}{dx}$

SELF-CHECK QUESTIONS

11.8 Total Revenue = $y = 20x - 2x^2$

(a) Find an expression for marginal revenue.
(b) Plot the total revenue and marginal revenue curves on a graph ($x = 0$ to $x = 8$)

11.9 Total Cost = $y = \dfrac{1}{3}x^3 - 3x^2 + 9x$

(a) Find an expression for marginal cost.
(b) Plot the total cost and marginal cost curves on a graph ($x = 0$ to $x = 6$)

Note: Answers can be found on p. 365.

Price elasticity of demand

Price elasticity of demand (PED) is a measure of the responsiveness of demand for a product to a change in its own price. It is an extremely important concept for business since its value will impact directly on the pricing strategy of the firm.

$$PED = \frac{\%\ \text{change in quantity demanded of } x}{\%\ \text{change in price of } x}$$

Here we use P for the original price and Q for the original quantity, and Δ for any change in that price or quantity. We can now say that:

$$PED = \frac{\dfrac{\Delta Q}{Q} \cdot 100}{\dfrac{\Delta P}{P} \cdot 100}$$

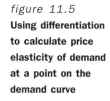

figure 11.5

Using differentiation to calculate price elasticity of demand at a point on the demand curve

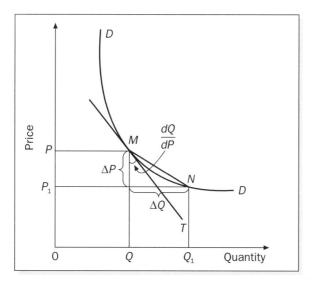

$$\text{PED} = \frac{\Delta Q}{Q} \div \frac{\Delta P}{P} \text{ (100s cancel out)}$$

$$\text{PED} = \frac{\Delta Q}{Q} \cdot \frac{P}{\Delta P} \text{ (to change divide to multiply, turn one fraction on its head)}$$

$$\text{PED} = \frac{P}{Q} \cdot \frac{\Delta Q}{\Delta P} \text{ (collect } \Delta \text{s on one side)}$$

Clearly the ratio $\Delta Q / \Delta P$ in Figure 11.5 will now vary depending on the *direction* of price change from P and on the *magnitude* of the price change from P.

However, at the point M there is a *unique* value for price elasticity of demand. In other words when demand is non-linear, only for infinitely small changes in price around the original price do we have a unique value of PED. We call this **point elasticity of demand** and it can be expressed as:

$$\text{Point price elasticity of demand} = \frac{P}{Q} \cdot \frac{dQ}{dP}$$

$$\left[\text{where } \frac{dQ}{dP} = \underset{\Delta P \to 0}{\text{limit}} \left(\frac{\Delta Q}{\Delta P} \right) \right]$$

In terms of Figure 11.5, as N approaches M (ΔP tends to zero), the slope of the chord *MN* (measured as angle *QMN*), namely $\Delta Q / \Delta P$, becomes closer and closer to the slope of the tangent *MT* (measured as angle *QMT*) at point M. In the *limit*, as N gets extremely close to M, we can regard the two slopes as identical, even though they will never quite be identical so long as N is a separate point from M on the demand curve.

In other words, at the *point* M, price elasticity of demand can be found by multiplying the ratio of initial price to initial quantity by the slope of the tangent (*MT*) to M. The slope of *MT* is expressed using derivatives (dQ/dP).

For anything other than an infinitely small change in price around the initial price, we must admit however that price elasticity of demand will vary with both the direction and magnitude of the price change.

WORKED EXAMPLE 11.6
••••••••••••••••

The quantity demanded (Q) of a product and its own price (P) are related in the following way

$$Q = 400 - P^2$$

where Q = quantity of x in units

P = price of x in £s

What is the (point) price elasticity of demand? Calculate this price elasticity at a price of £5.

Solution

$$\text{PED} = \frac{P}{Q} \cdot \frac{dQ}{dP}$$

where $\dfrac{dQ}{dP} = -2P$ (use our earlier 'rule' (p. 253) but Q replacing y and P replacing x)

So $\text{PED} = \dfrac{P}{Q} \cdot (-2P)$

At $P = £5$

$$Q = 400 - 5^2$$

i.e. $Q = 400 - 25 = 375$

So $\text{PED} = \dfrac{5}{375} \cdot (-10)$

So $\text{PED} = \dfrac{1}{75} \cdot (-10) = \dfrac{-10}{75}$

$\text{PED} = -0.13$

Strictly speaking price E of D is negative (−0.13 here) since the demand curve slopes downwards from left to right. However the negative sign is often ignored in practice. Any value for PED less than 1 implies a *relatively price inelastic* demand, and suggests that a price cut will reduce total revenue, whereas a price rise will increase total revenue.

Of course demand for a product depends on many variables other than its own price, such as the price of any substitutes or complements in consumption, the income of the household, etc. Often we want to find the rate of change between two variables (say quantity demanded of x and its own price) while assuming that the value of each of these other variables remains constant at some particular level. We are then involved in the process of **partial differentiation**, to which we now turn.

Inventory (stock) control

As we shall see (Box 3, p. 280) the use of differentiation can play an important part in deriving a formula for minimising the cost of holding **inventory** (stock).

A firm will need to hold inventories of its products for a variety of reasons.

▶ A stock of raw materials and work in progress is often needed so that the production sequence is not interrupted by shortages.
▶ A stock of finished goods can help by acting as a buffer between customer demand and the often erratic supply from the production process.
▶ A stock of tools and spare parts may be required for the maintenance of essential plant and machinery.

However stock represents cash tied up in either the production process or in goods on the shelves. There may therefore be a conflict between the financial department, which would like to keep stocks to a minimum in order to release as much capital for other uses, and the production and marketing departments which would like to see adequate levels of stocks to ensure against breakdown, down-time or late delivery. The purpose of inventory (stock) control is to find the *optimum* level of stocks which reconciles these two views.

Useful terminology

When considering inventory control, some important terms are frequently encountered.

▶ *Lead or procurement time* The period of time, often expressed in days, weeks, months, etc. between ordering and replenishment, i.e. when the goods become available for use.
▶ *Demand* The amount required by sales, production, etc. Usually expressed as a rate of demand per week, month, year, etc.
▶ *Usage rate* The number of stock items used per unit of time.
▶ *Economic order quantity (EOQ)* This is the ordering quantity which minimises the sum of inventory carrying costs and ordering costs.
▶ *Buffer stock or safety stock* A stock allowance to cover errors in forecasting the lead time or the demand during the lead time.

Figure 11.6 shows a simple stock-level diagram applying some of these ideas. Here the lead time and usage rates are constant and the goods arrive just as the minimum stock level is reached (i.e. replenishment is instantaneous at the end of the lead time).

We can calculate the *re-order level* in Figure 11.6 if we have information on usage rate and lead time.

figure 11.6
Stock model

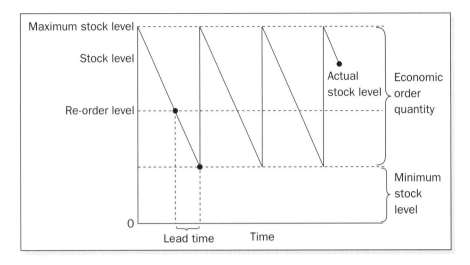

Calculate the re-order level in a situation where there is a constant usage rate of 30 items per week and a lead time of three weeks.

Solution

Re-order level = usage rate × lead time

Re-order level = 30 × 3

Re-order level = 90 units

When stocks reach 90 units a new order should be placed which will take three weeks to arrive, in which time the existing stock will be just enough to cover the usage rate of 30 per week. This assumes that the delivery will be exactly on time and that usage will be constant at 30 units per week. Any increase in the usage rate or delay in delivery will produce a stock-out; therefore most firms also carry a safety or buffer-stock. This is the minimum stock level held to cover any possible deviation in the average demand and supply.

There are three broad categories of costs involving inventories. The cost of holding stock (**carrying costs**), costs of obtaining stock (**ordering costs**) and the costs of failing to have adequate stock (**stock-out costs**).

Inventory costs include the following:

▶ **Holding or carrying costs.** These might include insurance, storage costs (staff, equipment, handling, deterioration, obsolescence, security). These might also include opportunity costs, i.e. the financial cost in terms of alternatives foregone (e.g. interest) through having capital tied up.

figure 11.7
Finding the economic order quantity (EOQ)

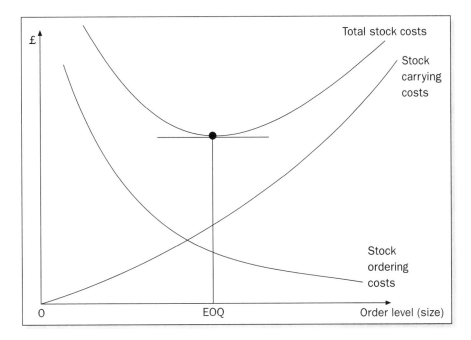

▶ **Order costs.** These occur when obtaining stock and might include the cost of clerical and administrative work in raising an order, any associated transport costs and inspection of stock on arrival, etc.

▶ **Stock – out costs.** These are difficult to quantify but might include the following:

stock-out of raw materials and work-in-progress, which may result in machine and operator idle time and possibly the need for overtime payments to catch up on missed production.

stock-out of finished goods, which may result in:

(i)   missed orders from occasional customers

(ii) missed delivery dates resulting in a deterioration in customer/ supplier relations

(iii) penalty clauses incurred for late delivery

stock-out of tools and spares, which may result in an increase in downtime of machinery and loss of production.

Stock carrying costs can be expected to *rise* as the order size increases, for reasons already discussed. However stock ordering costs can be expected to *fall* as the order size increases. (See Figure 11.7.)

If we ignore stock-out costs which are notoriously difficult to quantify, then total (inventory) costs can be regarded as the sum of the carrying and ordering costs. These will be at a minimum for the following value of Q (output).

Economic Order Quantity (EOQ)

$$Q = \sqrt{\frac{2 \cdot CoD}{Cc}}$$

where Q = economic order quantity
Co = ordering cost for one order
D = annual demand for stock
Cc = carrying cost for one item p.a.

Note: A proof of this formula can be found in Box 3 (p. 280).

WORKED
EXAMPLE **11.8**
· · · · · · · · · · · · · · · ·

A firm uses 100,000 components per annum in its manufacturing process each of which cost the firm £10 to purchase from its supplier. The carrying costs of stocking these components is estimated as 15 per cent per annum of the purchase price. The ordering costs are estimated at £200 per order. Find the economic order quantity.

Solution

$$EOQ = \sqrt{\frac{2 \cdot CoD}{Cc}}$$

where Co = £10 per order

D = 100,000 units p.a.

Cc = £10 × 0.15 = £1.50 per item per annum.

i.e. $EOQ = \sqrt{\dfrac{2 \cdot (10) \cdot (100,000)}{1.50}}$

i.e. EOQ = 1,155 units

Of course more complex inventory control situations with variable usage rates, variable lead times and gradual (rather than instantaneous) replenishment may be encountered by firms (See Further Study).

SELF-CHECK
QUESTIONS

11.10 Mondeo Ltd. produce transmission systems, assembling these using four main components, of which EL3 is one component. Since June, Mondeo has been using a new supplier who can supply EL3 at a much cheaper cost. The graph in Figure 11.8 shows stocks of EL3 for Mondeo Ltd., and indicates the usage of EL3 since January.

> **(a) Using the graph, find the:**
> > **(i)   lead time for EL3**
> > **(ii) minimum stock level**
> > **(iii) reorder quantity; and**
> > **(iv) stock-out point**
> **(b) (i) Explain the possible reasons for the change in the stock level after July.**

figure 11.8

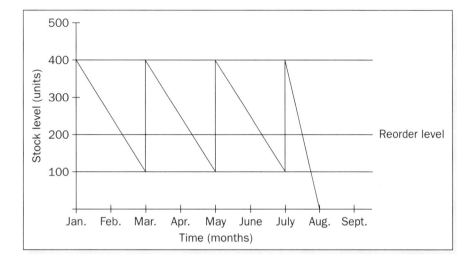

(ii) **What are the consequences for production from July of the change in stock levels?**

(c) **Calculate the economic order quantity if each order of EL3 components costs the firm £200, there is a carrying cost of £2 per EL3 component per annum and an annual demand for 5,000 EL3 components.**

PAUSE FOR THOUGHT 11.4 *What is meant by just-in-time manufacturing and how might Mondeo Ltd. benefit from its introduction?*

11.5 Partial differentiation

Many functions have *more than one* independent variable. A function with two independent variables could be expressed:

$y = f(x,z)$.

Similarly, a function with three independent variables could be expressed:

$y = f(w,x,z)$.

If we differentiate the function with respect to *one* of these variables, keeping *all other variables constant*, we are using the process of **partial differentiations** and are finding the partial derivatives.

We can illustrate the idea of partial differentiation using Figure 11.9 which shows a situation where the variable y depends upon two variables, x and z. Clearly we now have a three dimensional diagram.

▶ When we partially differentiate y with respect to x, we use the terminology $\frac{\partial y}{\partial x}$, replacing the letter d with ∂ to indicate partial differentiation. Essentially we are seeking to find the rate of change of y with respect to x, everything else (in this case z) assumed constant.

figure 11.9
**Using partial
differentiation to find
the gradient to a
segment of a surface
at a particular value
of some other
variable**

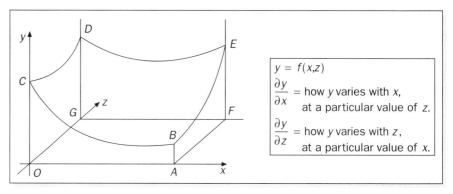

Suppose z is assumed to be constant at the specific value OG, then we are finding the gradient (rate of change) to segment DE of the surface at each value of x.

▶ Alternatively we may be seeking to partially differentiate y with respect to z, using the terminology $\dfrac{\partial y}{\partial z}$. In this case we are seeking to find the rate of change of y with respect to z, everything else (in this case x) assumed constant. Suppose x is assumed to be constant at the specific value OA, then we are finding the gradient (rate of change) to segment BE of the surface at each value of z. On the other hand, if x is assumed to be constant at the specific value 0 (zero), then we are finding the gradient (rate of change) to segment CD of the surface at each value of z.

Strictly speaking, finding *own-price elasticities of demand* often involves the 'other things equal' assumption for variables other than the price of the product in question, and is therefore a partial elasticity. The same is true of calculations involving *cross-elasticities of demand*, where only the price of the other product is allowed to change. The *particular values* of these other variables might then affect the own-price or cross-elasticity of demand calculations, as is illustrated in the following examples.

Calculating partial derivatives

To differentiate a function with respect to *one* of its variables, treat the remaining variables as constants and proceed in the usual way already considered for differentiation. Here the dependent variable (y) depends on two independent variables, x and z.

WORKED
EXAMPLE **11.9**
••••••••••••••••

Give the partial derivatives of

$$y = x^2 + 3xz - 4z^2$$

$$\frac{\partial y}{\partial x} = 2x + 3z \text{ (treat } z \text{ as a constant when differentiating)}$$

This measures the rate of change of y with respect to x, all other variables (here z) held constant.

$$\frac{\partial y}{\partial z} = 3x - 8z \text{ (treat } x \text{ as a constant when differentiating)}$$

This measures the rate of change of y with respect to z, all other variables (here x) held constant.

Note that the value of each partial derivative is influenced by the particular value of the 'other variable', whether z or x.

WORKED EXAMPLE 11.10

Give the partial derivatives of

$$y = w^3 - w^2x + x^2z - z^2$$

$$\frac{\partial y}{\partial w} = 3w^2 - 2wx \text{ (treat } x \text{ and } z \text{ as constants when differentiating)}$$

$$\frac{\partial y}{\partial x} = -w^2 + 2xz \text{ (treat } w \text{ and } z \text{ as constants when differentiating).}$$

$$\frac{\partial y}{\partial z} = x^2 - 2z \text{ (treat } w \text{ and } x \text{ as constants when differentiating)}$$

11.6 Integration

This is the *opposite* process to differentiation. As Figure 11.10 illustrates, if we have gone from a particular expression or function (e.g. $y = x^2$) to the first derivative (e.g. $\frac{dy}{dx} = 2x$) using *differentiation*, then we go backwards from $2x$ to x^2 using *integration*.

The function $y = x^2$ in Figure 11.10 is differentiated using our earlier 'rule' (p. 253) to give the gradient $\frac{dy}{dx} = 2x$. But suppose we are told that the result of differentiating some function is $2x$ and are asked to find the original function! In this case we must *reverse* the differentiation process in Figure 11.10 and instead use the integration process.

figure 11.10
Integration as the opposite of differentiation

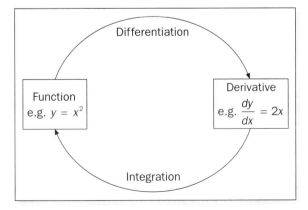

Unfortunately we will encounter an immediate problem in finding an *exact* original function whose derivative is $2x$. For example we could work back from $\dfrac{dy}{dx} = 2x$ to get *all* of the following original functions (y).

$\dfrac{dy}{dx}$	y
$2x$	$x^2 + 1$
$2x$	$x^2 + 2$
$2x$	$x^2 + 3$
.	.
.	.
.	.
$2x$	$x^2 + C$

So if we know the derivative $\left(\dfrac{dy}{dx}\right)$ of a function is $2x$, we must write that the original function (y) is $x^2 + C$ where C is any constant.

The standard symbol for the integration process is $\int$, which looks rather like an extended letter 's'. Whenever we are integrating we must also remember that we are integrating with respect to some variable; here the variable is x, so we must write dx at the end of the function to be integrated.

We can now write our integration as:

$$\int 2x\,dx = x^2 + C$$

Examples

$$\int 2x\,dx = x^2 + C$$

$$\int 4x\,dx = 2x^2 + C$$

$$\int 6x\,dx = 3x^2 + C$$

$$\int 8x\,dx = 4x^2 + C$$

Can you see a pattern emerging from these examples?

$\dfrac{dy}{dx}$	y
$2x^1$	$\dfrac{2x^2}{2} + C$
$4x^1$	$\dfrac{4x^2}{2} + C$
$6x^1$	$\dfrac{6x^2}{2} + C$
$8x^1$	$\dfrac{8x^2}{2} + C$

We can express this pattern as a general formula.

> General Formula for integration
>
> If $y = ax^n$
>
> $$\int y\,dx = \frac{ax^{n+1}}{n+1} + C$$
>
> for all values of n except $n = -1$

Of course you could *check* this general formula by reversing the process, i.e. differentiating

If $y = \frac{ax^{n+1}}{n+1} + C$

Then using our general formula for differentiating (p. 253)

$$\frac{dy}{dx} = \frac{(n+1)ax^n}{n+1} = ax^n$$

In other words, our process works both ways, except for the uncertainty as to C. We call C the **constant of integration**.

WORKED
EXAMPLE **11.11**

$$\int 3x^7 dx = \frac{3x^{7+1}}{7+1} + C = \frac{3x^8}{8} + C$$

WORKED
EXAMPLE **11.12**

$$\int 4x^8 dx = \frac{4x^{8+1}}{8+1} + C = \frac{4x^9}{9} + C$$

Integrating functions with more than one term

When the function has several terms, we apply our general formula to each term separately. However we only apply the constant of integration, C, at the end of the process.

WORKED
EXAMPLE **11.13**

$$y = \underset{\left(\begin{array}{c}a=8\\n=3\end{array}\right)}{8x^3} + \underset{\left(\begin{array}{c}a=6\\n=2\end{array}\right)}{6x^2} - \underset{\left(\begin{array}{c}a=5\\n=1\end{array}\right)}{5x} + \underset{\left(\begin{array}{c}a=8\\n=0\end{array}\right)}{8}$$

Note: 8 is the same as $8x^0$ (see Appendix 1, p. 293)

Solution

We can write this integration of each term separately, as:

$$\int 8x^3 dx + \int 6x^2 dx - \int 5x\,dx + \int 8\,dx + C$$

$$\int y dx = \frac{8x^{3+1}}{3+1} + \frac{6x^{2+1}}{2+1} - \frac{5x^{1+1}}{1+1} + \frac{8x^{0+1}}{0+1} + C$$

$$\int y dx = \frac{8x^4}{4} + \frac{6x^3}{3} - \frac{5x^2}{2} + 8x + C$$

$$\int y dx = 2x^4 + 2x^3 - 2.5x^2 + 8x + C$$

Finding the value of C

To find the value of C, the **constant of integration**, we need more specific information. In the example below we are given the co-ordinates to the curve at which the derivative $\left(\dfrac{dy}{dx}\right)$ has been calculated. We can then integrate the derivative and find C in the original function.

WORKED EXAMPLE **11.14**

Find the equation of the curve whose gradient at the point (1,1) is given by $1 - 3x^2$

Solution

Since $\dfrac{dy}{dx} = 1 - 3x^2$ then $y = \int (1 - 3x^2)\, dx$

$$\int 1 dx - \int 3x^2 dx + C$$

$$= \frac{x^{0+1}}{0+1} - \frac{3x^{2+1}}{2+1} + C$$

$$= x - \frac{3x^3}{3} + C$$

$$y = x - x^3 + C$$

When $x = 1$, $y = 1$ so $1 = 1 - 1 + C$

giving $C = 1$

The equation of the curve then is $y = x - x^3 + 1$

Definite integrals

So far we have only considered *indefinite integrals*, whereby the process of integration has resulted in a general function, with or without a specific value for C, the constant of integration.

However we are often interested in a *specific range* of a function. In this case we use the **definite integral** which evaluates the function at two specific points and allows us to find the difference between the value of the function at these points.

▶ $\int 4x\,dx = 2x^2 + C$ **Indefinite integral**

▶ $\int_1^3 4x\,dx = \left|2x^2\right|_1^3$ **Definite integral**

$$= 2(3)^2 - 2(1)^2$$

$$= 18 - 2$$

$$= 16$$

Notice that for the definite integral we place the specific values of the function around the integration sign. These specific values are often called the **limits of integration**. Here we are interested in finding the *difference* between the value of $\int 4x\,dx$ at $x = 3$ and at $x = 1$.

Because we are subtracting, the constant of integration, C, cancels out and can be ignored.

The indefinite integral, without the C, is then found and enclosed by vertical lines, with the limits of integration (the 3 and the 1) placed after the second vertical line. By convention we subtract the value of the integral at the bottom limit from the value of the integral at the top limit.

Using the definite integral helps us to eliminate C, and therefore avoid having to find it. A further benefit is that using the definite integral focuses on *summing* the function over particular values of the variable. This is required when we wish to calculate the *area beneath a curve* over a particular range of that curve. This is important in a variety of business applications, such as summing marginal revenue, marginal cost or marginal profit (all first derivatives) to find total revenue, total cost or total profit respectively.

Area under a curve

The area between a curve $y = f(x)$, the x axis and the lines $x = a$, $x = b$ is defined by $\int_a^b f(x)\,dx$.

The worked example which follows illustrates the use of integration in such situations.

figure 11.11
The definite integral and the area beneath a curve

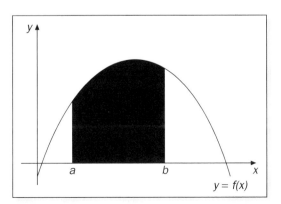

WORKED
EXAMPLE **11.15**
••••••••••••••••••

Find the area included between the curve $y = 2x + x^2 + x^3$, the x-axis and the lines $x = 1$ and $x = 2$.

Solution

$$\text{Area} = \int_1^2 (2x + x^2 + x^3) dx$$

$$\text{Area} = \left[\frac{2x^2}{2} + \frac{x^3}{3} + \frac{x^4}{4} \right]_1^2 = \left[x^2 + \frac{x^3}{3} + \frac{x^4}{4} \right]_1^2$$

$$\text{Area} = \left(4 + \frac{8}{3} + \frac{16}{4} \right) - \left(1 + \frac{1}{3} + \frac{1}{4} \right)$$

$$\text{Area} = 9\frac{1}{12} \text{ units}^2$$

**SELF-CHECK
QUESTIONS**

11.11 Solve the following indefinite integrations

(a) $\int 6x dx$ (b) $\int 3x^5 dx$ (c) $\int 4x^6 dx$

(d) $\int (4x^3 + 5x^2 - 3x + 4) dx$ (e) $\int (2x^4 - 4x^3 + 7x) dx$

11.12 Find the equation of the curve whose gradient at the point (1,1) is given by $2 - 4x^2$.

11.13 Find the area included between the curve $y = 3x + 2x^2 + x^3$, the x axis and the lines $x = 1$ and $x = 2$.

Note: Answers can be found on p. 366.

**REVIEW
QUESTIONS**

11.1 A firm has estimated that L workers on a production line will produce Q units per day where $Q = 80L^2 - 0.1L^4$. Find the number of workers that maximise output per day

11.2 The manager of a manufacturing company has estimated that the relationship between a firm's sales (X) and it's profits (Y) can be approximated by:

$Y = 0.6X - 0.002X^2$

where Y = profits (£000)
       X = sales (000 units)

Find the level of sales that would maximise the firm's profits.

11.3 For the straight line demand equation $P = 8 - 0.05Q$, verify that the demand is price elastic when P = 6 and price inelastic when P = 2. At what price does the demand curve have unitary elasticity?

Box 1

The relationship $y = x^2$ (See Figure 11.2, p. 252)

$$y^* + \Delta y = (x^* + \Delta x)^2$$

or

$$y^* + \Delta y = x^{*2} + 2x^*\Delta x + (\Delta x)^2 \text{ (see note below)}$$

but $\qquad y^* = x^{*2}$

Subtracting $\quad \Delta y = 2x^*\Delta x + (\Delta x)^2$

and dividing throughout by Δx

gives $\qquad \dfrac{\Delta y}{\Delta x} = 2x^* + \Delta x$

and $\quad \underset{\Delta x \to 0}{\text{limit}} \dfrac{\Delta y}{\Delta x} = 2x^*$

i.e. $\qquad \dfrac{dy}{dx} = 2x^*$

Note

$(x^* + \Delta x)(x^* + \Delta x)$

$x^{*2} + x^*\Delta x + x^*\Delta x + \Delta x \Delta x$

$x^{*2} + 2x^*\Delta x + (\Delta x)^2$

Box 2

The relationship $y = 3x^2$

$$y^* + \Delta y = 3(x^* + \Delta x)^2$$

or

$$y^* + \Delta y = 3x^{*2} + 6x^*\Delta x + 3(\Delta x)^2$$

but $\qquad y^* = 3x^{*2}$

Subtracting $\quad \Delta y = 6x^*\Delta x + 3(\Delta x)^2$

and dividing throughout by Δx

gives $\qquad \dfrac{\Delta y}{\Delta x} = 6x^* + 3\Delta x$

and $\quad \underset{\Delta x \to 0}{\text{limit}} \dfrac{\Delta y}{\Delta x} = 6x^*$

i.e. $\qquad \dfrac{dy}{dx} = 6x^*$

Box 3   Derivation of basic EOQ formula

Let D = annual demand

Q = order quantity

Co = cost of ordering for one order

Cc = carrying cost for one item p.a.

$$\text{Average Stock} = \frac{Q}{2}$$

$$\text{Total annual stock holding cost} = \frac{QCc}{2}$$

$$\text{Number of orders per annum} = \frac{D}{Q}$$

$$\text{Annual ordering costs} = \frac{DCo}{Q}$$

$$\text{Total (inventory) Cost} = \frac{QCc}{2} + \frac{D}{Q}Co$$

The order quantity which makes the total (inventory) cost (TC) a minimum is obtained by differentiating with respect to Q and equating the derivative to zero.

$$\frac{dTC}{dQ} = \frac{Cc}{2} - \frac{DCo}{Q^2}$$

and when $\dfrac{dTC}{dQ} = 0$ costs are at a minimum

$$\text{i.e. } 0 = \frac{Cc}{2} - \frac{DCo}{Q^2}$$

and to find Q

$$\frac{DCo}{Q^2} = \frac{Cc}{2}$$

$$2DCo = Q^2 Cc$$

$$\frac{2DCo}{Cc} = Q^2$$

$$Q \text{ (i.e. the EOQ)} = \sqrt{\frac{2 \cdot CoD}{Cc}}$$

11.4 Suppose a total cost function is given by TC = $0.01Q^2 + 5Q + 100$, where TC is total cost (£'s) and Q is output (units). Find the output level that minimises average total cost (ATC)

11.5 Investment in new machines increases output and hence revenue whilst at the same time increasing costs. Suppose each machine costs £1,800 and revenue (£) from sales occurs as follows, $R = 5,000X - 20X^2$ where X is the number of machines.

(a) Find the number of machines that maximise revenue.
(b) Find the number of machines that maximise profits (revenue – cost of machines)
(c) What is the break even number of machines?

11.6 A supply of 10 cm by 16 cm. tin plates is available to a manufacturer. Rectangular boxes are to be made by cutting out squares from each corner and then folding up the sides. How long should the sides of the square be if the manufacturer wishes to maximise the volume of the boxes?

11.7 The demand equation for a firm's product is given by P = $-5Q + 3,000$. The firm's total cost equation is given by TC = $50Q + 10,000$. All values are in £'s and quantities in units. Determine

(a) The quantity that maximises revenue.
(b) The quantity and price that maximise profits.
(c) The maximum profit.

11.8 Suppose the government wishes to discourage the consumption of the good produced by the firm in the previous example. It imposes a tax of £60 per unit produced, so that the new total cost relationship is TC = $50Q + 10,000 + 60Q = 110Q + 10,000$.

(a) How does this affect profit maximising output and price?
(b) What is the new maximum profit?
(c) What proportion of the tax is passed on to the consumer?

11.9 The total revenue a textile firm obtains from selling x football shirts and y cricket jumpers is given by the function

TR = $-2x^2 + 6x - 3y^2 + 6y + 10xy + 50$

Find

(a) the marginal revenue from selling 1 additional football shirt, when $x = 4$ and $y = 3$
(b) the marginal revenue from selling one extra cricket jumper when $x = 4$ and $y = 3$

11.10 The demand for a good depends on its own price (P), the income of consumers (Y) and the price of another good (P_B) The demand equation is given by

$$Q = -2P^2 + 4P_BY$$

if $P = 5$, $P_B = 4$ and $Y = 50$

Find

(a) the own price elasticity of demand
(b) the income elasticity of demand
(c) the cross elasticity of demand (CED). Are the goods substitutes or complements?

11.11 A firms production function is given $Q = 160K^{0.25}L^{0.75}$ where K and L are the number of machines and workers used. Find the marginal productivities of both factors when 400 units of capital and 81 units of labour are used.

11.12 The marginal revenue function for a firm is as follows:

$$MR = \frac{dTR}{dQ} = 100 - 40Q - 6Q^2$$

Find the firm's demand equation.

11.13 In the manufacture of a product, fixed costs are £500 per week. Suppose the marginal cost function of the manufacturer is given by $MC = 2.4Q^2 - 0.8Q + 10$, where Q is weekly output. Find the total cost of producing 100 units per week.

11.14 An economy's marginal propensity to save (MPS), depends on its national income(Y) in the following way:

$$MPS = 0.4 - 0.3Y^{-0.5}$$

If savings $(S) = 0$ when $Y = 100$, find

(a) the equation of total savings and
(b) savings when national income is 400

11.15 The management of an investment fund is considering investing in one of two possible firms in two years time when resources become available. Analysts have estimated that the equations for net profits over the next 8 years for the respective firms are as follows:

Y = net profits (£000,000) and X = the year in question from 1 to 8

Company A: $Y = 30 + 10X - X^2$

Company B: $Y = \dfrac{80}{X^2} + 8X - 10$

Calculate the total net profits that each firm is expected to make from the end of the second year to the end of the eighth year (i.e. evaluate from years 2 to 8).

11.16 A firm invests continuously over time. The rate of net investment (I) at time t (in years) is given by:

$$I = -t^2 + 6t + 10$$

Find out how much capital the firm will have accumulated

(a) in the first two years
(b) from years $t = 2$ to $t = 5$

11.17 A manufacturers marginal cost function is:

$$MC = \frac{dTC}{dQ} = 0.8Q + 9$$

Production is currently set at Q = 50 units per day. How much more would it cost to increase output to 80 units per day?

Further study and data
· ·

Texts

Bancroft, G. and O'Sullivan, G. (1993), *Quantitative methods for accounting and business studies*, 3rd edn, McGraw Hill, chapter 5.

Curwin, J. and Slater, R. (1996), *Quantitative methods for business decisions*, 4th edn, Chapman and Hall, chapter 8.

Swift, L. (1997), *Mathematics and statistics for business, management and finance*, Macmillan Parts A7 and B1.

Waters, D. (1997), *Quantitative methods*, 2nd edn, Addison Wesley Longman, chapter 12.

Wisniewski, M. with Stead, R. (1996), *Foundation quantitative methods for business*, Pitman, chapter 11.

Basic mathematics

Objectives
············

By the end of this appendix you should be able to:
- ▶ deal with arithmetic problems involving whole numbers, fractions and decimals;
- ▶ 'round off' to a given number of decimal places or significant figures;
- ▶ perform calculations involving percentages and ratios;
- ▶ handle expressions involving powers or roots of a variable;
- ▶ be familiar with the simple rules of algebra;
- ▶ draw graphs and solve problems involving linear and non-linear equations;
- ▶ solve pairs of simultaneous equations.

Introduction
··············

In this appendix we briefly review some of the key ideas in mathematics which are the building blocks for any course in quantitative methods. Many of these you will already have met in previous courses at school or college, though some may be new. The intention is to be *selective* rather than exhaustive and to give you the opportunity to revise and practice some important numerical skills. By following through the various Worked examples and trying the Self-check and Review questions (with answers) it is hoped that you will gain confidence in handling numbers and data, which is so important for your success in Quantitative methods.

Where you feel further help is required on any particular technique the 'Further reading' section (p. 313) will direct you to alternative sources.

Answers to the 'Self-check questions', responses to each 'Pause for thought' and answers to the 'Review questions' can be found at the end of the book.

A1 Whole numbers, fractions and decimals
···

Whole numbers

Numbers such as 3, 5, 9 are referred to as whole numbers or *integers*.

Such numbers can be positive (+3) or negative (−3).

Some simple rules apply to situations involving negative numbers.

Negative number arithmetic

* To *add two negative numbers*, add the 'numbers' and make the answer negative.

Example:

$-4 + -3$ or $-4 - 3 = -7$

▶ To *add a negative and a positive number*, take the smaller number away from the bigger number and give your result the sign of the 'bigger number'.

Examples:

$-11 + 4 = -(11 - 4) = -7$

$5 + -7$ or $5 - 7 = -(7 - 5) = -2$

▶ To *subtract a negative number*, you read the two minuses ($- -$) as a $+$

Example

$5 - -3 = 5 + 3 = 8$

These various rules involving negative numbers can usefully be illustrated by the *Number Line*. Look at the number line in Figure A1. The 0 is in the middle. All numbers to the right of 0 are the *positive* numbers, and all those to the left of 0 are the *negative* numbers.

▶ When we *add a negative number*, it is the same as *subtracting a positive number*: we always move towards the left on the number line. Check the following examples in Figure A1.

(a) $3 + -2 = 1$ or $3 - 2 = 1$
(b) $-1 + -3 = -4$ or $-1 - 3 = -4$
(c) $-2 + -3 = -5$ or $-2 - 3 = -5$

figure A1

Adding a negative number (same as subtracting a positive number)

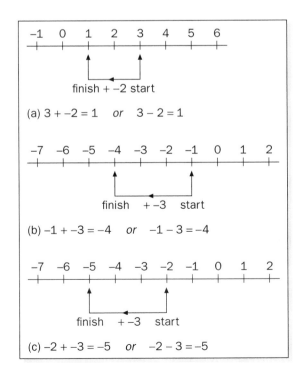

(a) $3 + -2 = 1$ *or* $3 - 2 = 1$

(b) $-1 + -3 = -4$ *or* $-1 - 3 = -4$

(c) $-2 + -3 = -5$ *or* $-2 - 3 = -5$

▶ When we *subtract a negative number*, it is the same as *adding a positive number*: we always move towards the right on the number line. Check the following example in Figure A2.

(a) $3 - -2 = 5$ or $3 + 2 = 5$
(b) $-6 - -4 = -2$ or $-6 + 4 = -2$
(c) $-1 - -3 = 2$ or $-1 + 3 = 2$

figure A2
Subtracting a negative number (same as adding a positive number)

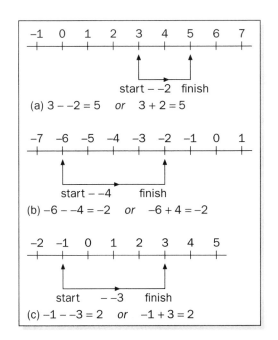

(a) $3 - -2 = 5$ *or* $3 + 2 = 5$

(b) $-6 - -4 = -2$ *or* $-6 + 4 = -2$

(c) $-1 - -3 = 2$ *or* $-1 + 3 = 2$

▶ The rules for *multiplying and dividing with negative numbers* are very easy after you have learnt the rules for addition and subtraction:
If the signs are the same, the answer is a positive
If the signs are different, the answer is a negative

Examples:

$2 \times 5 = 10$ $-3 \times -4 = 12$ $-18 \div -3 = 6$
$-2 \times 5 = -10$ $3 \times -4 = -12$ $18 \div -3 = -6$

Fractions

A **fraction** is usually part of something. It can be defined as the ratio of two numbers, one (the *numerator*) placed on top of another (the *denominator*).
Work through the following rules involving fractions.

Addition and subtraction of fractions

To add or subtract two fractions, change them to *equivalent fractions* (see below) with the same bottom number. Then we can add or subtract.

WORKED
EXAMPLE **A1**
················

$$\frac{1}{3} + \frac{2}{5} = \frac{5}{15} + \frac{6}{15} = \frac{11}{15}$$

We use 15 since it is the smallest multiple of both 3 and 5.

WORKED
EXAMPLE **A2**
················

$$\frac{7}{8} - \frac{5}{6} = \frac{21}{24} - \frac{20}{24} = \frac{1}{24}$$

We use 24 since it is the smallest multiple of both 8 and 6.

Multiplication of fractions

To multiply two fractions you simply need to multiply the top numbers and the bottom numbers of the fractions.

WORKED
EXAMPLE **A3**
················

$$\frac{3}{5} \times \frac{3}{4} = \frac{9}{20}$$

Division of fractions

To divide two fractions, you turn the second fraction upside-down and then multiply the two fractions together.

WORKED
EXAMPLE **A4**
················

$$\frac{2}{3} \div \frac{4}{5} = \frac{2}{3} \times \frac{5}{4} = \frac{10}{12} = \frac{5}{6}$$

Cancelling fractions

Worked example A4 illustrates the fraction 10/12 being cancelled down to 5/6 by dividing both top and bottom by the same number, in this case a 2.

Equivalent fractions

These are fractions that have the same value. For example, 1/4, 3/12, 6/24 are all equivalent to each other, and so are called equivalent fractions.

Decimals

Decimals are simply found by dividing the top (numerator) of the fraction by the bottom (denominator) of the fraction.

WORKED
EXAMPLE **A5**
················

Change $\frac{5}{8}$ to a decimal number. Divide 5 by 8 to give 0.625.

When a number is written in decimal form, the digits on the right-hand side of the decimal point are called the *decimal places*.

WORKED
EXAMPLE **A6**
············

83.7 is written to one decimal place (1 d.p.).
0.439 is written to three decimal places (3 d.p.).

A2 Rounding-off
·····················

In many tasks you will need to 'round-off' your answer to a suitable number of *decimal places* (d.p.) or *significant figures* (s.f.)

Decimal places

▶ Decide on the number of decimal places you wish to round-off to, say to two decimal places.
▶ Look at the number in the next (here third) decimal place.
▶ If it is less than 5, then the two decimal places remain the same.
▶ If it is 5 or more than 5, then think of the first two decimal place numbers as together forming a number between 1 and 99, and then add 1 to this. This new number now represents your two decimal places.

WORKED
EXAMPLE **A7**
············

9.5427 will round-off to 9.54 (the 2 of the third decimal place is less than 5, so we keep 54).

11.1873 will round-off to 11.19 (the 7 of the third decimal place is more than 5, so we need to add 1 to 18, making 19).

23.6154 will round-off to 23.62 (the 5 of the third decimal place causes us to add 1 to 61, making 62).

Significant figures

Counting the number of actual *digits* (numbers) will often tell us the number of significant figures involved.

WORKED
EXAMPLE **A8**
············

8	has 1 significant figure
9.3	has 2 significant figures
47.7	has 3 significant figures
0.1845	has 4 significant figures

However, when 0s are in the number, we must know when to count them as a significant figure and when not to.

▶ When the 0s come at the end of the number or at the beginning of the number, then we do *not* count them as significant figures.

WORKED
EXAMPLE **A9**
·············

60	has 1 significant figure
500	has 1 significant figure
57,000	has 2 significant figures
0.68	has 2 significant figures
0.009	has 1 significant figure
0.00013	has 2 significant figures

▶ When the 0s come between digits, we *do* count them as significant figures.

WORKED
EXAMPLE **A10**
···············

105 has 3 significant figures
2070 has 3 significant figures
5002 has four significant figures

The rules for rounding off for significant figures are similar to those for decimal places.

▶ Decide on the number of significant figures you wish to round-off to. Look at the next digit which then 'has to go'.
▶ If this is less than 5, then leave the digits on the left (if there are any) alone.
▶ If the digit is 5 or more than 5, then add 1 to the digit on the left.
▶ Then put 0's in to keep the place value of the original number.

WORKED
EXAMPLE **A11**
···············

832   to 1 s.f. is 800 since the 3 is less than 5
  8.7621 to 2 s.f. is 8.8 since the 6 is more than 5

Look at the following table to see how these rules work for the numbers chosen:

Number	Correct to 1 s.f.	Correct to 2 s.f.	Correct to 3 s.f.
34.87	30	35	34.9
159.2	200	160	159
10.942	10.000	11.000	10.900
0.07158	0.07	0.072	0.0716

A3 Percentages and ratios
·································

Percentages

A percentage means 'out of a hundred'. So:

▶ 1% means 1 out of a 100 or 1/100 or 0.01.
▶ 3% means 3 out of a 100 or 3/100 or 0.03.

Changes of form

Fractions to percentages
To change any *fraction* into a percentage, all you need to do is to multiply the fraction by 100. What this is doing is finding the fraction of 100.

For example:

$\frac{5}{8}$ would become $\frac{5}{8} \times 100 = 62.5\%$

You should know the common fractions expressed as a percentage.

$\frac{1}{2} = 50\%$ $\frac{1}{4} = 25\%$ $\frac{3}{4} = 75\%$ $\frac{1}{10} = 10\%$ $\frac{1}{5} = 20\%$ $\frac{1}{3} = 33\frac{1}{3}\%$

Percentages to fractions
To change a *percentage* into a fraction, simply express the percentage as a fraction over 100 and then cancel down. For example:

$45\% = \frac{45}{100} = \frac{9}{20}$ (cancelled by 5s)

$31\% = \frac{31}{100}$ (will not cancel)

Decimals to percentages
To change any *decimal* into a percentage, simply multiply by 100. For example:

0.35 becomes $0.35 \times 100 = 35\%$ as a percentage.
1.26 becomes $1.26 \times 100 = 126\%$ as a percentage.

Percentages to decimals
To change a *percentage* to a decimal, simply divide the percentage by 100. This is done by moving the decimal point two places to the left. For example:

35% becomes 0.35 as a decimal
6% becomes 0.06 as a decimal.

Percentage of
To calculate the *percentage of* something you first change the percentage to a decimal and then multiply.

WORKED
EXAMPLE **A12**
· · · · · · · · · · · · · · ·

Find 8% of £135.
Calculate $0.08 \times 135 = £10.80$. So 8% of £135 is £10.80.

Percentage increase
Change the percentage to a decimal, add 1, then multiply by the figure that needs increasing.

WORKED
EXAMPLE **A13**
················

Increase £6 by 5%.
Change 5% to a decimal, add 1, then multiply by £6.
1.05 × £6 = £6.30

Percentage decrease
Change the percentage to a decimal and take it away from 1, then multiply it
by the original figure.

WORKED
EXAMPLE **A14**
················

Decrease £8 by 4%. Change 4% to a decimal and take it away from 1.
1 − 0.04 = 0.96
Multiply this by the original
0.96 × £8 = £7.68

'As a percentage'
We express one quantity *as a percentage* of another by setting up the two
numbers as a fraction of each other and converting that fraction to a percentage by simply multiplying by 100.

WORKED
EXAMPLE **A15**
················

Express £7 as a percentage of £25

Set up the fraction $\dfrac{7}{25}$ and multiply by 100. This becomes (7 ÷ 25) × 100 = 28%

Reverse percentage
There are times when we know a certain percentage and we wish to get back to
the original amount.

WORKED
EXAMPLE **A16**
················

The 31 pupils who were absent represented only 4 per cent of the pupils in the
school. How many pupils should have been at school?
Since 4 per cent represents 31 pupils, then 1 per cent will represent 31 ÷ 4
pupils = 7.75, so 100 per cent will be represented by
(7.75 × 100) = 775 pupils

Ratios

To divide any amount in a given ratio, you simply multiply the amount by the
fraction of the ratio.

WORKED EXAMPLE **A17**
················

Divide £60 between John and Kevin in the ratio of 2:3.

From the ratio we see that John receives $\dfrac{2}{5}$ and Kevin receives $\dfrac{3}{5}$. Hence

John receives £60 $\times \dfrac{2}{5}$ = £24 and

Kevin receives £60 $\times \dfrac{3}{5}$ = £36

Sometimes you may know only part of the information.

WORKED EXAMPLE **A18**
················

Two business partners Sue and Trish divide their profits in the ratio 3 : 5. If Sue receives £1,800, how much does Trish receive?

Sue receives £1,800 which is $\dfrac{3}{8}$ of the whole profit. So $\dfrac{1}{8}$ = £1,800 ÷ 3 = £600.

So Trish's share which is $\dfrac{5}{8}$ will be £600 × 5 = £3,000.

SELF-CHECK QUESTIONS

A1 Solve

(a) −4 + −2   (b) −4 − −2   (c) −4 × −2
(d) −4 ÷ −2   (e) −16 × −6   (f) −81 ÷ −9

A2 Correct each of the following to the number of decimal places or significant figures indicated.

(a) 2.643 (2 d.p.)   (b) 1.338 (2 d.p.)   (c) 17.64 (1 d.p.)
(d) 7.5474 (2 s.f.)   (e) 17.6 (1 s.f.)   (f) 0.00587 (1 s.f.)

A3 Express each of the following as a percentage (to no more than 1 d.p.).

(a) £5 out of £24   (b) 4 kg out of 32 kg.
(c) 2.5 m out of 10 m.   (d) 40 cm out of 3 m.

A4 (a) Divide £3.25 in the ratio of 2 : 3
(b) Three footballers score 21, 15 and 9 goals respectively. Their club pays out £9,000 in bonus money to these players. They share the bonus in the same ratio as the goals they score. Calculate the share of the bonus for each player.

Note: Answers can be found on p. 367.

A4 Powers and roots
·····················

In the expressions x^4 and x^2, the letter x is called the *base* and the numbers 4 and 2 are called the *powers* (or *indices* or *exponents*).

$x^4 = x \times x \times x \times x$

$x^2 = x \times x$

Rules for powers

Whenever powers have the *same base,* then a number of rules can be applied. You should make sure that you are familiar with these simple rules.

Multiplying powers (indices)

$$4^3 \times 4^2 = (4 \times 4 \times 4) \times (4 \times 4) = 4 \times 4 \times 4 \times 4 \times 4 = 4^5$$

To multiply, just add the powers

i.e. $x^a \times x^b = x^{a+b}$

Dividing powers (indices)

$$3^5 \div 3^2 = \frac{3 \times 3 \times 3 \times 3 \times 3}{3 \times 3} = 3 \times 3 \times 3 = 3^3$$

To divide, just subtract the powers

i.e. $x^a \div x^b = x^{a-b}$

The power zero

e.g. $2^3 \div 2^3 = 2^{3-3} = 2^0$

but $2^3 \div 2^3 = \dfrac{8}{8} = 1$

so $2^0 = 1$

$x^0 = 1$

Negative powers

e.g. $3^1 \div 3^3 = 3^{1-3} = 3^{-2}$

but $3^1 \div 3^3 = \dfrac{3}{27} = \dfrac{1}{9} = \dfrac{1}{3^2}$

so $3^{-2} = \dfrac{1}{3^2}$

$x^{-a} = \dfrac{1}{x^a}$

Fractional powers

Fractional powers will be used to indicate *roots* (see below)

$$x^{\frac{1}{2}} = \sqrt{x}$$

$$x^{\frac{1}{3}} = \sqrt[3]{x}$$

$$x^{\frac{1}{n}} = \sqrt[n]{x}$$

and $x^{\frac{2}{3}} = \sqrt[3]{x^2} = \left(\sqrt[3]{x}\right)^2$

$$x^{\frac{m}{n}} = \sqrt[n]{x^m} = \left(\sqrt[n]{x}\right)^m$$

Roots

A root is the mathematical word for a solution of a *quadratic* equation.

Root of a number

The root of a number is generally taken to be the *square root*. So, root 9 will be 3 or −3.

The Nth root

The Nth root of a number A is that number which, when multiplied by itself *N* times, gives A.

Examples:

▶ The square root of 25: $\sqrt{25}$ = 5 or −5, because 5 × 5 = 25 and −5 × −5 = 25.
▶ The cube (3rd) root of 64 : $\sqrt[3]{64}$ = 4, because 4 × 4 × 4 = 64.
▶ The 4th root of 81, $\sqrt[4]{81}$ = 3 or −3, because 3 × 3 × 3 × 3 = 81 and −3 × −3 × −3 × −3 = 81.

You can use your calculator to find any root of any number by using the $x^{1/y}$ key, where *y* is the Nth root you want. You will most likely need to use the shift or inv or 2ndf key also. For example, if you want to find the 5th root of 7776, key in 7776 $x^{1/y}$ 5: this will give the result 6.

SELF-CHECK QUESTIONS

Solve the following using your knowledge of the rules for dealing with powers.

A5 (a) $t^3 \times t^4$ (b) $m^2 \times m$ (c) $3x^2 \times 2x^5$
      (d) $5p \times 3p^4$ (e) $7m^3 \times 4m$ (f) $3w \times 4w^2$

A6 (a) $x^7 \div x^3$ (b) $p^6 \div p^4$ (c) $8d^3 \div 2d$
      (d) $6m^4 \div 3m^3$ (e) $12c^3 \div 6c^3$ (f) $9m^4 \div 6m^3$

A7 (a) $3^8 \div 3^5$ (b) $2^9 \div 2^7$ (c) $10^3 \div 10^2$
      (d) $10^9 \div 10^3$ (e) $7^7 \div 7^6$ (f) $19^8 \div 19^7$

A8 Write the following in fraction form:

      (a) 7^{-2} (b) 8^{-3} (c) x^{-4} (d) m^{-1}

      (e) $4g^{-2}$ (f) $5m^{-2}$ (g) $(2t)^{-3}$ (h) $\frac{1}{2}t^{-4}$

A9 (a) $6m \div 3m^2$ (b) $8t^2 \div 6t^5$ (c) $9x^3 \div 6x^4$ (d) $cd^3 \div d^5$
      (e) $a^2b \div ab$ (f) $3ab \div b^2$ (g) $9q^2 \div 5q^3$ (h) $12m^2 \div 6mp$
      (i) $3x + 4x$ (j) $15x^2 \div 3x^2$ (k) $4t^2 \div 3t^{-1}$ (l) $5t^{-1} + 2t^{-1}$

A10 Write each of the following as a power

      (a) $\sqrt{3}$ (b) $\sqrt{4^2}$ (c) $\dfrac{1}{\sqrt{7}}$

      (d) $\dfrac{1}{\sqrt{5^2}}$ (e) $\sqrt[3]{3^2}$ (f) $\sqrt[4]{5^3}$

Note: **Answers can be found on p. 367.**

A5 Simple algebra
....

Algebra is the use of letters for numbers and is often known as the language of mathematics. A number of processes are often involved.

Substitution

One of the most important features of algebra is the use of expressions and formulae and the substitution of real numbers into them.

The value of an expression such as $3x + 2$ will change with the different values of x *substituted* into it.

WORKED
EXAMPLE **A19**
....

Suppose the formula is given by $A = \dfrac{h(a + b)}{2}$

Then if $a = 4$, $b = 7$ and $h = 8$

$$A = \frac{8(4 + 7)}{2} = 44$$

Transposition

It is often necessary to be able to change a formulae round to help you find a particular piece of information.

This changing round of formulae is called *transposition* of formulae and what we are doing is changing the subject of a formulae. The *subject* of a formula is the single letter, or word, usually on the left-hand side all by itself.

For example:

t is the subject of the formula $t = \dfrac{d}{v}$

Here are some rules for changing the subjects of formulae:

Rule 1
You can move any letter, or word, from one side of the equation to the other as long as it is operating on *all* the rest of that side.

For example, in the formula $v = u + 6t$, the u can be moved since it is adding to the rest of that side, but the t cannot be moved yet as it is only multiplying the 6.

This simple list of formulae should help you see when we can move terms:

▶ $v = u + 6t$ we could move either the u or the $6t$
▶ $A = lb$ we could move either the l or the b
▶ wage = hours × hourly rate   we could move either hours or hourly rate
▶ $t = \dfrac{d}{v}$ we could move either the d or the v
▶ $x = \dfrac{y + 1}{7}$ we could move either the 7 or the $(y + 1)$

▶ $w = n(y - 10)$ we could move either the n or the $(y - 10)$

Rule 2

When a letter, or word, has been moved from one side to the other, it does the *opposite thing* to the other side.

For example, if something was added, then when it moved it would be subtracted, or if something was multiplied then when it moved it would divide.

WORKED
EXAMPLE **A20**
•••••••••••••

The following examples will help to illustrate these points:

▶ $v = u + 6t$ can be changed to $v - u = 6t$

   or $v - 6t = u$

▶ $A = lb$ can be changed to $\dfrac{A}{l} = b$

   or $\dfrac{A}{b} = l$

▶ $t = \dfrac{d}{v}$ can be changed to $tv = d$

   or $\dfrac{t}{d} = \dfrac{1}{v}$

▶ $y = 6x - 10$ can be changed to $y + 10 = 6x$

   or $y - 6x = -10$

All your transposition or manipulation involving algebra can be summarised in the following principle.

> If it is doing what it is doing to everything else on that side of the equation, then it can be moved to the other side and perform the opposite job.

Simplification

This is what we do in algebra to make expressions look as simple as possible. Only *like* terms can be added or subtracted, as follows:

$3x + 4x = 7x$ $6x - 2x = 4x$ $3x^2 + 4x^2 = 7x^2$
$5y + y = 6y$ $4t - t = 3t$ $3y^3 + 2y^3 = 5y^3$

Simplification can also involve either the *expansion* of brackets or the opposite process, namely *factorisation*, whereby a more complex expression is reduced to a simpler one involving brackets.

Expansion

'Expand' in mathematics means to multiply out the brackets.

For example,

Expand $3(2x - 5)$

means multiply the 3 by everything inside the bracket to give $6x - 15$.

If you are asked to expand $(x + 6)(x + 4)$ you need to multiply everything inside the first bracket by everything inside the second bracket, i.e.

$$(x + 6)(x + 4) = x(x + 4) + 6(x + 4)$$
$$= x^2 + 4x + 6x + 24$$
$$= x^2 + 10x + 24$$

This can be illustrated with a diagram.

figure A3

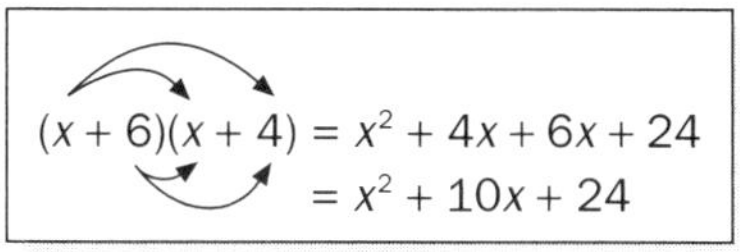

$$(x + 6)(x + 4) = x^2 + 4x + 6x + 24$$
$$= x^2 + 10x + 24$$

Factorisation

This means to separate an expression into the parts that will multiply together to give that expression. The two (or more) parts are usually connected by brackets.

For example

$4x + 8y$ would factorise and simplify to $4(x + 2y)$
$3y - 3x$ would factorise and simplify to $3(y - x)$

As we note below, these examples of factorisation involve *linear* expressions. However we are often faced with examples involving *quadratic* (highest power is a square) expressions.

Quadratic factorisation

For example:

Factorise and simplify the quadratic expression

$6x^2 + 5x - 6$

This process is the opposite to that shown in Figure A3 above for a quadratic expansion. We know that quadratic factorisation will involve *two* brackets. The quadratic expression can be thought to be of the general type:

$ax^2 + bx + c$

1 When the last sign in the quadratic $ax^2 + bx + c$ is *positive*, then both signs in the brackets are the *same as the first sign* in the quadratic. For example:

$$x^2 + 5x + 4 = (\ + \ )(\ + \ )$$
$$\text{and} \quad x^2 - 5x + 4 = (\ - \ )(\ - \ )$$

2 When the last sign in the quadratic $ax^2 + bx - c$ is *negative*, then the signs in the brackets are *different*. For example:

$$x^2 + 5x - 5 = (\ + \ )(\ - \ )$$
$$\text{or} = (\ - \ )(\ + \ )$$

Once you've sorted out the *signs*, then you need to look at the *numbers*. Follow through these two examples to see how to do this.

Factorise $6x^2 + 7x + 2$

Solution

By looking at the signs we see that the brackets both contain a '+', so:

$6x^2 + 7x + 2 = (\quad + \quad)(\quad + \quad)$.

We see that the end numbers in each bracket must multiply to give 2, and the only way to do this is to have 2×1.

Hence $6x^2 + 7x + 2 = (\quad + 2)(\quad + 1)$.

Now we see that the first numbers in each bracket must multiply to give 6, and we could have 3×2 or 2×3 or 6×1 or 1×6, but the combination we need must multiply with the 2 and the 1, so that their sum is 7. We ask ourselves which of the vertical pairs

$\{3 \times 1\} \{2 \times 1\} \{6 \times 1\}$ or $\{1 \times 1\}$

$\{2 \times 2\} \{3 \times 2\} \{1 \times 2\}$ $\{6 \times 2\}$

give a combined total of 7, and we see that the only one which does is

$\{3 \times 1\}$

$\{2 \times 2\}$

so the factorisation is $(3x + 2)(2x + 1)$

Factorise $2x^2 + 5x - 3$

Solution

We factorise by looking at the signs and noticing that both signs will be different, hence
$(\quad + \quad)(\quad - \quad)$. The -3 indicates we need a 3 and a 1 at the end of each bracket to give
$(\quad + 3)(\quad - 1)$ or $(\quad + 1)(\quad - 3)$. Now, a product of 2 for the first numbers in each bracket, i.e. 2 and 1, must combine with the 3 and 1 in such a way as to give a difference of $+5$. This will give us $(x + 3)(2x - 1)$.

A6 Solving equations
···························

To *solve* an equation is to find the value or values which satisfy that equation.

For example,

Solve $4x + 3 = 23$

This is a *linear* equation (highest power is 1) and has a unique solution, namely $4x = 23 - 3$, giving $x = 5$. Only when $x = 5$ is this equation satisfied. Linear equations have only one solution.

When we are solving *quadratic* equations, we may find up to two solutions, i.e. two values of the variable which satisfy that equation. In solving quadratic equations it is usual to use either *factorisation* or the *formula method*.

Factorising quadratic equations

Take the general form of the quadratic equation:

$ax^2 + bx + c = 0$

If we can *factorise* this equation, i.e. reduce it to two brackets multiplied together, then we can set *either* bracket $= 0$ and find a solution.

WORKED
EXAMPLE **A23**
················

Solve $x^2 + 2x - 15 = 0$

Solution

This factorises into $(x - 3)(x + 5) = 0$

The only way that this expression can ever equal 0 is if one of the brackets is worth 0. Hence either

$$(x - 3) = 0 \quad \text{or} \quad (x + 5) = 0$$

hence $x - 3 = 0$ or $x + 5 = 0$

hence $x = 3$ or $x = -5$

The solutions then are $x = 3$ and -5

Whether or not an equation will factorise, the next method will always give you the solution to a quadratic equation (where a solution exists!).

Formula for solving quadratic equations

A formula has been derived that can be used to solve any quadratic equation (or used to tell you that there is no solution). For a quadratic equation of the general form $ax^2 + bx + c = 0$:

$$x = \frac{-b \pm \sqrt{(b^2 - 4ac)}}{2a}$$

The use of the $\pm$ reflects the fact that a square root has a positive and a negative solution.

Solve the equation $3x^2 - 8x + 2 = 0$, correct to 2 d.p.

Solution

Use $x = \dfrac{-b \pm \sqrt{(b^2 - 4ac)}}{2a}$ where $a = 3$, $b = -8$ and $c = 2$

$\quad = \dfrac{8 \pm \sqrt{\{64 - 4(3)(2)\}}}{6}$

$\quad = \dfrac{8 \pm \sqrt{40}}{6} = \dfrac{8 + \sqrt{40}}{6}$ and $\dfrac{8 - \sqrt{40}}{6}$

$\quad = 2.39$ or 0.28

A7 Simultaneous equations
·····································

In business and economic situations we may, for example, need to find the price at which supply equals demand. We call this the *equilibrium price* as it balances both supply and demand. Put another way, it is the price which solves both the demand and supply equations *at the same time* (i.e. simultaneously).

It is therefore important that you know how to go about solving simultaneous equations. The idea in the example below is to *eliminate* either the *x* or the *y* variable, whether by addition or subtraction, so that we are left with one equation with one unknown variable. Having solved this equation we can then use the result to solve for the other unknown variable. Work through these examples yourself.

Solve the simultaneous equations $6x + y = 15$

$$4x + y = 11$$

Solution

Since both equations have a y term the same we can *subtract* one equation from the other to give

$$2x = 4$$

which solves to give $\qquad\qquad x = 2$

We now substitute $x = 2$ into one of the first equations (usually the one with the smallest numbers involved). So substitute $x = 2$ into $4x + y = 11$ to give $8 + y = 11$ which gives

$$y = 11 - 8$$

$$y = 3$$

We test our solution in the other initial equation.

Substitute $x = 2$ and $y = 3$ into $6x + y$ to give $12 + 3 = 15$, which is correct. So we can confidently say that our solution is $x = 2$ and $y = 3$.

WORKED
EXAMPLE **A26**
············

Solve the simultaneous equations $4x - 2y = 12$
$$2x + 2y = 18$$

Solution

Since both equations have a $2y$ term but one with a + and one with a − then we can *add* one equation to the other to give

$$6x = 30$$

$$x = 5$$

Substitute $x = 5$ into, say, the lower equation to get

$$2 \times 5 + 2y = 18$$

$$10 + 2y = 18$$

$$2y = 18 - 10 = 8$$

$$y = 4$$

The solution of $x = 5$ and $y = 4$ can be checked in the top equation to give

$$(4 \times 5) - (2 \times 4) = 20 - 8 = 12$$

which is correct. So our solution is $x = 5$ and $y = 4$.

WORKED
EXAMPLE **A27**
············

Solve the simultaneous equations $4x + 2y = 32$
$$3x - y = 19$$

Here we do not have any equal terms so we have to start creating them because that is the only way we can solve simultaneous equations. We can see that by multiplying *all* of the second equation by 2 we get

$$(3x - y = 19) \times 2 \Rightarrow 6x - 2y = 38$$

Our pair of equations is now $4x + 2y = 32$
$$6x - 2y = 38$$

and we can solve these as we did in Example 2 by *adding* them together.

WORKED
EXAMPLE **A28**
············

Solve the simultaneous equations $5x + 4y = 22$
$$2x + 3y = 16$$

Solution

Notice that we cannot simply multiply one equation by anything to give us equal terms. So we have to multiply *both* equations.

The choice is now up to us: we can either make the xs the same or the ys the same. Sometimes there is an obvious choice; sometimes it does not matter. In this example it does not matter which you do since there is no great advantage in choosing either.

Let us choose the xs to be made equal. We will have to multiply the first equation through by 2 and the second equation through by 5. This gives

$$(5x + 4y = 22) \times 2 \implies 10x + 8y = 44$$

and $(2x + 3y = 16) \times 5 \implies 10x + 15y = 80$

We now solve these in the same way as we did in Example 1 by *subtracting* them from each other.

A8 Inequalities
• • • • • • • • • • • • • • • • •

Inequalities behave similarly to normal equations. The difference is that they have an inequality sign instead of an equals sign.

Linear inequalities

For linear inequalities we use the same rules to solve inequalities as we do linear equations.

WORKED
EXAMPLE **A29**
• • • • • • • • • • • • •

Solve $\dfrac{5x + 7}{3} < 14$

Solution

$5x + 7 < 14 \times 3$

$5x + 7 < 42$

$\qquad 5x < 42 - 7$

$\qquad 5x < 35$

$\qquad x < 35 \div 5$

$\qquad x < 7$

WORKED
EXAMPLE **A30**
• • • • • • • • • • • • •

Solve the inequality $1 < 5x + 3 \leq 17$.

Solution

We need to treat each side separately as

$$\begin{array}{ll} 1 < 5x + 3 & 5x + 3 \leq 17 \\[4pt] 1 - 3 < 5x & 5x \leq 17 - 3 \\[4pt] -2 < 5x & 5x \leq 14 \\[4pt] \dfrac{-2}{5} < x & x \leq \dfrac{14}{5} \\[8pt] -0.4 < x & x \leq 2.8 \end{array}$$

Hence $-0.4 < x \leq 2.8$

Inequalities involving x^2

Consider $x^2 < 16$. Now, the solution to $x^2 = 16$ is $x = +4$ and $x = -4$. When we look at the $x = 4$ part we can see that, yes, $x < -4$ just does not work. In fact the solution to do with $x = -4$ needs the inequality sign changing round to give us the solution $x > -4$ which can be turned to give $-4 < x$.

Put all this on to a number line and you see the solution (Figure A4).

figure A4

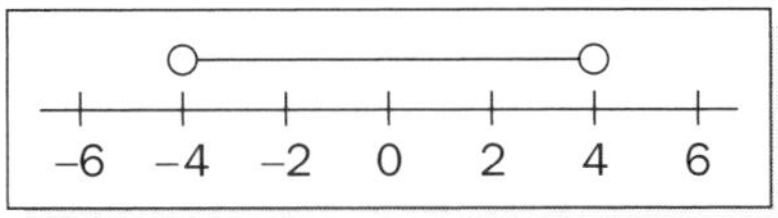

The solution is $-4 < x < 4$.

WORKED
EXAMPLE **A31**
....

Solve the inequality $x^2 > 25$

Solution

The solution to $x^2 > 25$ will be $x > 5$ and $x < -5$.
Notice the difference between the types $x^2 < a^2$ and the types $x^2 > a^2$.

A9 Graphs and functions
....

A *function* is a rule describing the relationship between variables. Using the notation $y = f(x)$, we are indicating, in a type of shorthand, that the variable y *depends upon* (is a function of) some other variable x. We could then say that y is the *dependent variable* and x the *independent variable*, though our study of economics will alert us to the fact that relationships between variables are rarely in a single direction only.

The function or rule describing the relationship between variables may be specified more precisely. Thus $y = f(x) = 3x + 2$, will tell us that y takes the value 2 when $x = 0$ and rises by 3 units for every unit rise in x. This is an example of a *linear function*, of the general form $y = mx + c$, where c is the vertical intercept and m is the slope or gradient.

Linear Function

Where the highest power of the independent variable is 1, as in $y = 3x^1 + 2$, then we have a linear function or relationship. A *graph* or picture of this linear relationship between the variables is shown in Figure A5.

Quadratic Function

Where the highest power of the independent variable is 2, as in the case of $y = ax^2 + bx + c$, then we have a quadratic function or relationship. A graph of such a quadratic relationship between the variables is shown in Figure A6. The shape of this graph is called a *parabola*, and will be $\cup$-shaped where a is positive and $\cap$-shaped where a is negative. The vertical intercept will again be determined by the value of c.

figure A5
Linear function

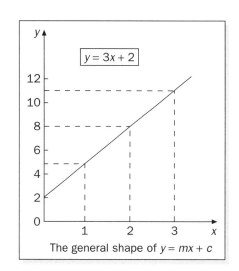

The general shape of $y = mx + c$

figure A6
Quadratic function

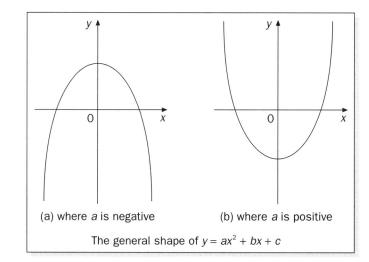

(a) where a is negative   (b) where a is positive

The general shape of $y = ax^2 + bx + c$

Cubic Function

Where the highest power of the independent variable is 3, as in the case of $y = ax^3 + bx^2 + cx + d$, then we have a cubic function or relationship. A graph of such a cubic relationship between the variables is shown in Figure A7.

You should, of course, be familiar with other functional relationships.

▶ **Exponential:** of the form $y = a^x$, where a is any constant > 1 and x is any variable. Figure A8 graphs the exponential relationship $y = 2^x$ over the values $x = 1$ to 5.

▶ **Reciprocal (Hyperbolic):** of the form $y = \dfrac{a}{x}$, where a is any constant and x any variable. Figure A9 graphs the reciprocal (hyperbolic) relationship of $y = \dfrac{6}{x}$ over the values $x = 1$ to 6.

figure A7
Cubic function

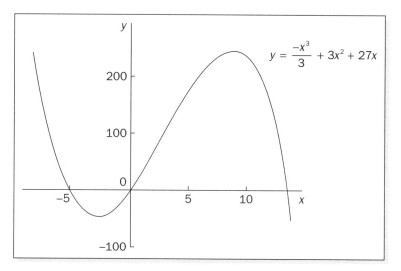

$$y = \frac{-x^3}{3} + 3x^2 + 27x$$

figure A8
Exponential function

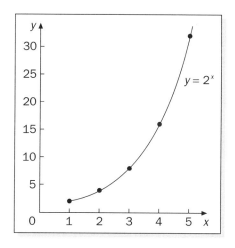

$y = 2^x$

figure A9
Reciprocal
(hyperbolic function)

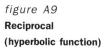
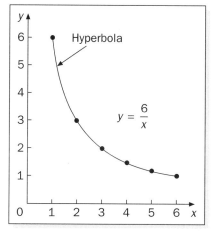

Hyperbola

$$y = \frac{6}{x}$$

Gradients to graphs

Linear Functions

The general form of the linear function is:

$y = mx + c$

where m is the gradient and c the vertical intercept.

The slope or gradient of the line joining two points measures how 'steep' the line is and is defined as the fraction:

$$\frac{\text{difference between the } y \text{ co-ordinates of the points}}{\text{difference between the } x \text{ co-ordinates of the points}}$$

Gradient between $(x_1 \ y_1)$, $(x_2 \ y_2)$

$$\text{Gradient} = \frac{(y_2 - y_1)}{(x_2 - x_1)}$$

$$\text{Gradient} = \frac{\text{vertical distance}}{\text{horizontal distance}}$$

In Figure A10

$$\text{Gradient} = \frac{7 - 3}{3 - 1} = \frac{4}{2} = +2$$

figure A10
Gradient of straight line

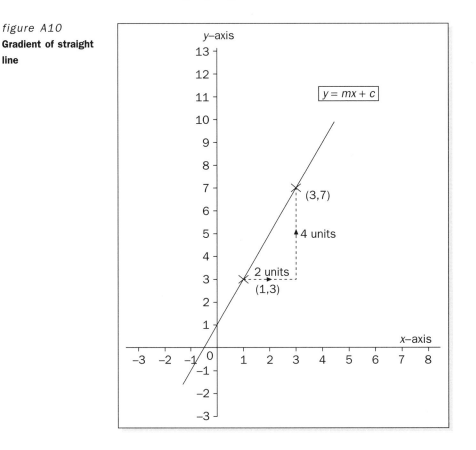

Non-linear Functions

Here we use *calculus* (see chapter 11) to find the gradient to a point on a curve. The process by which we *differentiate* the function will give us the required gradient.

ACTIVITY **8**
••••••••••••

A restaurant is considering a new vegetarian meal and has test marketed the product. The tests showed that if 280 pence is charged for the meal it will sell 1,600 units per restaurant per week, whilst at a price of 320 pence it sells 1,400 units.

Assuming that the demand curve for the product is linear, find its equation (i.e. find *m* and *c*).

$$P = c + mQ$$

1 Construct the demand schedule.
  (i) Label column **A**: **Quantity** and column **B**: **Price (in pence)**.
  (ii) Enter the price data from 600 to 0 in increments of –25.
  (iii) Use the demand equation formula to calculate how many units can be sold at each of these prices.
  This will be easier to accomplish if the demand equation is rewritten to make Q the subject of the equation.
2 Plot the demand curve.
3 In column **C** calculate the firm's total revenue at each price.
  What price will maximise the firm's total revenue?
4 In column **D** calculate the price elasticity of demand (P.E.D.) at each price where:

$$P.E.D. = \left(\frac{\Delta Q}{\Delta P}\right) \times \left(\frac{P}{Q}\right)$$

What is the price elasticity of demand when revenue is maximised?
5 Plot the graph showing the total revenue curve.
6 Using columns **E** and **F** construct data for total cost and profits at each potential level of output.
  The restaurant have estimated the total cost equation for the product (in pence) as:

$$TC = 100000 + 2Q + 0.1Q^2$$

Note that this is a quadratic equation where the 100,000 represents the fixed costs assigned to the product.

Which output and price maximises profits?
Is this the same output/price combination that maximises total revenue?

7 Plot a graph showing TR, TC and profits.
8 Use the spreadsheet to investigate changes in fixed costs on the profit maximising output/price combination – try increasing fixed costs by 20000.
9 Return fixed costs to their original level.

10 From the previous graph find the levels of output where the firm breaks even (this will be approximate).

Try to get a more accurate answer from the spreadsheet by altering *P*.

11 Use the formula:

Profit = TR − TC

to solve the quadratic profit equation which will disclose the break-even output.

Responses and solutions to this activity can be found on p. 471.

A10 Progressions
....

Two types of progression are frequently used in quantitative solutions, namely arithmetic and geometric progressions.

Arithmetic progressions (AP)

This is a sequence of terms in which an initial term, *a*, changes by a constant absolute amount, called the 'common difference' (*d*).

An **arithmetic progression** involving *n* terms takes the following form:

$a, a + d, a + 2d, a + 3d, a + 4d \ldots a + (n - 1)d$

Examples: $5, 7, 9, 11, 13 \ldots (a = 5, \quad d = +2)$

$\qquad 43, 39, 35, 31, 27 \ldots (a = 43, d = -4)$

Note that the third term is $a + 2d$, the fourth terms is $a + 3d$, and so on, so that the *n*th term is $a + (n - 1)d$, where *n* can be any number.

If we sum the *n* terms of an arithmetic progression (AP), then we can use the formula:

Sum of Arithmetic Progression

$S_n = \dfrac{n}{2}[2a + (n - 1)d]$

where S_n = sum of AP over *n* terms

$\qquad n$ = number of terms

$\qquad a$ = initial term

$\qquad d$ = common difference

WORKED
EXAMPLE **A32**
....

A businessman pays his employee a salary of £10,000 per annum; at the end of each year he receives an annual increment of £400.

Calculate (a) the employee's salary during the 6th year

$\qquad$ (b) the total salary received by the employee during the six years.

Solution

This is an arithmetic progression (AP) with an initial amount (a) of £10,000 which rises by a common difference (d) of £400 per annum.

(a) When $n = 6$, the sixth term of an AP will be $a + (n - 1)d$

$$= £10,000 + (6 - 1)£400$$

$$= £12,000$$

The employee receives £12,000 in the sixth year

(b) $S_n = \dfrac{n}{2}[2a + (n - 1)d]$

$S_6 = \dfrac{6}{2}[2(£10,000) + (6 - 1)£400]$

$S_6 = 3[£20,000 + £2,000]$

$S_6 = £66,000$

The employee receives £66,000 salary during the first six years of employment.

The box below gives a proof of the formula for summing an arithmetic progression

---

Proof of AP formula

$$S_n = a + [a + d] + [a + 2d] + \ldots [a + (n - 2)d] + [a + (n - 1)d]$$

S_n (backward) $= [a + (n - 1)d] + [a + (n - 2d)] + \ldots [a + d] + a$

∴ adding term by term

$$2S_n = [2a + (n - 1)d] + [2a + (n - 1)d] + [2a + (n - 1)d] + [2a + (n - 1)d] + [2a + (n - 1)d]$$

$$2S_n = n[2a + (n - 1)d]$$

$$S_n = \dfrac{n}{2}[2a + (n - 1)d]$$

Geometric progressions (GP)

A **geometric progression** occurs where an initial amount (a) changes by a 'common ratio' (r) in successive terms.

A geometric progression involving n terms takes the following form:

$a, ar, ar^2, ar^3 \ldots ar^{n-1}$

Examples

$3, 6, 12, 24, 48 \ldots (a = 3, r = 2)$

$200, 100, 50, 25, 12.5 \ldots (a = 200, r = \dfrac{1}{2})$

Note that the third term is ar^2, the fourth term is ar^3, and so on, so that the nth term is ar^{n-1}, where n can be any number.

If we sum the n terms of a geometric progression (GP), then we can use the formula

---

Sum of geometric progression

$$S_n = \frac{a(1 - r^n)}{(1 - r)}$$

where S_n = Sum of GP over n terms

n = number of terms

a = initial term

r = common ratio (as a fraction or a decimal)

WORKED
EXAMPLE **A33**
················

An employee makes an annual investment of £1,000 in shares this year. He instructs his broker to increase this annual investment by 5 per cent each year.

(a) How much does he invest in the sixth year?

(b) How much does he invest altogether over the first six years?

Solution

This is a GP, with a = £1,000 and r = 1.05

(a) When n = 6, the sixth term of a GP will be:

$ar^{n-1} = ar^{6-1} = ar^5$

£1,000$(1.05)^5$ = £1,276.28

He invests £1,276.28 in the sixth year

(b) $S_n = \dfrac{a(1 - r^n)}{(1 - r)}$

$S_6 = \dfrac{1,000[1 - (1.05)^6]}{(1 - 1.05)} = \dfrac{1,000[1 - 1.3401]}{-0.05}$

$S_6 = \dfrac{1,000[-0.3401]}{-0.05} = \dfrac{-340.1}{-0.05}$

S_6 = £6,802

He invests £6,802 over the six years.

The box below gives a proof of the formula for summing a geometric progression.

Proof of GP formula

$$S_n = a + ar + ar^2 + \ldots + ar^{n-2} + ar^{n-1}$$

$$\therefore rS_n = \quad\; ar + ar^2 + \ldots + ar^{n-2} + ar^{n-1} + ar^n$$

$$S_n - rS_n = a \hspace{7cm} - ar^n$$

---

i.e. $S_n(1 - r) = a - ar^n$

$$S_n = \frac{a(1 - r^n)}{(1 - r)}$$

SELF-CHECK QUESTIONS

A11 Make y the subject of the following formulae:

(a) $x = 2(y - 1)$ (b) $x = y(b + 7)$ (c) $t = 5y + \dfrac{p}{7}$

A12 Expand the following and simplify:

(a) $(2x - 3)(4x + 1)$ (b) $(3x + 5)(x - 3)$ (c) $p(2m + t) - t(3m - p)$

A13 Factorise the following:

(a) $3t + 7t^2$ (b) $2m^3 - 6m^2$ (c) $6mp^2 + 9m^2pt$

(d) $x^2 - 7x + 12$ (e) $x^2 - 25$ (f) $2x^2 - x - 15$

A14 Solve the following equations:

(a) $2x - 3 = 11$ (b) $3 - 5x = 8$ (c) $4(2x - 3) = 7$

A15 Solve the following quadratic equations, to 2 d.p. where necessary:

(a) $x^2 + 7x + 12 = 0$ (b) $5x^2 + 6x - 2 = 0$ (c) $x^2 + 4x - 117 = 0$

A16 Solve the following pairs of simultaneous equations:

(a) $5x + y = 0$ (b) $7x + 3y = 18$

     $3x - 2y = 13$ $x + y = 4$

A17 Solve the following inequalities:

(a) $5x > 32$ (b) $4t < 5t - 8$ (c) $x^2 < 36$ (d) $-2 \leq 5x + 3 < 4$

A18 Complete this table of values for $y = x^2 + x - 6$:

x	-4	-3	-2	-1	0	1	2	3
x^2		9			0		4	
$+x$	-4	-3				1	2	3
-6	-6	-6			-6		-6	
y	6		-4	-6				

(a) Use the table to draw the graph of $y = x^2 + x - 6$ as x takes values from -4 to 3.

(b) Use your graph to solve $y = x^2 + x - 6 = 0$

A19 Find the gradient of the straight line which connects the points $(-2, -3)$ and $(4, 9)$

A20 Use an appropriate *formula* to sum the following progressions to eight terms

    (a) 42, 46, 50, 54 ...
    (b) 200, 195, 190, 185 ...
    (c) 4, 6, 9, 13.5 ...
    (d) 1,000, 500, 250, 125 ...

Note: **Answers can be found on p. 368.**

Note: **Answers can be found on p. 368.**

REVIEW QUESTIONS

A1 Nearly a third of large and medium sized companies said they regarded overqualified (graduate) applicants for low level unskilled jobs as a problem. In reply it was argued that in 1980 one in eight school leavers went on to take a degree. Today (1997) the proportion is one in three, meaning that as a group they cannot be regarded as high fliers. Find

(a) how many of the 474 companies interviewed were concerned about this problem?
(b) if the number of school leavers was constant over the period at 900,000 how many went to university in 1980 and 1997?

A2 In a 1997 survey of British pop wealth in *Business Age* magazine, David Bowie came top with £550m, Paul McCartney came second with £520m and Gary Barlow 50th with £9.5m. The youngest person in the top 50 was Baby Spice with £14.5m.

(a) What percentage is Gary Barlow's wealth of Baby Spice's wealth?
(b) By what percentage would Paul McCartney's wealth have to increase by before it equalled that of David Bowie's?

A3 On Monday 27 October 1997 the Dow Jones share index in New York fell by 7 per cent to 7,161.15 (the biggest one day fall since Black Monday in 1987). What was the index at the start of the day?

A4 A company produces a product for which the variable cost per unit is £5 and the fixed costs are £20,000. If the selling price is £15 per unit

(a) how many units (Q)) does the company need to sell in order to make £8,000 profit?
(b) At what level of output would the firm break even (i.e. total revenue = total costs)
(c) New environmental legislation increases the company's fixed costs by 20 per cent, by what percentage does this increase the break even output?
(d) Plot the firms Fixed Costs, Total Costs (before and after the increase) and Total Revenue on a graph. Mark the break even outputs of b) and c) on the graph.
Make use the following relationships:

      Total cost   = fixed costs + variable costs
      Total revenue = price per unit × number of units sold
      Profit   = total revenue − total cost

A5 It is estimated that if a price of £15 per unit is charged for a product five units per period will be sold. If the price is lowered to £13, sales will be six units per period.

The supply curve for the product is given by P = 3Q + 5.

(a) Assuming that the demand relationship is linear, find the demand equation.
(b) Find the equilibrium price and quantity (i.e. the price where quantity demanded = quantity supplied).

A6 *Note:* the intention of Question A6 is to practice your mathematics and graph drawing and not break-even analysis (see chapter 10).

A firm's total revenue and total cost equations are given by:

Total costs = $Q^2 + 23$
Total revenue = $-2Q^2 + 26Q$

(a) Find the output levels at which the firm just breaks even.
(b) Plot the graph of total costs, total revenue and profits and show that the profit maximising output is mid-way between the break-even outputs.

Note: Answers to review questions can be found on p. 456.

Further study and data
....

Texts

Bancroft, G. and O'Sullivan, G. (1993), *Quantitative methods for accounting and business studies*, 3rd edn, McGraw Hill, chapters 1 and 2.

Curwin, J. and Slater, R. (1996), *Quantitative methods for business decisions*, 4th edn, Chapman and Hall, chapter 6.

Morris, C. (1996), *Quantitative approaches in business studies*, 4th edn, Pitman, chapter 1.

Swift, L. (1997), *Mathematics and statistics for business, management and finance*, Macmillan, parts A1 to A6.

Thomas, R. (1997), *Quantitative methods for business studies*, Prentice Hall, appendix.

Waters, D. (1997), *Quantitative methods*, 2nd edn, Addison Wesley Longman, chapters 1 and 2.

Wisniewski, M. with Stead, R. (1996), *Foundation quantitative methods for business*, Pitman, chapter 2.

Probabilities for the Normal distribution

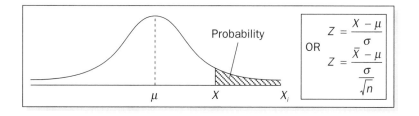

Z Score	0.00	0.01	0.02	0.03	0.04	0.05	0.06	0.07	0.08	0.09
0.0	0.5000	0.4960	0.4920	0.4880	0.4840	0.4801	0.4761	0.4721	0.4681	0.4641
0.1	0.4602	0.4562	0.4522	0.4483	0.4443	0.4404	0.4364	0.4325	0.4286	0.4247
0.2	0.4207	0.4168	0.4129	0.4090	0.4052	0.4013	0.3974	0.3936	0.3897	0.3859
0.3	0.3821	0.3783	0.3745	0.3707	0.3669	0.3632	0.3594	0.3557	0.3520	0.3483
0.4	0.3446	0.3409	0.3372	0.3336	0.3300	0.3264	0.3228	0.3192	0.3156	0.3121
0.5	0.3085	0.3050	0.3015	0.2981	0.2946	0.2912	0.2877	0.2843	0.2810	0.2776
0.6	0.2743	0.2709	0.2676	0.2643	0.2611	0.2578	0.2546	0.2514	0.2483	0.2451
0.7	0.2420	0.2389	0.2358	0.2327	0.2296	0.2266	0.2236	0.2206	0.2177	0.2148
0.8	0.2119	0.2090	0.2061	0.2033	0.2005	0.1977	0.1949	0.1922	0.1894	01867
0.9	0.1841	0.1814	0.1788	0.1762	0.1736	0.1711	0.1685	0.1660	0.1635	0.1611
1.0	0.1587	0.1562	0.1539	0.1515	0.1492	0.1469	0.1446	0.1423	0.1401	0.1379
1.1	0.1357	0.1335	0.1314	0.1292	0.1271	0.1251	0.1230	0.1210	0.1190	0.1170
1.2	0.1151	0.1131	0.1112	0.1093	0.1075	0.1056	0.1038	0.1020	0.1003	0.0985
1.3	0.0968	0.0951	0.0934	0.0918	0.0901	0.0885	0.0869	0.0853	0.0838	0.0823
1.4	0.0808	0.0793	0.0778	0.0764	0.0749	0.0735	0.0721	0.0708	0.0694	0.0681
1.5	0.0668	0.0655	0.0643	0.0630	0.0618	0.0606	0.0594	0.0582	0.0571	0.0559
1.6	0.0548	0.0537	0.0562	0.0516	0.0505	0.0495	0.0485	0.0475	0.0465	0.0455
1.7	0.0446	0.0436	0.0427	0.0418	0.0409	0.0401	0.0392	0.0384	0.0375	0.0367
1.8	0.0359	0.0351	0.0344	0.0336	0.0329	0.0322	0.0314	0.0307	0.0301	0.0294
1.9	0.0287	0.0281	0.0274	0.0268	0.0262	0.0256	0.0250	0.0244	0.0239	0.0233
2.0	0.0228	0.0222	0.0217	0.0212	0.0207	0.0202	0.0197	0.0192	0.0188	0.0183
2.1	0.0179	0.0174	0.0170	0.0166	0.0162	0.0158	0.0154	0.0150	0.0146	0.0143
2.2	0.0139	0.0136	0.0132	0.0129	0.0125	0.0122	0.0119	0.0116	0.0113	0.0110
2.3	0.0107	0.0104	0.0102	0.0099	0.0096	0.0094	0.0091	0.0089	0.0087	0.0084
2.4	0.0082	0.0080	0.0078	0.0075	0.0073	0.0072	0.0069	0.0068	0.0066	0.0064
2.5	0.0062	0.0060	0.0059	0.0057	0.0055	0.0054	0.0052	0.0051	0.0049	0.0048
2.6	0.0047	0.0045	0.0044	0.0043	0.0041	0.0040	0.0039	0.0038	0.0037	0.0036
2.7	0.0035	0.0034	0.0033	0.0032	0.0031	0.0030	0.0029	0.0028	0.0027	0.0026
2.8	0.0026	0.0025	0.0024	0.0023	0.0023	0.0022	0.0021	0.0021	0.0020	0.0019
2.9	0.0019	0.0018	0.0018	0.0017	0.0016	0.0016	0.0015	0.0015	0.0014	0.0014
3.0	0.0013	0.0013	0.0013	0.0012	0.0012	0.0011	0.0011	0.0011	0.0010	0.0010

Cumulative Binomial probabilities

		$p = 0.01$	0.05	0.10	0.20	0.30	0.40	0.45	0.50
$n = 5$	$r =$ 0	1.0000	1.0000	1.0000	1.0000	1.0000	1.0000	1.0000	1.0000
	1	0.0490	0.2262	0.4095	0.6723	0.8319	0.9222	0.9497	0.9688
	2	0.0010	0.0226	0.0815	0.2627	0.4718	0.6630	0.7438	0.8125
	3		0.0012	0.0086	0.0579	0.1631	0.3174	0.4069	0.5000
	4			0.0005	0.0067	0.0308	0.0870	0.1312	0.1875
	5				0.0003	0.0024	0.0102	0.0185	0.0313
$n = 10$	$r =$ 0	1.0000	1.0000	1.0000	1.0000	1.0000	1.0000	1.0000	1.0000
	1	0.0956	0.4013	0.6513	0.8926	0.9718	0.9940	0.9975	0.9990
	2	0.0043	0.0861	0.2639	0.6242	0.8507	0.9536	0.9767	0.9893
	3	0.0001	0.0115	0.0702	0.3222	0.6172	0.8327	0.9004	0.9453
	4		0.0010	0.0128	0.1209	0.3504	0.6177	0.7430	0.8281
	5		0.0001	0.0016	0.0328	0.1503	0.3669	0.4956	0.6230
	6			0.0001	0.0064	0.0473	0.1662	0.2616	0.3770
	7				0.0009	0.0106	0.0548	0.1020	0.1719
	8				0.0001	0.0016	0.0123	0.0274	0.0547
	9					0.0001	0.0017	0.0045	0.0107
	10						0.0001	0.0003	0.0010

where

p is the probability of a characteristic (e.g. a defective item),

n is the sample size and

r is the number with that characteristic.

Note: All probabilities are for 'r or more successes'. Only selected values for n and r are shown in this table.

Cumulative Poisson probabilities

		$\mu = 1.0$	2.0	3.0	4.0	5.0	6.0	7.0
$r =$	0	1.0000	1.0000	1.0000	1.0000	1.0000	1.0000	1.0000
	1	0.6321	0.8647	0.9502	0.9817	0.9933	0.9975	0.9991
	2	0.2642	0.5940	0.8009	0.9084	0.9596	0.9826	0.9927
	3	0.0803	0.3233	0.5768	0.7619	0.8753	0.9380	0.9704
	4	0.0190	0.1429	0.3528	0.5665	0.7350	0.8488	0.9182
	5	0.0037	0.0527	0.1847	0.3712	0.5595	0.7149	0.8270
	6	0.0006	0.0166	0.0839	0.2149	0.3840	0.5543	0.6993
	7	0.0001	0.0011	0.0335	0.1107	0.2378	0.3937	0.5503
	8		0.0002	0.0119	0.0511	0.1334	0.2560	0.4013
	9			0.0038	0.0214	0.0681	0.1528	0.2709
	10			0.0011	0.0081	0.0318	0.0839	0.1695
	11			0.0003	0.0028	0.0137	0.0426	0.0985
	12			0.0001	0.0009	0.0055	0.0201	0.0534
	13				0.0003	0.0020	0.0088	0.0270
	14				0.0001	0.0007	0.0036	0.0128
	15					0.0002	0.0014	0.0057
	16					0.0001	0.0005	0.0024
	17						0.0002	0.0010
	18						0.0001	0.0004
	19							0.0001

where
$\mu(=np)$ is the average number of times a characteristic occurs and
r is the number of occurrences.
Note: All probabilities are for 'r or more successes'.

Table of random numbers

83635	18471	01664	97316	13751	22904	46465	55782	13047	64812
66791	25482	48893	34611	07709	24016	81064	00876	11197	35664
46879	05246	13006	17669	16587	25597	24106	67913	05438	97013
98520	97410	96305	57421	23489	67492	31647	85500	69477	55523
68227	06488	52064	30027	66988	20333	47881	20944	67822	01668
20034	17909	14246	28346	10972	38106	20079	99555	24768	25009
03504	71668	64982	34679	97643	18164	28640	27913	64820	57913
59731	12389	60071	04587	32881	66749	12400	64478	94613	00457
00456	67910	17219	89404	62840	37898	74613	01346	78994	00657
98015	67623	15678	01541	34613	26546	51255	25245	53345	42031
19994	64313	43100	32065	40324	60354	60106	14659	01346	43213
79844	57645	00247	61683	09830	98401	87410	01964	30687	46280
19601	68163	54387	46338	46324	57621	05151	23544	57987	98037
69771	02344	00168	98884	23467	90120	34970	35668	76137	90173
14865	05576	58425	97031	26459	73156	87109	01348	76218	40245
83116	77102	00886	01134	46905	58766	41003	28979	84341	28752
46103	25571	93826	40319	73150	46283	79134	67229	87766	35441
90087	51685	24641	35794	58525	81000	17991	77851	00356	48440
16624	00975	11300	24687	12665	78941	12265	02399	54613	87291
03154	67913	83739	19726	48505	64213	58467	91349	72344	31164

Student *t* Critical values

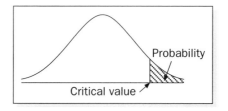

Probability

Critical value

Probability	0.10	0.05	0.025	0.01	0.005
v = 1	3.078	6.314	12.706	31.821	63.657
2	1.886	2.920	4.303	6.965	9.925
3	1.638	2.353	3.182	4.541	5.841
4	1.533	2.132	2.776	3.747	4.604
5	1.476	2.015	2.571	3.365	4.032
6	1.440	1.943	2.447	3.143	3.707
7	1.415	1.895	2.365	2.998	3.499
8	1.397	1.860	2.306	2.896	3.355
9	1.383	1.833	2.262	2.821	3.250
10	1.372	1.812	2.228	2.764	3.169
11	1.363	1.796	2.201	2.718	3.106
12	1.356	1.782	2.179	2.681	3.055
13	1.350	1.771	2.160	2.650	3.012
14	1.345	1.761	2.145	2.624	2.977
15	1.341	1.753	2.131	2.602	2.947
16	1.337	1.746	2.120	2.583	2.921
17	1.333	1.740	2.110	2.567	2.898
18	1.330	1.734	2.101	2.552	2.878
19	1.328	1.729	2.093	2.539	2.861
20	1.325	1.725	2.086	2.528	2.845
21	1.323	1.721	2.080	2.518	2.831
22	1.321	1.717	2.074	2.508	2.819
23	1.319	1.714	2.069	2.500	2.807
24	1.318	1.711	2.064	2.492	2.797
25	1.316	1.708	2.060	2.485	2.787
26	1.315	1.706	2.056	2.479	2.779
27	1.314	1.703	2.052	2.473	2.771
28	1.313	1.701	2.048	2.467	2.763
29	1.311	1.699	2.045	2.462	2.756
30	1.310	1.697	2.042	2.457	2.750
40	1.303	1.684	2.021	2.423	2.704
60	1.296	1.671	2.000	2.390	2.660
120	1.289	1.658	1.980	2.358	2.617
∞	1.282	1.645	1.960	2.326	2.576

where *v* is the number of degrees of freedom.

χ^2 **Critical values**

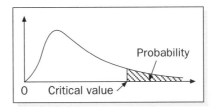

Probability v	0.250	0.100	0.050	0.025	0.010	0.005	0.001
1	1.32	2.71	3.84	5.02	6.63	7.88	10.8
2	2.77	4.61	5.99	7.38	9.21	10.6	13.8
3	4.11	6.25	7.81	9.35	11.3	12.8	16.3
4	5.39	7.78	9.49	11.1	13.3	14.9	18.5
5	6.63	9.24	11.1	12.8	15.1	16.7	20.5
6	7.84	10.6	12.6	14.4	16.8	18.5	22.5
7	9.04	12.0	14.1	16.0	18.5	20.3	24.3
8	10.2	13.4	15.5	17.5	20.3	22.0	26.1
9	11.4	14.7	16.9	19.0	21.7	23.6	27.9
10	12.5	16.0	18.3	20.5	23.2	25.2	29.6
11	13.7	17.3	19.7	21.9	24.7	26.8	31.3
12	14.8	18.5	21.0	23.3	26.2	28.3	32.9
13	16.0	19.8	22.4	24.7	27.7	29.8	34.5
14	17.1	21.1	23.7	26.1	29.1	31.3	36.1
15	18.2	22.3	25.0	27.5	30.6	32.8	37.7
16	19.4	23.5	26.3	28.8	32.0	34.3	39.3
17	20.5	24.8	27.6	30.2	33.4	35.7	40.8
18	21.6	26.0	28.9	31.5	34.8	37.2	42.3
19	22.7	27.2	30.1	32.9	36.2	38.6	43.8
20	23.8	28.4	31.4	34.2	37.6	40.0	45.3
21	24.9	29.6	32.7	35.5	38.9	41.4	46.8
22	26.0	30.8	33.9	36.8	40.3	42.8	48.3
23	27.1	32.0	35.2	38.1	41.6	44.2	49.7
24	28.2	33.2	36.4	39.4	43.0	45.6	51.2
25	29.3	34.4	37.7	40.6	44.3	46.9	52.6
26	30.4	35.6	38.9	41.9	45.6	48.3	54.1
27	31.5	36.7	40.1	43.2	47.0	49.6	55.5
28	32.6	37.9	41.3	44.5	48.3	51.0	56.9
29	33.7	39.1	42.6	45.7	49.6	52.3	58.3
30	34.8	40.3	43.8	47.0	50.9	53.7	59.7
40	45.6	51.8	55.8	59.3	63.7	66.8	73.4
50	56.3	63.2	67.5	71.4	76.2	79.5	86.7
60	67.0	74.4	79.1	83.3	88.4	92.0	99.6
70	77.6	85.5	90.5	95.0	100	104	112
80	88.1	96.6	102	107	112	116	125
90	98.6	108	113	118	124	128	137
100	109	118	124	130	136	140	149

where v is the number of degrees of freedom.

Answers to 'Self-check questions'

Chapter 1: Data presentation and collection

1.1 *Step 1* From the frequency table we can see that all the class intervals have a (standard) class width of £4.

Step 2 Enlarge the original table to include headings for:

Class width, No. of standard class widths, Height.

(1) Value (£)	(2) Frequency	(3) Class width	(4) No. of standard class widths	(5) Height (2) ÷ (4)
0–3.99	8	4	1	8
4–7.99	18	4	1	18
8–11.99	22	4	1	22
12–15.99	24	4	1	24
16–19.99	13	4	1	13
20–23.99	12	4	1	12
24–27.99	2	4	1	2
28–31.99	1	4	1	1

Note: Class width (3) is found by: upper class boundary – lower class boundary

Step 3 Construct the histogram

figure 1.13

Histogram showing the number and value of transactions between 17.00 and 22.00 hours

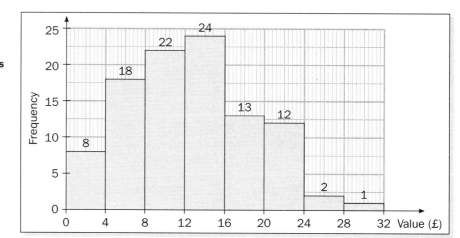

Because the class widths are equal, the heights of each rectangle correspond to class frequencies.

1.2

(1) Weekly income(£)	(2) F	(3) Class width	(4) No. of standard class widths	(5) Frequency density (2) ÷ (4)
75.5–100.5	6	25	1	6
100.5–125.5	8	25	1	8
125.5–150.5	17	25	1	17
150.5–200.5	8	50	2	4
200.5–300.5	6	100	4	1.5

Here the heights of each rectangle correspond to frequency densities.

figure 1.14
Unequal-width histogram

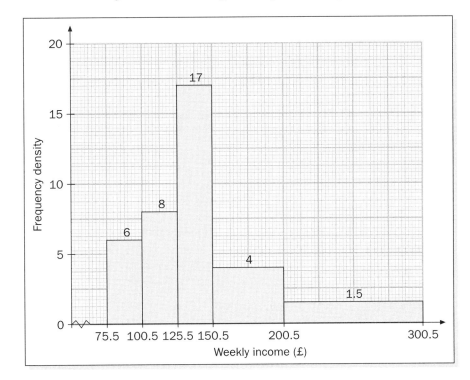

1.3

Less than	Cumulative frequency
19.5 years	8
39.5 years	34
59.5 years	144
79.5 years	272
99.5 years	328

Plot the points to draw a cumulative 'less than' frequency curve, as in Figure 1.15.

figure 1.15
Cumulative 'less than' frequency curve

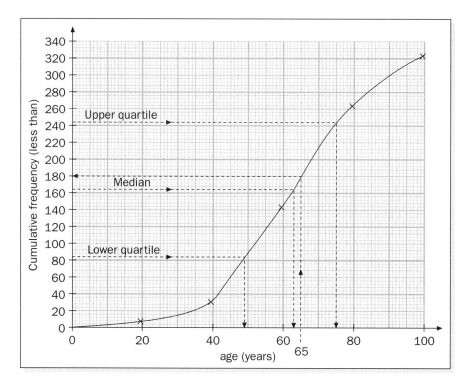

(i) The median corresponds to $\frac{1}{2}(n + 1) = \frac{328 + 1}{2} =$ the 164.5th person.

In Figure 1.15 this is estimated as an age of about 63 years.

(ii) The lower quartile corresponds to $\frac{1}{4}(n + 1) = \frac{329}{4} = 82.25$th person

$\rightarrow$ 49 years old.

The upper quartile corresponds to $\frac{3}{4}(n + 1) = \frac{3 \times 329}{4} = 246.75$th person

$\rightarrow$ 75 years old.

(iii) The number of people LESS than 65 is read off as 182 approx.

Hence there are 328 − 182 = 146 people OVER 65 years.

As a percentage, this is $\frac{146}{328} \times 100\% = 44.5\%$.

1.4 (a)

Height more than (m)	Cumulative frequency
0	100
1.95	85
2.45	42
2.95	12
3.45	2
4.55	0

(b) Plot on Figure 1.8 (p. 12) as requested (see Figure 1.16).

figure 1.16

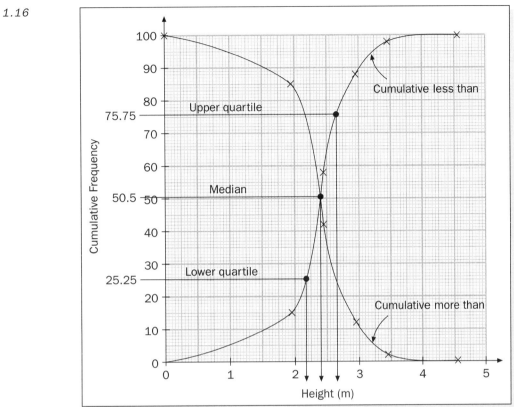

(c) The cumulative 'less than' and 'more than' curves intersect at the median. Where they intersect, the same number of persons are 'less than' a particular value as are 'more than' this value, which by definition is the median value (i.e. that value which divides the distribution in half).

1.5

Category	Road accident Casualties 1997 Number killed	Pie chart angle
Pedestrians	1,914	127°
Pedal cyclists	323	21°
Two wheeled motor vehicles	942	63°
Cars and taxis	2,019	134°
Others	226	15°
Total	5,424	360°

A completed pie chart from this table is shown in Figure 1.17.

figure 1.17
Pie chart

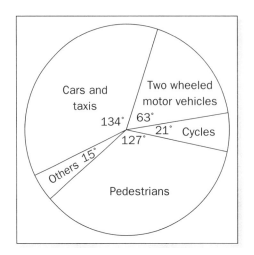

1.6 (a) Plot the Lorenz curve for 1979 on Figure 1.12 (p. 20) as requested
      (see Figure 1.18).
   (b) Note that the 1995 Lorenz curve lies outside the 1979 curve at all
      points, suggesting greater inequality in 1995 than in 1979 throughout
      the entire income distribution. The higher gini coefficient for 1995 is
      a useful indicator of greater inequality in this case since the respective
      Lorenz curves do not intersect.
   (c) In this case the respective Lorenz curves *would intersect*. We now have
      greater inequality in 1995 than in 1979 for the bottom 50 per cent of
      income receivers *but* greater equality in 1995 than in 1979 for the top
      50 per cent of income receivers.

figure 1.18

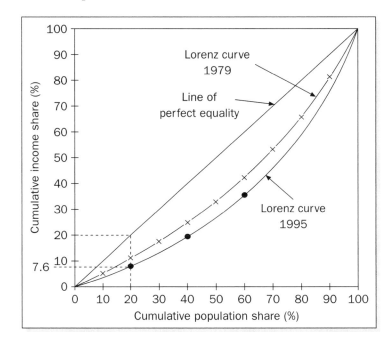

Chapter 2: Central location and dispersion
••

2.1 (a) $X_1 + X_2 + X_3 + X_4$
(b) $X_2 + X_3 + X_4 + X_5$
(c) $F_1X_1 + F_2X_2 + F_3X_3$
(d) $F_3X_3 + F_4X_4 + F_5X_5 + F_6X_6$

2.2 (a) $\sum_{i=1}^{5} X_i$ (b) $\sum_{i=5}^{7} X_i$

(c) $\sum_{i=1}^{4} F_iX_i$ (d) $\sum_{i=2}^{4} F_iX_i$

2.3 There are six different scores observed, so $j = 6$.
Let $X_1 = 1$ then $F_1 = 3$
       $X_2 = 2$ then $F_2 = 2$
       $X_3 = 3$ then $F_3 = 2$
       $X_4 = 4$ then $F_4 = 3$
       $X_5 = 5$ then $F_5 = 2$
       $X_6 = 6$ then $F_6 = 3$

$$\sum_{i=1}^{j} F_iX_i = \sum_{i=1}^{6} F_iX_i$$

i.e. $\sum_{i=1}^{6} F_iX_i = F_1X_1 + F_2X_2 + F_3X_3 + F_4X_4 + F_5X_5 + F_6X_6$

$$= (3 \times 1) + (2 \times 2) + (2 \times 3) + (3 \times 4) + (2 \times 5) + (3 \times 6)$$

$$= 3 + 4 + 6 + 12 + 10 + 18$$

$$= 53$$

2.4 (a) (i)   94.4 (000)
     (ii)   86.4 (000)
     (iii) 83.3 (000)

(b) $\overline{X} = \dfrac{\sum_{i=1}^{12} X_i}{n}$

$$= \frac{X_1 + X_2 + X_3 + X_4 + X_5 + X_6 + X_7 + X_8 + X_9 + X_{10} + X_{11} + X_{12}}{12}$$

$$= \frac{69.3 + 75.5 + 76.3 + 94.4 + 88.7 + 77.2 + 86.4 + 75.5 + 79 + 83.3 + 82.2 + 78.1}{12}$$

$$= \frac{965.9}{12} = 80.49(000)$$

(c) $\quad \bar{X} = \dfrac{\sum\limits_{i=7}^{12} X_i}{n}$

$\quad = \dfrac{X_7 + X_8 + X_9 + X_{10} + X_{11} + X_{12}}{6}$

$\quad = \dfrac{86.4 + 75.5 + 79 + 83.3 + 82.2 + 78.1}{6}$

$\quad = \dfrac{484.5}{6} = 80.75(000)$

(d) $\quad \bar{X} = \dfrac{\sum\limits_{i=4}^{9} X_i}{n}$

$\quad = \dfrac{X_4 + X_5 + X_6 + X_7 + X_8 + X_9}{6}$

$\quad = \dfrac{94.4 + 88.7 + 77.2 + 86.4 + 75.5 + 79}{6}$

$\quad = \dfrac{501.2}{6} = 83.53(000)$

2.5 Mean: $\bar{X} = \dfrac{\sum\limits_{i=1}^{n} X_i}{n} = \dfrac{375{,}975}{20} = £18{,}799$

Median:

Step 1 Place the salaries into an array:

14,375; 14,375; 14,375; 14,375; 14,375; 14,375; 15,180;
15,180; 15,180; 15,525; 15,767; 15,870; 16,767; 16,767;
17,880; 19,600; 19,870; 23,069; 36,938; 46,132.

Step 2 Find the median position:

Median position $= \dfrac{n+1}{2} = \dfrac{20+1}{2} = 10.5\text{th item}$

Step 3 Read the value of the 10.5th item in the array (the average of the 10th and 11th items):

Median $= \dfrac{15{,}525 + 15{,}767}{2} = £15{,}646$

Mode: The value occurring most often: £14,375 (occurs six times)

The mean salary of £18,799 appears flattering but a couple of unusually high salaries of £36,938 and £46,132 raise this type of average considerably. This distribution is skewed to the right – i.e. a few extreme high observations occur – and so the mean is pulled in the direction of the skew. The median value is the mid-point of the data: thus half the workers earn less than £15,646 whilst the other half earn more. In some ways this is the most representative type of average as it is unaffected by the few high salaries observed and lies below the mean. Six of the 20 workers earn the modal (most frequent) salary of £14,375 which is considerably lower than both the mean and the median value.

Management would probably use the mean figure to support a case that workers are well paid, whereas unions might prefer to use the median or mode figure to suggest that workers are less well paid. As in most cases when using income data, care must therefore be exercised when quoting averages. Statistics from other firms – or industry averages – would help in making more realistic comparisons.

2.6 (a) Calculate the mid-point values (X_i) of each class interval, then construct a table relevant to our formula for the mean with grouped data.

Class intervals	X_i (1)	F_i (2)	F_iX_i (1) × (2)
−5–0	−2.5	2	−5
0–5	2.5	32	80
5–10	7.5	25	187.5
10–15	12.5	10	125
15–20	17.5	8	140
20–25	22.5	3	67.5
25–30	27.5	2	55
30–35	32.5	5	162.5
35–40	37.5	4	150
40–100	70	3	210
100–172*	136	4	544
Sums		98	1,716.5

Note: * As the highest value recorded was 172 per cent; the upper class boundary of the last class interval = 172.

$$\overline{X} = \frac{\sum_{i=1}^{j} F_iX_i}{\sum_{i=1}^{j} F_i} = \frac{\sum_{i=1}^{11} F_iX_i}{\sum_{i=1}^{11} F_i} = \frac{\sum F_iX_i}{\sum F_i}$$

$$\overline{X} = \frac{1,716.5}{98}$$

$\overline{X} = 17.52$ per cent is the arithmetic mean

(b) Find the median position

$$\text{Median} = \frac{n+1}{2}$$

$$= \frac{98+1}{2}$$

$$= 49.5$$

The class interval in which the median (the 49.5th observation) lies is 5–10

Median =

$$\text{LCB} + \text{class width} \times \frac{\text{Number of observations to median position}}{\text{Total number of observations in median class interval}}$$

$$= 5 + \left(5 \times \frac{15.5}{25}\right)$$

$$= 5 + (5 \times 0.62)$$

$$= 5 + 3.1$$

Median = 8.1%

(c) The modal class interval is 0–5 (32 observations)

2.7 $s^2 = 43.6$ square cars
   $s = 6.6$ cars

2.8 $s^2 = 797.6$ square %
   $s = 28.2\%$

Chapter 3: Regression and correlation

3.1 *Approach 1*   *Approach 2*

X_i	Y_i	X_iY_i	X_i^2	x_i $X_i - 4.5$	y_i $Y_i - 9$	x_iy_i	x_i^2
1	2	2	1	−3.5	−7	+24.5	+12.25
2	5	10	4	−2.5	−4	+10.0	+6.25
3	6	18	9	−1.5	−3	+4.5	+2.25
4	7	28	16	−0.5	−2	+1.0	+0.25
5	9	45	25	+0.5	0	0	+0.25
6	12	72	36	+1.5	+3	+4.5	+2.25
7	15	105	49	+2.5	+6	+15.0	+6.25
8	16	128	64	+3.5	+7	+24.5	+12.25
36	72	408	204			84.0	42.0

$n = 8$ observations

$$m = \frac{n\sum XY - \sum X \sum Y}{n\sum X^2 - \left(\sum X\right)^2} \qquad \bar{X} = \frac{\sum X}{n} = \frac{36}{8} = 4.5$$

$$m = \frac{8(408) - (36)(72)}{8(204) - (36)^2}$$

$$\bar{Y} = \frac{\sum Y}{n} = \frac{72}{8} = 9$$

$$m = \frac{3{,}264 - 2{,}592}{1{,}632 - 1{,}296}$$

$$m = \frac{\sum xy}{\sum x^2}$$

$$m = \frac{672}{336}$$

$$m = \frac{84.0}{42.0}$$

$$\underline{m = +2.0}$$

$$\underline{m = +2.0}$$

$$\underline{c = \bar{Y} - m\bar{X}}$$

$$\underline{c = \bar{Y} - m\bar{X}}$$

$$\underline{c = 9 - 2(4.5)}$$

$$\underline{c = 9 - 2(4.5)}$$

$$\underline{c = 0}$$

$$\underline{c = 0}$$

$$\underline{\hat{Y} = 2X}$$

$$\underline{\hat{Y} = 2X}$$

So, whatever method we use, we obtain a least squares line which goes through the zero origin for its intercept and has a gradient (slope) of +2. When you plot this line on your scatter diagram it should fit the data very closely.

3.2 *Approach 1* *Approach 2*

X_i	Y_i	X_iY_i	X_i^2	x_i $(X_i - \bar{X})$	y_i $(Y_i - \bar{Y})$	$x_i y_i$	x_i^2
1	19	19	1	−4.5	+5.6	−25.2	20.25
2	18	36	4	−3.5	+4.6	−16.1	12.25
3	16	48	9	−2.5	+2.6	−6.5	6.25
4	16	64	16	−1.5	+2.6	−3.9	2.25
5	20	100	25	−0.5	+6.6	−3.3	0.25
6	13	78	36	+0.5	−0.4	−0.2	0.25
7	6	42	49	+1.5	−7.4	−11.1	2.25
8	6	48	64	+2.5	−7.4	−18.5	6.25
9	11	99	81	+3.5	−2.4	−8.4	12.25
10	9	90	100	+4.5	−4.4	−19.8	20.25
55	134	624	385			−113.0	82.50

$$m = \frac{n\sum XY - \sum X\sum Y}{n\sum X^2 - \left(\sum X\right)^2}$$

$$\bar{X} = \frac{\sum X}{n} = \frac{55}{10} = 5.5$$

$$m = \frac{10(624) - (55)(134)}{10(385) - (55)^2}$$

$$\bar{Y} = \frac{\sum Y}{n} = \frac{134}{10} = 13.4$$

$$m = \frac{6{,}240 - 7{,}370}{3{,}850 - 3{,}025}$$

$$m = \frac{\sum xy}{\sum x^2}$$

$$m = \frac{-1{,}130}{825}$$

$$m = \frac{-113.0}{82.5}$$

$m = -1.37$	$m = -1.37$
$c = \bar{Y} - m\bar{X}$	$c = \bar{Y} - m\bar{X}$
$c = 13.4 - (-1.37)5.5$	$c = 13.4 - (-1.37)5.5$
$c = 13.4 + 7.54$	$c = 13.4 + 7.54$
$c = 20.94$	$c = 20.94$
$\hat{Y} = -1.37X + 20.94$	$\hat{Y} = -1.37X + 20.94$

Notice that the gradient of the least squares line is negative in this example though the intercept on the vertical axis is positive. Every time the independent variable (X_i) rises by 1 unit, the dependent variable (Y_i) falls by 1.37 units.

3.3 Here we use Approach 1, original data. Either approach will give the same result.

X_i	Y_i	X_iY_i	X_i^2
4	47	188	16
5	111	555	25
6	124	744	36
12	240	2,880	144
13	211	2,743	169
13	205	2,665	169
16	276	4,416	256
16	305	4,880	256
17	309	5,253	289
17	302	5,134	289
18	259	4,662	324
19	334	6,346	361
20	302	6,040	400
22	371	8,162	484
24	241	5,784	576
222	3,637	60,452	3,794

$$m = \frac{n\sum XY - \sum X \sum Y}{n\sum X^2 - \left(\sum X\right)^2}$$

$$m = \frac{15(60,452) - (222)(3,637)}{15(3,794) - (222)^2}$$

$$m = \frac{906,780 - 807,414}{56,910 - 49,284}$$

$$m = \frac{99,366}{7,626}$$

$$\underline{m = 13.03}$$

$$c = \bar{Y} - m\bar{X}$$

$$\bar{Y} = \frac{\sum Y}{n} = \frac{3{,}637}{15} = 242.5$$

$$\bar{X} = \frac{\sum X}{n} = \frac{222}{15} = 14.8$$

$$c = 242.5 - 13.03(14.8)$$

$$c = 242.5 - 192.8$$

$$\underline{c = 49.7}$$

$$\underline{\hat{Y} = 13.03X + 49.7}$$

3.4 We need an extra column to those shown on p. 328 whichever approach we use.

Approach 1

Y_i^2
4
25
36
49
81
144
225
256
820

Approach 2

y_i^2 $(Y_i - \bar{Y})^2$
49
16
9
4
0
9
36
49
172

$$R^2 = \left[\frac{n\sum XY - \sum X \sum Y}{\sqrt{\left[n\sum X^2 - \left(\sum X\right)^2 \right] \times \left[n\sum Y^2 - \left(\sum Y\right)^2 \right]}} \right]^2$$

$$R^2 = \frac{\left[\sum xy\right]^2}{\left[\sum x^2\right]\left[\sum y^2\right]}$$

$$R^2 = \left[\frac{8(408) - (36)(72)}{\sqrt{\left[8(204) - (36)^2\right] \times \left[8(820) - (72)^2\right]}} \right]^2$$

$$R^2 = \frac{(84)^2}{(42)(172)}$$

$$R^2 = \left[\frac{3{,}264 - 2{,}592}{\sqrt{\left[1{,}632 - 1{,}296\right] \times \left[6{,}560 - 5{,}184\right]}} \right]^2$$

$$R^2 = \frac{7{,}056}{7{,}224}$$

$$R^2 = \left[\frac{672}{\sqrt{\left[336\right] \times \left[1{,}376\right]}} \right]^2$$

$$\underline{R^2 = 0.98}$$

$$R^2 = \left[\frac{672}{\sqrt{462{,}336}} \right]^2$$

$$\underline{R = \sqrt{R^2} = 0.99}$$

$$R^2 = \left[\frac{672}{680}\right]^2$$

$$R^2 = [0.988]^2$$

$$R^2 = 0.98$$

$$\underline{R = \sqrt{R^2} = 0.99}$$

From the value of R^2 we can see that 0.98 or 98 per cent of the total variation is 'explained' or accounted for by our regression line.

3.5 Again we need an extra column to those shown on p. 329 whichever approach we follow. Here Approach 2, the coding formula, is used: the results will be the same for either approach.

Approach 2

y_i^2 $(Y_i - \overline{Y})^2$
31.36
21.16
6.76
6.76
43.56
0.16
54.76
54.76
5.76
19.36
244.40

$$R^2 = \frac{\left(\sum xy\right)^2}{\left(\sum x^2\right)\left(\sum y^2\right)}$$

$$R^2 = \frac{(-113.0)^2}{(82.5)(244.4)}$$

$$R^2 = \frac{12{,}769}{20{,}163}$$

$$\underline{R^2 = 0.63}$$

$$\underline{R = \sqrt{0.63} = 0.80}$$

Here 63 per cent of the total variation is 'explained' or accounted for by the regression line.

3.6 (i) (1) The first step is to rank actual sales and the forecasts made by Method 1.

Region	Ranking actual sales	Ranking Method 1	d_i	d_i^2
A	6	7	1	1
B	4	4	0	0
C	2	5	3	9
D	7	3	4	16
E	1	1	0	0
F	8	6	2	4
G	3	2	1	1
H	5	8	3	9
				40

$$R_s = 1 - \frac{6\sum d_i^2}{n^3 - n}$$

$$R_s = 1 - \frac{6(40)}{8^3 - n}$$

$$R_s = 1 - \frac{240}{504}$$

$$R_s = 1 - 0.48$$

$$\underline{R_s = 0.52}$$

The Spearman coefficient of rank correlation is mid-way between 1 and 0, suggesting only a modest match between actual sales and forecasting Method 1.

(2) We now rank actual sales and the forecasts made by Method 2.

Region	Ranking actual sales	Ranking Method 2	d_i	d_i^2
A	6	7	1	1
B	4	5 =	1	1
C	2	3	1	1
D	7	8	1	1
E	1	1	0	0
F	8	5 =	3	9
G	3	2	1	1
H	5	4	1	1
				15

$$R_s = 1 - \frac{6\sum d_i^2}{n^3 - n}$$

$$R_s = 1 - \frac{6(15)}{8^3 - 8}$$

$$R_s = 1 - \frac{90}{504}$$

$$R_s = 1 - 0.18$$

$$\underline{R_s = 0.82}$$

The Spearman coefficient of rank correlation is high here, being quite close to 1, suggesting a close match between actual sales and forecasting Method 2.

(ii) The overall results from this data would indicate a clear preference for Method 2 for next years forecasts. Of course a more detailed comparison of the relative merits of each method for forecasting data for more than one year would allow us to be more confident in assessing the relative merits of each method.

Chapter 4: Time series and forecasting

4.1

Year and quarter	Y	4 quarter moving total	4 quarter moving average	Centred 4 quarter moving average
1995 Q1	44			
Q2	80			
		304	76.0	
Q3	120			77.00
		312	78.0	
Q4	60			79.00
		320	80.0	
1996 Q1	52			80.75
		326	81.5	
Q2	88			81.75
		328	82.0	
Q3	126			83.00
		336	84.0	
Q4	62			85.25
		346	86.5	
1997 Q1	60			88.25
		360	90.0	
Q2	98			90.75
		366	91.5	
Q3	140			
Q4	68			

The centred 4 quarter moving average gives you the trend points, which can then be plotted on a scatter diagram containing the original data (all values 100,000 passengers).

4.2

Year and quarter	Y	4 quarter moving total	4 quarter moving average	Centred 4 quarter moving average (T)	(Y − T)
1995 Q1	66				
Q2	106				
		394	98.50		
Q3	140			99.38	40.62
		401	100.25		
Q4	82			101.88	−19.88
		414	103.50		
1996 Q1	73			106.63	−33.63
		439	109.75		
Q2	119			110.88	8.12
		448	112.00		
Q3	165			113.50	51.50
		460	115.00		
Q4	91			116.38	−25.38
		471	117.75		
1997 Q1	85			122.75	−37.75
		511	127.75		
Q2	130			128.88	1.12
		520	130.00		
Q3	205				
Q4	100				

(a) The centred 4 quarter moving average provides the values (100,000 units) for the trend component.

(b) The trend values and the original Y values can be plotted on a scatter diagram.

(c) We can use either of the approaches in Chapter 3 to find the least squares line. Let the first trend estimate for the independent variable (time) equal 1, i.e. let Q3 of 1995 equal 1.

Year and quarter	Y (centred 4 qr moving average	X (Time)	XY	X^2	Y^2
1995 Q3	99.38	1	99.38	1	9,876.4
Q4	101.88	2	203.76	4	10,379.5
1996 Q1	106.63	3	319.89	9	11,370.0
Q2	110.88	4	443.52	16	12,294.4
Q3	113.50	5	567.50	25	12,882.3
Q4	116.38	6	698.28	36	13,544.3
1997 Q1	122.75	7	859.25	49	15,067.6
Q2	128.88	8	1,031.04	64	16,610.1
	900.28	36	4,222.62	204	102,024.6

Using Approach 1, original data

$$m = \frac{n\sum XY - \sum X\sum Y}{n\sum X^2 - \left(\sum X\right)^2}$$

$$m = \frac{8(4{,}222.62) - (36)(900.28)}{8(204) - (36)^2}$$

$$m = \frac{33{,}780.96 - 32{,}410.08}{1{,}632 - 1{,}296}$$

$$m = \frac{1{,}370.88}{336} = 4.08$$

$$m = 4.08$$

$$c = \bar{Y} - m\bar{X}$$

$$\bar{Y} = \frac{900.28}{8} = 112.5$$

$$\bar{X} = \frac{36}{8} = 4.5$$

$$c = 112.5 - 4.08(4.5)$$

$$c = 112.5 - 18.4$$

$$\underline{c = 94.1}$$

(d) We can estimate $S + I$ by subtracting T, the centred 4 quarter moving average, from Y and then averaging to remove I.

$$Y - T = T + S + I - T = S + I \text{ (ignoring the cycle, } C)$$

	Q1	Q2	Q3	Q4
1995			+40.62	−19.88
1996	−33.63	+8.12	+51.50	−25.38
1997	−37.75	+1.12		
Average	−35.69	+4.62	+46.06	−22.63

If we sum the averages for S for each quarter we get

$$-35.69 + 4.62 + 46.06 + (-22.63) = -7.64$$

So to *adjust* the S factors we add $+\dfrac{7.64}{4} = 1.91$ to each quarter.

This gives the adjusted S factors as:

[Q1] −33.78   [Q2] 6.53   [Q3] 47.97   [Q4] 20.72

(e) $\hat{Y}_{T+S}$ is the trend forecast

$(\hat{Y}_T)$ + the adjusted seasonal variation factor for that quarter

(i) Q1, year 2000 gives $X = 19$ (Q2, 1995 = 0)

So $\hat{Y}_T = 4.08(19) + 94.1$

i.e. $\hat{Y}_T = 77.5 + 94.1 = 171.6$

$\underline{S \text{ for Q1} = -33.78}$

So $\hat{Y}_{T+S} = 171.6 + (-33.78)$

$\underline{\hat{Y}_{T+S} = 137.82}$

Forecast for Q1, year 2000 is 137.82.
Since units are 100,000, this gives 13,782,000 units.

(ii) Q3, Year 2000 gives $X = 21$ (Q2, 1995 = 0)

$\hat{Y}_T = 4.08(21) + 94.1$

$\underline{\hat{Y}_T = 85.7 + 94.1 = 179.8}$

$\underline{S \text{ for Q3} = +47.97}$

So $\hat{Y}_{T+S} = 179.8 + 47.97$

$\underline{\hat{Y}_{T+S} = 227.77}$

Forecast for Q3, year 2000 is 227.77
Since units are 100,000. this gives 22,777,000 units.

(f) Finding R^2, the coefficient of determination will help us decide how confident we can be in our forecast for the trend value.

Again, using Approach 1, original data.

$$R^2 = \left[\frac{n\sum XY - \sum X \sum Y}{\sqrt{\left[n\sum X^2 - \left(\sum X\right)^2\right] \times \left[n\sum Y^2 - \left(\sum Y\right)^2\right]}} \right]^2$$

$$R^2 = \left[\frac{8(4,222.62) - (36)(900.28)}{\sqrt{\left[8(204) - (36)^2\right] \times \left[8(102,024.6) - (900.28)^2\right]}} \right]^2$$

$$R^2 = \left[\frac{33,780.96 - 32,410.08}{\sqrt{[336] \times [5,692.7]}} \right]^2$$

$$R^2 = \left[\frac{1,370.88}{1,383.02} \right]^2$$

$$R^2 = [0.99]^2$$

$$\underline{R^2 = 0.98}$$

We can have considerable confidence in using the least squares regression line of forecasting future trend values since 98 per cent of total variation is 'explained' or accounted for by the trend regression line. Of course the overall forecast also includes our adjusted seasonal variation factors. Nevertheless this is an encouraging background for such forecasts.

Chapter 5: Probability
••••••••••••••••••••••••

5.1 (a) $\dfrac{1}{6}$ (b) $1 - \dfrac{1}{6} = \dfrac{5}{6}$ (c) $\dfrac{3}{6} = \dfrac{1}{2}$ (d) $\dfrac{2}{6} = \dfrac{1}{3}$

(e) $\dfrac{4}{52} = \dfrac{1}{13}$ (f) $\dfrac{39}{52} = \dfrac{3}{4}$ (g) 0   (h) 1

(i) 0.5   (j) $\dfrac{2}{9}$ (k) $\dfrac{7}{9}$ (l) $\dfrac{6}{7}$

5.2 (a) $\dfrac{10}{20} = \dfrac{1}{2}$ (b) $\dfrac{2}{20} = \dfrac{1}{10}$ (c) $\dfrac{5}{20} = \dfrac{1}{4}$

(d) $\dfrac{3}{20} + \dfrac{2}{20} = \dfrac{5}{20} = \dfrac{1}{4}$ (e) $1 - \dfrac{5}{20} = \dfrac{15}{20} = \dfrac{3}{4}$

5.3 (a) (2,6)   (3,6)   (4,6)   (5,6)   (6,6)
        (2,5)   (3,5)   (4,5)   (5,5)   (6,5)
        (2,4)   (3,4)   (4,4)   (5,4)   (6,4)
        (2,3)   (3,3)   (4,3)   (5,3)   (6,3)
                  (4,2)   (5,2)   (6,2)

(b) (i) $\dfrac{1}{36}$ (ii) $\dfrac{2}{36} = \dfrac{1}{18}$ (iii) $\dfrac{3}{36} = \dfrac{1}{12}$

(iv) $\dfrac{5}{36}$ (v) $\dfrac{6}{36} = \dfrac{1}{6}$ (vi) $\dfrac{5}{36}$

(vii) $\dfrac{3}{36} = \dfrac{1}{12}$ (viii) $\dfrac{1}{36}$

(c) $1 - \dfrac{1}{6} = \dfrac{5}{6}$

5.4 P(A OR B) = P(A) + P(B) as events mutually exclusive.

P(A OR B) = 0.3 + 0.5 = 0.8

5.5 (a) See Figure 5.6. Venn diagram since events not mutually exclusive.

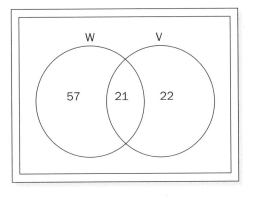

figure 5.6

Venn diagram:
W = work
experience,
V = vocational exam

(b) From Venn diagram, number of applicants with either W or V is
57 + 21 + 22 = 100

$$\text{Probability} = \frac{100}{140} = \frac{5}{7} = 0.71$$

In terms of our formula:

$$P(W \text{ or } V) = P(W) + P(V) - P(WV)$$
$$= \frac{78}{140} + \frac{43}{140} - \frac{21}{140}$$
$$= \frac{100}{140} = 0.71$$

5.6 P(GGGGG), where G = good (non-defective)

$$G = 1 - 0.03 = 0.97$$

AND rule for independent events, so multiply probabilities

$0.97 \times 0.97 \times 0.97 \times 0.97 \times 0.97 = 0.86$ probability

5.7 Need probability of seed germinating
AND being a blue flower.

$0.95 \times 0.4 = 0.38$ probability

5.8 Independent events – so AND rule

(a) $\dfrac{3}{4} \times \dfrac{9}{10} = \dfrac{27}{40} = 0.675$

(b) $\dfrac{1}{4} \times \dfrac{1}{10} = \dfrac{1}{40} = 0.025$

(c) $\dfrac{27}{40} = 0.675$

5.9 (a) 'Good' (G) $= 1 - \dfrac{6}{20} = \dfrac{14}{20}$

$$P(GGG) = \frac{14}{20} \times \frac{14}{20} \times \frac{14}{20} = 0.343$$

(b) $\quad P(GGG) = \dfrac{14}{20} \times \dfrac{13}{19} \times \dfrac{12}{18} = 0.319$

5.10

figure 5.7

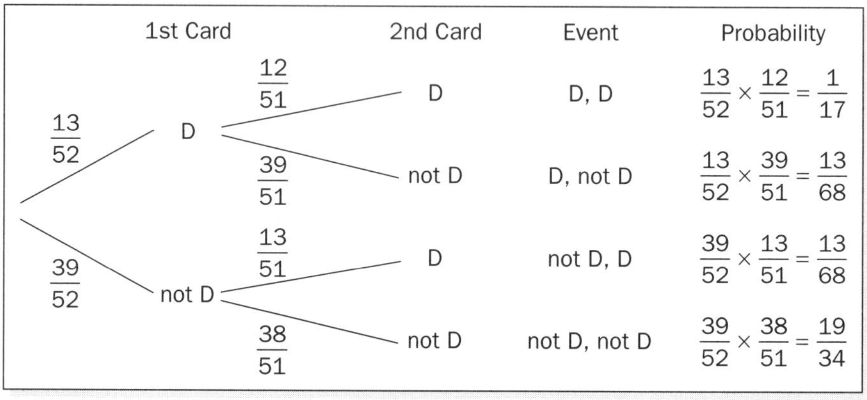

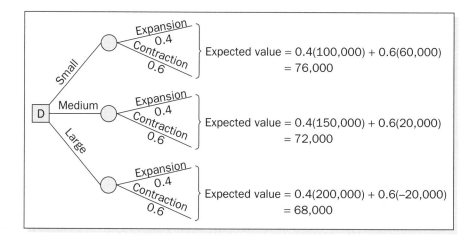

(a) Probability of both being a diamond is found as $\dfrac{1}{17}$

(b) The probability of one of them being a diamond is from either (D, not D) OR (not D, D), hence we ADD their probabilities

$$\frac{13+13}{68} = \frac{13}{34}$$

(c) The probability of neither being a diamond is found as $\dfrac{19}{34}$

5.11 (a) P (defective) = $\dfrac{35}{2,000}$ = 0.0175

(b) Expected number of defective items per 4,500 produced is 4,500 × 0.0175 = 79 to nearest whole item.

5.12

figure 5.8

The decision tree analysis leads us to recommend the small computer system.

5.13

figure 5.9

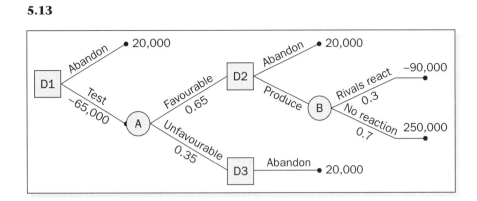

Expected value at Node B = 0.7 (250,000) + 0.3 (–90,000)

$$= 148,000$$

Comparison at D2 is 20,000 and 148,000

Therefore produce

Expected value at Node A = 0.65 (148,000) + 0.35 (20,000)

$$= 103,200$$

Comparison at D1 is 103,200 – 65,000 = 38,200 and 20,000

Therefore test market and produce if the test market is favourable

5.14 (a) As the selected elements are to be ranked, order is important. Therefore we want the number of permutations of three elements taken from eight elements, or

$_8P_3$ i.e. $\dfrac{8!}{(8-3)!} = \dfrac{8!}{5!} = 336$ ways

(b) As order is not important in this part of the question, we want the number of combinations of three elements taken from eight elements, or

$_8C_3$ i.e. $\dfrac{8!}{(8-3)! \times 3!} = \dfrac{8!}{5! \times 3!} = 56$ ways

5.15 (a) Order is not important in this question therefore we are looking for the number of possible combinations of 5 from 20.

$_{20}C_5$ i.e. $\dfrac{20!}{(20-5)! \times 5!} = \dfrac{20!}{15! \times 5!} = 15,504$ ways

(b) In this case we are interested in selecting only non-defectives in the sample. As there are 16 non-defectives we are looking for the number of different ways 5 can be selected from 16, order unimportant.

$_{16}C_5$ i.e. $\dfrac{16!}{(16-5)! \times 5!} = \dfrac{16!}{11! \times 5!} = 4,368$ ways

5.16 (a) Order of selection is not important here (ABC would be the same committee as BAC). Therefore we want the number of combinations of 3 from 5.

$$_5C_3 \quad \text{i.e.} \quad \frac{5!}{(5-3)! \times 3!} = \frac{5!}{2! \times 3!} = \text{ten ways}$$

(b) In this case, order is relevant (ABC as chairperson, treasurer and secretary respectively is a different line up to BAC as chairperson, treasurer and secretary respectively). Therefore we need the number of permutations of 3 from 5.

$$_5P_3 \quad \text{i.e.} \quad \frac{5!}{(5-3)!} = \frac{5!}{2!} = 60 \text{ different ways}$$

Chapter 6: Probability distributions

6.1 (a) $0.5000 - 0.4207 = 0.0793$
(b) $0.3085 - 0.1587 = 0.1498$
(c) $0.1711 - 0.0054 = 0.1657$
(d) $0.0606 - 0.000 = 0.0606$

In questions (e), (f) and (g) the areas involve the *left-hand* tail of the distribution.

(e) $0.5000 - 0.0668 = 0.4332$
(f) $0.1469 - 0.0322 = 0.1147$
(g) $0.0606 - 0.000 = 0.0606$

6.2 (a) $Z_1 = \dfrac{X_1 - \mu}{\sigma} = \dfrac{28{,}000 - 20{,}000}{4{,}000}$

$$Z_1 = \frac{8{,}000}{4{,}000} = +2$$

$\underline{P_1 = 0.0228}$

There is a 0.0228 (2.28 per cent) probability that more than 28,000 persons will attend.

(b) $Z_2 = \dfrac{X_2 - \mu}{\sigma} = \dfrac{14{,}000 - 20{,}000}{4{,}000}$

$$Z_2 = \frac{-6{,}000}{4{,}000} = -1.5$$

$\underline{P_2 = 0.0668}$

There is a 0.0668 (6.68 per cent) probability that less than 14,000 persons will attend.

(c)

figure 6.10

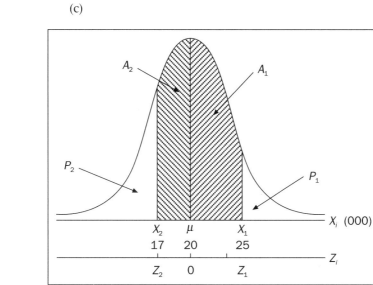

$$Z_1 = \frac{X_1 - \mu}{\sigma} = \frac{25{,}000 - 20{,}000}{4{,}000}$$

$$Z_1 = \frac{5{,}000}{4{,}000} = +1.25$$

$$\underline{P_1 = 0.1056}$$

$$A_1 = 0.5000 - 0.1056$$

$$\underline{A_1 = 0.3944}$$

$$Z_2 = \frac{X_2 - \mu}{\sigma} = \frac{17{,}000 - 20{,}000}{4{,}000}$$

$$Z_2 = \frac{-3{,}000}{4{,}000} = -0.75$$

$$\underline{P_2 = 0.2266}$$

$$A_2 = 0.5000 - 0.2266$$

$$\underline{A_2 = 0.2734}$$

$$\text{Required area} = A_1 + A_2$$
$$= 0.3944 + 0.2734$$
$$\underline{= 0.6678}$$

There is a 0.6678 (66.78 per cent) probability that between 17,000 and 25,000 persons will attend.

6.3 (a) $Z_1 = \dfrac{X_1 - \mu}{\sigma}$

From the *body* of the Z tables we can find the Z statistic which gives 0.05 in the *right-hand* tail.

$$+1.645 = \dfrac{X_1 - 20{,}000}{4{,}000}$$

$$+1.645(4{,}000) = X_1 - 20{,}000$$

$$+1.645(4{,}000) + 20{,}000 = X_1$$

$$\underline{26{,}580 = X_1}$$

(b) $Z_2 = \dfrac{X_2 - \mu}{\sigma}$

From the *body* of the Z tables we can find the Z statistic which gives 0.01 in the *left-hand* tail.

$$-2.33 = \dfrac{X_2 - 20{,}000}{4{,}000}$$

$$-2.33(4{,}000) = X_2 - 20{,}000$$

$$-2.33(4{,}000) + 20{,}000 = X_2$$

$$\underline{10{,}680 = X_2}$$

6.4 (a) $\dfrac{3!}{(3-2)!2!} = \dfrac{3 \times 2 \times 1}{1 \times 2 \times 1} = 3$

(b) $\dfrac{10!}{(10-7)!7!} = \dfrac{10 \times 9 \times 8 \times 7 \times 6 \times 5 \times 4 \times 3 \times 2 \times 1}{(3 \times 2 \times 1) \times (7 \times 6 \times 5 \times 4 \times 3 \times 2 \times 1)}$

$$= \dfrac{10 \times 9 \times 8}{3 \times 2 \times 1}$$

$$\underline{= 120}$$

(c) This reduces to

$$\dfrac{12 \times 11 \times 10 \times 9 \times 8}{5 \times 4 \times 3 \times 2 \times 1} = 792$$

(d) This reduces to

$$\dfrac{14 \times 13 \times 12 \times 11 \times 10 \times 9 \times 8 \times 7}{8 \times 7 \times 6 \times 5 \times 4 \times 3 \times 2 \times 1} = 3{,}003$$

6.5 (a) $\qquad P(r) = {}_nC_r p^r q^{n-r}$

where $p = 0.10$ and $q = 0.90$

$$P(2) = {}_6C_2 0.10^2 0.90^4$$

i.e. $P(2) = \dfrac{6 \times 5}{2 \times 1} \times 0.01 \times 0.6561$

$\underline{P(2) = 0.0984}$

There is a 0.0984 (9.84%) probability of two items being defective.

(b) $P(3) = {_6}C_3 0.10^3 0.90^3$

$P(3) = \dfrac{6 \times 5 \times 4}{3 \times 2 \times 1} \times 0.001 \times 0.729$

$\underline{P(3) = 0.0146}$

There is a 0.0146 (1.46%) probability of three items being defective.

6.6 P (less than 3) = P (3 or more)

p (error) = 0.05

$n = 10$, $r = 3$

From the Cumulative Binomial

Probabilities table (p. 315)

P (3 or more) = 0.0115

∴ P (less than 3) = 1–0.0115 = 0.9885

6.7 With continuity correction

(a) To find $P(X \geq 25)$ given that $\mu = 20$ and $\sigma = 4$ using the Normal approximation

$Z = \dfrac{X - \mu}{\sigma} = \dfrac{24.5 - 20}{4} = 1.125$ (i.e 1.13 rounded)

From the Z tables, probability = 0.1292

There is a 0.1292 (12.9%) probability of 25 or more bookings.

(b) $P(X \geq 16)$ given that $\mu = 20$ and $\sigma = 4$ using the Normal approximation

$Z = \dfrac{X - \mu}{\sigma} = \dfrac{15.5 - 20}{4} = -1.125$ (i.e. –1.13 rounded)

From the Z tables, probability = 0.1292 in left-hand tail.

The probability that there will be 16 or more bookings is 1 – 0.1292 = 0.8708 (87.1%)

(c) $P(X < 14)$ given that $\mu = 20$ and $\sigma = 4$ using the Normal approximation

$Z = \dfrac{X - \mu}{\sigma} = \dfrac{13.5 - 20}{4} = -1.625$ (i.e. –1.63 rounded)

From the Z tables, probability = 0.0516

The probability that there will be less than 14 bookings is 0.0516 (5.2%)

6.8 With continuity correction

(a) $P(X = 14) = P(13.5 < X < 14.5)$ given

$$\mu = np = 121 \times 0.10 = 12.1 \text{ and } \sigma = \sqrt{npq} = \sqrt{121 \times 0.10 \times 0.90} = 3.3$$

$P(X > 13.5)$ is found from $Z = \dfrac{X - \mu}{\sigma} = \dfrac{13.5 - 12.1}{3.3} = 0.4242$

From the Z tables, probability = 0.3372

$P(X > 14.5)$ is found from $Z = \dfrac{X - \mu}{\sigma} = \dfrac{14.5 - 12.1}{3.3} = 0.7273$

From the Z tables, probability = 0.2327

The probability that exactly 14 houses have alarms is $(0.3372 - 0.2327) = 0.1045(10.5\%)$

(b) $P(X < 10)$ is $P(X \leq 9.5)$

$$Z = \frac{X - \mu}{\sigma} = \frac{9.5 - 12.1}{3.3} = -0.7879$$

From the Z tables, probability = 0.2148

The probability that less than 10 homes have alarms is 0.2148(21.5%)

(c) $P(7 \leq X \leq 11) = P(6.5 < X < 11.5)$

$P(X < 11.5)$ is found from $Z = \dfrac{X - \mu}{\sigma} = \dfrac{11.5 - 12.1}{3.3} = -0.1818$

From the Z tables, probability = 0.4286 in left-hand tail

$P(X < 6.5)$ is found from $Z = \dfrac{X - \mu}{\sigma} = \dfrac{6.5 - 12.1}{3.3} = -1.6970$

From the Z tables, probability = 0.0446

The probability that between seven to 11 houses inclusive have alarms is $0.4286 - 0.0446 = 0.384(38.4\%)$

(d) $P(9 \leq X \leq 13) = P(8.5 < X < 13.5)$

$P(X < 8.5)$ is found from

$$Z = \frac{X - \mu}{\sigma} = \frac{8.5 - 12.1}{3.3} = -1.0909$$

From the Z tables, probability = 0.1379

$P(X > 13.5)$ is found from $Z = \dfrac{X - \mu}{\sigma} = \dfrac{13.5 - 12.1}{3.3} = 0.4242$

From the Z tables, probability = 0.3372

Therefore the probability that between nine and 13 houses inclusive have alarms = $(1 - 0.1379 - 0.3372) = 0.5249(52.5\%)$

6.9 (a) $P(X = 0) = \dfrac{e^{-0.2}0.2^0}{0!} = 0.8187$

(b) $P(X = 4) = \dfrac{e^{-0.2}0.2^4}{4!} = 0.0001$

(c) $P(X > 1) = 1 - P(0) - P(1) = 1 - 0.8187 - \dfrac{e^{-0.2}0.2^1}{1!}$

$= 1 - 0.8187 - 0.1637 = 0.0176$

(d) $P(X \leq 4) = P(0) + P(1) + P(2) + P(3) + P(4) = 0.8187 + 0.1637 + 0.0164$
$+ 0.0011 + 0.0001 = 1.0$

6.10 (a) mean number of trips per year, $\mu = 0.7$, therefore $P(0) = \dfrac{e^{-\mu}\mu^r}{r!} =$
$\dfrac{e^{-0.7}0.7^0}{0!} = 0.4966$. The probability of a family not making a trip last
year is 0.4966 (49.7%)

(b) $P(1) = \dfrac{e^{-\mu}\mu^r}{r!} = \dfrac{e^{-0.7}0.7^1}{1!} = 0.3476$

The probability of the family making one trip last year is 0.3476
(34.8%)

(c) Mean number of trips per three-year period μ is $3 \times 0.7 = 2.1$

$P(X \leq 3) = P(0) + P(1) + P(2) + P(3) = \dfrac{e^{-2.1}2.1^0}{0!} + \dfrac{e^{-2.1}2.1^1}{1!} +$

$\dfrac{e^{-2.1}2.1^2}{2!} + \dfrac{e^{-2.1}2.1^3}{3!} = 0.8386$

The probability that the family had made three or less trips per
three-year period is 0.8386 (83.9%)

(d) The mean number of trips per six-year period μ is $6 \times 0.7 = 4.2$

$P(X = 4) = \dfrac{e^{-4.2}4.2^4}{4!} = 0.1944$

The probability of exactly four trips per six-year period is
0.1944(19.4%)

Chapter 7: Sampling and tests of hypotheses

7.1 (a) $Z_1 = \dfrac{\overline{X}_1 - \mu}{\dfrac{\sigma}{\sqrt{n}}} = \dfrac{98 - 100}{\dfrac{10}{\sqrt{100}}} = \dfrac{-2}{1} = -2$

$\underline{P_1 = 0.0228}$ (2.28%)

(b) $Z_2 = \dfrac{\bar{X}_2 - \mu}{\dfrac{\sigma}{\sqrt{n}}} = \dfrac{103 - 100}{\dfrac{10}{\sqrt{100}}} = \dfrac{3}{1} = 3$

$\underline{P_2 = 0.0013}$ (0.13%)

7.2 (a) $Z_1 = \dfrac{\bar{X}_1 - \mu}{\dfrac{\sigma}{\sqrt{n}}} = \dfrac{9.50 - 10.00}{\dfrac{2}{\sqrt{36}}} = \dfrac{-0.50}{0.33} = -1.52$

$\underline{P_1 = 0.0643}$ (6.43%)

(b) $Z_2 = \dfrac{\bar{X}_2 - \mu}{\dfrac{\sigma}{\sqrt{n}}} = \dfrac{10.75 - 10.00}{\dfrac{2}{\sqrt{36}}} = \dfrac{0.75}{0.33} = 2.27$

$\underline{P_2 = 0.0116}$ (1.16%)

(c) $Z_3 = \dfrac{\bar{X}_3 - \mu}{\dfrac{\sigma}{\sqrt{n}}} = \dfrac{11.00 - 10.00}{\dfrac{2}{\sqrt{36}}} = \dfrac{1.00}{0.33} = 3.03$

$\underline{P_3 = 0.0012}$ (0.12%)

7.3 (a) $Z_1 = \dfrac{\bar{X}_1 - \mu}{\dfrac{\sigma}{\sqrt{n}}} = \dfrac{340.75 - 340}{\dfrac{8}{\sqrt{64}}} = \dfrac{0.75}{1} = 0.75$

$\underline{P_1 = 0.2266}$ (22.66%)

(b) $Z_2 = \dfrac{\bar{X}_2 - \mu}{\dfrac{\sigma}{\sqrt{n}}} = \dfrac{338.5 - 340}{\dfrac{8}{\sqrt{64}}} = \dfrac{-1.5}{1} = -1.5$

$\underline{P_2 = 0.0668}$ (6.68%)

(c) $Z_1 = \dfrac{339 - 340}{\dfrac{8}{\sqrt{64}}} = \dfrac{-1}{1} = -1$

$\underline{P_1 = 0.1587}$ (15.87%)

$A_1 = 0.5000 - 0.1587 = 0.3413$ (34.13%)

$Z_2 = \dfrac{342 - 340}{\dfrac{8}{\sqrt{64}}} = \dfrac{2}{1} = 2$

$\underline{P_2 = 0.0228}$ (2.28%)

$A_2 = 0.5000 - 0.0228 = 0.4772$ (47.72%)

Solution is $\underline{A_1 + A_2 = 0.8185}$ (81.85%)

7.4 (a) 95 per cent confidence interval for sample mean

$$\bar{X}_i = \mu \pm 1.96\left(\frac{\sigma}{\sqrt{n}}\right)$$

$$\bar{X}_i = 550 \pm 1.96\left(\frac{120}{\sqrt{144}}\right)$$

$$\bar{X}_i = 550 \pm 1.96(10)$$

$$\underline{\bar{X}_i = £530.40 \text{ to } £569.60}$$

(b) 99 per cent confidence interval for sample mean

$$\bar{X}_i = \mu \pm 2.58\left(\frac{\sigma}{\sqrt{n}}\right)$$

$$\bar{X}_i = 550 \pm 2.58\left(\frac{120}{\sqrt{144}}\right)$$

$$\bar{X}_i = 550 \pm 2.58(10)$$

$$\underline{\bar{X}_i = £524.20 \text{ to } £575.80}$$

7.5 (a) 95 per cent confidence interval for population mean

$$\mu = \bar{X}_i \pm 1.96\left(\frac{s}{\sqrt{n}}\right)$$

$$\mu = 6.15 \pm 1.96\left(\frac{1.30}{\sqrt{64}}\right)$$

$$\mu = 6.15 \pm 1.96\left(\frac{1.30}{8}\right)$$

$$\mu = 6.15 \pm 1.96(0.1625)$$

$$\mu = 6.15 \pm 0.32$$

$$\underline{\mu = £5.83 \text{ to } £6.47}$$

(b) 99 per cent confidence interval for population mean

$$\mu = \bar{X}_i \pm 2.58\left(\frac{s}{\sqrt{n}}\right)$$

$$\mu = 6.15 \pm 2.58\left(\frac{1.30}{\sqrt{64}}\right)$$

$$\mu = 6.15 \pm 2.58(0.1625)$$

$$\mu = 6.15 \pm 0.42$$

$$\underline{\mu = £5.73 \text{ to } £6.57}$$

7.6 *Step 1* $H_0 : \mu = 1{,}000$ hours

$H_1 : \mu \neq 1{,}000$ hours

We use a *two-tailed* test since variation either side of 1,000 hours will cause us to reject H_0.

Step 2 (a) 5 per cent (0.05) level of significance
and
(b) 1 per cent (0.01) level of significance

Step 3 Critical values: two-tailed tests

(a)   5 per cent : $Z = \pm 1.96$
(b)   1 per cent : $Z = \pm 2.58$

Step 4 For sample data

$$Z = \frac{\bar{X} - \mu}{\dfrac{s}{\sqrt{n}}} = \frac{940 - 1{,}000}{\dfrac{126}{\sqrt{36}}}$$

$$Z = \frac{-60}{21} = -2.86$$

Step 5 (a) −2.86 is outside −1.96
(b) −2.86 is outside −2.58

Step 6 (a) Reject H_0 at 5 per cent (0.05) level of significance for a two-tailed test
(b) Reject H_0 at 1 per cent (0.01) level of significance for a two-tailed test

Step 7 Evidence does not support the sales manager's claims that the average life of light bulbs is 1,000 hours.

7.7 *Step 1* $H_0 : \mu = 14$ hours
$H_1 : \mu \neq 14$ hours

This is a *two-tailed* test since variation either side of 14 hours a day will cause us to reject H_0.

Step 2 5 per cent (0.05) level of significance
Step 3 Critical value: two-tailed test ±1.96
Step 4 For sample data

$$Z = \frac{\bar{X} - \mu}{\dfrac{s}{\sqrt{n}}} = \frac{13.33 - 14.00}{\dfrac{3}{\sqrt{64}}}$$

$$Z = \frac{-0.67}{0.38} = -1.76$$

Step 5 −1.76 is inside −1.96
Step 6 Accept H_0
Step 7 Evidence is insufficient for us to reject the factory manager's claim that the average running time of machines is 14 hours a day, so we accept that claim.

7.8 *Step 1* $\mu = 100$ hours

$\mu > 100$ hours

This is a *one-tailed* test. as we place all our 'risk' on one side of the distribution only.

Step 2 5% (0.05)

Step 3 Critical value: one-tailed test = +1.65

Step 4 For sample data

$$Z = \frac{\bar{X} - \mu}{\frac{\sigma}{\sqrt{n}}} = \frac{104 - 100}{\frac{14}{\sqrt{49}}} = \frac{4}{2} = +2$$

Note: here we are given σ rather than s.

Step 5 +2 is outside +1.65

Step 6 Reject H_0

Step 7 Evidence does support the suggestion that the new technique has produced longer lasting components.

7.9 $H_0 : \mu = 18$ $H_1 : \mu > 18$ hrs.

Critical value $t_{0.05,24} = 1.711$

From sample $t = \dfrac{\bar{X} - \mu}{\dfrac{s}{\sqrt{n}}} = \dfrac{18.6 - 18.0}{\dfrac{1.02}{\sqrt{25}}} = 2.94$

As 2.94 is outside 1.711 we reject H_0, in other words we conclude that the evidence supports the view that the mean library time is greater than 18 hours.

7.10 $H_0 : \mu = 15\%$ $H_1 : \mu < 15\%$

Critical value $t_{0.01,7} = -2.998$

From sample $t = \dfrac{\bar{X} - \mu}{\dfrac{s}{\sqrt{n}}} = \dfrac{14.3 - 15.0}{\dfrac{0.96}{\sqrt{8}}} = -2.06$

As −2.06 is inside −2.998 we cannot reject H_0. In other words we cannot conclude from the evidence that the fat content is less than 15 per cent.

7.11 $H_0 : \mu = 154$ $H_1 : \mu < 154$

Critical value $t_{0.01,19} = -2.539$

From sample $t = \dfrac{\bar{X} - \mu}{\dfrac{s}{\sqrt{n}}} = \dfrac{141 - 154}{\dfrac{12}{\sqrt{20}}} = -4.84$

As −4.84 is outside −2.539 we reject H_0. In other words we conclude that the evidence supports the view that the training package improves worker performance.

Chapter 8: Index numbers

8.1 (a) Laspeyres (base-weighted) price index $= \dfrac{\Sigma P_n Q_0}{\Sigma P_0 Q_0} \times 100$

where $\Sigma P_n Q_0 =$ value of base year basket of items in year n.

$\Sigma P_0 Q_0 =$ value of base year basket of items in base year 0.

Materials	Year 0			Year 2		
	P_0	Q_0	$P_0 Q_0$	P_2	Q_0	$P_2 Q_0$
Plastic	1.20	4,000	4,800	2.50	4,000	10,000
Steel tubing	5.30	1,000	5,300	5.80	1,000	5,800
Cloth	2.30	2,000	4,600	2.70	2,000	5,400
			$\Sigma P_0 Q_0 = 14{,}700$			$\Sigma P_2 Q_0 = 21{,}200$

Year	$\dfrac{\Sigma P_n Q_0}{\Sigma P_0 Q_0}$	Laspeyres price index
0	14,700/14,700 = 1.00	100
2	21,200/14,700 = 1.44	144

Paasche (current-weighted) price index $= \dfrac{\Sigma P_n Q_n}{\Sigma P_0 Q_n}$

where $\Sigma P_n Q_n =$ value of the basket of items bought in year n at year n prices.

$\Sigma P_0 Q_n =$ value of the basket of items bought in year n at year 0 prices.

Materials	Year 0			Year 2			
	P_0	Q_0	$P_0 Q_0$	P_2	Q_2	$P_2 Q_2$	$P_0 Q_2$
Plastic	1.20	4,000	4,800	2.50	2,000	5,000	2,400
Steel tubing	5.30	1,000	5,300	5.80	800	4,640	4,240
Cloth	2.30	2,000	4,600	2.70	4,000	10,800	9,200
			$\Sigma P_0 Q_0 = 14{,}700$			$\Sigma P_2 Q_2 = 20{,}440$	$\Sigma P_0 Q_2 = 15{,}840$

Year	$\dfrac{\Sigma P_n Q_n}{\Sigma P_0 Q_n}$	Paasche price index
0	14,700/14,700 = 1.00	100
2	20,440/15,840 = 1.29	129

(b) Laspeyres (base-weighted) quantity index $= \dfrac{\Sigma P_0 Q_n}{\Sigma P_0 Q_0} \times 100$

where $\Sigma P_0 Q_n =$ value of year n basket of items at prices in base year (year 0)

$\Sigma P_0 Q_0 =$ value of base year basket of items at prices in base year (year 0)

Materials	Year 0			Year 2		
	P_0	Q_0	P_0Q_0	P_0	Q_2	P_0Q_2
Plastics	1.20	4,000	4,800	1.20	2,000	2,400
Steel tubing	5.30	1,000	5,300	5.30	800	4,240
Cloth	2.30	2,000	4,600	2.30	4,000	9,200
			$\Sigma P_0Q_0 = 14,700$			$\Sigma P_0Q_2 = 15,840$

Year	$\dfrac{\Sigma P_0Q_n}{\Sigma P_0Q_0}$	Laspeyres quantity index
0	14,700/14,700 = 1.00	100
2	15,840/14,700 = 1.08	108

Paasche (current-weighted) quantity index $= \dfrac{\Sigma P_nQ_n}{\Sigma P_nQ_0} \times 100$

where ΣP_nQ_n = value of year n basket of items at prices in year n.
ΣP_nQ_0 = value of base year basket of items at prices in year n.

Materials	Year 0			Year 2			
	P_0	Q_0	P_0Q_0	P_2	Q_2	P_2Q_2	P_2Q_0
Plastics	1.20	4,000	4,800	2.50	2,000	5,000	10,000
Steel tubing	5.30	1,000	5,300	5.80	800	4,640	5,800
Cloth	2.30	2,000	4,600	2.70	4,000	10,800	5,400
			$\Sigma P_0Q_0 = 14,700$			$\Sigma P_2Q_2 = 20,440$	$\Sigma P_2Q_0 = 21,200$

Year	$\dfrac{\Sigma P_nQ_n}{\Sigma P_nQ_0}$	Paasche quantity index
0	14,700/14,700 = 1.00	100
2	20,440/21,200 = 0.96	96

(c) The Laspeyres price index (144) is considerably higher than the Paasche price index (129), suggesting a higher price inflation for material costs for the motor component industry over the two year period. This is typically the case since the Paasche price index tends to *understate* the true increase in prices as it uses current year quantities as weights. Note also that the Paasche price index is not, strictly, a 'pure' price index since it involves changes in *both* prices and quantities from year to year.

The Laspeyres quantity index (108) is also higher than the Paasche quantity index (96), suggesting an increase rather than decrease in the volume of materials used in the production of motor components over the two year period. Again, arguably the Paasche quantity index, being a mixture of both changes in price and quantities from year to year is a less 'pure' quantity index than is the Laspeyres version.

8.2 New index = old index × scaling factor

New index =

old index × $\dfrac{\text{value in period } T_1 \ (\text{value of old index in original base year})}{\text{value in period } T_2 \ (\text{value of old index in new base year})}$

From Table 8.8 (p. 189), the 'scaling factor' is $\dfrac{100}{132}$

The new Laspeyres quantity index with Year 1 as base is as follows:

Year 0 $100 \times \dfrac{100}{132} = 76$

Year 1 $132 \times \dfrac{100}{132} = 100$

Year 2 $159 \times \dfrac{100}{132} = 120$

8.3 Same procedure as for the previous answer except this time, from Table 8.9 (p. 190) the 'Scaling factor' is $\dfrac{100}{130}$

The new Paasche quantity index with Year 1 as base is as follows.

Year 0 $100 \times \dfrac{100}{130} = 77$

Year 1 $130 \times \dfrac{100}{130} = 100$

Year 2 $156 \times \dfrac{100}{130} = 120$

8.4 Weighted index of quantity = $\dfrac{\Sigma WR}{\Sigma W}$

where R = quantity relative for each item (1990 = 100)
        W = weight for each item

W	R	WR
264	101	26,664
25	82	2,050
41	88	3,608
68	95	6,460
325	84	27,300
99	92	9,108
52	82	4,264
126	83	10,458
1,000		89,912

Weighted index of quantity = $\dfrac{89{,}912}{1{,}000} = 89.912$

Clearly the current output of the bundle of various products of the multinational has fallen since 1990 by over 10 per cent.

Chapter 9: Time value of money

9.1 (a) £2,078.90   (b) £10,834.70   (c) £16,366.50
     (d) £237,376.30   (e) £9,313.20   (f) £2,619,996.30

9.2 (a) £80,000   (b) £62,090   (c) £7,250
     (d) £48,100   (e)   £6,110   (f) £1,050

9.3

| Time (year) | Nominal Cash Flow (NCF) | | | Discounted Cash Flow (DCF) | |
	NCF (£m) Project A	NCF (£m) Project B	Discount Factor	DCF (£m) Project A	DCF (£m) Project B
0	−1,000	−1,000	1.000	−1,000	−1,000
1	400	400	0.909	363.6	363.6
2	500	400	0.826	413	330.4
3	350	400	0.751	262.9	300.4
4	300	400	0.683	204.9	273.2
			NPV	+244.4	+267.6

NPV of Project B at £267.6m is higher than that of Project A at £244.4m. If you have to choose between the projects, then B is preferred to A. If you have enough capital to undertake *both* projects, then each might be implemented.

9.4

| Year | Nominal cash flow (NCF) | | Discount factor* | Discounted cash flow (DCF) | |
	Project I	Project II		Project I	Project II
0	−100,000	−100,000	1.000	−100,000	−100,000
1	38,000	5,000	0.909	34,542	4,545
2	30,000	57,000	0.826	24,780	47,082
3	23,000	60,000	0.751	17,273	45,060
4	22,500	12,000	0.683	15,368	8,196
5	22,500	1,000	0.621	13,973	621
	+36,000	+35,000	NPV	+5,936	+5,504

Note: * Discount rate (i) = 0.10 (10%)

Payback   *Project I*   three years and $\dfrac{9,000}{22,500}$ of year 4 (on pro rata assumption)

                i.e. 3.4 years

        Project II   two years and $\dfrac{38,000}{60,000}$ of year 3 (on pro rata assumption)

                i.e. 2.4 years

So Project II preferred to Project I on payback.

Average Rate of Return (ARR)

$$Project\ I \quad \frac{136{,}000 - 100{,}000}{100{,}000} \times 100 \div 5$$

i.e. 7.2% per annum

$$Project\ II \quad \frac{135{,}000 - 100{,}000}{100{,}000} \times 100 \div 5$$

i.e. 7% per annum

So marginal preference for Project I on ARR

NPV

Various discount factors could be applied to formula.

$$\text{discount factor} = \frac{1}{(1 + i)^{t}}$$

Here use $i = 0.10$ (10%) for purpose of illustration, giving the column shown in the table above.

Project I   NPV = +£5,936

Project II   NPV = +£5,504

Marginal preference for Project I via NPV

Internal Rate of Return (IRR)

Using a spreadsheet package we find the IRR for each project as follows (i.e. the rate of discount at which NPV = zero).

Project I   IRR = 12.32%

Project II   IRR = 12.35%

Marginal preference for Project II via IRR.

Overall Project II is narrowly favoured on two of the four investment criteria, and Project I on the other two criteria. On this evidence there would seem to be little to choose between the two projects.

Chapter 10: Linear programming and break even analysis

10.1 $Z = 4A + 3B$

Maximise Z subject to:

$1A + 2B \leq 110$ (labour constraint)
$A \leq 70$ (capacity constraint)
$B \leq 150$ (capacity constraint)
$A \geq 0 , B \geq 0$

figure 10.9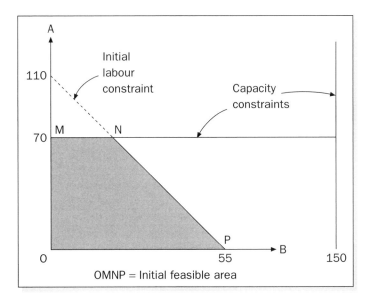

OMNP = Initial feasible area

(i) At M(A = 70, B = 0)   Z = 4(70) + 3(0) = 280
     At P(A = 0, B = 55)   Z = 4(0) + 3(55) = 165

At N   1A + 2B = 110 ... (1)
              1A = 70   ... (2)

Subtract   2B = 40
               B = 20

Substitute B = 20 in (1)

1A + 2(20) = 110

  1A + 40 = 110

      1A = 70

So N has (A = 70, B = 20)   So Z = 4(70) + 3(20) = 340

Z is a maximum N with value at 340, producing 70A and 20B

(ii) (a) Z = 4A + 2B

         At M, Z = 280

         At P, Z = 110

         At N, Z = 320

         Z is a maximum at N, with value at 320, still producing 70A
         and 20B

    (b) Change labour constraint to 1A + 2B = 120 (shifts outwards)

         Maximum now occurs at a new corner point with B = 25, A = 70

         So Z = 4 (70) + 3 (25) = 355

(c) Change labour constraint to: $1.1A + 2B = 110 \ldots (1)$ (i.e. pivots inwards around P)

$$1A = 70 \ \ldots (2)$$

$(2) \times 1.1$ $\qquad$ $1.1A = 77 \ \ldots (3)$

subtract (3) from (1) $\qquad$ $2B = 33$

$$\underline{B = 16.5} \quad \underline{A = 70}$$

Maximum now occurs at a new corner point B = 16.5, A = 70

$$Z = 4(70) + 3(16.5)$$

$$\underline{Z = 329.5}$$

10.2 $Z = 2X + 3Y$

Minimise Z (Total Cost in £s)

$1X + 1Y \geq 10 \ldots$ (protein constraint)

$1X + 2Y \geq 14 \ldots$ (vitamin constraint)

$X \geq 0 \quad Y \geq$ (non-negative constraints)

The feasible region is as shown in Figure 10.10, where we graph the equalities for the two constraints.

figure 10.10
Feasible region in a minimisation problem

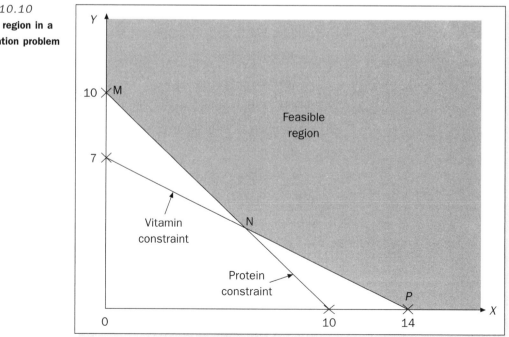

The minimum value for Z must occur at one (or more) of the corner points M, N or P in the feasible area.

At M($X = 0$, $Y = 10$) $Z = 2(0) + 3(10) = 30$

At P($X = 14$, $Y = 0$) $Z = 2(14) + 3(0) = 28$

At N $1X + 1Y = 10 \ldots (1)$

$\qquad 1X + 2Y = 14 \ldots (2)$

Subtract $-1Y = -4$

i.e. $Y = 4$

Substituting $Y = 4$ in (1)

$\qquad 1X + 1(4) = 10$

$\qquad\qquad X = 6$

So the co-ordinates at N are $X = 6$, $Y = 4$

$Z = 2(6) + 3(4) = 24$

$\underline{Z = £24}$

Clearly the company can minimise its total costs by using six units of input X and four units of input Y. This gives the lowest cost (£24) possible for producing the foodstuff while still meeting its protein and vitamin requirements.

10.3 (a) (i) *Initial situation*

$$\text{BEP} = \frac{\text{TFC}}{\text{c/u}}$$

$\text{c/u} = \text{AR} - \text{AVC}$
$\underline{\text{c/u} = £4 - £2 = £2}$
$\underline{\text{TFC} = £15,000}$
$\text{BEP} = \dfrac{£15,000}{£2} = 7,500$

▶ $\underline{\text{BEP} = 7,500 \text{ units}}$
     Budgeted profit = TR − TC at budgeted output
     Budgeted profit = TR − (TFC + TVC)
     Budgeted profit = (£4 × 8,000) − [£15,000 + (£2 × 8,000)]
▶ $\underline{\text{Budgeted profit} = £1,000}$

     $\text{Margin of safety} = \dfrac{\text{budgeted output} - \text{BEP}}{\text{budgeted output}} \times 100$

     $\text{Margin of safety} = \dfrac{8,000 - 7,500}{8,000} \times 100$

▶ $\underline{\text{Margin of safety} = 6.25\%}$

(ii) *After new technology*

If new technology reduces variable costs to £1.50 per unit but raises TFC to £20,000, then:

$$\text{BEP} = \frac{£20,000}{\text{c/u}} = \frac{£20,000}{£4 - £1.50}$$

$$\text{BEP} = \frac{£20,000}{£2.50}$$

▶   BEP = 8,000
  Budgeted profit = TR − TC at budgeted output
  Budgeted profit = (£4 × 8,000) − [£20,000 + (£1.50 × 8,000)]
▶   Budgeted profit = £0
▶   Margin of safety = $\dfrac{8,000 - 8,000}{8,000} \times 100$
▶   Margin of safety = 0%

It would seem that the initial solution, prior to new technology, is preferable as it has a lower BEP, a higher budgeted profit and higher margin of safety.

(b) The linearity assumption implies constant prices as output increases, which may be unrealistic for substantial changes in output for a firm in some type of imperfect competition. Further, linearity assumes constant returns to factors (e.g. constant AVC), which again may be unrealistic for substantial changes in output where diminishing returns may exist (short-run rises in AVC) or economies of scale exist (long-run falls in AVC).

Chapter 11: Calculus and business applications

11.1 (a) 9
(b) $8x$
(c) $9x^2$
(d) $20x^3$

(e) x^2
(f) x^3
(g) $\dfrac{1}{2}x^{-\frac{1}{2}} = \dfrac{1}{2\sqrt{x}}$

(h) $\dfrac{1}{3}x^{-\frac{2}{3}} = \dfrac{1}{3\sqrt[3]{x^2}}$
(i) $\dfrac{2}{3}x^{-\frac{1}{3}} = \dfrac{2}{3\sqrt[3]{x}}$
(j) 0

11.2 (a) (i) 9 (ii) 9
(b) (i) 8 (ii) 16
(c) (i) 9 (ii) 36

(d) (i) 20 (ii) 160
(e) (i) 1 (ii) 4
(f) (i) 1 (ii) 8

(g) (i) $\dfrac{1}{2}$ (ii) 0.354
(h) (i) $\dfrac{1}{3}$ (ii) 0.210

(i) (i) $\dfrac{2}{3}$ (ii) 0.529
(j) both zero

11.3 (a) $\dfrac{dy}{dx} = 2x - 10 = 0$ for turning point

$$2x = 10$$

$$\underline{x = 5}$$

$$\frac{d^2y}{dx^2} = +2$$

So $x = 5$ is a turning point, and this is a minimum since 2nd derivative is positive.

(b) $\dfrac{dy}{dx} = -6 + 2x = 0$ for turning point

$$2x = 6$$

$$\underline{x = 3}$$

$$\frac{d^2y}{dx^2} = +2$$

So $x = 3$ is a minimum turning point since 2nd derivative is positive

(c) $\dfrac{dy}{dx} = 4 - 2x = 0$ for a turning point

$$4 = 2x$$

$$\underline{2 = x}$$

$$\frac{d^2y}{dx^2} = -2$$

So $x = 2$ is a maximum turning point since the second derivative is negative.

(d) $\dfrac{dy}{dx} = 3x^2 - 27 = 0$ for a turning point

$$3x^2 = 27$$

$$\underline{x = \pm 3}$$

$$\frac{d^2y}{dx^2} = 6x$$

▶ when $x = +3$, 2nd derivative is positive (+18), so minimum turning point.
▶ when $x = -3$, 2nd derivative is negative (−18), so maximum turning point.

(e) $\dfrac{dy}{dx} = 3x^2 - 6x = 0$ for a turning point

$$x(3x - 6) = 0$$

which solves when $x = 0$ or $+2$

$$\frac{d^2y}{dx^2} = 6x - 6$$

▶ when $x = 0$, 2nd derivative is negative (-6), so maximum turning point.

▶ when $x = +2$, 2nd derivative is positive $(+6)$, so minimum turning point.

(f) $\dfrac{dy}{dx} = x^2 - 7x + 12 = 0$ for a turning point

$$(x - 3)(x - 4) = 0$$

This solves for either <u>$x = +3$ or $x = +4$</u>

$$\dfrac{d^2 y}{dx^2} = 2x - 7$$

▶ Second derivative is negative (-1) when $x = +3$, so maximum turning point.

▶ Second derivative is positive $(+1)$ when $x = +4$, so minimum turning point.

11.4 (a) $\dfrac{dy}{dx} = \dfrac{du}{dx} + \dfrac{dv}{dx} = 35x^4 + 6x$

(b) $\dfrac{dy}{dx} = \dfrac{du}{dx} - \dfrac{dv}{dx} = 20x^4 - 12x^2$

(c) $\dfrac{dy}{dx} = u\dfrac{dv}{dx} + v\dfrac{du}{dx}$

$u = 2x + 3, \dfrac{du}{dx} = 2$

$v = 2x^3, \dfrac{dv}{dx} = 6x^2$

$\dfrac{dy}{dx} = (2x + 3) \cdot (6x^2) + (2x^3) \cdot (2)$

$\dfrac{dy}{dx} = 12x^3 + 18x^2 + 4x^3 = 16x^3 + 18x^2$

(d) Using above approach

$\dfrac{dy}{dx} = (3x + 4)(12x^3) + (3x^4) \cdot (3)$

$\dfrac{dy}{dx} = 36x^4 + 48x^3 + 9x^4 = 45x^4 + 48x^3$

(e) $y = \dfrac{u}{v}$, so $\dfrac{dy}{dx} = \dfrac{u\dfrac{dv}{dx} - v\dfrac{du}{dx}}{v^2}$

$\dfrac{dy}{dx} = \dfrac{(2x + 3)(4x) - (2x^2) \cdot (2)}{(2x^2)^2} = \dfrac{8x^2 + 12x - 4x^2}{4x^4}$

$\dfrac{dy}{dx} = \dfrac{4x^2 + 12x}{4x^4} = \dfrac{4x + 12}{4x^3}$

(f) Using above approach

$$\frac{dy}{dx} = \frac{(4x^2 - 2) \cdot (4x) - (2x^2 + 4) \cdot (8x)}{(2x^2 + 4)^2}$$

$$\frac{dy}{dx} = \frac{16x^3 - 8x - 16x^3 - 32x}{4x^4 + 16x^2 + 16}$$

$$\frac{dy}{dx} = \frac{-40x}{4x^4 + 16x^2 + 16}$$

(g) $y = f(u)$ where $u = f(x)$

$$\frac{dy}{dx} = \frac{dy}{du} \cdot \frac{du}{dx}$$

$y = u^2$ where $u = (2x^2 + 3)$

$$\frac{dy}{dx} = 2u \cdot 4x$$

i.e. $\dfrac{dy}{dx} = 2(2x^2 + 3) \cdot 4x = 16x^3 + 24x$

(h) Using above approach

$$\frac{dy}{dx} = 3u^2 \cdot 9x^2$$

$$\frac{dy}{dx} = 3(3x^3 + 4)^2 \cdot 9x^2 = 3(9x^6 + 24x^3 + 16) \cdot 9x^2$$

$$\frac{dy}{dx} = 243x^8 + 648x^5 + 432x^2$$

11.5 (a) (i) TR = AR × output

TR = $[32 - \dfrac{2}{3}x^2]x$

TR = $32x - \dfrac{2}{3}x^3$

(ii) TC = ATC × output

TC = $[\dfrac{1}{3}x^2 - x + 11] \cdot x$

TC = $\dfrac{1}{3}x^3 - x^2 + 11x$

(iii) TP = TR − TC

TP = $32x - \dfrac{2}{3}x^3 - [\dfrac{1}{3}x^3 - x^2 + 11x]$

TP(y) = $-x^3 + x^2 + 21x$

(b) $\dfrac{dy}{dx} = 0$ for a turning point

$-3x^2 + 2x + 21 = 0$ for a turning point

$(-3x - 7)(x - 3) = 0$

i.e. when $-3x - 7 = 0$ $x = -2\frac{1}{3}$

and when $x - 3 = 0$ $x = 3$

2nd derivative $\dfrac{d^2y}{dx^2} = -6x + 2$

when $x = +3$, the 2nd derivative $= -16$

when $x = -2\frac{1}{3}$, the 2nd derivative $= +16$

so the turning point $\underline{x = +3 \text{ is the maximum}}$

▶ Producing three units of output will maximise total profit.
▶ At this output total profit $(y) = -(3^3) + 3^2 + 21(3) = \text{£45}.$
▶ Price = AR $= 32 - \dfrac{2}{3}(3^2) = \text{£26}.$

11.6 (a) TP (y) = TR − TC

$$y = (40x - 8x^2) - (8 + 16x - x^2)$$

$$y = -7x^2 + 24x - 8$$

$$\frac{dy}{dx} = 0 \text{ for a turning point}$$

i.e. $-14x + 24 = 0$ for a turning point

$$24 = 14x$$

$$\frac{24}{14} = x$$

$$\underline{1\frac{5}{7} = x}$$

2nd derivative $\dfrac{d^2y}{dx^2} = -14$

So turning point $x = 1\dfrac{5}{7}$ is a maximum

Maximum Total Profit is earned at an output of $1\dfrac{5}{7}$ (000) units.

Price = AR $= \dfrac{\text{TR}}{\text{output}} = \dfrac{\text{TR}}{x} = \dfrac{40x - 8x^2}{x} = 40 - 8x$

Price $= 40 - 8\left(1\dfrac{5}{7}\right)$

Price $= \text{£}26\dfrac{2}{7}$

Total profit $(y) = -7\left(1\dfrac{5}{7}\right)^2 + 24\left(1\dfrac{5}{7}\right) - 8$

$$y = \frac{-144}{7} + \frac{288}{7} - 8$$

$$y = 20\frac{4}{7} - 8$$

$$y = 12\frac{4}{7}$$

Total profit is £$12\frac{4}{7}$ 000

(b) We now seek to maximise total revenue

$\text{TR}(y) = 40x - 8x^2$

$\dfrac{dy}{dx} = 40 - 16x = 0$ for a turning point

$16x = 40$

$x = 2.5$

2nd derivative $\dfrac{d^2y}{dx^2} = -16$, so $x = 2.5$ is a maximum

The output which maximises total revenue is 2.5 (000) units, which is greater than the $1\frac{5}{7}$ (000) units which maximises total profit.

The total profit earned would be:

(TP) $y = -7(2.5)^2 + 24(2.5) - 8$

$y = -43.75 + 60 - 8$

$y = 8.25$

Total profit is £8,250

This is less than the total profit (£$12\frac{4}{7}$, 000) earned by the profit maximising firm, as we should expect.

11.7 $\text{ATC}(y) = \dfrac{x^2}{3} - x + 11$

$\dfrac{dy}{dx} = \dfrac{2}{3}x - 1 = 0$ for t.p.

$x = \dfrac{3}{2}$ for t.p. Since 2nd derivative positive $(+\dfrac{2}{3})$ then ATC is minimum at 1,500 units of output.

11.8 (a) Marginal revenue (MR) $= \dfrac{dy}{dx} = 20 - 4x$

(b) MR should be negatively sloped and intersect the horizontal axis at $x = 5$. At this output total revenue (TR) should be at its maximum value of 50.

11.9 (a) $\text{MC} = \dfrac{dy}{dx} = x^2 - 6x + 9$

(b) Total cost is entirely variable here, so the total cost curve goes through the origin. The marginal cost curve reaches a minimum at $x = 3$

11.10 (a) (i) Lead time is approximately two weeks.
(ii) Minimum stock level is 100 units.
(iii) Reorder quantity is 300 units.
(iv) Stock-out occurs at the beginning of August.

(b) (i) Stock have gone below the safety limit presumably because the new supplier was unable to respond to the increased usage rate and to deliver the goods on time. Opting for a cheaper supplier does not necessarily mean a better service or more reliable deliveries.
(ii) The lack of a component will cause a stock-out if delivery is not immediate at the start of August. This in turn will result in production delays, machine downtime and possible delays in completing orders for customers. An inability to meet delivery deadlines could lead to a permanent loss of customers to rival firms.

(c) $\text{EOQ} = \sqrt{\dfrac{2CoD}{Cc}}$

$\text{EOQ} = \sqrt{\dfrac{2 \cdot (200) \cdot (5,000)}{2}}$

$\underline{\text{EOQ} = 1,000 \text{ components}}$

11.11 (a) $3x^2 + C$

(b) $\dfrac{1}{2}x^6 + C$

(c) $\dfrac{4}{7}x^7 + C$

(d) $x^4 + \dfrac{5}{3} \cdot x^3 - \dfrac{3}{2}x^2 + 4x + C$

(e) $\dfrac{2}{5}x^5 - x^4 + \dfrac{7}{2}x^2 + C$

11.12 $y = \displaystyle\int (2 - 4x^2)dx$

$y = \displaystyle\int 2dx - \int 4x^2 dx + C$

$y = 2x - \dfrac{4}{3}x^3 + C$

when $x = 1$, $y = 1$

so $\qquad 1 = 2(1) - \dfrac{4}{3}(1)^3 + C$

$1 - 2 + \dfrac{4}{3} = C$

$\underline{\dfrac{1}{3} = C}$

The equation of the curve is $y = 2x - \dfrac{4}{3}x^3 + \dfrac{1}{3}$

11.13
$$\int_{1}^{2}(3x + 2x^2 + x^3)\,dx = \left| \frac{3}{2}x^2 + \frac{2}{3}x^3 + \frac{1}{4}x^4 \right|_{1}^{2}$$

$$= \left(6 + 5\frac{1}{3} + 4 \right) - \left(\frac{3}{2} + \frac{2}{3} + \frac{1}{4} \right)$$

$$= 15\frac{4}{12} - 2\frac{5}{12}$$

$$= 12\frac{11}{12} \text{ units}^2$$

Appendix: Basic mathematics

A1 (a) −6 (b) −2 (c) +8
 (d) 2 (e) 96 (f) 9

A2 (a) 2.64 (b) 1.34 (c) 17.6
 (d) 7.5 (e) 20.0 (f) 0.006

A3 (a) 20.8% (b) 12.5 (c) 25% (d) 13.3%

A4 (a) £1.30 : £1.95 (b) £4,200 : £3,000 : £1,800

A5 (a) t^7 (b) m^3 (c) $6x^7$
 (d) $15p^5$ (e) $28m^4$ (f) $12w^3$

A6 (a) x^4 (b) p^2 (c) $4d^2$

 (d) $2m$ (e) 2 (f) $1\frac{1}{2}m$

A7 (a) 27 (b) 4 (c) 10
 (d) 1,000,000 (e) 7 (f) 19

A8 (a) $\dfrac{1}{49}$ (b) $\dfrac{1}{512}$ (c) $\dfrac{1}{x^4}$ (d) $\dfrac{1}{m}$

 (e) $\dfrac{4}{g^2}$ (f) $\dfrac{5}{m^2}$ (g) $\dfrac{1}{8t^3}$ (h) $\dfrac{1}{2t^4}$

A9 (a) $\dfrac{2}{m}$ (b) $\dfrac{4}{3t^3}$ (c) $\dfrac{3}{2x}$ (d) $\dfrac{c}{d^2}$

 (e) a (f) $\dfrac{3a}{b}$ (g) $\dfrac{9}{5q}$ (h) $\dfrac{2m}{p}$

 (i) $\dfrac{3}{4}$ (j) 5 (k) $\dfrac{4t^3}{3}$ (l) $\dfrac{5}{2}$

A10 (a) $3^{\frac{1}{2}}$ (b) 4^1 (c) $7^{-\frac{1}{2}}$

      (d) 5^{-1} (e) $3^{\frac{2}{3}}$ (f) $5^{\frac{3}{4}}$

A11 (a) $y = \dfrac{x+2}{2}$ (b) $y = \dfrac{x}{b+7}$ (c) $y = \dfrac{t}{5} - \dfrac{p}{35}$

A12 (a) $8x^2 - 12x + 2x - 3 = 8x^2 - 10x - 3$ (b) $3x^2 - 4x - 15$

      (c) $2pm + pt - 3tm + pt = 2pm + 2pt - 3tm$

A13 (a) $t(3 + 7t)$ (b) $2m^2(m - 3)$ (c) $3mp(2p + 3mt)$

      (d) $(x - 4)(x - 3)$ (e) $(x + 5)(x - 5)$ (f) $(2x + 5)(x - 3)$

A14 (a) $x = 7$ (b) $x = -1$ (c) $x = \dfrac{19}{8}$

A15 (a) $(x + 4)(x + 3) = 0$, so $x = -4$ and -3

      (b) Use formula method, with $a = 5$, $b = 6$, $c = -2$

$$x = \frac{-6 \pm \sqrt{36 - 4(5)(-2)}}{10}$$

$$x = \frac{-6 \pm \sqrt{76}}{10} = \frac{-6 \pm 8.7}{10}$$

$$x = \frac{-14.7}{10} \text{ or } \frac{+2.87}{10} = -1.47 \text{ or } +0.29$$

      (c) Use formula method, with $a = 1$, $b = 4$, $c = -117$

$$x = \frac{-4 \pm \sqrt{16 - 4(1)(-117)}}{2}$$

$$x = \frac{-4 \pm \sqrt{484}}{2} = \frac{-4 \pm 22}{2}$$

$$x = \frac{-26}{2} \text{ or } +\frac{18}{2} = -13 \text{ or } +9$$

A16 (a) $5x + y = 0$ ... (1)

                $3x - 2y = 13$ ... (2)

      (1) $\times$ 2 $\underline{10x + 2y = 0}$ ... (3)

      (2) + (3) $13x = 13$

                   $\underline{x = 1}$

      substitute $x = 1$ in equation (1)

             $5(1) + y = 0$

                 $y = -5$

      Solutions are $x = 1$ and $y = -5$

(b) $7x + 3y = 18$ . . . (1)

$x + y = 4$ . . . (2)

(2) × 3 $3x + 3y = 12$ . . . (3)

(1) − (3) $4x = 6$

$x = 1.5$

Substitute $x = 1.5$ in equation (2)

$1.5 + y = 4$

$y = 2.5$

Solutions are $x = 1.5$ and $y = 2.5$

A17 (a) $x > \dfrac{32}{5}$ (b) $t < \dfrac{5t}{4} - 2$ (c) $-6 < x < 6$

(d) Treat each side separately

$-2 \le 5x + 3$ $5x + 3 < 4$

$-2 - 3 \le 5x$ $5x < 4 - 3$

$-\dfrac{5}{5} \le x$ $5x < 1$

$-1 \le x$ $x < \dfrac{1}{5}$

Hence $-1 \le x < \dfrac{1}{5}$

A18

x	−4	−3	−2	−1	0	1	2	3
x^2	16	9	4	1	0	1	4	9
$+x$	−4	−3	−2	−1	0	1	2	3
−6	−6	−6	−6	−6	−6	−6	−6	−6
y	6	0	−4	−6	−6	−4	0	6

(a) Your graph should look similar to Figure A6(b) (p. 304).

(b) Solutions are $x = -3$ and $x = +2$

A19 Gradient $= \dfrac{(y_2 - y_1)}{(x_2 - x_1)} = \dfrac{9 - -3}{4 - -2} = \dfrac{12}{6} = +2$

A20 Note (a) and (b) use arithmetic progression formula

(a) $S_8 = \dfrac{8}{2}[84 + 7(4)] = 448$

(b) $S_8 = \dfrac{8}{2}[400 + 7(-5)] = 1{,}460$

Note (c) and (d) use geometric progression formula

(d) $S_8 = \dfrac{4(1 - 1.5^8)}{(1 - 1.5)} = \dfrac{4(1 - 25.63)}{-0.5} = \dfrac{4(-24.63)}{-0.5} = 197.04$

(e) $S_8 = \dfrac{1{,}000(1 - 0.5^8)}{(1 - 0.5)} = \dfrac{1{,}000(1 - 0.0039)}{0.5} = \dfrac{1{,}000(0.9961)}{0.5} = 1{,}992.2$

Responses to 'Pause for thought'

Chapter 1: Data presentation and collection
• •

Pause for thought 1.1

Many possibilities here: *discrete data*, number of persons in a class, number of cars in a garage, etc. *continuous data*, speed on a speedometer, distance travelled on a mileometer, etc.

Pause for thought 1.2

Check your solution with the answer to Self-check question 1.4 on p. 322.

Pause for thought 1.3

The median value. Where the respective cumulative frequency curves intersect, there will be the same number of observations above that value as there are below that value.

Chapter 2: Central location and dispersion
• •

Pause for thought 2.1

The UK income distribution is skewed to the right, as the tail of the distribution is to the right. A few, high income earners pull the arithmetic mean income *above* the median income.

Pause for thought 2.2

The distribution is skewed to the right, with a few high values. We should expect the mean to be higher than the median. Check your calculation when you tackle this question.

Pause for thought 2.3

Various possibilities here. One important change is the growth in the elderly in the UK. In 1951 only 11 per cent of the UK population was over 65 years, today it is 15 per cent and by 2011 it is expected to be 20 per cent. Since the 'spread' of ages around the average is likely to rise (even if the average itself rises) we should expect the mean deviation to rise.

Chapter 3: Regression and correlation

Pause for thought 3.1

If the least squares line fits the data very well, then we can have more confidence in using it for prediction (see section on correlation, p. 58). Even if there is a good fit, if the underlying relationship between the variables changes in the future, then any predictions can still be unreliable.

Pause for thought 3.2

Total Variation is the sum of the squared deviations from the mean, **Variance** (see p. 42) is the *average* of the sum of the squared deviations from the mean.

Pause for thought 3.3

Yes, since the actual observations are extremely close to the least squares line.

Chapter 4: Time series and forecasting

Pause for thought 4.1

Many possibilities here. For example chocolate (Easter and Christmas peaks), Sun lotion (Summer), gloves (Autumn and Winter), Hotels (Summer and festivals), swimwear (Spring and Summer), freelance gardeners (Spring and Summer), etc.

Pause for thought 4.2

Many possibilities here. For example the exit of sterling from the exchange rate mechanism (ERM) in 1992 (helped UK exporters, harmed UK importers), the financial problems in many of the Pacific Rim countries in 1997 (harmed UK exporters and reduced inward investment from that region into the UK), the impacts of global warming on weather patterns (less rain creating problems for water companies), etc.

Pause for thought 4.3

Many possibilities here. For example three products with a well-established upward sales trend might include mobile telephones, designer clothes and cinema attendance. On the other hand three products with a well-established downward sales trend might include coal, anoraks, cassette tapes, etc.

Chapter 5: Probability

Pause for thought 5.1

Many possibilities here. For example, the theoretical probabilities of:

▶ tossing a coin and getting a head $= \dfrac{1}{2}$

▶ picking one card from a (shuffled) pack and getting an ace $= \dfrac{4}{52} = \dfrac{1}{13}$

▶ choosing one red ball from a bag containing four red balls and six white balls $= \dfrac{4}{10} = \dfrac{2}{5}$

Pause for thought 5.2

Many possibilities here. For example:

▶ tossing a coin and getting head or a tail $= \dfrac{1}{2} + \dfrac{1}{2} = 1$

▶ picking one card from a (shuffled) pack and getting an ace or a king $= \dfrac{4}{52} + \dfrac{4}{52} = \dfrac{8}{52} = \dfrac{2}{13}$

▶ choosing one ball from a bag containing four red balls, six white balls and five blue balls and getting a red or a white ball $= \dfrac{4}{15} + \dfrac{6}{15} = \dfrac{10}{15} = \dfrac{2}{3}$

Chapter 6: Probability distributions

Pause for thought 6.1

Many possibilities here; for example IQ scores, heights of a population (say, male adults), etc.

Pause for thought 6.2

Many possibilities here; for example;

▶ tossing a coin a given number of times and getting a particular number of heads (heads = 'success')

▶ selecting a particular number of a type of card (or cards) from a pack with replacement (so that the probability of 'success' or 'failure' is constant) after a given number of attempts.

▶ selecting a particular number of defective items in a sample of given size when the proportion of defective items overall (i.e. in the population) is known. (Again sampling with replacement will keep the probability of 'success' or 'failure' constant.)

Chapter 7: Sampling and tests of hypotheses

Pause for thought 7.1

Many possibilities here, but the key idea is that the product (good or service) should be consumed in similar quantities by most segments of a population. Examples might include products such as chocolate, confectionery, ice-cream, etc.

Pause for thought 7.2

Many possibilities here, but the key idea is that the product should be consumed in substantially different quantities by different segments of a population. Examples might include products such as pipes, carpet slippers, baby food, etc.

Chapter 8: Index numbers

Pause for thought 8.1

Many possibilities here. Three cheaper products in real terms than 20 years ago might include various types of computer, international telephone calls, price of energy sources such as oil, coal, gas (which are now in more plentiful supply relative to demand), etc. Three more expensive products might included houses, water rates, electricity prices, etc.

Pause for thought 8.2

One obvious problem involves products for which the *quality* has changed substantially over time. For example a wide range of electronic items are immensely more powerful today (in terms of the number of operations they can perform per unit of time, area, etc.) than they were even a few years ago.

Chapter 9: Time value of money

Pause for thought 9.1

$133.1 + 133.1(0.10) = 133.1(1 + 0.10) = 100(1 + 0.10)^4 = £146.41$

Pause for thought 9.2

The two projects have very similar values for the IRR. The respective NPV curves intersect, but *below* the horizontal axis.

Pause for thought 9.3

Two projects might have similar NPVs but the *dispersion* of the future returns might be very different. Arguably, the greater the dispersion, the greater the risk. So, if we regard the NPV as a type of 'average' return, we might calculate the variance or standard deviation of the discounted cash flows around that average. Even where projects have different 'averages' (NPVs), we might calculate the Coefficient of Variation (see chapter 2, p. 46) as a measure of *relative* dispersion.

Chapter 10: Linear programming and break – even analysis

Pause for thought 10.1

For example, $B = 10$, $D = 5$ would use up 65 units of capital ($10 \times 4 + 5 \times 5$), *less than* the 100 units of capital available. However $B = 20$, $D = 10$ would use up 130 units of capital ($20 \times 4 + 10 \times 5$), *more than* the 100 units of capital available.

Pause for thought 10.2

Using Figure 10.3 (p. 228) we can say that:

▶ combinations of B and D *inside* MVW do not have enough capital available to produce them, though they do have enough labour.
▶ combinations of B and D *inside* WXN do not have enough labour, but do have enough capital.
▶ combinations of B and D *to the right* of segment MWN do not have enough capital or labour to make these outputs feasible.

Pause for thought 10.3

For example, take the combination of vehicles 15A and 5B. This will permit only 900 passengers ($15 \times 40 + 5 \times 60$) to be carried, which is less than the minimum 960 which must be carried per journey, though this combination of vehicles can better the baggage constraint since 525 ($15 \times 30 + 5 \times 15$) tons of baggage exceeds the minimum 360 tons which must be carried per journey. Any combination of vehicles you select to the left of segment QRS in Figure 10.6 (p. 237) will fail to meet one or more of the two constraints.

Chapter 11: Calculus and business applications

Pause for thought 11.1

Many possibilities here. All of the following suggest zero as the *limit* to which something tends, though it never actually gets there:

▶ Zero is the limit of ($\frac{1}{2}^{n}$) as *n* rises to infinity.
▶ Zero is the limit to which the slope of a unit elastic demand curve tends as output rises to infinity.
▶ Zero is the limit to which the slope of an average fixed cost curve tends as output rises to infinity. etc.

Pause for thought 11.2

The rate of change of the curves identified give us:

(a) Marginal cost
(b) Marginal revenue
(c) Marginal profit.

Pause for thought 11.3

By finding the turning point for the equation relating total revenue to output, they can find where total revenue is a maximum, should they be interested in a sales revenue maximising output. Also total profit = total revenue – total cost, so this equation can be worked out, and the turning point calculated for which total profit is a maximum. In these ways the levels of output which achieve maximum revenue, maximum profit, etc. can be estimated.

Pause for thought 11.4

Just-in-time manufacturing is a production system, which is designed to mini-mise stock-holding costs by carefully planning the flow of resources through the production process. It requires a highly efficient ordering system and reli-able delivery, often directly to the production line. This type of system is highly sensitive to customer demand. In some cases production only begins when an order is placed. The system originated in Japan in the 1950s but is now uni-versally applied, especially in firms using flow production such as car assembly, electronics and bottling plants.

Benefits to Mondeo from its introduction include the following:

▶ Improved cash flow since money is no longer tied up in stocks.
▶ Reduced waste from obsolete or damaged stock.
▶ Reduced cost of handling stock (e.g. in terms of space, shelving, security, store personnel).
▶ Less space required for stock holding therefore more available for production.
▶ Relationships with suppliers are improved.
▶ More scope for use of computerised information system to improve integration of departments.
▶ Workforce is given more responsibility and encouraged to work in teams or 'cells'. This should improve motivation.

Answers to 'Review questions'

Chapter 1 : Data presentation and collection

1.1 This is an unequal width histogram.

Step 1 From the frequency table decide on a standard class width = 10 years.

Step 2 Enlarge the original table as follows:

Class	Frequency	Class width	No of std widths	Frequency density
0–5	41	5	0.5	82
5–15	142	10	1	142
15–25	63	10	1	63
25–35	70	10	1	70
35–45	105	10	1	105
45–55	102	10	1	102
55–65	177	10	1	177
65–95	138	30	3	46

Step 3 Construct the histogram and frequency polygon.

figure R1.1
Histogram and frequency polygon showing age distribution of a village's population

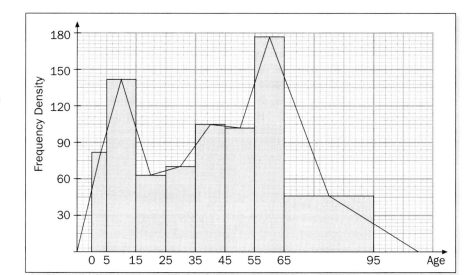

1.2 (a) *Step 1* Maximum = 73;   Minimum = 1; Range = 72

Step 2 The class intervals can reflect the interests of those conducting the survey. The raw data shows that the maximum distance travelled is 73 kilometres – so the final class interval can be set at 30–75. Therefore:

Class	Tally	Frequency
0–5	ЖІ ЖІ ЖІ ІІ	17
5–10	ЖІ ЖІ І	11
10–30	ЖІ ЖІ ІІ	12
30–75	ЖІ ЖІ	10

(b) *Step 1* From the frequency table decide on a standard class width – 10 kilometres.

Step 2 Enlarge the original table as indicated below:

Distance	Frequency	Class width	No of std widths	Height
0–5	17	5	0.5	34
5–10	11	5	0.5	22
10–30	12	20	2	6
30–75	10	45	4.5	2.2

Step 3 Construct the histogram.

figure R1.2
Histogram showing distance travelled to work

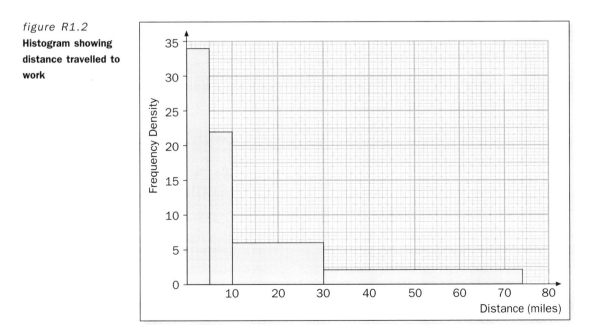

1.3 (a) *Step 1* Construct a cumulative frequency table. Here we construct a cumulative 'less than' frequency table:

Time to Load (minutes)	Cumulative frequency
less than 45	4
less than 50	17
less than 55	34
less than 60	78
less than 70	137
less than 80	144

Step 2 Construct the cumulative 'less than' ogive, as indicated.

figure R1.3
Cumulative 'less than' ogive showing number of vehicles

Notes: **(i) the median loading time is 59.5 minutes**
(ii) the interquartile range is 65.5 − 55.25 = 10.25 minutes
(iii) the number of vehicles loaded in under 52 minutes is 24 vehicles

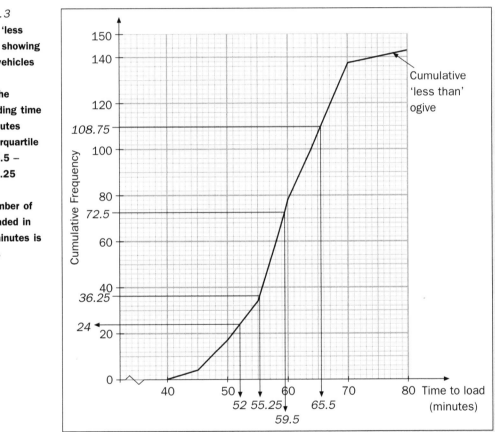

Step 3 Identify the positions corresponding to the lower and upper quartiles and the median.

Note that we use the continuity correction (see p. 13) to identify the observation which corresponds to each quartile and the median.

Step 4 Read off the appropriate values from the diagram as shown in Figure R1.3.

1.4 As there is a figure for the total amount of expenditure a pie chart is particularly useful in illustrating how it can be divided into its constituent parts. Thus:

Step 1 Find the total expenditure – given (£1,438,667).

Step 2 Find the angles of the circle.

Cost centre	Expenditure (£)	Angle
Employees	1,139,410	$\dfrac{1,139,410}{1,438,667} \times 360° = 285°$
Premises	69,004	$\dfrac{69,004}{1,438,667} \times 360° = 17°$
Transport	52,524	$\dfrac{52,524}{1,438,667} \times 360° = 13°$
Raw materials	83,205	$\dfrac{83,205}{1,438,667} \times 360° = 21°$
Admin	23,242	$\dfrac{23,242}{1,438,667} \times 360° = 6°$
Capital financing costs	71,282	$\dfrac{71,282}{1,438,667} \times 360° = 18°$

Step 3 Construct the pie chart.

figure R1.4
Annual expenditure in the form of a pie chart

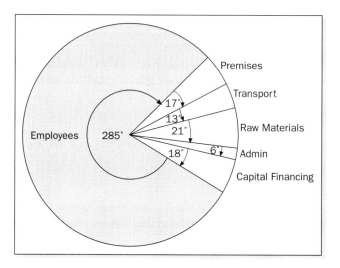

1.5 Note that there are gaps between the bars (unlike the histogram) and that there is no scale on the horizontal axis.

figure R1.5
Imports into target market 1988–1997 by value ($bn)

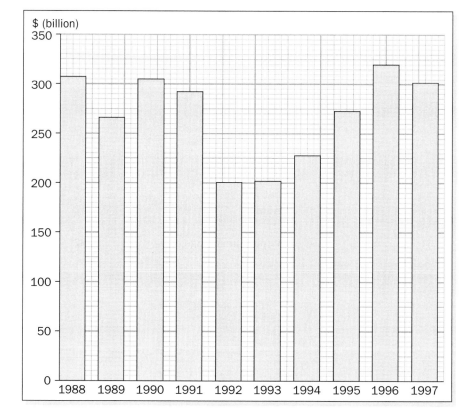

1.6 A useful way of illustrating the data is by means of a component bar-chart, which could be shown horizontally or vertically.

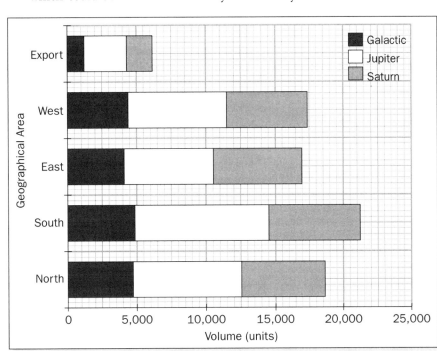

figure R1.6 (a)
Component bar chart (horizontal): sales by volume (units) and geographical area

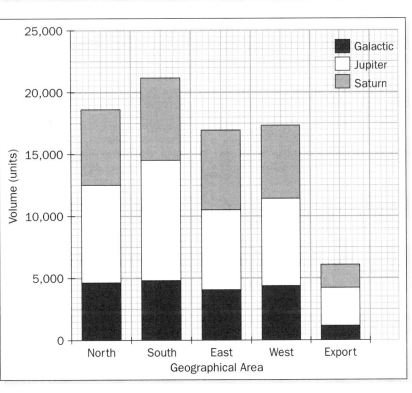

figure R1.6 (b)
Component bar chart (vertical): sales by volume (units) and geographical area

The same data can be displayed using a multiple bar chart.

figure R1.7 (a)
Multiple bar chart (horizontal)

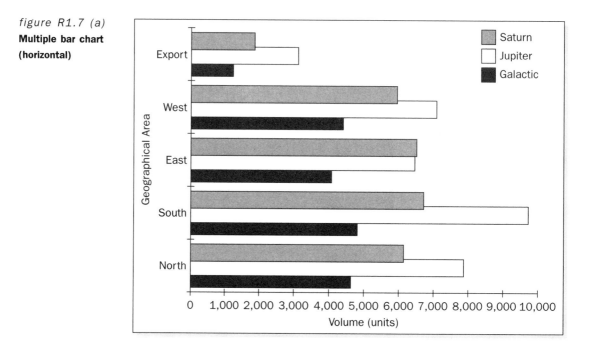

figure R1.7 (b)
Multiple bar chart (vertical)

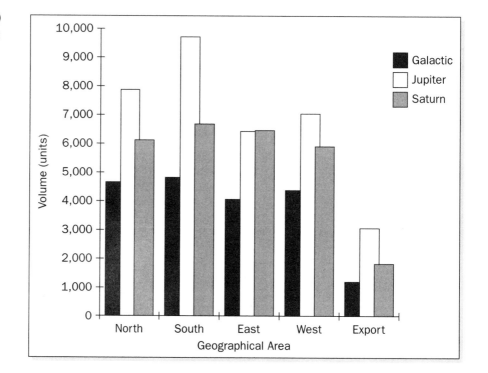

1.7 Again this table lends itself to a component bar chart, which can usefully be displayed horizontally and in a manner which represents both total passengers and their split between international and domestic markets. Figure R1.8 shows the main strengths of each market. For example, although British Airways is only rated eleventh in the total passengers carried, the graph shows that it is the largest international carrier. The strength of Delta in its domestic market (USA) is also evident.

figure R1.8
Number of passengers carried by 20 largest airlines

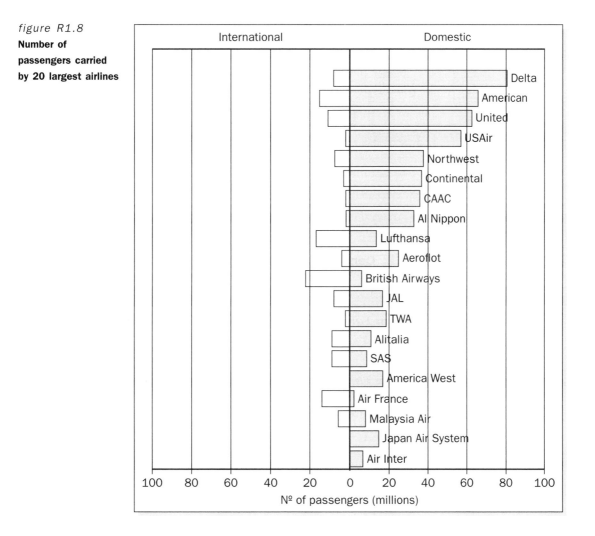

In contrast the component bar chart displayed vertically in Figure R1.9 illustrates the overall strength of the combined markets. Although the chart shows the different contributions of the two markets, it is the combination of them both which is the most striking feature of this presentation. Clearly, the particular type of visual presentation used may depend on the features you may wish to highlight.

figure R1.9
Number of passengers carried by 20 largest airlines

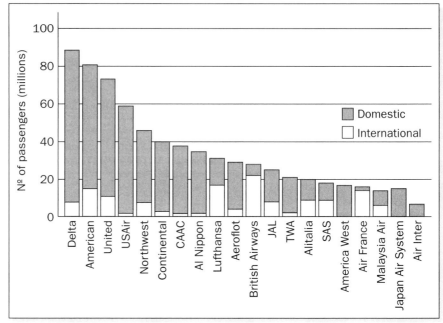

Chapter 2: Central location and dispersion

· ·

2.1 (a) ***Mean Farm A*** $= \dfrac{\sum\limits_{i=1}^{n} X_i}{n} = \dfrac{4{,}604.49}{14} = 328.89$ ***tonnes***

Mean Farm B $= \dfrac{\sum\limits_{i=1}^{n} X_i}{n} = \dfrac{4{,}553.21}{14} = 325.23$ ***tonnes***

(b) Arrange the data into an array

Farm A

| 229.88 | 259.43 | 262.8 | 309.42 | 319.95 | 329.33 | 330.33 |
| 332.04 | 337.99 | 341.27 | 357.38 | 383.31 | 398.46 | 412.9 |

Range farm A = highest value – lowest value
$$= 412.9 - 229.88$$
$$= 183.02$$

Farm B

| 290.43 | 291.21 | 291.99 | 295.18 | 306.03 | 314.39 | 315.25 |
| 324.79 | 333.81 | 343.87 | 348.88 | 352.92 | 364.32 | 380.14 |

Range farm B = highest value – lowest value
$$= 380.14 - 290.43$$
$$= 89.71$$

(c) First, calculate the value of the upper quartile (Q_3).

$$Q_3 \; position = \frac{3}{4}(n + 1) = \frac{3}{4}(15) = 11.25$$

Farm A

The upper quartile is the 11.25th observation – or 0.25 of the way between the 11th and 12th observation in the above array.

    To calculate this value:

(i)   calculate the difference between the 12th and 11th values:
383.31 – 357.38 = 25.93
(ii) multiply the difference by 0.25:
25.93 × 0.25 = 6.48
(iii) add 6.48 to the 11th observation:
357.38 + 6.48 = 363.86

Q_3 *of Farm A* = **363.86**

Farm B

$$Q_3 \; position = \frac{3}{4}(n + 1) = \frac{3}{4}(15) = 11.25$$

The upper quartile is the 11.25th observation – or 0.25 of the way between the 11th and 12th observation in the above array.

    To calculate this value:

(i)   calculate the difference between the 12th and 11th values:
352.92 – 348.88 = 4.04
(ii) multiply the difference by 0.25:
4.04 × 0.25 = 1.01
(iii) add 1.01 to the 11th observation:
348.88 + 1.01 = 349.89

Q_3 *of Farm B* = **349.89**

Second, calculate the value of the lower quartile (Q_1)

Farm A

$$Q_1 \; position = \frac{1}{4}(n + 1) = \frac{1}{4}(15) = 3.75$$

The lower quartile is the 3.75th observation – or 0.75 of the way between the 3rd and 4th observation in the above array.

    To calculate this value:

(i)   calculate the difference between the 4th and 3rd values:
309.42 – 262.80 = 46.62
(ii) multiply the difference by three-quarters (0.75):
46.62 × 0.75 = 34.97
(iii) add 34.97 to the 3rd observation:
262.80 + 34.97 = 297.77

Q_1 *of Farm A* = **297.77**

Farm B

$Q_1 \ position = \dfrac{1}{4}(n + 1) = \dfrac{1}{4}(15) = 3.75$

The upper quartile is the 3.75th observation – or 0.75 of the way between the 3rd and 4th observation in the above array.

To calculate this value:

(i) calculate the difference between the 4th and 3rd values:
   295.18 – 291.99 = 3.19
(ii) multiply the difference by 0.75:
   $3.19 \times 0.75 = 2.39$
(iii) add 2.39 to the 3rd observation:
   291.99 + 2.39 = 294.38

$Q_1 \ of \ Farm \ B = \mathbf{294.38}$

Finally, calculate the interquartile range as follows:

interquartile range of **Farm A** $= Q_3 - Q_1 = 363.86 - 297.77 = \mathbf{66.09}$

interquartile range of **Farm B** $= Q_3 - Q_1 = 349.89 - 294.38 = \mathbf{55.51}$

(d) *semi-interquartile range of* **Farm A** $= \dfrac{Q_3 - Q_1}{2} = \dfrac{66.09}{2} = \mathbf{33.05}$

semi-interquartile range of **Farm B** $= \dfrac{Q_3 - Q_1}{2} = \dfrac{55.51}{2} = \mathbf{27.75}$

(e) Although the mean daily supply of peas from both farmers is similar the data suggest that the supply of peas from Farm A is more erratic.

The range of data from Farm A is around double that of Farm B (183.02 tonnes compared to 89.71 tonnes). This shows that Farm A's supply has reached more extreme values over the two week period.

The interquartile range is also greater for Farm A's supply (66.09 compared to 55.51). This demonstrates that dispersion of the data around the mean is greater for Farm A than for Farm B. This pattern is also reflected in the quartile deviation (the semi-interquartile range).

Therefore Farm B would seem to provide a more consistent supply, at least over the two week period in question.

2.2 (a) *mean deviation* $= \dfrac{\sum\limits_{i=1}^{n}|X_i - \bar{X}|}{n}$

To calculate the mean deviation:

Step 1 Calculate the mean value
Step 2 Find the absolute deviation (but ignore the sign) of each observation from the mean
Step 3 Sum the absolute deviations (ignoring signs)
Step 4 Divide this sum by the number of observations

Farm A

Step 1 The mean for Farm A's supply was previously calculated as 328.89 tonnes.

Step 2 Construct a table of two columns with the values of X_i in one column and the absolute deviations from the mean $|X_i - \bar{X}|$ in the other, ignoring the sign:

X_i	$|X_i - \bar{X}|$ $|X_i - 328.89|$
229.88	99.01
259.43	69.46
262.8	66.09
309.42	19.47
319.95	8.94
329.33	0.44
330.33	1.44
332.04	3.15
337.99	9.10
341.27	12.38
357.38	28.49
383.31	54.42
398.46	69.57
412.9	84.01
	525.97

Step 3 = 525.97

Step 4

$$MD = \frac{\sum\limits_{i=1}^{n}|X_i - \bar{X}|}{n} = \frac{525.97}{14} = 37.57 \; tonnes$$

This suggests that Farm A has a mean daily supply of 328.89 ± 37.57 tonnes of peas:

Farm B

Step 1 The mean for Farm B's supply was previously calculated as 325.23 tonnes

Step 2 construct a table of two columns

X_i	$|X_i - \bar{X}|$ $|X_i - 325.23|$
364.32	39.09
295.18	30.05
352.92	27.69
380.14	54.91
314.39	10.84
343.87	18.64
290.43	34.80
291.21	34.02
306.03	19.20
348.88	23.65
333.81	8.58
291.99	33.24
324.79	0.44
315.25	9.98
	345.13

Step 3 = 345.13

Step 4

$$MD = \frac{\sum_{i=1}^{n}|X_i - \bar{X}|}{n} = \frac{345.13}{14} = 24.65 \ tonnes$$

This suggests that Farm B has a mean daily supply of 325.23 ± 24.65 tonnes of peas.

(b) As noted in the answer to question 2.1, both farmers have a mean supply of approximately the same daily amount, but the larger mean deviation for Farm A (37.57 tonnes compared with 24.65 tonnes) reveals that the data for Farm A has a greater average deviation around the mean supply than that for Farm B. The mean deviation has the advantage of comparing the dispersion of **all** items of data for each farm, rather than selecting specific points only (e.g. quartiles) in the respective distributions for comparison.

2.3 The question can by interpreted as: *'What is the hourly mean temperature of the cabinet and by how much, on average, does it deviate from the mean?'* In other words find the mean hourly temperature and the mean deviation.
The data are grouped therefore:

Step 1 Calculate the mean from the table below:

$$\bar{X} = \frac{\sum_{i=1}^{n}F_iX_i}{\sum_{i=1}^{n}F_i}$$

where: F_i = frequency of *i*th class

X_i = class mid-point

$$\bar{X} = \frac{2676}{720}$$

$$= 3.72°C$$

Step 2 Enlarge the original table with two extra columns as follows:

Temperature (°C)	Class mid-point X_i	Frequency F_i	F_iX_i	$|X_i - \bar{X}|$	$F_i|X_i - \bar{X}|$
0–1	0.5	1	0.5	3.22	3.22
1–2	1.5	11	16.5	2.22	24.42
2–3	2.5	123	307.5	1.22	150.06
3–4	3.5	322	1,127	0.22	70.84
4–5	4.5	223	1,003.5	0.78	173.94
5–6	5.5	39	214.5	1.78	69.42
6–7	6.5	1	6.5	2.78	2.78
		720	2,676		494.68

Step 3 Calculate the mean deviation:

$$mean\ deviation = \frac{\sum_{i=1}^{j} F_i |X_i - \bar{X}|}{\sum_{i=1}^{j} F_i}$$

where: j = number of class intervals

$$MD = \frac{494.68}{720}$$

$$= 0.69°C$$

The mean temperature of 3.72°C, although slightly low, is close to the company's standard. However, the mean deviation of 0.69°C exceeds the limit of 0.5°C. Therefore, the equipment does **not** comply with the company's policy.

2.4

Visitors(000s)	Class mid-point X_i	Frequency F_i	F_iX_i	$F_iX_i^2$
6–8	7	4	28	196
8–10	9	17	153	1,377
10–12	11	61	671	7,381
12–14	13	47	611	7,943
14–16	15	18	270	4,050
16–18	17	3	51	867
		150	1,784	21,814

Calculate the mean

$$\bar{X} = \frac{\sum_{i=1}^{j} F_i X_i}{\sum_{i=1}^{j} F_i}$$

where: F_i = frequency of ith class

X_i = class mid-point

$$\bar{X} = \frac{1,784}{150}$$

$$= 11,893\ visitors$$

Calculate the variance

$$s^2 = \frac{\sum F_i X_i^2}{\sum F_i} - \left(\frac{\sum F_i X_I}{\sum F_i}\right)^2$$

$$s^2 = \frac{21,814}{150} - \left(\frac{1,784}{150}\right)^2$$

$$s^2 = 145.43 - 141.45$$

$$s^2 = 3.98$$

Calculate the standard deviation

standard deviation $s = \sqrt{s^2}$
$$s = \sqrt{3.98}$$
$$s = 1.99$$

The standard deviation = 1.99

As the standard deviation and variance can be linked directly to the arithmetic mean they provide a measure of dispersion. They are not, however, an appropriate measure of relative dispersion between data sets with different arithmetic means. In this case, the coefficient of variation would be more useful (see below).

2.5 If the first set of data is labelled A and the second set labelled B. Then

$$C\ of\ V_A = \frac{s}{\overline{X}} = \frac{standard\ deviation}{mean}$$

$$= \frac{21.48}{196}$$

$$= 0.11$$

$$C\ of\ V_B = \frac{12.62}{94}$$

$$= 0.13$$

In other words although the absolute dispersion (s) had fallen over the two time periods the relative dispersion indicted by the coefficient of variation had actually risen. This is because the mean value for the rejection rate had fallen even faster over the successive time periods than had the absolute dispersion around the respective means. As a consequence the relative dispersion had risen over the two time periods.

2.6

figure R2.1
Chart showing distribution of the value of lager sales in two supermarkets

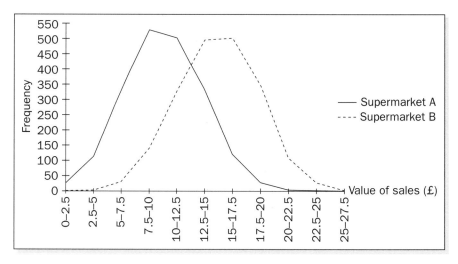

Supermarket A

Sales value of lager (£)	Frequency F_i	mid-point X_i	F_iX_i	$F_iX_i^2$
0–2.5	27	1.25	33.75	42.19
2.5–5	114	3.75	427.5	1,603.13
5–7.5	333	6.25	2,081.25	13,007.81
7.5–10	530	8.75	4,637.5	40,578.13
10–12.5	504	11.25	5,670.0	63,787.5
12.5–15	334	13.75	4,592.5	63,146.88
15–17.5	121	16.25	1,966.25	31,951.56
17.5–20	29	18.75	543.75	10,195.31
20–22.5	5	21.25	106.25	2,257.81
22.5–25	2	23.75	47.5	1,128.13
25–27.5	1	26.25	26.25	689.06
	2,000		20,132.5	228,387.51

$$\bar{X}_A = \frac{\sum F_iX_i}{\sum F_i}$$

$$\bar{X}_A = \frac{20,132.5}{2,000}$$

Mean = £10.07

$$\text{Variance } (s^2) = \frac{\sum F_iX_i^2}{\sum F_i} - \left(\frac{\sum F_iX_i}{\sum F_i}\right)^2$$

$$= \frac{228,387.51}{2,000} - \left(\frac{20,132.5}{2,000}\right)^2$$

$$= 114.19 - 10.07^2$$

$$= 114.19 - 101.4$$

Variance = 12.79 *square pounds*

Standard deviation = $\sqrt{12.79}$ = £3.58

Supermarket B

Sales value of lager (£)	Frequency F_i	mid-point X_i	F_iX_i	$F_iX_i^2$
0–2.5	1	1.25	1.25	1.56
2.5–5	3	3.75	11.25	42.19
5–7.5	31	6.25	193.75	1,210.94
7.5–10	142	8.75	1,242.5	10,871.88
10–12.5	328	11.25	3,690.0	41,512.50
12.5–15	498	13.75	6,847.5	94,153.13
15–17.5	504	16.25	8,190.0	133,087.50
17.5–20	351	18.75	6,581.25	123,398.44
20–22.5	110	21.25	2,337.5	49,671.88
22.5–25	29	23.75	688.75	16,357.81
25–27.5	3	26.25	78.75	2,067.19
	2,000		29,862.50	472,375.02

$$\overline{X}_B = \frac{\sum F_i X_i}{\sum F_i}$$

$$\overline{X}_B = \frac{29{,}862.25}{2{,}000}$$

Mean = £14.93

$$\text{Variance } (s^2) = \frac{\sum F_i X_i^2}{\sum F_i} - \left(\frac{\sum F_i X_i}{\sum F_i} \right)^2$$

$$= \frac{472{,}375}{2{,}000} - \left(\frac{29{,}862.25}{2{,}000} \right)^2$$

$$= 236.19 - 14.93^2$$

$$= 236.19 - 222.9$$

Variance = 13.29 *square pounds*

Standard deviation = $\sqrt{13.29}$ = £3.65

Coefficient of variation

$$C \text{ of } V_A = \frac{s}{\overline{X}} = \frac{standard\ deviation}{mean}$$

$$= \frac{3.58}{10.07}$$

$$= 0.36$$

$$C \text{ of } V_B = \frac{3.65}{14.93}$$

$$= 0.24$$

The mean amount spent by those buying lager in store A is lower than that of store B whilst the variability of the data measured by both the variance and standard deviation are almost identical. The coefficient of variation, however, shows that the *relative* dispersion of store A is greater than that of store B. From the data provided from that particular weekend it would appear that store B would be the best location to promote the new lager.

Chapter 3: Regression and correlation

Note: For the answer to question 1 we present both approaches (see pp. 53 and 55). Thereafter we use only the coding method, though either approach is equally valid.

3.1 Using original data (Approach 1).

	X_i	Y_i	X_iY_i	X_i^2	Y_i^2
	1	89	89	1	7,921
	2	74	148	4	5,476
	3	92	276	9	8,464
	4	123	492	16	15,129
	5	102	510	25	10,404
	6	139	834	36	19,321
	7	152	1,064	49	23,104
	8	128	1,024	64	16,384
	9	183	1,647	81	33,489
	10	148	1,480	100	21,904
	11	166	1,826	121	27,556
	12	179	2,148	144	32,041
Sums	78	1,575	11,538	650	221,193

$$\bar{X} = \frac{78}{12} = 6.5$$

$$\bar{Y} = \frac{1,575}{12} = 131.25$$

$$m = \frac{n\sum_{i=1}^{n} X_iY_i - \sum_{i=1}^{n} X_i \sum_{i=1}^{n} Y_i}{n\sum_{i=1}^{n} X_i^2 - \left(\sum_{i=1}^{n} X_i\right)^2}$$

$$m = \frac{12(11,538) - (78)(1,575)}{12(650) - 78^2}$$

$$m = \frac{138,456 - 122,850}{7,800 - 6,084}$$

$$m = \frac{15,606}{1,716}$$

$$m = 9.0944$$

$$c = \bar{Y} - m\bar{X}$$

$$c = 131.25 - (9.0944 \times 6.5)$$

$$c = 72.1364$$

$$\hat{Y} = 9.0944X + 72.1364$$

$$R^2 = \left[\frac{n\sum_{i=1}^{n} X_iY_i - \sum_{i=1}^{n} X_i \sum_{i=1}^{n} Y_i}{\sqrt{\left[n\sum_{i=1}^{n} X_i^2 - \left(\sum_{i=1}^{n} X_i\right)^2\right] \times \left[n\sum_{i=1}^{n} Y_i^2 - \left(\sum_{i=1}^{n} Y_i\right)^2\right]}}\right]^2$$

$$R^2 = \left[\frac{12(11{,}538) - (78)(1{,}575)}{\sqrt{\left[12(650) - (78)^2\right] \times \left[12(221{,}193) - (1{,}575)^2\right]}}\right]^2$$

$$R^2 = \left[\frac{138{,}456 - 122{,}850}{\sqrt{\left[7{,}800 - 6{,}084\right] \times \left[2{,}654{,}316 - 2{,}480{,}625\right]}}\right]^2$$

$$R^2 = \left[\frac{15{,}606}{\sqrt{1{,}716 \times 173{,}691}}\right]^2$$

$$R^2 = \left[\frac{15{,}606}{17{,}264.23}\right]^2$$

$R^2 = [0.9039]^2$
$R^2 = 0.8171$

When $X = 13$ then: $\hat{Y} = (9.0944 \times 13) + 72.1364 = \mathbf{190.36}$

When $X = 14$ then: $\hat{Y} = (9.0944 \times 14) + 72.1364 = \mathbf{199.46}$

When $X = 15$ then: $\hat{Y} = (9.0944 \times 15) + 72.1364 = \mathbf{208.55}$

As R^2 is relatively high (81.71 per cent can be explained by the regression model) then the forecast can be considered quite reliable.

Using redefined data (Approach 2)

X	Y	x_i	y_i	$x_i y_i$	x_i^2	y_i^2
1	89	−5.5	−42.25	232.375	30.25	1,785.0625
2	74	−4.5	−57.25	257.625	20.25	3,277.5625
3	92	−3.5	−39.25	137.375	12.25	1,540.5625
4	123	−2.5	−8.25	20.625	6.25	68.0625
5	102	−1.5	−29.25	43.875	2.25	855.5625
6	139	−0.5	7.75	−3.875	0.25	60.0625
7	152	0.5	20.75	10.375	0.25	430.5625
8	128	1.5	−3.25	−4.875	2.25	10.5625
9	183	2.5	51.75	129.375	6.25	2,678.0625
10	148	3.5	16.75	58.625	12.25	280.5625
11	166	4.5	34.75	156.375	20.25	1,207.5625
12	179	5.5	47.75	262.625	30.25	2,280.0625
			Sums	1,300.5	143	14,474.25

$\hat{Y} = mX + c$

$$m = \frac{\sum x_i y_i}{\sum x_i^2}$$

$$m = \frac{1{,}300.5}{143}$$

$m = 9.0944$
$c = \hat{Y} - m\bar{X}$
$c = 131.25 - (9.0944 \times 6.5)$

$c = 72.1364$

$\hat{Y} = 9.0944X + 72.1364$

$$R^2 = \frac{\left(\sum x_i y_i\right)^2}{\left(\sum x_i^2\right)\left(\sum y_i^2\right)}$$

$$R^2 = \frac{1{,}300.5^2}{143 \times 14{,}474.25}$$

$R^2 = 0.8171$

When $X = 13$ then: $\hat{Y} = (9.0944 \times 13) + 72.1364 =$ **190.36**

When $X = 14$ then: $\hat{Y} = (9.0944 \times 14) + 72.1364 =$ **199.46**

When $X = 15$ then: $\hat{Y} = (9.0944 \times 15) + 72.1364 =$ **208.55**

As R^2 is relatively high (81.71 per cent can be explained by the regression model) then the forecast can be considered quite reliable.

3.2

X	Y	x_i	y_i	$x_i y_i$	x_i^2	y_i^2
10	103	−7	40.07	−280.47	49	1,605.34
11	104	−6	41.07	−246.40	36	1,686.47
12	95	−5	32.07	−160.33	25	1,028.27
13	83	−4	20.07	−80.27	16	402.67
14	81	−3	18.07	−54.20	9	326.40
15	75	−2	12.07	−24.13	4	145.60
16	68	−1	5.07	−5.07	1	25.67
17	47	0	−15.93	0	0	253.87
18	53	1	−9.93	−9.93	1	98.67
19	40	2	−22.93	−45.87	4	525.94
20	43	3	−19.93	−59.80	9	397.34
21	40	4	−22.93	−91.73	16	525.94
22	38	5	−24.93	−124.67	25	621.67
23	39	6	−23.93	−143.60	36	572.80
24	35	7	−27.93	−195.53	49	780.27
			Sums	−1,522	280	8,996.93

In your scatter diagram you should have placed average daily sales on the vertical axis (Y). This is because we are treating sales as the *dependent variable*, i.e. sales depend on the average daily temperature. We therefore place temperature (°C) on the horizontal axis (X) and treat it as the *independent variable*. You should have plotted 12 points on your scatter diagram. The points plotted should give the idea of an indirect (negative) relationship, with sales generally falling as temperature increases.

$$\overline{X} = 17 \quad \overline{Y} = 62.93$$

$$\hat{Y} = mX + c$$

$$m = \frac{\sum x_i y_i}{\sum x_i^2}$$

$$m = \frac{-1,522}{280}$$

$$m = -5.4357$$

$$c = \overline{Y} - m\overline{X}$$

$$c = 62.93 - (-5.4357 \times 17)$$

$$c = 155.3369$$

$$\hat{Y} = -5.4357X + 155.3369$$

$$R^2 = \frac{\left(\sum x_i y_i\right)^2}{\left(\sum x_i^2\right)\left(\sum y_i^2\right)}$$

$$R^2 = \frac{-1,522^2}{280 \times 8,996.9326}$$

$$R^2 = 0.9196$$

When $X = 25$ then: $\hat{Y} = (-5.4357 \times 25) + 155.3369 = \textbf{19.44}$

3.3

X	Y	x_i	y_i	$x_i y_i$	x_i^2	y_i^2
1	1,459	−3.8	706.25	−2,683.75	14.44	498,789.0625
3	395	−1.8	−357.75	643.95	3.24	127,985.0625
0	534	−4.8	−218.75	1,050	23.04	47,851.5625
2	641	−2.8	−111.75	312.9	7.84	12,488.0625
7	927	2.2	174.25	383.35	4.84	30,363.0625
3	650	−1.8	−102.75	184.95	3.24	10,557.5625
4	447	−0.8	−305.75	244.6	0.64	93,483.0625
5	392	0.2	−360.75	−72.15	0.04	130,140.5625
0	569	−4.8	−183.75	882	23.04	33,764.0625
11	713	6.2	−39.75	−246.45	38.44	1,580.0625
1	401	−3.8	−351.75	1,336.65	14.44	123,728.0625
12	2,691	7.2	1,938.25	13,955.4	51.84	3,756,813.0625
1	443	−3.8	−309.75	1,177.05	14.44	95,945.0625
7	883	2.2	130.25	286.55	4.84	16,965.0625
12	1,577	7.2	824.25	5,934.6	51.84	679,388.0625
11	147	6.2	−605.75	−3,755.65	38.44	366,933.0625
7	568	2.2	−184.75	−406.45	4.84	34,132.5625
2	455	−2.8	−297.75	833.7	7.84	88,655.0625
3	632	−1.8	−120.75	217.35	3.24	14,580.5625
4	531	−0.8	−221.75	177.4	0.64	49,173.0625
			Sums	20,456	311.2	6,213,315.75

Your scatter diagram should have the number of passengers on the vertical axis (Y), since the train operator believes that the number of passengers depends on the lateness of trains in the terminus (final destination). In other words we are treating the number of passengers as the *dependent variable*, placing the number of minutes late on the horizontal axis (X) as we are treating this as the *independent variable*. The 20 points plotted should indicate a generally direct (positive) relationship, with passengers rising as lateness increases.

$\bar{X} = 4.8 \quad \bar{Y} = 752.75$

$\hat{Y} = mX + c$

$$m = \frac{\sum x_i y_i}{\sum x_i^2}$$

$$m = \frac{20{,}456}{311.2}$$

$m = 65.7326$

$c = \bar{Y} - m\bar{X}$

$c = 752.75 - (65.7326 \times 4.8)$

$c = 437.2335$

$\hat{Y} = 65.7326X + 437.2335$

$$R^2 = \frac{\left(\sum x_i y_i\right)^2}{\left(\sum x_i^2\right)\left(\sum y_i^2\right)}$$

$$R^2 = \frac{20{,}456^2}{311.2 \times 6{,}213{,}315.75}$$

$R^2 = 0.2164$

The low coefficient of determination (R^2) suggests that the relationship between the number of passengers and the lateness of the trains is extremely weak.

The *dependent variable* (Y) is sales, so we place this on the vertical axis. The *independent variable* (X) is advertising, so we place this on the horizontal axis. Your scatter diagram should have eight points plotted on it. It should show a generally direct (positive) relationship between the two variables, with sales value rising as advertising value increases.

X	Y	x_i	y_i	x_iy_i	x_i^2	y_i^2
8.73	40.285	−1.86	−8.606	16.008	3.460	74.070
8.78	39.423	−1.81	−9.468	17.138	3.276	89.650
9.25	47.389	−1.34	−1.502	2.013	1.796	2.257
9.54	45.707	−1.05	−3.184	3.344	1.103	10.140
10.29	47.711	−0.3	−1.180	0.354	0.090	1.393
11.22	52.5	0.63	3.609	2.273	0.397	13.022
12.92	53.727	2.33	4.836	11.267	5.429	23.383
13.99	64.389	3.4	15.498	52.692	11.560	240.176
			Sums	105.089	27.111	454.091

$\bar{X} = 10.59 \quad \bar{Y} = 48.891$

$\hat{Y} = mX + c$

$m = \dfrac{\sum x_i y_i}{\sum x_i^2}$

$m = \dfrac{105.089}{27.111}$

$m = 3.876$

$c = \bar{Y} - m\bar{X}$

$c = 48.891 - (3.876 \times 10.59)$

$c = 7.844$

(b) Hence the linear equation that best fits the data is

$$\hat{Y} = 3.876X + 7.844$$

$$R^2 = \frac{\left(\sum x_i y_i\right)^2}{\left(\sum x_i^2\right)\left(\sum y_i^2\right)}$$

$$R^2 = \frac{105.089^2}{27.111 \times 454.091}$$

$$R^2 = 0.8971$$

(c) Hence the estimated sales revenue when advertising is £11,000 is £50,480, and so on

When $X = 11,000$ then: $\hat{Y} = (3.876 \times 11) + 7.844 = $ **£50,480**

When $X = 13,500$ then: $\hat{Y} = (3.876 \times 13.5) + 7.844 = $ **£60,170**

When $X = 15,000$ then: $\hat{Y} = (3.876 \times 15) + 7.844 = $ **£65,984**

(d) The relatively high value of R^2 implies that this model could be used as a predictive tool.

3.5

X	Y	x_i	y_i	$x_i y_i$	x_i^2	y_i^2
103	1,188	−4.643	−219.5	1,019.107	21.556	48,180.25
104	1,224	−3.643	−183.5	668.464	13.270	33,672.25
104	1,243	−3.643	−164.5	599.250	13.270	27,060.25
105	1,239	−2.643	−168.5	445.321	6.985	28,392.25
105	1,242	−2.643	−165.5	437.393	6.985	27,390.25
107	1,138	−0.643	−269.5	173.250	0.413	72,630.25
108	1,481	0.357	73.5	26.250	0.128	5,402.25
108	1,562	0.357	154.5	55.179	0.128	23,870.25
109	1,554	1.357	146.5	198.821	1.842	21,462.25
109	1,566	1.357	158.5	215.107	1.842	25,122.25
110	1,598	2.357	190.5	449.036	5.556	36,290.25
111	1,562	3.357	154.5	518.679	11.270	23,870.25
112	1,609	4.357	201.5	877.964	18.985	40,602.25
112	1,499	4.357	91.5	398.679	18.985	8,372.25
			Sums	6,082.501	121.215	422,317.5

$\bar{X} = 107.643 \quad \bar{Y} = 1,407.5$

$\hat{Y} = mX + c$

$$m = \frac{\sum x_i y_i}{\sum x_i^2}$$

$$m = \frac{6,082.501}{121.215}$$

$$m = 50.179$$

$$c = \bar{Y} - m\bar{X}$$

$$c = 1{,}407.5 - (50.179 \times 107.643)$$

$$c = 3{,}993.918$$

$$\hat{Y} = 50.179X + 3{,}993.918$$

$$R^2 = \frac{\left(\sum x_i y_i\right)^2}{\left(\sum x_i^2\right)\left(\sum y_i^2\right)}$$

$$R^2 = \frac{6{,}082.501^2}{121.215 \times 422{,}317.5}$$

$$R^2 = 0.7227$$

Some 72.27 per cent of the total variation can be explained by the regression line whilst 27.73 per cent can be explained by other factors.

3.6

X	Y	x_i	y_i	$x_i y_i$	x_i^2	y_i^2
60	2.3	−37.5	−1.45	54.375	1,406.25	2.1025
65	2.5	−32.5	−1.25	40.625	1,056.25	1.5625
70	2.7	−27.5	−1.05	28.875	756.25	1.1025
75	2.9	−22.5	−0.85	19.125	506.25	0.7225
80	3.2	−17.5	−0.55	9.625	306.25	0.3025
85	3.6	−12.5	−0.15	1.875	156.25	0.0225
90	3.5	−7.5	−0.25	1.875	56.25	0.0625
95	3.7	−2.5	−0.05	0.125	6.25	0.0025
100	4.0	2.5	0.25	0.625	6.25	0.0625
105	4.4	7.5	0.65	4.875	56.25	0.4225
110	4.3	12.5	0.55	6.875	156.25	0.3025
115	4.6	17.5	0.85	14.875	306.25	0.7225
120	4.7	22.5	0.95	21.375	506.25	0.9025
125	3.3	27.5	−0.45	−12.375	756.25	0.2025
130	5.1	32.5	1.35	43.875	1,056.25	1.8225
135	5.2	37.5	1.45	54.375	1,406.25	2.1025
			Sums	291	8,500	12.42

$$\bar{X} = 97.5 \quad \bar{Y} = 3.75$$

$$\hat{Y} = mX + c$$

$$m = \frac{\sum x_i y_i}{\sum x_i^2}$$

$$m = \frac{291}{8{,}500}$$

$$m = 0.0342$$

$$c = \bar{Y} - m\bar{X}$$

$$c = 3.75 - (0.0342 \times 97.5)$$

$$c = 0.4155$$

$$\hat{Y} = 0.0342X + 0.4155$$

$$R^2 = \frac{\left(\sum x_i y_i\right)^2}{\left(\sum x_i^2\right)\left(\sum y_i^2\right)}$$

$$R^2 = \frac{291^2}{8{,}500 \times 12.42}$$

$$R^2 = 0.8021$$

Some 80.21 per cent of the total variation can be explained by the regression line whilst 19.79 per cent can be explained by other factors.

It must be borne in mind that correlation, not causation, is being measured. Therefore, although the correlation between the length of the work period and the rejection rate is strong, it does not prove long work periods cause an increased rejection rate.

The error of assuming that causation is invariably implied by correlation between variables is frequently made by managers.

3.7

Product	Northern Panel	Southern Panel	d_i	d_i^2
A	3	2	1	1
B	4	4	0	0
C	5	3	2	4
D	2	6	4	16
E	6	5	1	1
F	1	1	0	0

$$R_s = 1 - \frac{6\sum_{i=1}^{n} d_i^2}{n^3 - n}$$

$$R_s = 1 - \frac{6(22)}{6^3 - 6}$$

$$R_s = 1 - \frac{132}{210}$$

$$R_s = 1 - 0.6286$$

$$R_s = 0.3714$$

The low Spearman correlation co-efficient of 0.3714 suggests that the two rankings are not a very good match. In other words the evidence suggests that the tastes of consumers may indeed be related to geographical region.

3.8

Product	Lab 1	Lab 2	d_i	d_i^2
Chimera 205	1	2	1	1
Apollo T7	6	5	1	1
Pastiche	7	8	1	1
Ganymede	4	6	2	4
Callisto LX	3	4	1	1
QM4	5	3	2	4
Alfredo GTi	8	7	1	1
Arctura	2	1	1	1

$$R_s = 1 - \frac{6\sum_{i=1}^{n} d_i^2}{n^3 - n}$$

$$R_s = 1 - \frac{6(14)}{8^3 - 8}$$

$$R_s = 1 - \frac{84}{504}$$

$$R_s = 1 - 0.1667$$

$$R_s = 0.8333$$

The high Spearman correlation coefficient of 0.8333 suggests that the different testing procedures in each laboratory still result in similar rankings of the eight models.

Chapter 4: Time series and forecasting
· ·

4.1 (a) *Step 1* Construct a table as follows:

(1) Yr	Qtr	(2) Book issues (**Y**)	(3) 4 qtr moving total	(4) 4 qtr moving average	(5) Centred 4 qtr moving average (**Trend**)
1995	1	2,542			
	2	2,826			
	3	2,991			
	4	2,644			
1996	1	2,766			
	2	2,905			
	3	3,048			
	4	3,137			
1997	1	2,944			
	2	3,140			
	3	3,333			
	4	3,125			

Step 2 Calculate the four quarter moving totals by summing the first four quarters:

2,542 + 2,826 + 2,991 + 2,644 = 11,003.

This value can then be entered into the table. Strictly speaking this value should be entered *between* the rows containing the second and third quarterly values However, with the increasing use of personal computers it has become accepted practice to place the value in the row containing either the second or third quarterly value.

The next four quarter moving total uses the 2nd to the 5th items of data:

2,826 + 2,991 + 2,644 + 2,766 = 11,227.

The other four quarter moving totals can then be completed by summing the 3rd to the 6th items of data, followed by the 4th to the 7th, and so on, up to the 9th to the 12th values.

In the following table the personal computer aligns the first four quarter moving total with the second quarterly value even though it strictly falls between the second and third values.

(1)		(2)	(3)	(4)	(5)
Yr	Qtr	Book issues	4 qtr moving total	4 qtr moving average	Centred 4 qtr moving average
		(Y)			*(Trend)*
1995	1	2,542			
	2	2,826	11,003		
	3	2,991	11,227		
	4	2,644	11,306		
1996	1	2,766	11,363		
	2	2,905	11,856		
	3	3,048	12,034		
	4	3,137	12,269		
1997	1	2,944	12,554		
	2	3,140	12,542		
	3	3,333			
	4	3,125			

Step 3 The column containing the moving averages can now be completed by simply dividing the values in column (3) by 4.

Therefore the first four quarter moving average: 11,003/4 = 2,750.75

Again, strictly speaking this value should be placed between rows 2 and 3.

The second four quarter moving average: 11,227/4 = 2,806.75

The remainder of the column is then completed.

(1) Yr	Qtr	(2) Book issues (Y)	(3) 4 qtr moving total	(4) 4 qtr moving average	(5) Centred 4 qtr moving average (Trend)
1995	1	2,542			
	2	2,826	11,003	2,750.75	
	3	2,991	11,227	2,806.75	
	4	2,644	11,306	2,826.50	
1996	1	2,766	11,363	2,840.75	
	2	2,905	11,856	2,964.00	
	3	3,048	12,034	3,008.50	
	4	3,137	12,269	3,067.25	
1997	1	2,944	12,554	3,138.50	
	2	3,140	12,542	3,135.50	
	3	3,333			
	4	3,125			

Step 4 Calculate the centred four quarter moving average, or the trend, by simply calculating the mean of the first two values in column (4) i.e.

$$\frac{2{,}750.75 + 2{,}806.75}{2} = 2{,}778.750$$

Place the value in the *third* row of the table in column (5). This is important because, strictly speaking, we are taking the average of the two items of data *between* the second and third rows and *between* the third and fourth rows. The result will then align with the third row (see p. 81).

The next value of the trend is then obtained by finding the mean of the 2nd and 3rd values in column (4) i.e.

$$\frac{2{,}806.75 + 2{,}826.5}{2} = 2{,}816.625$$

The process is continued by finding the mean of the 3rd and 4th values in column (4), and so on, until the column is completed:

(1) Yr	Qtr	(2) Book issues (Y)	(3) 4 qtr moving total	(4) 4 qtr moving average	(5) Centred 4 qtr moving average (Trend)
1995	1	2,542			
	2	2,826	11,003	2,750.75	
	3	2,991	11,227	2,806.75	2,778.750
	4	2,644	11,306	2,826.50	2,816.625
1996	1	2,766	11,363	2,840.75	2,833.625
	2	2,905	11,856	2,964.00	2,902.375
	3	3,048	12,034	3,008.50	2,986.250
	4	3,137	12,269	3,067.25	3,037.875
1997	1	2,944	12,554	3,138.50	3,102.875
	2	3,140	12,542	3,135.50	3,137.000
	3	3,333			
	4	3,125			

(b) The values in columns (1), (2) and (5) can now be used to construct the scatter diagram as in Figure R4.1.

figure R4.1

Graph showing book issues over a three year period

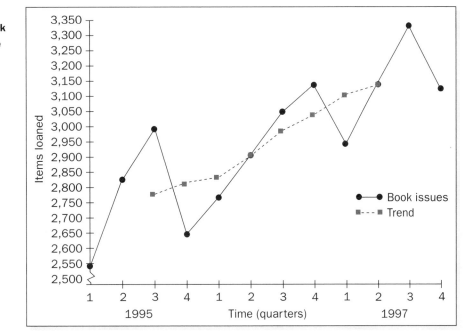

(c) Add an extra column to the table and subtract the trend values in column (5) from the original data in column (2). This gives column (6):

(1) Yr	Qtr	(2) Book issues (**Y**)	(3) 4 qtr moving total	(4) 4 qtr moving average	(5) Centred 4 qtr moving average (**Trend**)	(6) S + I (2)–(5)
1995	1	2,542				
	2	2,826	11,003	2,750.75		
	3	2,991	11,227	2,806.75	2,778.750	212.25
	4	2,644	11,306	2,826.50	2,816.625	−172.63
1996	1	2,766	11,363	2,840.75	2,833.625	−67.63
	2	2,905	11,856	2,964.00	2,902.375	2.63
	3	3,048	12,034	3,008.50	2,986.250	61.75
	4	3,137	12,269	3,067.25	3,037.875	99.13
1997	1	2,944	12,554	3,138.50	3,102.875	−158.88
	2	3,140	12,542	3,135.50	3,137.000	3.00
	3	3,333				
	4	3,125				

Column (6) is $S + I$. Averaging for each quarter will help remove I, the irregular factor, giving S (unadjusted):

	Q1	Q2	Q3	Q4
1995			212.25	−172.63
1996	−67.63	2.63	61.75	99.13
1997	−158.88	3.00		
Total	−226.51	5.63	274.00	−73.50
Average	−113.25	2.82	137.00	−36.75

Because the unadjusted values for S, when added together give −10.18 rather than zero, we adjust them by:

$$\frac{10.18}{4} = 2.55 \text{ being added to each quarter.}$$

4.2 (a) Construct and complete the table as follows. Before making the appropriate centring adjustment in column (5) we follow the convention, often adopted for personal computers, of aligning the first four quarter moving total and moving average respectively with the second quarter value:

(1) Yr Qtr		(2) Sales volume (000's) (Y)	(3) 4 qtr moving total	(4) 4 qtr moving average	(5) 4 qtr centred average (T)	(6) $Y - T =$ $S + I$ (2)−(5)
1	1	441.1				
	2	397.7	1,707.7	426.93		
	3	396.1	1,743.0	435.75	431.34	−35.24
	4	472.8	1,799.7	449.93	442.84	29.96
2	1	476.4	1,854.4	463.60	456.76	19.64
	2	454.4	1,935.1	483.78	473.69	−19.29
	3	450.8	2,039.4	509.85	496.81	−46.01
	4	553.5	2,158.2	539.55	524.70	28.80
3	1	580.7	2,279.0	569.75	554.65	26.05
	2	573.2	2,429.1	607.28	588.51	−15.31
	3	571.6	2,540.4	635.10	621.19	−49.59
	4	703.6	2,643.7	660.93	648.01	55.59
4	1	692.0	2,732.0	683.00	671.96	20.04
	2	676.5	2,781.2	695.30	689.15	−12.65
	3	659.9				
	4	752.8				

Column (5) provides the trend line values whilst column (6) is required for part (c)

(b)

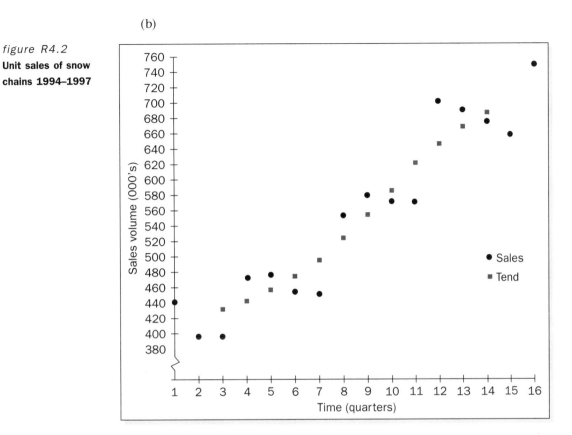

figure R4.2
Unit sales of snow chains 1994–1997

(c) Column (6) is obtained by subtracting column (5) from column (2) and provides the seasonal and the irregular values $(S + I)$. We now need to average the data for each quarter in order to eliminate the irregular factor, I, and leave the seasonal variation factors, S.

Step 1 Construct a new table using the quarterly values from column (6) above:

	Q1	Q2	Q3	Q4
Year 1			−35.24	29.96
Year 2	19.64	−19.29	−46.01	28.8
Year 3	26.05	−15.31	−49.59	55.59
Year 4	20.04	−12.65		

Step 2 Add a 'total' row to the bottom of the table then sum the columns:

	Q1	Q2	Q3	Q4
Year 1			−35.24	29.96
Year 2	19.64	−19.29	−46.01	28.8
Year 3	26.05	−15.31	−49.59	55.59
Year 4	20.04	−12.65		
Total	65.73	−47.25	−130.84	114.35

Step 3 Add another row to the bottom of the table to average the respective quarterly values, giving the unadjusted seasonal variation factors (*S*). Calculate *S* by dividing the total by the number of quarterly values in each column. Therefore *S* for quarter 1 equals: 65.73/3 = 21.91.

Step 4 Find the net value by summing the contents of the 'average' row:

Enter this figure for net value into the table:

	Q1	Q2	Q3	Q4	Net value
Year 1			−35.24	29.96	
Year 2	19.64	−19.29	−46.01	28.8	
Year 3	26.05	−15.31	−49.59	55.59	
Year 4	20.04	−12.65			
Total	65.73	−47.25	−130.84	114.35	
Average (S)	21.91	−15.75	−43.61	38.12	**+0.67**

Step 5 Add two rows to the bottom of the table – labelled *Adjustment* and *Adjusted (S)*. If the net value does not come to zero, then we must *adjust* the seasonal variation factors as discussed in the text (p. 85).

In the row labelled *Adjustment* calculate the adjustment i.e. −0.67/4 = −0.17. Enter this value in each of the four columns.

In the next row labelled *Adjusted (S)* calculate the seasonal adjusted values by subtracting 0.17. Note, because the net value sign was +, this means that our adjustment must be – *(as the net value is positive)* from the values in the row above:

	Q1	Q2	Q3	Q4	Net value
Year 1			−35.24	29.96	
Year 2	19.64	−19.29	−46.01	28.8	
Year 3	26.05	−15.31	−49.59	55.59	
Year 4	20.04	−12.65			
Total	65.73	−47.25	−130.84	114.35	
Unadjusted (S)	21.91	−15.75	−43.61	38.12	+0.67
Adjustment	−0.17	−0.17	−0.17	−0.17	
Adjusted (S)	**21.74**	**−15.92**	**−43.78**	**37.95**	

Step 6 Eliminate the seasonal variation by subtracting the adjusted seasonal variation factor (*S*) from its original data:

Yr	Qtr	Y	S	Y – S
1	1	441.1	21.74	419.36
	2	397.7	–15.92	413.62
	3	396.1	–43.78	439.88
	4	472.8	37.95	434.85
2	1	476.4	21.74	454.66
	2	454.4	–15.92	470.32
	3	450.8	–43.78	494.58
	4	553.5	37.95	515.55
3	1	580.7	21.74	558.96
	2	573.2	–15.92	589.12
	3	571.6	–43.78	615.38
	4	703.6	37.95	665.65
4	1	692	21.74	670.26
	2	676.5	–15.92	692.42
	3	659.9	–43.78	703.68
	4	752.8	37.95	714.85

Note: Column **S** contains the four adjusted seasonal variation factors for each quarter, repeated for each successive year.

4.3 If we ignore the cycle (C) we can state that:

$Y = T + S + I$ (additive)

$Y = T \times S \times I$ (multiplicative)

Here we use the additive approach (see below for reasons)

Step 1 Construct a standard table for the decomposition of time series data as follows:

(1) Yr Qtr	(2) Sales volume (000's) (Y)	(3) 4 qtr moving total	(4) 4 qtr moving average	(5) 4 qtr centred average (T)	(6) Y – T = S + I
1 1	349.4				
2	295.5	1,231.1	307.78		
3	196.9	1,329.2	332.30	320.04	–123.14
4	389.3	1,451.7	362.93	347.62	41.68
2 1	447.5	1,578.9	394.73	378.83	68.67
2	418.0	1,646.0	411.50	403.11	14.89
3	324.1	1,749.1	437.28	424.39	–100.29
4	456.4	1,859.7	464.93	451.10	5.30
3 1	550.6	1,950.8	487.70	476.31	74.29
2	528.6	2,109.7	527.43	507.56	21.04
3	415.2				
4	615.3				

A scatter diagram of the data (using columns (1), (2) and (3)) suggests that that the deviations from the trend line are of a similar *absolute* magnitude therefore the additive model is the most appropriate. Column (6) is thus calculated using $Y - T$.

Step 2 Calculate the adjusted seasonal variation factors from $S + I$ [column (6)]

	Q1	Q2	Q3	Q4	Net value
Year 1			−123.14	41.68	
Year 2	68.67	14.89	−100.29	5.30	
Year 3	74.29	21.04			
Total	142.96	35.93	−223.43	46.98	
Unadjusted (S)	71.48	17.97	−111.72	23.49	+1.22*
adjustment	−0.31	−0.31	−0.31	−0.31	
Adjusted (S)	**71.17**	**17.66**	**−112.03**	**23.18**	

Note: * As the net value is positive *then* subtract *the adjustment from the row containing the unadjusted seasonal variation factors.*

Step 3 Using the eight trend values calculate a least squares regression line. Here we use approach 2, the coding formula (see chapter 3). However either approach will give the same result. Note that we let the first trend observation (qtr 3, yr 1) have the value 1, and so on for each successive quarter.

X	Y	x_i	y_i	$x_i y_i$	x_i^2	y_i^2
1	320.04	−3.5	−93.58	327.53	12.25	8,757.22
2	347.62	−2.5	−66.00	165.00	6.25	4,356.00
3	378.83	−1.5	−34.79	52.19	2.25	1,210.34
4	403.11	−0.5	−10.51	5.26	0.25	110.46
5	424.39	0.5	10.77	5.39	0.25	115.99
6	451.10	1.5	37.48	56.22	2.25	1,404.75
7	476.31	2.5	62.69	156.73	6.25	3,930.04
8	507.56	3.5	93.94	328.79	12.25	8,824.72
			Sums	1,097.11	42	28,709.52

$$\bar{X} = \frac{36}{8} = \textbf{4.5}$$

$$\bar{Y} = \frac{3{,}308.96}{8} = \textbf{413.62}$$

$$\hat{Y}_T = mX + c$$

$$m = \frac{\sum x_i y_i}{\sum x_i^2}$$

$$m = \frac{1{,}097.11}{42}$$

$$m = \textbf{26.12}$$

$$c = \bar{Y} - m\bar{X}$$

$$c = 413.62 - (26.12 \times 4.5)$$

$$c = \textbf{296.08}$$

$$\hat{Y}_T = \textbf{26.12X + 296.08}$$

Step 4 Test for the goodness of fit

$$R^2 = \frac{\left(\sum x_i y_i\right)^2}{\left(\sum x_i^2\right)\left(\sum y_i^2\right)}$$

$$R^2 = \frac{1,097.11^2}{42 \times 28,709.52}$$

$$R^2 = \frac{1,203,650.35}{1,205,799.84}$$

$$R^2 = \mathbf{0.998}$$

With an R^2 value of 0.998 the trend line is a very good fit with 99.8 per cent of the total variation 'explained' or accounted for by the regression line. Forecasting using this trend regression line can be undertaken with some confidence. Therefore:

Step 4 Forecast the trend for the following year (4 quarters) by extrapolating the trend line:

When X = 11 (year 4 quarter 1) then:

$\hat{Y}_T = (26.12 \times 11) + 296.08 = 583.4$

When X = 12 (year 4 quarter 2) then:

$\hat{Y}_T = (26.12 \times 12) + 296.08 = 609.52$

When X = 13 (year 4 quarter 3) then:

$\hat{Y}_T = (26.12 \times 13) + 296.08 = 635.64$

When X = 14 (year 4 quarter 4) then:

$\hat{Y}_T = (26.12 \times 14) + 296.08 = 661.76$

Step 5 Add the 4 seasonally adjusted quarterly values to the forecast trend values:

Q 1   583.4 + 71.17 = 654.57
Q 2   609.52 + 17.66 = 627.18
Q 3   635.64 + –112.03 = 523.61
Q 4   661.76 + 23.18 = 684.94

The forecast demand (000's) for torches in the fourth year is:

Year 4	Q1	Q2	Q3	Q4
	654.57	627.18	523.61	684.94

4.4 As there are no previous forecasts then a problem of initialising the forecast data exists. There are several methods used to initialise forecasts, for example, using the first value of the Y data (3.85 in this case). For the purposes of this example we will use the mean value for the known values of Y to initialise the forecast.

Thus

Construct a table with five columns labelled t, Y, $\hat{Y}$, E_t and E_t^2 and insert the original data as follows:

t	Y	$\hat{Y}$	E_t	E_t^2
(1)	(2)	(3)	(4)	(5)
1	3.85			
2	3.22			
3	3.18			
4	3.61			
5	3.62			
6	3.48			
7	3.53			
8	3.62			
9	3.36			
10	3.58			
11	3.62			
12	3.24			
13				

Calculate the mean of the actual (Y) data.

$$\frac{\sum_{i=1}^{n} Y_i}{n} = \frac{41.91}{12} = 3.49$$

Then enter this as the first value of the forecast data ($\hat{Y}$) to initialise the forecast:

t	Y	$\hat{Y}$	E_t	E_t^2
(1)	(2)	(3)	(4)	(5)
1	3.85	3.49		
2	3.22			
3	3.18			
4	3.61			
5	3.62			
6	3.48			
7	3.53			
8	3.62			
9	3.36			
10	3.58			
11	3.62			
12	3.24			
13				

Calculate the second value of $\hat{Y}$ using $\alpha = 0.2$ and the first forecast value of 3.49

$$\hat{Y}_{t+1} = \hat{Y}_t + \alpha(Y_t - \hat{Y}_t)$$

$$\hat{Y}_2 = \hat{Y}_1 + \alpha(Y_1 - \hat{Y}_1)$$

$$\hat{Y}_2 = 3.49 + 0.2(3.85 - 3.49)$$

$$\hat{Y}_2 = 3.56$$

Calculate the next forecast ($t = 3$)

$$\hat{Y}_{t+1} = \hat{Y}_t + \alpha(Y_t - \hat{Y}_t)$$

$$\hat{Y}_3 = \hat{Y}_2 + \alpha(Y_2 - \hat{Y}_2)$$

$$\hat{Y}_3 = 3.56 + 0.2(3.22 - 3.56)$$

$$\hat{Y}_3 = 3.492$$

Complete the remainder of the forecasts up to $t = 13$:

t (1)	Y (2)	$\hat{Y}$ (3)	E_t (4)	E_t^2 (5)
1	3.85	3.49		
2	3.22	3.56		
3	3.18	3.49		
4	3.61	3.43		
5	3.62	3.47		
6	3.48	3.50		
7	3.53	3.50		
8	3.62	3.51		
9	3.36	3.53		
10	3.58	3.50		
11	3.62	3.52		
12	3.24	3.54		
13		**3.48**		

The forecast for the 13th period is therefore **3.48**.

To examine whether the α of 0.2 is better than one of 0.3 the errors can be calculated to give firstly the mean absolute error. Therefore, in column (4) calculate all the errors (E_t)

where $E_t = Y_t - \hat{Y}_t$

$$= 3.22 - 3.56$$

$$= -0.34$$

and

$$= 3.18 - 3.49$$

$$= -0.31$$

The table now resembles:

t (1)	Y (2)	$\hat{Y}$ (3)	E_t (4)	E_t^2 (5)
1	3.85	3.49		
2	3.22	3.56	−0.34	
3	3.18	3.49	−0.31	
4	3.61	3.43	0.18	
5	3.62	3.47	0.15	
6	3.48	3.50	−0.02	
7	3.53	3.50	0.03	
8	3.62	3.51	0.11	
9	3.36	3.53	−0.17	
10	3.58	3.50	0.08	
11	3.62	3.52	0.10	
12	3.24	3.54	−0.30	
13		**3.48**		

$$MAE = \frac{\sum_{i=1}^{n} |E_t|}{n}$$

$$= \frac{1.79}{11}$$

$$= 0.1627$$

A further check of α would be to calculate mean square error (E_t^2). Therefore, in column (5) calculate all the errors ($Y_t - \hat{Y}_t$) then square them (E_t^2) as follows:

$E_t = (Y_t - \hat{Y}_t)^2$
    $= (3.22 - 3.56)^2$
    $= 0.1156$

and

$E_t = (Y_t - \hat{Y}_t)^2$
    $= (3.18 - 3.49)^2$
    $= 0.0961$

Complete the remainder of the column:

t (1)	Y (2)	$\hat{Y}$ (3)	E_t (4)	E_t^2 (5)
1	3.85	3.49		
2	3.22	3.56	−0.34	0.1156
3	3.18	3.49	−0.31	0.0961
4	3.61	3.43	0.18	0.0324
5	3.62	3.47	0.15	0.0225
6	3.48	3.50	−0.02	0.0004
7	3.53	3.50	0.03	0.0009
8	3.62	3.51	0.11	0.0121
9	3.36	3.53	−0.17	0.0289
10	3.58	3.50	0.08	0.0064
11	3.62	3.52	0.10	0.0100
12	3.24	3.54	−0.30	0.0900
13		**3.48**		

$$MSE = \frac{\sum_{i=1}^{n} E_t^2}{n}$$

$$= \frac{0.4153}{11}$$

$$= 0.0378$$

The same procedure will need to be repeated for the value of $\alpha = 0.3$. On completion the table should resemble:

t	Y	$\hat{Y}$	E_t	E_t^2
(1)	(2)	(3)	(4)	(5)
1	3.85	3.49		
2	3.22	3.60	−0.38	0.14
3	3.18	3.49	−0.31	0.09
4	3.61	3.39	0.22	0.05
5	3.62	3.46	0.16	0.03
6	3.48	3.51	−0.03	0.00
7	3.53	3.50	0.03	0.00
8	3.62	3.51	0.11	0.01
9	3.36	3.54	−0.18	0.03
10	3.58	3.49	0.09	0.01
11	3.62	3.52	0.10	0.01
12	3.24	3.55	−0.31	0.09
13		**3.45**		

$$MAE = \frac{\sum_{i=1}^{n}|E_t|}{n}$$

$$= \frac{1.92}{11}$$

$$= 0.1745$$

$$MSE = \frac{\sum_{i=1}^{n}E_t^2}{n}$$

$$= \frac{0.46}{11}$$

$$= 0.0418$$

In this example there is no conflict between the two measures (MAE and MSE). The MAE suggests that an α of 0.2 is the better smoothing constant and MSE would also suggest that an α of 0.2 provides a better smoothing constant. As the MSE penalises large deviations, then most observers would suggest that the MSE would provide a better test.

Therefore, an α of 0.2 (MSE = 0.0378 < 0.0418) would be the better value.

Chapter 5: Probability

5.1 (a) P(claim) = 1/50 × 1,600 = 32. Given that the people who bought insurance represent typical risks the company should expect 32 claims per year.

(b) 32 claims × £750 = £24,000 divided among 1,600 policy holders = £15 annual premium.

5.2 (a) P(at least nine sales) = 1 − 0.60 = 0.40
   (b) P(at most 12 sales) = 0.60 + 0.35 = 0.95
   (c) P(more than 12 sales) = 1 − (0.60 + 0.35) = 1 − 0.95 = 0.05

5.3 (a) P(4 defectives with replacement) = 8/32 × 8/32 × 8/32 × 8/32 = 0.00391
   (b) P(4 non-defectives with replacement) = 24/32 × 24/32 × 24/32 × 24/32
        = 0.3164
   (c) P(4 defectives without replacement) = 8/32 × 7/31 × 6/30 × 5/29 =
        0.00195
        P(4 non-defectives without replacement) = 24/32 × 23/31 × 22/30 ×
        21/29 = 0.2955

5.4 (a) P(male) = 86/200 = 0.43
   (b) P(female) = 114/200 = 0.57
   (c) P(marketing stream) = 160/200 = 0.80
   (d) P(male and marketing) = P(male) × P(marketing | male) = 0.43 × (70/86)
        = 0.35
   (e) P(non-marketing | female), using Bayes' theorem

$$= \frac{P(nm) \times P(f|nm)}{P(f)} = \frac{(40/200) \times 24/40)}{(114/200)} = 0.2105$$

5.5 (a) P(day shift and defective) = P(day) × P(defective | day) = $\dfrac{2,000}{2,800} \times \dfrac{2}{100} =$
        0.0143

   (b) P(night shift and def.) = P(night) × P(def. | night shift) = $\dfrac{800}{2,800} \times \dfrac{4}{100} =$
        0.0114

   (c) P(defective): expected number of defectives from day shift = (0.02 ×
        2,000) = 40
        expected number of defectives from night shift = (0.04 ×
        800) = 32
        Total defects expected is 72 per 2,800 output; the probability of a
        defective therefore is

        given by $\dfrac{72}{2,800}$ = 0.0257   This is same as the sum of (a) and (b)

   (d) Applying Bayes' theorem

        $$P(\text{day shift} \mid \text{defective}) = \frac{P(day) \times P(def|dayshift)}{P(def)} = \frac{0.7143 \times 0.02}{0.0257}$$

        = 0.5559

   (e) P(night | defective) = $\dfrac{P(night) \times P(def|night)}{P(def)} = \dfrac{0.2857 \times 0.04}{0.0257} = 0.4447$

        (the answers to (d) and (e) should of course sum to one, subject to
        rounding)

5.6 (a) P(good service) = $\dfrac{66}{100}$ = 0.66

(b) P(independent and good service) is from table, $\dfrac{26}{100}$ = 0.26 alternatively

P(independent and good service) = P(ind) × P(good service | independent)

$$= \dfrac{36}{100} \times \dfrac{26}{36} = 0.26$$

(c) P(poor service | high street chain) = from table, $\dfrac{24}{64}$ = 0.375

alternatively using Bayes theorem

P(poor service | high street chain)

$$= \dfrac{\text{P(poor service)} \times \text{P(High st chain | provides poor service)}}{\text{P(High st)}}$$

$$= \dfrac{0.34 \times 0.706}{0.64} = 0.375$$

5.7

figure R5.1

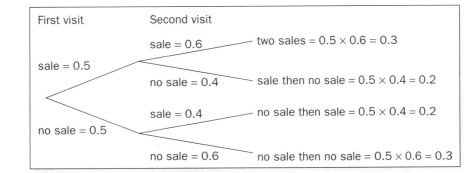

probability of just one sale = 0.2 + 0.2 = 0.4

5.8

figure R5.2

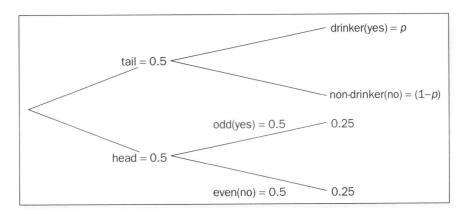

Proportion answering yes = 0.37, therefore $0.25 + 0.5p = 0.37$

p (probability of a drinker) $= (0.37 - 0.25)/0.5 = 0.24$ We estimate that 24 per cent of employees drink regularly at lunch time.

5.9

figure R5.3

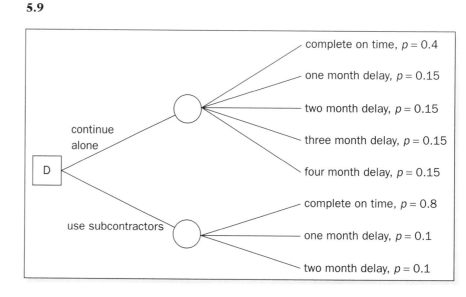

Estimated value of continuing without subcontractors:

$0.4(100,000) + 0.15(100,000 - 8,000) + 0.15(100,000 - 16,000) + 0.15(100,000 - 24,000) + 0.15(100,000 - 32,000)$

$= £88,000$

Estimated value using subcontractors:

$0.8(100,000 - 18,000) + 0.1(100,000 - 18,000 - 8,000) + 0.1(100,000 - 18,000 - 16,000)$

$= £79,600$

The calculation suggest that the firm should continue without subcontractors.

5.10 As six different numbers are selected from 49 different possibilities the number of combinations (order not important) are

$$_{49}C_6 = \frac{49!}{(49 - 6)! \times 6!} = \frac{49!}{43! \times 6!} = 13,983,816$$

5.11 The number of different three button possibilities where order is important is given by

$$_{10}P_3 = \frac{10!}{(10 - 3)!} = 720 \quad \text{The probability is } 1/720$$

5.12 (a) Six programmes taken from 15, order not important. Possible combinations

$$_{15}C_6 = \frac{15!}{(15-6)! \times 6!} = 5{,}005 \text{ possible combinations}$$

(b) If 900 of the combinations are not appropriate the probability of selecting an appropriate combination of six programmes at random is given by $(5{,}005 - 900)/5{,}005 = 0.82$

5.13 Order does not matter, therefore combinations

The different number of combinations of five colours from eight is given by:

$$_8C_5 = \frac{8!}{(8-5)!5!} = 56 \text{ combinations can be advertised}$$

Chapter 6: Probability distributions
....

6.1 (a) 0.0808   (b) 0.6554   (c) 0.1587
(d) 0.3848   (e) 0.0792   (f) 0.8041

6.2 (a) 0.44
(b) 1.93. This is the same as $P(Z > Z_1) = 0.0268$
(c) 0.92. This is the same as $P(Z > Z_1) = 0.1788$
(d) 0.12. This is the same as $P(Z > Z_1) = 0.4522$

6.3 (a) To find $P(X_1 > 144)$, $Z_1 = \dfrac{X_1 - \mu}{\sigma} = \dfrac{144 - 130}{7} = 2$

From the Z tables we find that $Z_1 = 2$ gives 0.0228 in the right-hand tail.

$4{,}000 \times 0.0228 = 91.2$

We would expect around 91 children to have a height over 144 cm.

(b) To find $P(X_1 < 123)$, $Z_1 = \dfrac{X_1 - \mu}{\sigma} = \dfrac{123 - 130}{7} = -1$

From the Z tables we find that $Z_1 = -1$ gives 0.1587 in the left-hand tail.

$4{,}000 \times 0.1587 = 634.8$

We would expect around 635 children to have a height less than 123 cm.

(c) (i) $Z_1 = \dfrac{X_1 - \mu}{\sigma} = \dfrac{137 - 130}{7} = +1$

From the Z tables, we find that $Z_1 = +1$ gives 0.1587 in the right-hand tail.

Area A_1 is therefore $0.5000 - 0.1587 = 0.3413$

(ii) $Z_2 = \dfrac{X_2 - \mu}{\sigma} = \dfrac{126.5 - 130}{7} = -0.5$

From the Z tables, we find that $Z_2 = -0.5$ gives 0.3085 in the left-hand tail.

Area A_2 is therefore $0.5000 - 0.3085 = 0.1915$

Total area is $A_1 + A_2 = 0.3413 + 0.1915 = 0.5328$.

$4{,}000 \times 0.5328 = 2{,}131.2$

We would expect around 2,131 children to have a height between 126.5 cm and 137 cm.

(d) Upper quartile height, X_1, has P = 0.25 in right-hand tail.

$Z_1 = \dfrac{X_1 - \mu}{\sigma}$

The value of Z_1 which gives $P = 0.25$ in the right-hand tail is approximately +0.67

$+0.67 = \dfrac{X_1 - 130}{7}$

$7\,(+0.67) = X_1 - 130$

$4.69 + 130 = X_1$

$\underline{134.69 \text{ cm} = X_1}$

Lower quartile height, X_2, has P = 0.25 in left-hand tail

$Z_2 = \dfrac{X_2 - \mu}{\sigma}$

The value of Z_2 which gives P = 0.25 in the left-hand tail is approximately −0.67.

$-0.67 = \dfrac{X_2 - 130}{7}$

$7(-0.67) = X_2 - 130$

$-4.69 + 130 = X_2$

$\underline{125.31 \text{ cm} = X_2}$

So the upper quartile height is 134.69 cm and the lower quartile height is 125.31 cm.

6.4 (a) $\dfrac{X_1 - \mu}{\sigma} = \dfrac{9.00am - 9.40am}{20} = \dfrac{-40}{20} = -2$

From the Z tables we find that $Z_1 = -2$ gives 0.0228 in the left-hand tail

$250 \times 0.0228 = 5.7$

We estimate that on around six occasions in the year the mail arrives before the main gates open at 9 a.m.

(b) $Z_1 = \dfrac{X_1 - \mu}{\sigma} = \dfrac{9.20am - 9.40am}{20} = \dfrac{-20}{20} = -1$

From the Z tables we find that $Z_1 = -1$ gives 0.1587 in the left-hand tail. If 0.1587 is the probability of the mail arriving *before* 9.20 a.m., then 1.0000 − 0.1587 is the probability of the mail arriving *after* 9.20 a.m., i.e. 0.8413.

$250 \times 0.8413 = 210.325$

We estimate that on around 210 occasions the mail will arrive after 9.20 a.m.

(c) $Z_1 = \dfrac{X_1 - \mu}{\sigma} = \dfrac{10.00am - 9.40am}{20} = \dfrac{20}{20} = +1$

From the Z tables, $Z_1 = +1$ gives 0.1587 in the right-hand tail.

$Z_2 = \dfrac{X_2 - \mu}{\sigma} = \dfrac{10.20am - 9.40am}{20} = \dfrac{40}{20} = +2$

From the Z tables, $Z_2 = +2$ gives 0.0228 in the right-hand tail.
Required probability is $0.1587 - 0.0228 = 0.1359$

$250 \times 0.1359 = 33.98$

We estimate that on around 34 occasions the mail will arrive between 10 a.m. and 10.20 a.m.

6.5 (a) $Z_1 = \dfrac{X_1 - \mu}{\sigma} = \dfrac{24 - 25}{0.5} = -2$

(Note that all units must be the same, either hours or minutes – here hours)

$P(Z_1) = 0.0228$ in left-hand tail

$Z_2 = \dfrac{X_1 - \mu}{\sigma} = \dfrac{24.5 - 25}{0.5} = -1$

$P(Z_2) = 0.1587$ in left-hand tail

Required probability $= 0.1587 - 0.0228 = 0.1359$
In other words there is a 13.59 per cent chance of a randomly selected component lasting between 24 and 24.5 hours.

(b) $Z_1 = \dfrac{X_1 - \mu}{\sigma} = \dfrac{24.25 - 25}{0.5} = -1.5$

$P(Z_1) = 0.0668$ in left-hand tail

$Z_2 = \dfrac{24.75 - 25}{0.5} = -0.5$

$P(Z_2) = 0.3085$ in left-hand tail

Required probability $= 0.3085 - 0.0668 = 0.2417$

In other words there is a 24.17 per cent chance of a randomly selected component lasting between 24.25 and 24.75 hours.

(c) From (a), the probability of *less than* 24.5 hours is 0.1587 (left-hand tail). Therefore the probability of *more than* 24.5 hours is 1.0000 − 0.1587 = 0.8413. In other words there is an 84.13 per cent chance of a randomly selected component lasting more than 24.5 hours.

(d) Note that 24 hours 15 minutes is 24.25 hours. From (b), the probability of *less than* 24.25 hours is 0.0668 (left-hand tail).

(e) The Z value which gives 0.281 in the left-hand tail is −0.58.

$$Z_1 = \frac{K - \mu}{\sigma}$$

$$-0.58 = \frac{K - 25}{0.5}$$

$$-0.58(0.5) + 25 = K$$

$$\underline{24.71 = K}$$

In other words 28.1 per cent of the components last less than 24.71 hours.

6.6 To find $P(157.5 < X_1)$, $Z_1 = \dfrac{X_1 - \mu}{\sigma} = \dfrac{157.5 - 160.9}{6.0} = -0.57$

from the Z tables we find that $Z_1 = -0.57$ gives 0.2843 as the area in the left-hand tail. The implication being that just over 28 per cent of women would be excluded from buying the car because of a difficult driving position.

6.7 (a) To find $P(X_1 > 45,000)$, $Z_1 = \dfrac{X_1 - \mu}{\sigma} = \dfrac{45,000 - 42,000}{4,000} = 0.75$

From the Z tables we find that $Z_1 = 0.75$ gives 0.2266 as the area in the right-hand tail. Nearly 23 per cent of tyres will last for more than 45,000 miles.

(b) The Z value associated with 4 per cent (0.04) in the left hand-tail is found from the *body* of the Z tables; i.e. $Z = -1.75$

Using $Z = \dfrac{X_1 - \mu}{\sigma}$ then $-1.75 = \dfrac{X_1 - 42,000}{4,000} = (-1.75 \times 4,000) +$

$42,000 = 35,000$

The guaranteed tyre life must be 35,000 miles to keep replacements at or below 4 per cent.

6.8 (a) The proportion of jars with less than 100g is $\dfrac{1{,}500}{50{,}000} = 0.03$. This is the proportion in the left-hand tail below 100g. From the *body* of the Z tables we find that a Z value of 1.88 is associated with a probability of 0.03 and as our X value is below the mean, $Z = -1.88$. Using $Z = \dfrac{X_1 - \mu}{\sigma}$ then $-1.88 = \dfrac{100 - 100.50}{\sigma}$ so $\sigma = \dfrac{-0.50}{-1.88} = 0.27$g. The standard deviation of jar weights is <u>0.27g</u>.

(b) The firm wishes to save £400 per week on rejects. At 80p per reject this represents $\dfrac{400}{0.80} = 500$ rejects. The firm must therefore reduce its rejects to 1,000 jars per week. This is a reject rate of $\dfrac{1{,}000}{50{,}000} = 0.02$. From the *body* of the Z tables we find that a Z value of 2.05 is associated with a probability of 0.02.

Using $Z = \dfrac{X_1 - \mu}{\sigma}$ then $-2.05 = \dfrac{100 - \mu}{0.27}$ (Z is negative because $X < \mu$) so $-2.05 \times 0.27 = 100 - \mu$, so $\mu = 100 + 0.55 = 100.55$g. The mean fill has to be increased by 0.05g per jar to reduce reject costs by £400 per week.

6.9 Let p = probability that a booked passenger turns up = 0.85 therefore $q = 0.15$

$P(X = 16$ or 15 either all sixteen or fifteen passengers turn up)

$P(X \geq 15) = {}_{16}C_{16}\,p^{16} + {}_{16}C_{15}\,p^{15}q = (0.85^{16}) + (16 \times 0.85^{15} \times 0.15) = 0.2839$

There is a 28.4 per cent chance that the plane will be overbooked.

6.10 Let p = probability of a defective component = 0.2. and q the probability of a non-defective = 0.8. The batch is accepted if $P(X \leq 1) = P(0) + P(1) = 10pq^9 + q^{10} = (10 \times 0.2 \times 0.8^9) + (0.8^{10}) = 0.3758$

There is a 37.6 per cent chance of accepting a batch with 20 per cent defectives.

6.11 (a) $P(8) = {}_{24}C_8\,p^8 q^{16} = \dfrac{24!}{(16!)(8!)}(0.40)^8(0.60)^{16} = 0.136$ or 13.6%

(b) Mean $\mu = np = (24 \times 0.40) = 9.6$ and standard deviation $\sigma = \sqrt{npq} = \sqrt{24 \times 0.60 \times 0.40} = 2.4$. To find $P(X = 8)$ we need to find the area under the normal curve between 7.5 and 8.5.

$Z_1 = \dfrac{8.5 - 9.6}{2.4} = -0.4583$

From the Z tables this gives 0.3228 in the left-hand tail

$Z_2 = \dfrac{7.5 - 9.6}{2.4} = -0.875$

From the Z tables this gives 0.1894 in the left-hand tail.

The proportion between 7.5 and 8.5 is therefore $0.3228 - 0.1894 = 0.1334$ or 13.3 per cent (approx.)

6.12 Let X be the number of passengers that choose chicken. X has a binomial distribution with a mean $\mu = np = (180 \times 0.65) = 117$ and a standard deviation $\sigma = \sqrt{npq} = \sqrt{180 \times 0.65 \times 0.35} = 6.40$. We need P($X > 125$)

with continuity correction:

$$Z = \frac{125.5 - 117}{6.40} = 1.33$$

From the Z tables, area in right-hand tail is 0.0918.

There is a 9.2 per cent chance of more than 125 passengers choosing chicken on any flight.

6.13 (a) P($X = 4$) = $\dfrac{e^{-4} \cdot 4^4}{4!}$ = 0.1954(19.54%)

(b) P($X > 1$) = 1 − P(0) − P(1) = $1 - \dfrac{e^{-4}4^0}{0!} - \dfrac{e^{-4}4^1}{1!}$ = 1 − 0.0183 − 0.0733 = 0.9084(90.8%)

(c) The mean arrivals per ten minute period is 8, P($X = 6$) = $\dfrac{e^{-8}8^6}{6!}$ = 0.1221(12.2%)

6.14 (a) P($X = 0$) = $\dfrac{e^{-2}2^0}{0!}$ = 0.1353(13.5%). So 13.5 per cent of the samples will have no blemishes.

(b) The mean number of blemishes per 30 metre sample is 6

P($X > 7$) = 1 − P($X \leq 7$) =

$$1 - \left[\frac{e^{-6}6^0}{0!} + \frac{e^{-6}6^1}{1!} + \frac{e^{-6}6^2}{2!} + \frac{e^{-6}6^3}{3!} + \frac{e^{-6}6^4}{4!} + \frac{e^{-6}6^5}{5!} + \frac{e^{-6}6^6}{6!} + \frac{e^{-6}6^7}{7!} \right]$$

1 − (0.0025 + 0.0149 + 0.0446 + 0.0892 + 0.1339 + 0.1606 + 0.1606 + 0.1377) = 0.2560

We would expect more than seven blemishes per 30 metre sample about 26 per cent of the time.

6.15 Mean number of defectives per box = $0.006 \times 250 = 1.5$

P($X > 3$) = 1 − P($X \leq 3$) =

$$1 - \left[\frac{e^{-1.5}1.5^0}{0!} + \frac{e^{-1.5}1.5^1}{1!} + \frac{e^{-1.5}1.5^2}{2!} + \frac{e^{-1.5}1.5^3}{3!} \right] = 1 - 0.93436 = 0.06564$$

The probability of a box being replaced is 0.06564. Out of 250 boxes this is 16.4 and at a cost of £4 per box this represents a mean replacement cost of £65.60 per 250 boxes.

The new scheme costs 10p per box or £25 per 250 boxes. It would appear that the new inspection scheme would save costs.

Chapter 7: Sampling and tests of hypotheses

....

7.1 (a) $P(\bar{X} < 3{,}100)$, $Z_1 = \dfrac{\bar{X}_1 - \mu}{\sigma/\sqrt{n}} = \dfrac{3{,}100 - 3{,}130}{115/\sqrt{25}} = -1.304$ from Z tables $=$

0.0968. There is a 9.7 per cent chance that the sample mean will be less than £3,100. (Note: we are told the distribution is Normal, so Z tables).

(b) $P(\bar{X} > 3{,}190)$, $Z_1 = \dfrac{\bar{X}_1 - \mu}{\sigma/\sqrt{n}} = \dfrac{3{,}190 - 3{,}130}{115/\sqrt{25}} = 2.609$ from Z tables $=$

0.0045. There is a 0.5 per cent chance that the sample mean will be greater than £3,190.

(c) $P_1(3{,}110 < \bar{X})$ $Z_1 = \dfrac{\bar{X}_1 - \mu}{\sigma/\sqrt{n}} = \dfrac{3{,}110 - 3{,}130}{115/\sqrt{25}} = -0.8696$, $P_1 = 0.1922$

$A_1 = 0.5000 - 0.1922 = 0.3078$

$P_2(\bar{X} > 3{,}180)$ $Z_2 = \dfrac{\bar{X}_2 - \mu}{\sigma/\sqrt{n}} = \dfrac{3{,}180 - 3{,}130}{115/\sqrt{25}} = 2.1739$, $P_2 = 0.0150$

$A_2 = 0.5000 - 0.0150 = 0.4850$

$A_1 + A_2 = 0.3078 + 0.4850 = 0.7928$.

There is a 79.28% chance that the sample mean will be between £3,110 and £3,180.

7.2 $P(\bar{X} \geq 13{,}000)$ $Z_1 = \dfrac{\bar{X}_1 - \mu}{\sigma/\sqrt{n}} = \dfrac{13{,}000 - 12{,}500}{1{,}300/\sqrt{49}} = 2.6923$ from Z tables $= 0.0036$.

There is 0.36 per cent chance that the sample mean will be at least £13,000.

7.3 95 per cent confidence interval for μ

$\mu = \bar{X}_1 \pm 1.96\left(\dfrac{s}{\sqrt{n}}\right) = 58 \pm 1.96\left(\dfrac{10}{\sqrt{49}}\right) = 58 \pm 1.96(1.429) = 58 \pm 2.801$

$\mu = 55.2$ to 60.8

99 per cent confidence interval for μ

$\mu = \bar{X}_1 \pm 2.58\left(\dfrac{s}{\sqrt{n}}\right) = 58 \pm 2.58\left(\dfrac{10}{\sqrt{49}}\right) = 58 \pm 2.58(1.429) = 58 \pm 3.687$

$\mu = 54.3$ to 61.7

7.4 99 per cent confidence interval for μ

$\mu = \bar{X}_1 \pm 2.58\left(\dfrac{s}{\sqrt{n}}\right) = 8.6 \pm 2.58\left(\dfrac{2.3}{\sqrt{60}}\right) = 8.6 \pm 2.58(0.297) = 8.6 \pm 0.766$

$\mu = 7.8$ to 9.4

7.5 (a) 99 per cent confidence interval for μ

$$\mu = \bar{X}_1 \pm 2.58\left(\frac{s}{\sqrt{n}}\right) = 39.8 \pm 2.58\left(\frac{6.0}{\sqrt{45}}\right) = 39.8 \pm 2.58(0.894) =$$

39.8 ± 2.307

$\mu = 37.5$ to 42.1 kilos

(b) 90 per cent confidence interval for μ

$$\mu = \bar{X}_1 \pm 1.65\left(\frac{s}{\sqrt{n}}\right) = 39.8 \pm 1.65\left(\frac{6.0}{\sqrt{45}}\right) = 39.8 \pm 1.65(0.894) =$$

39.8 ± 1.475

$\mu = 38.3$ to 41.3 kilos

(c) To find the sample size (n) that gives 2 kilo margin of error at the 99 per cent level.

$$2.58\left(\frac{s}{\sqrt{n}}\right) = 2 \quad 2.58\left(\frac{6.0}{\sqrt{n}}\right) = 2 \quad \frac{2.58 \times 6.0}{2} = \sqrt{n} \quad \text{therefore } n = (7.74)^2$$

$= 59.9$

The sample size should be 60.

7.6 (a) To find the sample size (n) that gives a margin of error of 3 at the 95 per cent level

$$1.96\left(\frac{s}{\sqrt{n}}\right) = 3 \quad 1.96\left(\frac{14}{\sqrt{n}}\right) = 3 \quad \frac{1.96 \times 14}{3} = \sqrt{n} \quad \left(\frac{1.96 \times 14}{3}\right)^2 = n$$

$= 83.66$

sample size $= 84$

(b) 95 per cent confidence interval for μ

$$\mu = \bar{X}_1 \pm 1.96\left(\frac{s}{\sqrt{n}}\right) = 22.4 \pm 1.96\left(\frac{15}{\sqrt{160}}\right) = 22.4 \pm 1.96(1.186) =$$

22.4 ± 2.325

$\mu = 20.1$ to 24.7 trips per week.

7.7 $H_0 : \mu = £50.00$, $H_1 : \mu \neq £50.00$, 5 per cent level, critical value for $Z = 1.96$

From sample $Z = \dfrac{\bar{X} - \mu}{\dfrac{s}{\sqrt{n}}} = \dfrac{53.70 - 50.00}{\dfrac{7.80}{\sqrt{40}}} = 3.00$

As 3.00 is outside 1.96 we therefore reject H_0 at the 5 per cent level.

The evidence suggests that the mean is not £50.00.

7.8 $H_0 : \mu = 32.5 mpg$, $H_1 : \mu < 32.5 mpg$, 1 per cent critical value for $Z = -2.33$

From sample, $Z = \dfrac{\bar{X} - \mu}{\dfrac{s}{\sqrt{n}}} = \dfrac{30.4 - 32.5}{\dfrac{5.3}{\sqrt{50}}} = -2.80$

As -2.80 is outside -2.33 we therefore reject the H_0. There is sufficient evidence to suggest the *mpg* is less than 32.5.

7.9 $H_0 : \mu = 90,000$ miles, $H_1 : \mu > 90,000$ miles, 1 per cent level, critical value for $Z = 2.33$

From sample $Z = \dfrac{\overline{X} - \mu}{\dfrac{s}{\sqrt{n}}} = \dfrac{96,700 - 90,000}{\dfrac{37,500}{\sqrt{190}}} = 2.46$

As 2.46 is outside 2.33 we therefore reject H_0. There is sufficient evidence from the sample to suggest that the mean engine life is above 90,000 miles.

7.10 $H_0 : \mu = 40$ days, $H_1 : \mu > 40$ days, 5 per cent level critical value for $Z = 1.65$ (one-tailed test)

From sample $Z = \dfrac{\overline{X} - \mu}{\dfrac{s}{\sqrt{n}}} = \dfrac{45 - 40}{\dfrac{20}{\sqrt{64}}} = 2.00$

As 2.00 is outside 1.65 we reject H_0. The sample evidence suggests that the mean sales time is greater than 40 days.

7.11 $H_0 : \mu = 7.5$ $H_1 : \mu < 7.5$ CDs, 1 per cent level critical value for $Z = -2.33$

From sample $Z = \dfrac{\overline{X} - \mu}{\dfrac{s}{\sqrt{n}}} = \dfrac{7.01 - 7.50}{\dfrac{3.74}{\sqrt{121}}} = -1.44$

As -1.44 is inside -2.33 we cannot reject the H_0. There is insufficient evidence to support the claim that the mean is less than 7.5 CDs per year.

7.12 This is a sample less than 32 in size, so t test.
$H_0 : \mu = 8.75$cms 0 $\quad H_1 : \mu < 8.75$cms $\quad t_{0.01,7} = -2.998$
From sample $\overline{X} = 8.6$cms, $s = 0.227$cms

$t = \dfrac{\overline{X} - \mu}{\dfrac{s}{\sqrt{n}}} = \dfrac{8.6 - 8.75}{\dfrac{0.227}{\sqrt{8}}} = -1.869$

As this value is inside -2.998 we cannot reject H_0. The sample does not show that the mean length is less than 8.75cms.

7.13 $H_0 : \mu = 20$ days $\quad H_1 : \mu < 20$ days $\quad t_{0.05,16} = -1.746$

$t = \dfrac{\overline{X} - \mu}{\dfrac{s}{\sqrt{n}}} = \dfrac{18 - 20}{\dfrac{2.5}{\sqrt{17}}} = -3.296$

As this is outside -1.746 we reject the H_0. The new procedure significantly reduces dispatch delay.

7.14 This is a sample less than 32 in size, so t test.

$H_0 : \mu = £900$ $H_1 : \mu > £900$ $t_{0.10,19} = 1.328$

$$t = \frac{\bar{X} - \mu}{\dfrac{s}{\sqrt{n}}} = \frac{1{,}050 - 900}{\dfrac{290}{\sqrt{20}}} = 2.313$$

As this is outside 1.328 we reject H_0. The evidence suggests that the mean monthly rental is more than £900.

7.15 *Step 1* H_0: There is no association between smoking and lung cancer.

H_1: There is an association between smoking and lung cancer.

Step 2 5% (0.05)

Step 3 $v = (r - 1)(c - 1)$

$v = (2 - 1)(2 - 1)$

$v = 1$

$\chi^2_{0.05,1} = 3.84$

figure 7.18

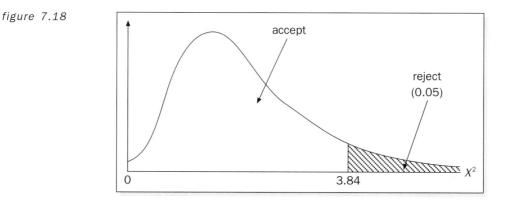

Step 4 Expected frequencies

$$\text{row total} \times \frac{\text{column total}}{\text{grand total}}$$

▶ Cancer sufferers: smokers

$$400 \times \frac{350}{1{,}000} = 140$$

▶ Cancer sufferers: non-smokers

$$400 \times \frac{650}{1{,}000} = 260$$

▶ Non-sufferers: smokers

$$600 \times \frac{350}{1,000} = 210$$

▶ Non-sufferers: non-smokers

$$600 \times \frac{650}{1,000} = 390$$

Expected value table

	Smokers	Non-smokers	Totals
Cancer sufferers	140	260	400
Non-sufferers	210	390	600
Totals	350	650	1,000

Calculating Chi-squared $= \sum\limits_{i=1}^{n} \dfrac{(O - E)^2}{E}$

O	E	$(O - E)$	$(O - E)^2$	$\dfrac{(O - E)^2}{E}$
200	140	60	3,600	25.71
150	210	−60	3,600	17.14
200	260	−60	3,600	13.85
450	390	60	3,600	9.23
				$\Sigma = 65.93$

Step 5 65.93 > 3.84

Step 6 Reject H_0

Step 7 There is enough evidence to link smoking with lung cancer.

Chapter 8: Index numbers

8.1 Simple price index $= \dfrac{P_n}{P_0} \times 100$

Index 1992 $= \dfrac{P_{1992}}{P_{1992}} \times 100 = \dfrac{66.90}{66.90} \times 100 = 100$

Index 1993 $= \dfrac{P_{1993}}{P_{1992}} \times 100 = \dfrac{69.20}{66.90} \times 100 = 103$

Index 1994 $= \dfrac{P_{1994}}{P_{1992}} \times 100 = \dfrac{71.30}{66.90} \times 100 = 107$

Index 1995 $= \dfrac{P_{1995}}{P_{1992}} \times 100 = \dfrac{72.70}{66.90} \times 100 = 109$

Index 1996 $= \dfrac{P_{1996}}{P_{1992}} \times 100 = \dfrac{78.40}{66.90} \times 100 = 117$

Index 1997 $= \dfrac{P_{1997}}{P_{1992}} \times 100 = \dfrac{81.60}{66.90} \times 100 = 122$

8.2 New index = old index ×

$$\frac{\text{value in period } T_1 \text{ (value of old index in original base year = 100)}}{\text{value in period } T_2 \text{ (value of old index in new base year)}}$$

Year	1992	1993	1994
old index (1992 = 100)	100	103	107
new index (1995 = 100)	$100 \times \dfrac{100}{109} = 92$	$103 \times \dfrac{100}{109} = 94$	$107 \times \dfrac{100}{109} = 98$

Year	1995	1996	1997
old index (1992 = 100)	$109 \times \dfrac{100}{109} = 100$	$117 \times \dfrac{100}{109} = 107$	$122 \times \dfrac{100}{109} = 112$
new index (1995 = 100)	100	107	112

8.3 Simple aggregate price index $= \dfrac{\Sigma P_n}{\Sigma P_0} \times 100 = \dfrac{\Sigma P_n}{\Sigma P_{1995}}$

Price index for 1995 $= \dfrac{\Sigma P_{1995}}{\Sigma P_{1995}} \times 100 = \dfrac{1{,}249}{1{,}249} \times 100 = 100.0$

Price index for 1996 $= \dfrac{\Sigma P_{1996}}{\Sigma P_{1995}} \times 100 = \dfrac{1{,}280}{1{,}249} \times 100 = 102.5$

Price index for 1997 $= \dfrac{\Sigma P_{1997}}{\Sigma P_{1995}} \times 100 = \dfrac{1{,}523}{1{,}249} \times 100 = 121.9$

8.4 (a) Laspeyres price index $= \dfrac{\Sigma P_n Q_0}{\Sigma P_0 Q_0} \times 100$ substituting

Index 1995 $= \dfrac{(304)(15) + (135)(30) + (205)(12) + (147)(24) + (458)(19)}{(304)(15) + (135)(30) + (205)(12) + (147)(24) + (458)(19)}$
$\times 100 = 100.0$

Index 1996 $= \dfrac{(327)(15) + (146)(30) + (197)(12) + (155)(24) + (455)(19)}{(304)(15) + (135)(30) + (205)(12) + (147)(24) + (458)(19)}$
$\times 100 = 103.1$

Index 1997 $= \dfrac{(452)(15) + (154)(30) + (221)(12) + (164)(24) + (532)(19)}{(304)(15) + (135)(30) + (205)(12) + (147)(24) + (458)(19)}$
$\times 100 = 120.6$

(b) Paasche price index $= \dfrac{\Sigma P_n Q_n}{\Sigma P_0 Q_n} \times 100$ substituting

Index 1995 $= \dfrac{(304)(15) + (135)(30) + (205)(12) + (147)(24) + (458)(19)}{(304)(15) + (135)(30) + (205)(12) + (147)(24) + (458)(19)}$
$\times 100 = 100.0$

$$\text{Index } 1996 = \frac{(327)(18) + (146)(24) + (197)(18) + (155)(20) + (455)(20)}{(304)(18) + (135)(24) + (205)(18) + (147)(20) + (458)(20)}$$
$$\times 100 = 102.6$$

$$\text{Index } 1997 = \frac{(452)(12) + (154)(35) + (221)(10) + (164)(22) + (532)(21)}{(304)(12) + (135)(35) + (205)(10) + (147)(22) + (458)(21)}$$
$$\times 100 = 119.5$$

8.5 (a) Laspeyres quantity index $= \dfrac{\sum P_0 Q_n}{\sum P_0 Q_0} \times 100$ substituting

$$\text{Index } 1995 = \frac{(50)(200) + (80)(100) + (100)(300)}{(50)(200) + (80)(100) + (100)(300)} \times 100 = \frac{48{,}000}{48{,}000} \times 100$$
$$= 100.0$$

$$\text{Index } 1996 = \frac{(50)(300) + (80)(200) + (100)(400)}{(50)(200) + (80)(100) + (100)(300)} \times 100 = \frac{71{,}000}{48{,}000} \times 100$$
$$= 147.9$$

$$\text{Index } 1997 = \frac{(50)(300) + (80)(300) + (100)(500)}{(50)(200) + (80)(100) + (100)(500)} \times 100 = \frac{89{,}000}{48{,}000} \times 100$$
$$= 185.4$$

(b) Paasche quantity index $= \dfrac{\sum P_n Q_n}{\sum P_n Q_0} \times 100$ substituting

$$\text{Index } 1995 = \frac{(50)(200) + (80)(100) + (100)(300)}{(50)(200) + (80)(100) + (100)(300)} \times 100 = \frac{48{,}000}{48{,}000} \times 100$$
$$= 100.0$$

$$\text{Index } 1996 = \frac{(60)(300) + (100)(200) + (120)(400)}{(60)(200) + (100)(100) + (120)(300)} \times 100 = \frac{86{,}000}{58{,}000} \times 100$$
$$= 148.3$$

$$\text{Index } 1997 = \frac{(80)(300) + (120)(300) + (150)(500)}{(80)(200) + (120)(100) + (150)(300)} \times 100 = \frac{135{,}000}{73{,}000} \times 100$$
$$= 184.9$$

8.6 To rebase the RPI making 1990 = 100 we can use:

New index = old index $\times$

$$\frac{\text{value in period } T_1 \text{ (value of old index in original base year)}}{\text{value in period } T_2 \text{ (value of old index in new base year)}}$$

$$1990 = 126.1 \times \frac{100}{126.1} = 100.0$$

$$1993 = 140.7 \times \frac{100.0}{126.1} = 111.6$$

$$1994 = 144.1 \times \frac{100.0}{126.1} = 114.3$$

$$1995 = 149.1 \times \frac{100.0}{126.1} = 118.2$$

$$1996 = 152.7 \times \frac{100.0}{126.1} = 121.1$$

$$1997 = 157.5 \times \frac{100.0}{126.1} = 124.9$$

From this we can see that prices rose, on average, by 24.9 per cent from 1990 to 1997, whereas earnings rose by 37 per cent, implying that real earnings had risen over the period.

8.7 Weighted index of price relatives $= \dfrac{\sum WR}{W} = \dfrac{\sum W\left(\dfrac{P_n}{P_0}\right)}{\sum W}$ weight are given by expenditure $P_0 \times Q_0$

Index for 1997 $= \dfrac{(40 \times 30)\left(\dfrac{45}{30}\right) + (80 \times 40)\left(\dfrac{50}{40}\right) + (50 \times 20)\left(\dfrac{25}{20}\right)}{(40 \times 30) + (80 \times 40) + (50 \times 20)} = 1.35056$

or 135.1

Prices have risen by 35 per cent since 1995.

8.8 Weighted index of price relatives $= \dfrac{\sum WR}{W} = \dfrac{\sum W\left(\dfrac{P_n}{P_0}\right)}{\sum W}$

$$\frac{136\left(\dfrac{142.2}{141.0}\right) + 49\left(\dfrac{182.7}{179.2}\right) + \ldots + 47\left(\dfrac{123.9}{123.7}\right) + 59\left(\dfrac{182.5}{177.8}\right)}{1,000} = \frac{1,020.064}{1,000} = 1.02$$

Therefore the index for July 1997 $= 154.4 \times 1.02 = 157.5$

Chapter 9: Time value of money

9.1 $A_t = P(1 + i)^t$
$= 20,500(1 + 0.12)^3$
$= 20,500 \times 1.404928$
$= £28,801.02$

9.2 $APR = [1(1 + i)^{12} - 1] \times 100$
$= [1(1 + 0.025)^{12} - 1] \times 100$
$= [(1.025)^{12} - 1] \times 100$
$= 0.3449 \times 100$
$= 34.49\%$

9.3 (a)
$$CI_t = P(1 + i)^t - P$$
$$= 12,000(1 + 0.229)^3 - 12,000$$
$$= 12,000 \times 1.856332 - 12,000$$
$$= £22,275.98 - 12,000$$

Compound interest = £10,275.98

(b) There are 30 monthly payments at 1.73% therefore:
$$A_t = P(1 + i)^t$$
$$= 12,000(1 + 0.0173)^{30}$$
$$= 12,000 \times 1.674359$$
$$= £20,092.31$$

(c) Interest paid over $2\frac{1}{2}$ years:
$$£20,092.31 - £12,000 = £8,092.31$$
Interest paid over 3 years = £10,275.98
Therefore difference $\quad = £10,275.98 - £8,092.31 = £2,183.67$
Note: Monthly interest rate can be calculated by:

$$i_m = \left(\sqrt[12]{1 + APR} - 1\right)$$
$$= [(1 + APR)^{1/12} - 1]$$

where: $\quad i_m$ = monthly interest rate
$\qquad APR$ = the annual percentage rate (expressed as a decimal)
Therefore 22.9% APR = 0.229
$$\therefore i_m = \left(\sqrt[12]{1.229} - 1\right)$$
$$= 0.01733$$
$$= 1.73\%$$

9.4 The present value of Waffle's offer:

$$PV = £A_t \times \frac{1}{(1 + i)^t}$$
$$= 96,600 \times \frac{1}{(1 + 0.085)^4}$$
$$= 96,600 \times 0.72157$$
$$= £69,704.08$$

The present value of Blarney's offer:

$$PV = £A_t \times \frac{1}{(1 + i)^t}$$
$$= 105,000 \times \frac{1}{(1 + 0.085)^5}$$
$$= 105,000 \times 0.665045$$
$$= £69,829.77$$

The present value of Blarney's offer is marginally better than that of Waffle's. However, as the difference is only £125.69 then the risk associated with an extra year's delay in payment must be considered. A risk-averse manager is likely to accept Waffle's offer.

9.5 (a) $Annual\ depreciation = \dfrac{initial\ value\ of\ capital - scrap\ value}{estimated\ life\ of\ capital}$

$$= \frac{147{,}000 - 20{,}000}{8}$$

$$= \frac{127{,}000}{8}$$

Annual depreciation = £15,875 per annum

(b) $Annual\ depreciation = \dfrac{initial\ value\ of\ capital - scrap\ value}{estimated\ life\ of\ capital}$

$$= \frac{147{,}000 - 40{,}000}{8}$$

$$= \frac{107{,}000}{8}$$

Annual depreciation = £13,375 per annum

(c) $A_t = P \times (1 - i)^t$
$A_8 = P \times (1 - 0.18)^8$
$\quad = £30{,}048.87$

At an annual depreciation rate of 18 per cent then the book value of the asset after 8 years would be £30,048.87

(d) $\quad 40{,}000 = 147{,}000 \times (1 - i)^8$
$\quad 0.2721 = (1 - i)^8$
$\sqrt[8]{0.2721} = (1 - i)$
$\quad 0.8499 = 1 - i$
$\qquad\quad i = 1 - 0.8499$
$\qquad\quad i = 0.1501$
$\qquad\quad i = 15.01\%$

9.6 (a) By adding the nominal values to give the net revenues (£m), the table below shows that projects A & B pay back in year 5, project B earlier on in the year, and project B provides a greater revenue stream. Project C's payback period is in year 4 but has a lower revenue stream than B.

Year	Project A	Project B	Project C
0	−24	−20	−15.5
1	−23.98	−19.91	−14.21
2	−20.6	−16.05	−9.45
3	−14.62	−9.24	−2.24
4	−6.8	−0.3	6.4
5	2.1	9.95	15.45
6	11.32	20.69	23.89
7	20.1	31.1	30.7
8	27.68	40.36	34.86
9	33.3	47.65	35.35

The table shows that project C would be selected using the payback method. However, the total *nominal* value of each project rates project B first (£47.65 m), project C second (£35.35 m) and the more capital intensive project A last (£33.3 m).

(b) $ARR = \dfrac{total\ return\ -\ initial\ capital\ outlay}{initial\ capital\ outlay} \times \dfrac{100}{time\ period\ of\ project}$

Project A:

$ARR = \dfrac{33.3 - 24}{24} \times \dfrac{100}{9}$

$= 0.3875 \times 11.1111$

$= 4.31\%$

Project B:

$ARR = \dfrac{47.65 - 20}{20} \times \dfrac{100}{9}$

$= 1.3825 \times 11.1111$

$= 15.36\%$

Project C:

$ARR = \dfrac{35.35 - 15.5}{15.5} \times \dfrac{100}{9}$

$= 1.2807 \times 11.1111$

$= 14.23\%$

The ARR method would suggest that project B provides the best return on investment.

(c) To calculate NPV construct a table from the given data as follows:

	Nominal cash flow			Discount factor	Discounted cash flow		
		Project		8.25%		Project	
Year	A	B	C		A	B	C
0	−24	−20	−15.5				
1	0.02	0.09	1.29				
2	3.38	3.86	4.76				
3	5.98	6.81	7.21				
4	7.82	8.94	8.64				
5	8.9	10.25	9.05				
6	9.22	10.74	8.44				
7	8.78	10.41	6.81				
8	7.58	9.26	4.16				
9	5.62	7.29	0.49				

Complete the discount factor (df) column (5) using:

$df = \dfrac{1}{(1 + i)^t}$

df for year 0:

$= \dfrac{1}{(1 + 0.0825)^0} = 1$

df for year 1:

$$= \frac{1}{(1 + 0.0825)^1} = 0.924$$

Complete the remainder of the column increasing the power (t) by 1 for each successive year

| | Nominal cash flow | | | Discount factor | Discounted cash flow | | |
| | | Project | | | | Project | |
Year	A	B	C	8.25%	A	B	C
0	−24	−20	−15.5	1			
1	0.02	0.09	1.29	0.924			
2	3.38	3.86	4.76	0.853			
3	5.98	6.81	7.21	0.788			
4	7.82	8.94	8.64	0.728			
5	8.9	10.25	9.05	0.673			
6	9.22	10.74	8.44	0.621			
7	8.78	10.41	6.81	0.574			
8	7.58	9.26	4.16	0.530			
9	5.62	7.29	0.49	0.490			

The remainder of the table can be completed by multiplying the nominal value by the discount factor. Thus:

column (6) is calculated as follows:

column (2) × column (5) = −24 × 1

column (7) is calculated

column (3) × column (5) = −20 × 1

column (8) is calculated

column (4) × column (5) = −15.5 × 1

Thus for year 2, project A's DCF = 0.02 × 0.924 = 0.018
Complete the remainder of the table:

| | Nominal cash flow | | | Discount factor | Discounted cash flow | | |
| | | Project | | | | Project | |
Year	A	B	C	8.25%	A	B	C
0	−24	−20	−15.5	1	−24	−20	−15.5
1	0.02	0.09	1.29	0.924	0.018	0.083	1.192
2	3.38	3.86	4.76	0.853	2.883	3.293	4.060
3	5.98	6.81	7.21	0.788	4.712	5.366	5.681
4	7.82	8.94	8.64	0.728	5.693	6.508	6.290
5	8.9	10.25	9.05	0.673	5.990	6.898	6.091
6	9.22	10.74	8.44	0.621	5.726	6.670	5.241
7	8.78	10.41	6.81	0.574	5.040	5.975	3.909
8	7.58	9.26	4.16	0.530	4.017	4.908	2.205
9	5.62	7.29	0.49	0.490	2.754	3.572	0.240
				NPV	12.833	23.273	19.409

Sum the DCF columns for each of the projects. The NPV for each project is as follows:

Project A £12.833 m
Project B £23.273 m
Project C £19.409 m

As all the projects' NPVs are positive all are worth undertaking. However, if they are mutually exclusive so that only one project can be undertaken, the venture with the highest NPV should be selected. Therefore choose project B.

(d) The calculation for the IRR is unwieldy. However, with the increasing use of personal computers, it has become relatively straightforward. The solution to this problem will be undertaken using a spreadsheet package where the problem is solved initially using first principles and then using a spreadsheet's in-built functions (programs) to confirm the solution.

Step 1 Calculate the discount factors for each of the time periods using various discount rates of 10%, 15%, 20%, 25%, 30%, 35%.

$$df = \frac{1}{(1 + i)^t}$$

df for year 0:

$$= \frac{1}{(1 + 0.1)^0} = 1$$

df for year 1:

$$= \frac{1}{(1 + 0.1)^1} = 0.909$$

Complete the remainder of the columns increasing the power (*t*) by 1 for each successive year, and the discount rates by 5 per cent up to 35 per cent:

Year	NCF*	Discount rates and Discount factors					
		0.1	0.15	0.2	0.25	0.3	0.35
0	−24	1	1	1	1	1	1
1	0.02	0.909	0.870	0.833	0.800	0.769	0.741
2	3.38	0.826	0.756	0.694	0.640	0.592	0.549
3	5.98	0.751	0.658	0.579	0.512	0.455	0.406
4	7.82	0.683	0.572	0.482	0.410	0.35	0.301
5	8.90	0.621	0.497	0.402	0.328	0.269	0.223
6	9.22	0.564	0.432	0.335	0.262	0.207	0.165
7	8.78	0.513	0.376	0.279	0.210	0.159	0.122
8	7.58	0.467	0.327	0.233	0.168	0.123	0.091
9	5.62	0.424	0.284	0.194	0.134	0.094	0.067

Note: * Nominal cash flow

Step 2 Complete the table by multiplying the nominal values by the appropriate discount factor as in (c) above:

Project A

Year	NCF*	Discount factors						Discounted cash flow (£m)					
		0.1	0.15	0.2	0.25	0.3	0.35	10	15	20	25	30	35
0	−24	1	1	1	1	1	1	−24	−24	−24	−24	−24	−24
1	0.02	0.909	0.870	0.833	0.800	0.769	0.741	0.018	0.017	0.017	0.016	0.015	0.015
2	3.38	0.826	0.756	0.694	0.640	0.592	0.549	2.792	2.555	2.346	2.163	2.001	1.856
3	5.98	0.751	0.658	0.579	0.512	0.455	0.406	4.491	3.935	3.462	3.062	2.721	2.428
4	7.82	0.683	0.572	0.482	0.410	0.35	0.301	5.341	4.473	3.769	3.206	2.737	2.354
5	8.90	0.621	0.497	0.402	0.328	0.269	0.223	5.527	4.423	3.578	2.919	2.394	1.985
6	9.22	0.564	0.432	0.335	0.262	0.207	0.165	5.200	3.983	3.089	2.416	1.909	1.521
7	8.78	0.513	0.376	0.279	0.210	0.159	0.122	4.504	3.301	2.450	1.844	1.396	1.071
8	7.58	0.467	0.327	0.233	0.168	0.123	0.091	3.540	2.479	1.766	1.273	0.932	0.690
9	5.62	0.424	0.284	0.194	0.134	0.094	0.067	2.383	1.596	1.090	0.753	0.528	0.377
							NPV	9.796	2.762	−2.433	−6.348	−9.366	−11.704

Step 3 Plot the NPV and discount rates (%) as a scatter graph and join the points (see Figure R9.1)

Step 4 Repeat the process for each of the projects.

Project B

Year	NCF	Discount factors						Discounted cash flow (£m)					
		10	15	20	25	30	35	10	15	20	25	30	35
0	−20	1	1	1	1	1	1	−20	−20	−20	−20	−20	−20
1	0.09	0.909	0.87	0.833	0.8	0.769	0.741	0.082	0.078	0.075	0.072	0.069	0.067
2	3.86	0.826	0.756	0.694	0.64	0.592	0.549	3.188	2.918	2.679	2.47	2.285	2.119
3	6.81	0.751	0.658	0.579	0.512	0.455	0.406	5.114	4.481	3.943	3.487	3.099	2.765
4	8.94	0.683	0.572	0.482	0.41	0.35	0.301	6.106	5.114	4.309	3.665	3.129	2.691
5	10.25	0.621	0.497	0.402	0.328	0.269	0.223	6.365	5.094	4.121	3.362	2.757	2.286
6	10.74	0.564	0.432	0.335	0.262	0.207	0.165	6.057	4.64	3.598	2.814	2.223	1.772
7	10.41	0.513	0.376	0.279	0.21	0.159	0.122	5.34	3.914	2.904	2.186	1.655	1.27
8	9.26	0.467	0.327	0.233	0.168	0.123	0.091	4.324	3.028	2.158	1.556	1.139	0.843
9	7.29	0.424	0.284	0.194	0.134	0.094	0.067	3.091	2.07	1.414	0.977	0.685	0.488
							NPV	19.669	11.338	5.201	0.589	−2.958	−5.699

Plot the NPV and discount rates (%) as a scatter graph and join the points (see Figure R9.1)

Project C

Year	NCF	Discount factors						Discounted cash flow (£m)					
		10	15	20	25	30	35	10	15	20	25	30	35
0	−15.5	1	1	1	1	1	1	−15.5	−15.5	−15.5	−15.5	−15.5	−15.5
1	1.29	0.909	0.87	0.833	0.8	0.769	0.741	1.173	1.122	1.075	1.032	0.992	0.956
2	4.76	0.826	0.756	0.694	0.64	0.592	0.549	3.932	3.599	3.303	3.046	2.818	2.613
3	7.21	0.751	0.658	0.579	0.512	0.455	0.406	5.415	4.744	4.175	3.692	3.281	2.927
4	8.64	0.683	0.572	0.482	0.41	0.35	0.301	5.901	4.942	4.164	3.542	3.024	2.601
5	9.05	0.621	0.497	0.402	0.328	0.269	0.223	5.62	4.498	3.638	2.968	2.434	2.018
6	8.44	0.564	0.432	0.335	0.262	0.207	0.165	4.76	3.646	2.827	2.211	1.747	1.393
7	6.81	0.513	0.376	0.279	0.21	0.159	0.122	3.494	2.561	1.9	1.43	1.083	0.831
8	4.16	0.467	0.327	0.233	0.168	0.123	0.091	1.943	1.36	0.969	0.699	0.512	0.379
9	0.49	0.424	0.284	0.194	0.134	0.094	0.067	0.208	0.139	0.095	0.066	0.046	0.033
							NPV	16.944	11.111	6.647	3.187	0.437	−1.750

(e) Plot the NPV and discount rates (%) as a scatter graph and join the points (see Figure R9.1 below)

If the NPV curves are plotted on the same graph then the result is as shown in Figure R9.1

figure R9.1

Diagram showing the NPV of three investment opportunities

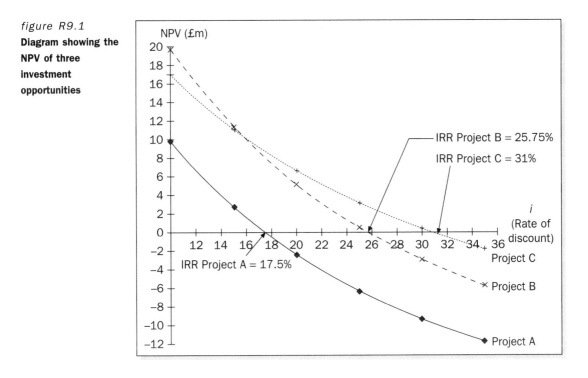

Using the spreadsheet function, IRR results in the following internal rates of return:

Project A   **17.47%**
Project B   **25.74%**
Project C   **30.93%**

The decision rule when using IRR is that a firm should undertake a project if the annualized return in the form of the IRR is greater than the annual cost of capital (the rate of interest). In the three projects the IRR exceeds the cost of the capital (8.25 per cent < 17.5 per cent, 25.7 per cent and 30.9 per cent respectively). If the IRR was less the than the interest rate used to calculate NPV (8.25 per cent in this case) then the company should not undertake the project. In other words if IRR is less than the annual cost of capital (interest rate) then the company should avoid such capital expenditures.

All three projects are therefore viable but the NPV for project B is the highest whereas the IRR for project C is highest. As we can see from Figure R9.1 the respective NPV curves for projects B and C intersect, causing the NPV and IRR criteria to conflict.

9.7 To calculate NPV construct a table from the given data as follows:

Year	NCF (£000)	Discount factor (0.135)	Discounted cash flow (£000)
0	−450		
1	−15		
2	105		
3	105		
4	105		
5	105		
6	105		
7	105		
8	105		
9	105		
10	105		

Complete the discount factor (*df*) column (3) using:

$$df = \frac{1}{(1 + i)^t}$$

df for year 0:

$$= \frac{1}{(1 + 0.135)^0} = 1$$

df for year 1:

$$= \frac{1}{(1 + 0.135)^1} = 0.881$$

Complete the remainder of the column increasing the power (*t*) by 1 for each successive year.

Year	NCF (£000)	Discount factor (0.135)	Discounted cash flow (£000)
0	−450	1	−450
1	−15	0.881	−13.215
2	105	0.776	81.48
3	105	0.684	71.82
4	105	0.603	63.315
5	105	0.531	55.755
6	105	0.468	49.14
7	105	0.412	43.26
8	105	0.363	38.115
9	105	0.32	33.6
10	105	0.282	29.61
		NPV	2.88

The discounted cash flow column of the table can be completed by multiplying the nominal value by the discount factor.

Sum the DCF column.

Thus the NPV of the project at a 13.5 per cent discount rate is £2,880 and, as NPV is positive, then the project is worth undertaking (or at least considering undertaking).

At a discount rate of 14 per cent

Year	NCF (£000)	Discount factor (0.14)	Discounted cash flow (£000)
0	−450	1	−450
1	−15	0.877	−13.155
2	105	0.769	80.745
3	105	0.675	70.875
4	105	0.592	62.16
5	105	0.519	54.495
6	105	0.456	47.88
7	105	0.4	42
8	105	0.351	36.855
9	105	0.308	32.34
10	105	0.27	28.35
			−7.455

At a discount rate of 14 per cent however the NPV is £−7,455 and would represent an overall loss. The project at this discount rate should not be undertaken.

Chapter 10: Linear programming and break-even analysis

10.1 Maximise $Z = 70X + 100Y$

Subject to:

$12X + 3Y \leq 1{,}080$ (labour constraint)

$3X + 5Y \leq 450$ (machine constraint)

$1X + 1Y \leq 100$ (land constraint)

$X \geq 0 \ Y \geq 0$ (land constraint)

OMNPQ = Feasible region (see Figure R10.1)

figure R10.1

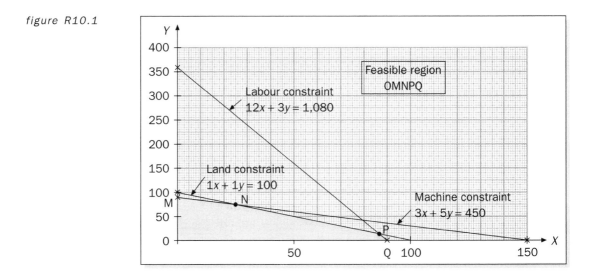

Solving at corner point:

▶ **At M** $Z_M = 70(0) + 100(90)$

$\underline{Z_M = 9000}$

▶ **At Q** $Z_Q = 70(90) + 100(0)$

$\underline{Z_Q = 6{,}300}$

▶ **At N** Using simultaneous equations

$3X + 5Y = 450 \ldots (1)$

$1X + 1Y = 100 \ldots (2)$

$(2) \times 3$ $\underline{3X + 3Y = 300} \ldots (3)$

$(1) - (3)$ $2Y = 150$

$\underline{Y = 75}$

Subst $Y = 75$ in (1)

$$3X + 5(75) = 450$$

$$3X = 75$$

$$\underline{X = 25}$$

So coordinates of N are $X = 25$, $Y = 75$

$Z_N = 70(25) + 100(75)$

$\underline{Z_N = 9,250}$

▶ **At P**   Using simultaneous equations

$$12X + 3Y = 1080. \ldots (1)$$

$$1X + 1Y = 100 \ldots (2)$$

(2) × 3 $3X + 3Y = 300 \ldots (3)$

(1) − (3) $9X + = 780$

$$\underline{X = 86\frac{2}{3}}$$

Substitute $X = 86\frac{2}{3}$ in (2)

$$86\frac{2}{3} + 1Y = 100$$

$$\underline{Y = 13\frac{1}{3}}$$

$Z_p = 70(86\frac{2}{3}) + 100(13\frac{1}{3})$

$Z_p = 6,066.2 + 1,333.3$

$\underline{Z_p = 7,399.5}$

So Z (Net profit, £s) is a maximum at corner point N, giving £9,250 net profit. Here 25 acres are devoted to potatoes (X) and 75 acres to barley (Y).

10.2 In this case a summary table of the information given in the question might help clarify the situation.

Variable	Name	E 132 content	E 320 content	Maximum production	Profit per unit
R	Rockets	2.5 g	5.0 g	10,000	£0.05
S	Starships	5.0 g	2.5 g	no max^{im}	£0.02

Maximise $Z = 0.05R + 0.02S$

where Z = profit (£'s)

Subject to:

$2.5R + 5.0S \leq 80,000$ (E 132 constraint)

$5.0R + 2.5S \leq 70,000$ (E 320 constraint)

$R \leq 10,000$ (marketing constraint)

$R \geq 0, \ S \geq 0$ (non − negative constraints)

The feasible region is area OMBAN as shown in Figure R10.2

figure R10.2

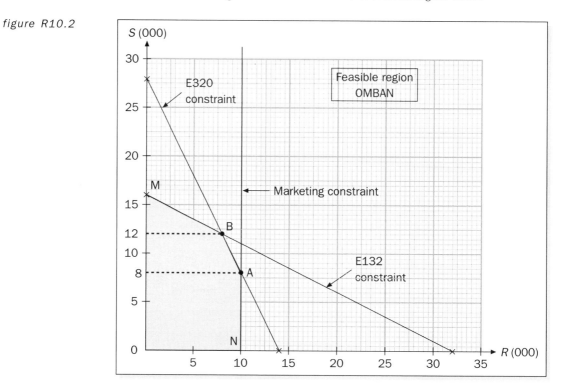

Solving at this corner points.

► **At M** $Z_M = 0.05(0) + 0.02(16,000)$

   $\underline{Z_M = £320}$

► **At N** $Z_N = 0.05(10,000) + 0.02(0)$

   $\underline{Z_N = £500}$

► **At B**   Using simultaneous equations

   $2.5R + 5.0S = 80,000 \ldots (1)$

   $5.0R + 2.5S = 70,000 \ldots (2)$

(1) × 2 $5.0R + 10.0S = 160,000 \ldots (3)$

(2) − (3) $-7.5S = -90,000$

   $\underline{S = 12,000}$

Substitute $S = 12,000$ in (1)

   $2.5R + 5.0(12,000) = 80,000$

   $2.5R = 20,000$

   $\underline{R = 8,000}$

Co-ordinates at B are $R = 8,000$, $S = 12,000$

$Z_B = 0.05(8,000) + 0.02(12,000)$

$\underline{Z_B = £640}$

► **At A** $5.0R + 2.5S = 70,000 \ldots$ (1)

$1.0R = 10,000 \ldots$ (2)

$(2) \times 5$ $5.0R = 50,000 \ldots$ (3)

$(1) - (3)$ $2.5S = 20,000$

$\underline{S = 8,000}$

$\underline{R = 10,000}$

$Z_A = 0.05(10,000) + 0.02(8,000)$

$\underline{Z_A = £660}$

So profit is a maximum at corner point A, with 10,000 units of Starships produced and 8,000 units of Rockets. Total profit is £660 on each production run.

10.3 Maximise $Z = 3,700X + 3,600Y$

where $X = 1,500$ cc motorcycle

$Y = 2,000$ cc motorcycle

$Z = $ Total net profit (£)

Subject to:

$600X + 1,200Y \le 9,000$ (assembly constraint)

$300X + 300Y \le 3,000$ (component constraint)

$900X \le 6,300$ (engine shop constraint)

The feasible region OABCD is shown in Figure R.10.3.

figure R10.3

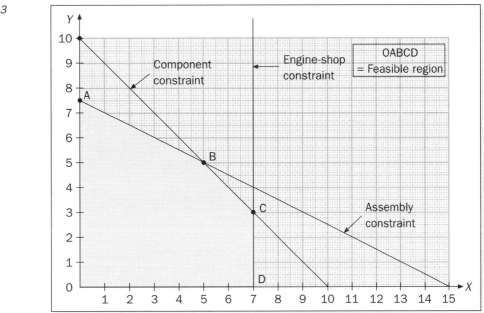

Solving Z for the corner points

► **At A** $Z_A = 3,700(0) + 3,600(7.5)$

$\underline{Z_A = £27,000}$

► **At D** $Z_D = 3,700(7) + 3,600(0)$

$\underline{Z_D = £25,900}$

► **At B**   Using simultaneous equations

$600X + 1,200Y = 9,000 \ldots (1)$

$300X + 300Y = 3,000 \ldots (2)$

$(2) \times 2$ $\underline{600X + 600Y = 6,000 \ldots (3)}$

$(1) - (3)$ $600Y = 3,000$

$\underline{Y = 5}$

Substitute $Y = 5$ in (1)

$600X + 1,200(5) = 9,000$

$600X = 3,000$

$\underline{X = 5}$

$Z_B = 3,700(5) + 3,600(5)$

$\underline{Z_B = £36,500}$

► **At C** $300X + 300Y = 3,000 \ldots (1)$

$900X = 6,300 \ldots (2)$

$(1) \times 3$ $\underline{900X + 900Y = 9,000 \ldots (3)}$

$(2) - (3)$ $-900Y = -2,700$

$\underline{Y = 3}$

Substitute $Y = 3$ in (1)

$300X + 300(3) = 3,000$

$300X = 2,100$

$\underline{X = 7}$

$Z_C = 3,700(7) + 3,600(3)$

$\underline{Z_C = £36,700}$

The producer will maximise net profit by producing seven motorcycles of the 1,500 cc type and 3 motorcycles of the 2,000 cc type each month, making a total net profit of £36,700 per month.

10.4 Minimise $Z = 120X + 110Y$

where Z = Total cost of foodstuffs (£)

Subject to:

$3X + 10Y \geq 9$ ... (vitamin constraint)

$3X + 3Y \geq 6$ ... (protein constraint)

$8X + 3Y \geq 12$ ... (starch constraint)

$X \geq 0$, $Y \geq 0$ ... (non-negative constraints)

The shaded feasible region is shown in Figure R10.4

figure R10.4
Minimisation problem: feasible region on or to right of segments ABCD

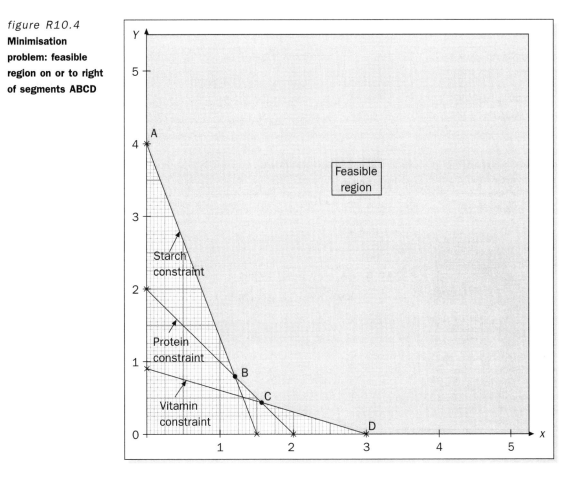

To fulfil all our constraints in this minimisation problem we must be on, or to the right, of segments ABCD.

Solving Z for corner points.

▶ **At A** $Z_A = 120(0) + 110(4)$

$\underline{Z_A = £440}$

▶ **At D** $Z_D = 120(3) + 110(0)$

$\underline{Z_D = £360}$

▶ **At C** Using simultaneous equations

$$3X + 10Y = 9 \ldots (1)$$

$$3X + 3Y = 6 \ldots (2)$$

$(1) - (2)$ $7Y = 3$

$$\underline{Y = \frac{3}{7}}$$

Substitute $Y = \frac{3}{7}$ in (1)

$$3X + 10\left(\frac{3}{7}\right) = 9$$

$$3X = 9 - 4\frac{2}{7}$$

$$X = 4\frac{5}{7} \div 3$$

$$\underline{X = 1\frac{4}{7}}$$

$$Z_C = 120\left(1\frac{4}{7}\right) + 110\left(\frac{3}{7}\right)$$

$$Z_C = 188.6 + 47.1$$

$$\underline{Z_C = £235.7}$$

▶ **At B** $3X + 3Y = 6 \ldots (1)$

$8X + 3Y = 12 \ldots (2)$

$(1) - (2)$ $-5X = -6$

$$\underline{X = 1\frac{1}{5}}$$

Substitute $X = 1\frac{1}{5}$ in (1)

$$3\left(1\frac{1}{5}\right) + 3Y = 6$$

$$3Y = 2\frac{2}{5}$$

$$\underline{Y = \frac{4}{5}}$$

$$Z_B = 120\left(1\frac{1}{5}\right) + 110\left(\frac{4}{5}\right)$$

$$\underline{Z_B = £232}$$

The farmer should use a mix of $1\frac{1}{5}$ tons of foodstuff X with $\frac{4}{5}$ ton of foodstuff Y in order to minimise the total cost of foodstuff (£232) while still meeting all the nutrient requirements.

10.5 (a) $\text{BEP} = \dfrac{\text{total fixed costs (TFC)}}{\text{Contribution per unit (c/u)}}$

c/u = AR − AVC

c/u = £600 − £200

<u>c/u = £400</u>

$\text{BEP} = \dfrac{£12,000}{£400} = 30$

<u>Break-even output occurs at 30 kitchen units</u>

Budgeted profit = TR − TC at budgeted output
$$= P \cdot (Q) - [\text{TFC} + \text{TVC}]$$
$$= £600(60) - [£12,000 + 200(60)]$$
$$= £36,000 - £24,000$$

<u>Budgeted profit = £12,000</u>

$\text{Margin of safety} = \dfrac{\text{budgeted output} - \text{BEP}}{\text{budgeted output}} \times 100$

$\qquad\qquad\qquad = \dfrac{60 - 30}{60} \times 100$

<u>Margin of safety = 50%</u>

(b) $\text{BEP} = \dfrac{\text{TFC}}{\text{c/u}}$

c/u = £600 − £100 = £500

$\text{BEP} = \dfrac{£25,000}{£500} = 50$

<u>BEP = 50 kitchen units</u>

Budgeted profit = TR − TC at budgeted output
$$= £600(60) - [£25,000 + 100(60)]$$
$$= £36,000 - [£31,000]$$

<u>Budgeted profit = £5,000</u>

$\text{Margin of safety} = \dfrac{60 - 50}{60} \times 100$

<u>Margin of safety = 16.66%</u>

It would seem that the original manufacturing process is to be preferred as it gives a lower BEP, a higher budgeted profit and a higher margin of safety. Only if the new technique in addition to reducing average variable cost, improved quality, raised price and/or raised budgeted output, might it be considered for implementation.

10.6 (a) AVC = £200

$$\text{c/u} = \text{AR} - \text{AVC}$$

$$\text{c/u} = £300 - £200$$

$$\text{c/u} = £100$$

$$\text{BEP} = \frac{\text{TFC}}{\text{c/u}} = \frac{£40,000}{£100}$$

BEP = 400 bicycles per week

Budgeted profit = TR − TC at budgeted output
$$= £300(500) - [£40,000 + £200(500)]$$
$$= £150,000 - £140,000$$

Budgeted profit = £10,000

$$\text{Margin of safety} = \frac{\text{Budgeted output} - \text{BEP}}{\text{Budgeted output}} \times 100$$

$$= \frac{500 - 400}{500} \times 100$$

Margin of safety = 20%

(b) Price = £400

$$\text{c/u} = £400 - £200$$

$$\text{c/u} = £200$$

$$\text{BEP} = \frac{\text{TFC}}{\text{c/u}} = \frac{£40,000}{£200}$$

BEP = 200 bicycles per week

Budgeted profit = TR − TC at budgeted output
$$= £400\,(300) - [£40,000 + £200\,(300)]$$
$$= £120,000 - £100,000$$

Budgeted profit = £20,000

$$\text{Margin of safety} = \frac{300 - 200}{300} \times 100$$

Margin of safety = 33.3%

Raising price to £400 and selling 300 bicycles seems an attractive strategy since there is a lower number of bicycles for BEP, with a higher budgeted profit and greater margin of safety.

(c) Price = £300

$$\text{c/u} = £300 - £150$$

$$\text{c/u} = £150$$

$$\text{BEP} = \frac{£60,000}{£150}$$

BEP = 400 bicycles per week

Budgeted profit = TR − TC at budgeted output

$$= £300(500) − [£60,000 + £150(500)]$$
$$= £150,000 − £135,000$$
$$= \underline{£15,000}$$

$$\text{Margin of safety} = \frac{500 − 400}{500} \times 100$$

Margin of safety = 20%

As compared with the strategy in (a), using the more capital intensive process would raise the budgeted profit, while giving the same BEP and margin of safety, and would therefore seem attractive.

Chapter 11: Calculus and business applications

11.1
$$Q = 80L^2 − 0.1L^4$$

$$\frac{dQ}{dL} = 0 \qquad \text{for a turning point}$$

i.e. $160L − 0.4L^3 = 0$

$160L = 0.4L^3$ divide both sides by L gives $160 = 0.4L^2$,

$L^2 = 400$ $L = \pm 20$

Obviously labour input cannot be −20 therefore the labour input that maximises or minimises daily Q is 20 units.

Find whether maximum or minimum via sign of second derivative

$$\frac{d^2Q}{dL^2} = 160 − 1.2L^2, = −320 \quad \text{when} \quad L = 20$$

Therefore 20 workers will maximise output per day.

11.2 $\dfrac{dY}{dX} = 0$ for a turning point

$0 = 0.6 − 0.004X$ $X = 0.6/0.004 = 150$

The sales output that maximises or minimises profits is 150 units.

Second derivative

$$\frac{d^2Y}{dX^2} = −0.004 \therefore \text{ maximum profit at the sales output of 150 units}$$

11.3 $\dfrac{P}{Q} \cdot \dfrac{dQ}{dP} = PED$ and in order to evaluate $\dfrac{dQ}{dP}$ we need to make Q the subject of the equation or invert the result of $\dfrac{dP}{dQ}$

Either way the result is −20 therefore $PED = \dfrac{P}{Q} \cdot (−20)$

▶ when $P = 6$, $6 = 8 - 0.05Q$ so $Q = 40$ and PED $= (6/40) \times (-20) = -3$ so price elastic
▶ when $P = 2$, $2 = 8 - 0.05Q$ so $Q = 120$ and PED $= (2/120) \times (-20) = -0.33$ so price inelastic

To find the price where the demand curve has unitary elasticity

$-1 = P/Q \times (-20)$ so $-1/-20 = P/Q = 0.05$ and $P = 0.05Q = 0.05(160 - 20P)$

$P = 8 - P$ therefore $P = 4$ is where the demand curve has unitary elasticity.

11.4 ATC $= $ TC/Q $= 0.01Q + 5 + 100Q^{-1}$

$$\frac{d\text{ATC}}{dQ} = 0 \text{ for a turning point}$$

$$0 = 0.01 - 100Q^{-2} \quad 100/Q^2 = 0.01$$

Therefore $Q^2 = 100/0.01 = 10{,}000$ $Q = \pm100$ for a turning point. Obviously output cannot be -100 therefore the output that minimises or maximises cost per unit is likely to be 100. Check that this is the minimum we required by finding the second derivative

$$\frac{d^2\text{ATC}}{dQ^2} = 200Q^{-3}, = +0.0002$$

Since positive sign for second derivative, $Q = +100$ is the output that minimises ATC.

11.5 (a) $\dfrac{dR}{dX} = 0$ for a turning point

$$0 = 5{,}000 - 40X, \quad 40X = 5{,}000 \quad \text{therefore} \quad X = 125$$

The number of machines that maximise revenue is 125. The second derivative (-40) is negative. Therefore maximum revenue at $X = 125$.

(b) Total profit (TP) $=$ revenue $-$ costs $= (5{,}000X - 20X^2) - 1800X$
$$= 3{,}200X - 20X^2$$

$$\frac{d\text{TP}}{dX} = 0 \text{ for a turning point}$$

$$0 = 3{,}200 - 40X, \quad 40X = 3{,}200 \quad \text{therefore} \quad X = 80$$

Check second derivative to find if maximum or minimum turning point. This is -40, so maximum at $X = 80$.
The number of machines that maximise profits $= 80$

(c) Break even is where revenue $=$ costs, $\quad 5{,}000X - 20X^2 = 1{,}800X$
$$3{,}200X = 20X^2, \quad 3{,}200 = 20X, \quad X = 160$$
The break-even number of machines is 160.

11.6 Let the side of the square $= x$ cm. The sides of the rectangular box will be $10 - 2x$ cm, and $16 - 2x$ cm respectively and its depth will be x cm.

Vol. of box (V) $= (16 - 2x)(10 - 2x)(x) = 160x - 52x^2 + 4x^3$

$\dfrac{dV}{dx} = 0$ for a turning point

$160 - 104x + 12x^2 = 0$; dividing by 4 gives $40 - 26x + 3x^2 = 0$

i.e. $(2 - x)(20 - 3x) = 0$, therefore $x = 2$ or 6.667.

To find which turning point is the maximum we take the second derivative.

$\dfrac{dV^2}{d^2 x} = -104 + 24x$

When $x = 2$ the second derivative $= -56$, when $x = 6.667$ the second derivative $= +56$.

The value of x that maximises the volume of the box is therefore 2 cm.

11.7 (a) TR $= P.Q = -5Q^2 + 3,000Q$. A turning point $\dfrac{d\,\text{TR}}{dQ} = 0$

Therefore $-10Q + 3,000 = 0$, i.e. $Q = 300$. The output level that maximises revenue is 300 units, since the second derivative is -10, indicating a maximum turning point.

(b) Profit (TP) $=$ TR $-$ TC $= (-5Q^2 + 3,000Q) - (50Q + 10,000)$

TP $= -5Q^2 + 2,950Q - 10,000$. At a turning point $\dfrac{d\,\text{TP}}{dQ} = 0$

Therefore $-10Q + 2,950 = 0$, giving $Q = 295$.

The output level that maximises profits is 295 units (since second derivative is -10, indicating a maximum turning point)

Price charged $P = -5Q + 3,000 = -5(295) + 3,000 = £1,525$

(c) Maximum profit $= -5Q^2 + 2,950Q - 10,000 = -5(295)^2 + 2,950(295) - 10,000$

Maximum profit $= £425,125$.

11.8 (a) Profit (TP) $= (-5Q^2 + 3,000Q) - (110Q + 10,000) = -5Q^2 + 2,890Q - 10,000$

At a turning point $\dfrac{d\,\text{TP}}{dQ} = 0$

Therefore $-10Q + 2,890 = 0$ and $Q = 289$.

The output that maximises profit is 289 units (since the second derivative is -10).

Price charged $P = -5Q + 3,000 = -5(289) + 3,000 = £1,555$

(b) New profit $= -5Q^2 + 2,890Q - 10,000 = -5(289)^2 + 2,890(289) - 10,000$

Maximum profit is $£407,605$ (a reduction of $£17,520$)

(c) Price increase to customer = 1,555 − 1,525 = £30. The tax is £60 per unit, therefore 50 per cent or one half of the tax is passed on to the customer.

11.9 The solution to this problem involves the use of *partial differentiation* (see p. 271).

(a) The marginal revenue from the sale of one extra football shirt

$$= \frac{\partial TR}{\partial x} = -4x + 6 + 10y = -4(4) + 6 + 10(3) = 20$$

(b) The marginal revenue from the sale of one extra cricket jumper

$$= \frac{\partial TR}{\partial y} = -6y + 6 + 10x = -6(3) + 6 + 10(4) = 28$$

11.10 The solution to this question involves partial differentiation (p. 271).

(a) $\quad Q = -2(5)^2 + 4(4)(50) = 750$

$$PED = \frac{P}{Q} \times \frac{\partial Q}{\partial P} = \frac{5}{750} \times -4P = \frac{5}{750} \times -4(5) = -0.1333 \text{ (inelastic)}$$

(b) $\quad IED = \frac{Y}{Q} \times \frac{\partial Q}{\partial Y} = \frac{50}{750} \times 4P_B = \frac{50}{750} \times 4(4) = 1.0667 \text{ (normal good)}$

(c) $\quad CED = \frac{P_B}{Q} \times \frac{\partial Q}{\partial P_B} = \frac{4}{750} \times 4Y = \frac{4}{750} \times 4(50) = 1.0667$

This is positive and therefore the goods are substitutes.

11.11 The solution to this question involves partial differentiation (see p. 271).

▶ Marginal product of labour (MPL) =

$$\frac{\partial Q}{\partial L} = (0.75)(160)K^{0.25}L^{(0.75-1)} = 120K^{0.25}L^{-0.25}$$

$$= 120\left(\frac{K}{L}\right)^{0.25} = 120\left(\frac{400}{81}\right)^{0.25} = 178.89$$

One extra worker contributes 178.89 extra units of output (given L = 81 and K = 400)

▶ Marginal product of capital (MPK) =

$$\frac{\partial Q}{\partial K} = (0.25)(160)K^{(0.25-1)}L^{0.75} = 40K^{-0.75}L^{0.75}$$

$$= 40\left(\frac{L}{K}\right)^{0.75} = 40\left(\frac{81}{400}\right)^{0.75} = 12.07$$

One extra machine contributes 12.07 extra units of output (given L = 81 and K = 400).

11.12 dTR/dQ is the first derivative of total revenue (TR)

We can therefore use *integration* (p. 273) to find the total revenue function.

$$TR = \int (100 - 40Q - 6Q^2)dQ = 100Q - 40\frac{Q^2}{2} - 6\frac{Q^3}{3} + C$$

$$TR = 100Q - 20Q^2 - 2Q^3 + C$$

If $Q = 0$ we can assume that TR = 0 hence C in our equation = 0 and TR is

$$TR = 100Q - 20Q^2 - 2Q^3$$

To find the demand (AR) equation we use the relationship AR = TR/Q

Therefore demand (AR) = price $= \dfrac{100Q - 20Q^2 - 2Q^3}{Q} = 100 - 20Q - 2Q^2$

11.13 MC $= \dfrac{d\text{TC}}{dQ}$ in order to find TC we therefore need to *integrate* the MC function

$$\int (2.4Q^2 - 0.8Q + 10)\,dQ = 2.4\frac{Q^3}{3} - 0.8\frac{Q^2}{2} + 10Q + C$$

TC $= 0.8Q^3 - 0.4Q^2 + 10Q + C$ where C represents the fixed costs of 500

TC $= 0.8Q^3 - 0.4Q^2 + 10Q + 500$ and when $Q = 100$

TC $= 0.8(100)^3 - 0.4(100)^2 + 10(100) + 500 = 797,500$

11.14 (a) MPS $= \dfrac{dS}{dY}$. In order to find the savings equation we need to *integrate* MPS

$$\int (0.4 - 0.3Y^{-0.5})dY = 0.4Y - 0.3\frac{Y^{0.5}}{0.5} + C = 0.4Y - 0.6Y^{0.5} + C$$

We can find the vertical intercept, C by finding the value of savings when $Y = 0$

$0 = 0.4(100) - 0.6(100)^{0.5} + C$ therefore $C = -34$

Savings $S = 0.4Y - 0.6Y^{0.5} - 34$ and when $Y = 400$,

$S = 0.4(400) - 0.6(400)^{0.5} - 34 = 114$

11.15 ▶ Profit from end of year 2 to end of year 8, company A:

$$\int_2^8 (30 + 10X - X^2)dx = \left[30X + 5X^2 - \frac{X^3}{3} \right]_2^8$$
$$= (240 + 320 - 170.67) - (60 + 20 - 2.67)$$
$$= 312 \text{ i.e. total net profit for A is £312m}$$

▶ Profit from end of year 2 to end of year 8, company B:

$$\int_{2}^{8}\left(\frac{80}{X^2} + 8X - 10\right)dx = \left[\frac{-80}{X} + 4X^2 - 10X\right]_{2}^{8}$$

$$= (-10 + 256 - 80) - (-40 + 16 - 20)$$

$$= 210, \text{ i.e. total net profit for B is £210 m}$$

11.16 (a) Capital accumulated in the first two years ($t = 0$ to $t = 2$)

$$\int_{0}^{2}\left(-t^2 + 6t + 10\right)dt = \left[\frac{-t^3}{3} + 3t^2 + 10t\right]_{0}^{2}$$

$$= (-2.67 + 12 + 20) - (0) = 29.33 \text{ units of capital}$$

(b) Capital accumulated from $t = 2$ to $t = 5$

$$\int_{2}^{5}\left(-t^2 + 6t + 10\right)dt = \left[\frac{-t^3}{3} + 3t^2 + 10t\right]_{2}^{5}$$

$$= (-41.67 + 75 + 50) - (29.33) = 54 \text{ units of capital}$$

11.17 We need to find:

$$TC(80) - TC(50) = \int_{50}^{80}\frac{dTC}{dQ}dQ = \int_{50}^{80}(0.8Q + 9)dQ$$

$$= \left[0.4Q^2 + 9Q\right]_{50}^{80} = (2{,}560 + 720) - (1{,}000 + 450)$$

$$= 1{,}830$$

If TC is in £s, then the additional cost of increasing daily output is £1,830.

Appendix 1: Basic mathematics
....

A1 (a) $\frac{1}{3} \times 474 = 158$ companies were concerned

(b) In 1980 $\frac{1}{8} \times 900{,}000 = 112{,}500$ school leavers go to university.

In 1997 $\frac{1}{3} \times 900{,}000 = 300{,}000$ go to university

A2 (a) Gary Barlow's wealth as a percentage of David Bowie's

$$= \frac{9.5}{14.5} \times 100 = 65.5\%$$

(b) The percentage increase necessary is $\frac{(550 - 520)}{520} \times 100 = 5.8\%$

A3 Let index at start of day be x then

$$\left(1 - \frac{7}{100}\right) \times x = 7161.15 \text{ therefore } x = \frac{7161.15}{0.93} = 7700.16$$

A4 (a) Total cost = fixed costs + variable costs = 20,000 + 5Q

Total revenue = price × quantity = 15Q

Profit = total revenue – total cost = 15Q – (20,000 + 5Q)
= 15Q – 20,000 – 5Q

Therefore profit = 10Q – 20,000

If profit is to equal 8,000 then

8,000 = 10Q – 20,000

28,000 = 10Q   so   Q = 2,800

The level of output required to produce £8,000 profit is 2,800 units

(b) In order to break even (profit = 0)

0 = 10Q – 20,000

20,000 = 10Q therefore Q = 2,000.

Break even output is 2,000 units.

(c) Increase fixed costs by 20 per cent. New fixed costs = 20,000(1 + 20/100)

▶ new fixed costs = 24,000
▶ new profits = 10Q – 24,000
▶ new break even output is given by 0 = 10Q – 24,000 and Q = 2,400

Break even output increases by (400/2,000) × 100% = 20%

A 20% increase in fixed costs causes break even output to increase by 20%.

(d)

figure R12.1
Break-even graph

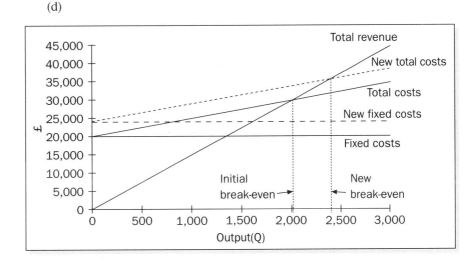

A5 (a) The general equation of a straight line is $y = mx + c$ where m is the gradient and c and is the intercept. In this specific example the equation is $P = mQ + c$ and the gradient is found from:

$$m = \frac{y_2 - y_1}{x_2 - x_1} \text{ or in this case } \frac{P_2 - P_1}{Q_2 - Q_1} = \frac{15 - 13}{5 - 6} = -2$$

The demand equation is therefore $P = -2Q + c$.

To find c substitute one point into this equation.

$15 = -2(5) + c$ therefore $c = 25$.

The demand equation is: $P = -2Q + 25$

(b) The equilibrium price and quantity is where the two lines intersect

▶ $P = 3Q + 5$ Supply equation
▶ $P = -2Q + 25$ Demand equation

These can be solved simultaneously by subtracting demand from supply.

$0 = 3Q - (-2Q) + 5 - 25$

$0 = 5Q - 20$

Therefore $Q = 4$.

Substituting 4 for Q in the demand equation gives the equilibrium price

$P = -2(4) + 25 = 17$

A6 (a) Break-even output is where TR = TC

$-2Q^2 + 26Q = Q^2 + 23$ To solve for Q we need to rearrange:

$$0 = 3Q^2 - 26Q + 23.$$

This quadratic will not factorise easily, so use the formula method

$$Q = \frac{-b \pm \sqrt{b^2 - 4ac}}{2a} \text{ where } a = 3, b = -26 \text{ and } c = 23$$

$$Q = \frac{-(-26) \pm \sqrt{(-26)^2 - 4(3)(23)}}{2(3)} = \frac{26 \pm \sqrt{400}}{6} = \frac{26 \pm 20}{6}$$

$Q = 6/6 = 1$ and $46/6 = 7.67$.

Break-even outputs are $Q = 1$ and $Q = 7.67$ (or 8 units).

(b)

figure R12.2
Break-even output

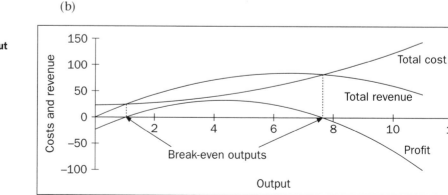

Responses to activities

Response to Activity 1

The formula used by the *Excel* spreadsheet in cell **D5** to create a cumulative less than frequency is:

= **D4** + **B5**

The equal sign has the same function as the @ in some spreadsheet packages and signifies that a calculation or a built-in function is to follow. As the formula in cell D5 is copied down to cell D12 then the spreadsheet now resembles:

	A	B	C	D	E	F
2				cum. total		cum. %age
3	Class	000	Upper boundary	(less than)	%age	(less than)
4	0 to 9	1,160	9.5	1,160	11.37	11.37
5	10 to 19	1,425	19.5	2,585	13.97	25.34
6	20 to 29	1,544	29.5	4,129	15.14	40.48
7	30 to 39	1,428	39.5	5,557	14.00	54.48
8	40 to 49	1,263	49.5	6,820	12.38	66.86
9	50 to 59	1,305	59.5	8,125	12.79	79.66
10	60 to 69	1,081	69.5	9,206	10.60	90.25
11	70 to 79	663	79.5	9,869	6.50	96.75
12	80 and over	331	89.5	10,200	3.25	100.00

The ogive can now be constructed by using the values in cells **C4** to **D12**. With the aid of the computer's drawing facilities the population below the age of 25 can be estimated by drawing a vertical line (using the rectangle drawing tool) from mid-way between 20 and 30 on the X axis class boundary up to the ogive and then extending it to the Y axis to read off the value. The ogive shows that approximately 3.4 million of the population are under 25 years old.

figure A1.1

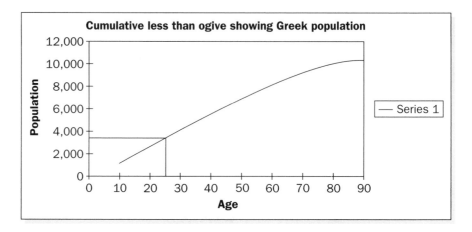

Cells **E4 to E12** are used to derive the percentage of the total appropriate to each class interval. This can readily be converted to a cumulative *percentage* less than ogive in cells **F4** to **F12.** Note that around 36 per cent of the Greek population are under 25 years of age.

figure A1.2

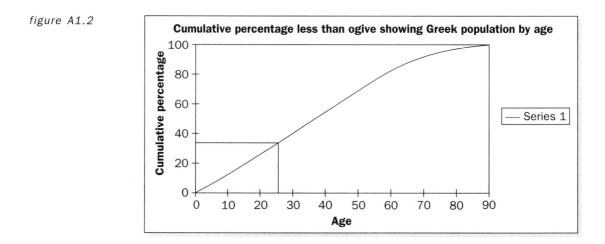

The values for the pie chart are those in cells **B4** to **B12** and, when coupled with the class boundaries as labels in cells **A4** to **A12**, the following chart results:

figure A1.3

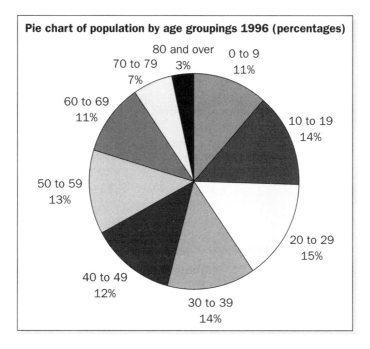

Pie chart of population by age groupings 1996 (percentages)

The pie chart shows the breakdown of the population by ten year age groups up to 80 years and the percentage of that population in each group. The age of the Greek population which is of particular interest to the company can be highlighted by exploding (i.e. separating the relevant segment from the chart). Therefore if the company was interested in, say, the 20 to 39 age group, then the pie chart showing this broader age grouping could be exploded.

Responses to Activity 2

There are several formulae for calculating the percentage change. Among them are those based on the difference between the previous population and the new population, whilst the second uses a ratio of the change in population.

▶ Using the difference based calculation, the formula for the spreadsheet entered in cell **C8** is:

$$= \textbf{(B8-B7)/B7*100.}$$

as the cell references are relative then when copied down to cell **C20**.

▶ The same result will be obtained using the ratio method where the spreadsheet formula used is:

= (B8/B7-1)*100

Through multiplying by 100 the change in population is converted to a percentage.

▶ To calculate the population density, divide the population by the area. Thus in cell **D7** enter:

= B7/$B$3

and copy to **D20**

▶ See graph in Figure A2.1(a)

▶ The mean percentage change in population can then be found either by summing all the values contained in cells **C8** to **C20** then dividing by the number of values or by using a spreadsheet function. Therefore in cell **C23** enter one of the following formulae:

= SUM(C8:C20)/13
= SUM(C8:C20)/COUNT(C8:C20)
= AVERAGE(C8:C20)

All the above will calculate the mean percentage change as 0.601 (correct to 3 decimal places). The spreadsheet should now resemble:

Greece: Population 1983–1996

Area (Sq Km)	131,908		
	population	% change	Pop. density
1983	9,642,505		73.10022895
1984	9,729,350	0.901	73.75860448
1985	9,789,513	0.618	74.21470267
1986	9,846,627	0.583	74.64768627
1987	9,895,801	0.499	75.02047639
1988	9,934,249	0.389	75.31195227
1989	9,963,604	0.295	75.53449374
1990	9,983,490	0.200	75.68525033
1991	10,004,401	0.209	75.84377748
1992	10,038,672	0.343	76.10358735
1993	10,088,700	0.498	76.48285168
1994	10,200,000	1.103	77.32662158
1995	10,311,300	1.091	78.17039148
1996	10,422,600	1.079	79.01416139
		Mean % change	
		0.601	

To apply the percentage change as an estimate for the population over the next three years, do the following.

(i)   In cells **A21** to **A23** insert the values 1997, 1998 and 1999.
(ii) The value of the percentage change needs to be converted back into a decimal (divided by 100) before it can be applied to the last known population (the value in cell **C20**). Therefore, in cell **B21** enter the formula = **B20*(1 + $C$23/100)**
(iii) Copy the formula down to cell **C23**.

The spreadsheet now resembles:

Greece: Population 1983–1996

Area (Sq Km)	131,908		
	population	**% change**	**Pop. density**
1983	9,642,505		73.10022895
1984	9,729,350	0.901	73.75860448
1985	9,789,513	0.618	74.21470267
1986	9,846,627	0.583	74.64768627
1987	9,895,801	0.499	75.02047639
1988	9,934,249	0.389	75.31195227
1989	9,963,604	0.295	75.53449374
1990	9,983,490	0.200	75.68525033
1991	10,004,401	0.209	75.84377748
1992	10,038,672	0.343	76.10358735
1993	10,088,700	0.498	76.48285168
1994	10,200,000	1.103	77.32662158
1995	10,311,300	1.091	78.17039148
1996	10,422,600	1.079	79.01416139
1997	10,485,213		
1998	10,548,201	Mean % change	
1999	10,611,568	0.601	

Here a combination graph, making use of *both* vertical axes, has been presented and shows the actual population on the left hand axis and the percentage change on the right-hand axis. The graph shows that although the population (represented by the bars) was increasing every year the rate at which it was increasing was falling up to 1990. During 1991 the growth rate stabilised, followed by population growth at an increasing rate.

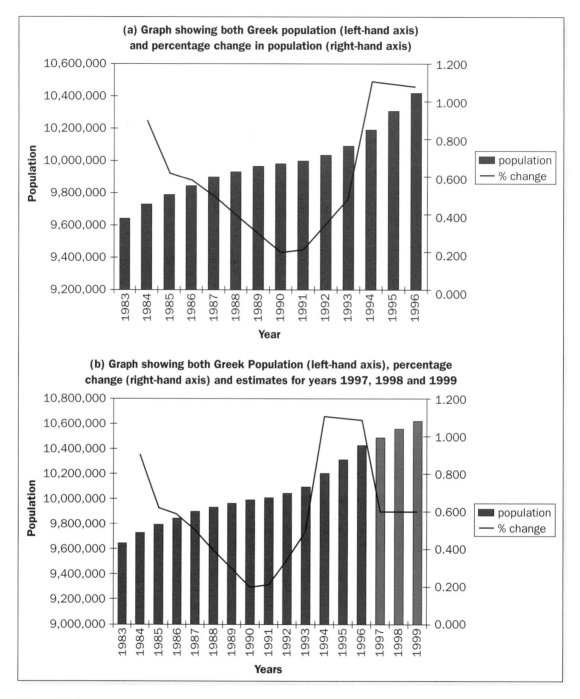

figure A2.1

Responses to Activity 3
....

▶ **Solving from first principles**
Figure A3.3 shows the complete solution

figure A3.3

	Xbar	Ybar		m (slope)	c (intercept)		R^2
	1989.5	9989343.714		50277.52967	−90037801.56		0.944379874
	X	Y					
y hat	year	population	xi	yi	xiyi	xi^2	yi^2
9,662,540	1983	9,642,505	−6.5	−346838.7143	2254451.643	42.25	1.20297E+11
9,712,817	1984	9,729,350	−5.5	−259993.7143	1429965.429	30.25	67596731468
9,763,095	1985	9,789,513	−4.5	−199830.7143	899238.2143	20.25	39932314372
9,813,372	1986	9,846,627	−3.5	−142716.7143	499508.5	12.25	20368060537
9,863,650	1987	9,895,801	−2.5	−93542.71429	233856.7857	6.25	8750239396
9,913,927	1988	9,934,249	−1.5	−55094.71429	82642.07143	2.25	3035427542
9,964,205	1989	9,963,604	−0.5	−25739.71429	12869.85714	0.25	662532891.5
10,014,482	1990	9,983,490	0.5	−5853.714286	−2926.857143	0.25	34265970.94
10,064,760	1991	10,004,401	1.5	15057.28571	22585.92857	2.25	226721853.1
10,115,038	1992	10,038,672	2.5	49328.28571	123320.7143	6.25	2433279772
10,165,315	1993	10,088,700	3.5	99356.28571	347747	12.25	9871671511
10,215,593	1994	10,200,000	4.5	210656.2857	947953.2857	20.25	44376070711
10,265,870	1995	10,311,300	5.5	321956.2857	1770759.571	30.25	1.03656E+11
10,316,148	1996	10,422,600	6.5	433256.2857	2816165.857	42.25	1.87711E+11
10,366,425	**1997**			**Sums**	11438138	227.5	6.08951E+11
10,416,703	**1998**						
10,466,980	**1999**						

▶ **Using in-built functions**
Figure A3.4 shows the complete solution

figure A3.4

	B	C	D
2	**Slope**	**Intercept**	**R^2**
3	50277.52967	−90037801.56	0.944379874
4			
5	**Y**	**X**	
6	**Population**	**Year**	**Y hat**
7	9,642,505.00	1983	9,662,539.77
8	9,729,350.00	1984	9,712,817.30
9	9,789,513.00	1985	9,763,094.83
10	9,846,627.00	1986	9,813,372.36
11	9,895,801.00	1987	9,863,649.89
12	9,934,249.00	1988	9,913,927.42
13	9,963,604.00	1989	9,964,204.95
14	9,983,490.00	1990	10,014,482.48
15	10,004,401.00	1991	10,064,760.01
16	10,038,672.00	1992	10,115,037.54
17	10,088,700.00	1993	10,165,315.07
18	10,200,000.00	1994	10,215,592.60
19	10,311,300.00	1995	10,265,870.13
20	10,422,600.00	1996	10,316,147.66
21		1997	10,366,425.19
22		1998	10,416,702.72
23		1999	10,466,980.25

In most spreadsheets there are other functions that would provide the same results but these have been selected as providing the solutions to the regression equation.

Responses Activity 4

figure A4.1

	B	C	D	E	F	G	H	I	J
2			Value	4 Quarter	Moving	Centre	Variable		
3				Total	Average	TREND	S + I	Adj (S)	Y – S
4		Q1	196.9						
5		Q2	295.5						
6		Q3	349.4	1,231.1	307.78	323.68	25.72	19.85	329.55
7		Q4	389.3	1,358.3	339.58	354.89	34.41	29.68	359.62
8		Q1	324.1	1,480.8	370.20	382.47	–58.37	–67.87	391.97
9		Q2	418.0	1,578.9	394.73	403.12	14.88	18.36	399.64
10		Q3	447.5	1,646.0	411.50	422.89	24.61	19.85	427.65
11		Q4	456.4	1,737.1	434.28	448.11	8.29	29.68	426.72
12		Q1	415.2	1,847.7	461.93	474.82	–59.62	–67.87	483.07
13		Q2	528.6	1,950.8	487.70	507.57	21.03	18.36	510.24
14		Q3	550.6	2,109.7	527.43	539.73	10.87	19.85	530.75
15		Q4	615.3	2,208.1	552.03	567.31	47.99	29.68	585.62
16		Q1	513.6	2,330.3	582.58	597.58	–83.98	–67.87	581.47
17		Q2	650.8	2,450.3	612.58	629.97	20.83	18.36	632.44
18		Q3	670.6	2589.4	647.35				
19		Q4	754.4						
20									
21									
22				QI	QII	QIII	QIV		
23	Year	1				25.72	34.41		
24	Year	2		–58.37	14.88	24.61	8.29		
25	Year	3		–59.62	21.03	10.87	47.99		
26	Year	4		–83.98	20.83				
27	**total**			–201.97	56.74	61.20	90.69		
28	**average**			–67.32	18.91	20.40	30.23		
29	**adjustment**			–0.55	–0.55	–0.55	–0.55		
30	**Factors**			–67.87	18.36	19.85	29.68		

figure A4.2

Row	B	C	D (Value)	E (4 Quarter / Total)	F (Moving / Average)	G (Centre / TREND)	H (Variable / S + 1)	I (2 / AOJ (S))	J (2 / Y - S)
1									
2			Value	4 Quarter	Moving	Centre	Variable	2	2
3				Total	Average	TREND	S + 1	AOJ (S)	Y - S
4	Q	1					=IF(G4="","",ROUND(D4-G4,$I$1))	=$E$30	=ROUND(D4-I4,$J$1)
5	Q	2					=IF(G5="","",ROUND(D5-G5,$I$1))	=$F$30	=ROUND(D5-I5,$J$1)
6	Q	3			=IF(E6<>"",E6/4,"")		=IF(G6="","",ROUND(D6-G6,$I$1))	=$G$30	=ROUND(D6-I6,$J$1)
7	Q	4		=IF(D7="",SUM(D4:D7))	=IF(E7<>"",E7/4,"")	=IF(F7<>"",(F6+F7)/2,"")	=IF(G7="","",ROUND(D7-G7,$I$1))	=$H$30	=ROUND(D7-I7,$J$1)
8	Q	1		=IF(D8<>"",SUM(D5:D8),"")	=IF(E8<>"",E8/4,"")	=IF(F8<>"",(F7+F8)/2,"")	=IF(G8="","",ROUND(D8-G8,$I$1))	=$E$30	=ROUND(D8-I8,$J$1)
9	Q	2		=IF(D9<>"",SUM(D6:D9),"")	=IF(E9<>"",E9/4,"")	=IF(F9<>"",(F8+F9)/2,"")	=IF(G9="","",ROUND(D9-G9,$I$1))	=$F$30	=ROUND(D9-I9,$J$1)
10	Q	3		=IF(D10<>"",SUM(D7:D10),"")	=IF(E10<>"",E10/4,"")	=IF(F10<>"",(F9+F10)/2,"")	=IF(G10="","",ROUND(D10-G10,$I$1))	=$G$30	=ROUND(D10-I10,$J$1)
11	Q	4		=IF(D11<>"",SUM(D8:D11),"")	=IF(E11<>"",E11/4,"")	=IF(F11<>"",(F10+F11)/2,"")	=IF(G11="","",ROUND(D11-G11,$I$1))	=$H$30	=ROUND(D11-I11,$J$1)
12	Q	1		=IF(D12<>"",SUM(D9:D12),"")	=IF(E12<>"",E12/4,"")	=IF(F12<>"",(F11+F12)/2,"")	=IF(G12="","",ROUND(D12-G12,$I$1))	=$E$30	=ROUND(D12-I12,$J$1)
13	Q	2		=IF(D13<>"",SUM(D10:D13),"")	=IF(E13<>"",E13/4,"")	=IF(F13<>"",(F12+F13)/2,"")	=IF(G13="","",ROUND(D13-G13,$I$1))	=$F$30	=ROUND(D13-I13,$J$1)
14	Q	3		=IF(D14<>"",SUM(D11:D14),"")	=IF(E14<>"",E14/4,"")	=IF(F14<>"",(F13+F14)/2,"")	=IF(G14="","",ROUND(D14-G14,$I$1))	=$G$30	=ROUND(D14-I14,$J$1)
15	Q	4		=IF(D15<>"",SUM(D12:D15),"")	=IF(E15<>"",E15/4,"")	=IF(F15<>"",(F14+F15)/2,"")	=IF(G15="","",ROUND(D15-G15,$I$1))	=$H$30	=ROUND(D15-I15,$J$1)
16	Q	1		=IF(D16<>"",SUM(D13:D16),"")	=IF(E16<>"",E16/4,"")	=IF(F16<>"",(F15+F16)/2,"")	=IF(G16="","",ROUND(D16-G16,$I$1))		=ROUND(D16-I16,$J$1)
17	Q	2		=IF(D17<>"",SUM(D14:D17),"")	=IF(E17<>"",E17/4,"")	=IF(F17<>"",(F16+F17)/2,"")	=IF(G17="","",ROUND(D17-G17,$I$1))		=ROUND(D17-I17,$J$1)
18	Q	3		=IF(D18<>"",SUM(D15:D18),"")	=IF(E18<>"",E18/4,"")	=IF(F18<>"",(F17+F18)/2,"")	=IF(G18="","",ROUND(D18-G18,$I$1))		=ROUND(D18-I18,$J$1)
19	Q	4		=IF(D19<>"",SUM(D16:D19),"")	=IF(E19<>"",E19/4,"")	=IF(F19<>"",(F18+F19)/2,"")	=IF(G19="","",ROUND(D19-G19,$I$1))		=ROUND(D19-I19,$J$1)
20				=IF(D20<>"",SUM(D17:D20),"")		=IF(F20<>"",(F19+F20)/2,"")			
21									
22				QI	QII	QIII	QIV		
23	year	1		=H4	=H5	=H6	=H7		
24	year	2		=H8	=H9	=H10	=H11		
25	year	3		=H12	=H13	=H14	=H15		
26	year	4		=H16	=H17	=H18	=H19		
27	total			=SUM(E23:E26)	=SUM(F23:F26)	=SUM(G23:G26)	=SUM(H23:H26)		
28	average			=IF(E27=0,"",E27/COUNT(E23:E26))	=IF(F27=0,"",F27/COUNT(F23:F26))	=IF(G27=0,"",G27/COUNT(G23:G26))	=IF(H27=0,"",H27/COUNT(H23:H26))	=SUM(E28:H28)	
29	adjustment			=IF(($I$28/4)<>0,($I$28/4)*-1,0)	=IF(($I$28/4)<>0,($I$28/4)*-1,0)	=IF(($I$28/4)<>0,($I$28/4)*-1,0)	=IF(($I$28/4)<>0,($I$28/4)*-1,0)		
30	Factors			=SUM(E28:E29)	=SUM(F28:F29)	=SUM(G28:G29)	=SUM(H28:H29)		

Responses to Activity 5

The final completed spreadsheet should resemble:

	C	D	E	F	G	H	I
2		**Sample**	**1**	**2**			
3		Size	60	120			
4		Median	299.75	300.05			
5		Mean	300.00	300.00			
6		Stdev	8.00	8.00			
7		Stderror	1.03	0.73			
8		Variance	64.05	63.99			
9		Min	284.20	276.40			
10		Max	316.10	321.60			
11		Range	31.90	45.20			
12							
13							
14				**Sample 1**			
15		Conf level %	Z	Z*SE	lower	upper	interval
16		90	1.645	1.6944	298.3056	301.6944	3.3888
17		95	1.960	2.0188	297.9812	302.0188	4.0376
18		99	2.575	2.6523	297.3477	302.6523	5.3046
19							
20				**Sample 2**			
21		Conf level %	Z	Z* SE	lower	upper	interval
22		90	1.645	1.2009	298.7991	301.2009	2.4018
23		95	1.960	1.4308	298.5692	301.4308	2.8616
24		99	2.575	1.8798	298.1202	301.8798	3.7596

Note that the mean and median are almost identical in each sample, as indeed are the absolute measures of dispersion involving the variance and standard deviation, though the range of respective samples differs substantially. However, the standard error differs markedly between the samples because of the different sample sizes.

The relevant confidence intervals for each sample can be extracted from the lower and upper confidence limits at each confidence level.

Sample 1

- ▶ The 90% confidence interval is 298.3056 to 301.6944.
- ▶ The 95% confidence interval is 297.9812 to 302.0188.
- ▶ The 99% confidence interval is 297.3477 to 302.6523.

Sample 2

- ▶ The 90% confidence interval is 298.7991 to 301.2009.
- ▶ The 95% confidence interval is 298.5692 to 301.4308.
- ▶ The 99% confidence interval is 298.1202 to 301.8798.

Response to Activity 6

Where the significance level = 0.05

		F	G	H	I
2	**H0:**		Average equals		1.48
3	**H1:**		Average is not equal		1.48
4					
5	**Sig level**	0.05			
6					
7	**Critical values**	**Lower**	**Upper**		
8		−0.67449037	0.67449037		
9					
10	**Z statistic**	−0.95170524			
11					
12	**Compare**	**REJECT**			

Where the significance level = 0.1

		F	G	H	I
2	**H0:**		Average equals		1.48
3	**H1:**		Average is not equal		1.48
4					
5	**Sig level**	0.1			
6					
7	**Critical values**	**Lower**	**Upper**		
8		−1.644853	1.644853		
9					
10	**Z statistic**	−0.95170524			
11					
12	**Compare**	**ACCEPT**			

Responses Activity 7

Let b = *basic and* d = *deluxe then:*

Maximize

$z = 5.5b + 9.5d$ ... **the linear objective function**

Subject to:

Process I	$12b + 16d \leq 480$	
Process II	$10b + 10d \leq 600$	**the linear structural constraints**
Process III	$10b + 20d \leq 480$	

and

$b \geq 0, \quad d \geq 0$ ... **the non-negativity constraints**

The following solution is illustrated using the 'Solver' tool in *Excel*.

The first stage is to prepare for the optimisation process as follows:

1 Set up the maximising table:

Label three cells: **Model   Contribution   Quantity**.

Place the coefficients of the objective function into the **Contribution** column i.e. 5.5 and 9.5.

Set any value in the **Quantities** column (they will change) – 0 is the simplest option for the initial entry.

For ease of reading, label the corresponding rows with the terms from the objective function i.e. **b (basic)** and **d (deluxe)**

2 Translate the objective function into a spreadsheet formula:

From $z = 5.5b + 9.5d$
to   =(B4*C4)+(B5*C5)
if   **A3 to C5** contains the maximising table.

3 Construct a table of linear structural constraints – for this you need three columns:

Label cells in the last two rows of the
constraints table: **Constraints Quantities**.

The next three rows calculate the constraints i.e. $12b + 16d$ etc.

Use the cells that contains the quantities of b and d in your *Excel* formula even though they still contain zero at this point. Therefore if **A3 to C5** contains the maximising table then the next row should contain three cells as follows:

Process 1 = (12*$C$4) + (16*$C$5)   480

Enter the respective formulae for the remaining two processes.

4 Your spreadsheet should now resemble:

	A	B	C
3	**Model**	**Contribution**	**Quantities**
4	b	5.5	0
5	d	9.5	0
6			
7			
8	**Objective Function**	0	
9			
10		**Constraints**	**Quantities**
11	Process 1	0	480
12	Process 2	0	600
13	Process 3	0	480

5 From the **Tools** on menu bar select **Solver**.

6   Complete the entry boxes:

Set target cell to: ....the cell that contains the objective function (B8 in the above)

Equal to: ....as the aim is to maximise the objective function select **Max**

By changing cells: ....The values that can be changed are the quantities of *b* and *d*. i.e. the values in cells **C4** & **C5**.

Subject to the constraints: ..... Click the Add icon and enter all the constraints including the non-negativity constraints e.g. **$B$11 <= $C$11** etc.

When you have finished entering all 5 constraints (3 process and 2 non-negativity) enter **OK**

Finally, click on the **Options** icon and ensure that the **Assume linear model** is selected – leave the other options in their default setting.

Select **Solve** and the dialogue box should resemble that shown on p. 236.

7   A menu box entitled **Solver Results** will appear and as we are at this level not carrying out any sensitivity analysis select **Keep Solver** Solution and press the **OK** icon

8   You should find the optimal solution as:
    Profit maximise when we produce 12 *deluxe* and 24 *basic* units
    Profit will be £246.

Response to Activity 8

Making Q the subject of the equation:

$$P = c + mQ$$

$$P - c = mQ$$

$$Q = \frac{P - c}{m}$$

$$Q = (P - c)/m$$

In cell A5 *m* is solved using the formula:

= (A2 – A3)/(B2 – B3)

whilst in B5 c is calculated by:

= 280 – (A5*1600)

The demand curve is calculated from columns A (X axis) and B (Y axis) – following Marshallian convention.

figure A7.1

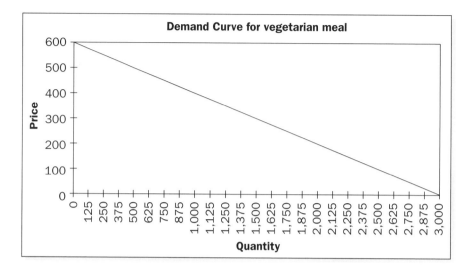

The completed spreadsheet now resembles:

P	Q			Fixed Costs	100,000
280	1,600			Q1	2
320	1,400			Q2	0.1

m	c
−0.2	600

Quantity	Price	TR	PED	TC	Profit
0	600	0		100,000.00	−100,000.00
125	575	71,875	−23	101,812.50	−29,937.50
250	550	137,500	−11	106,750.00	30,750.00
375	525	196,875	−7	114,812.50	82,062.50
500	500	250,000	−5	126,000.00	124,000.00
625	475	296,875	−3.8	140,312.50	156,562.50
750	450	337,500	−3	157,750.00	179,750.00
875	425	371,875	−2.42857	178,312.50	193,562.50
1,000	400	400,000	−2	202,000.00	198,000.00
1,125	375	421,875	−1.66667	228,812.50	193,062.50
1,250	350	437,500	−1.4	258,750.00	178,750.00
1,375	325	446,875	−1.18182	291,812.50	155,062.50
1,500	300	450,000	−1	328,000.00	122,000.00
1,625	275	446,875	−0.84615	367,312.50	79,562.50
1,750	250	437,500	−0.71429	409,750.00	27,750.00
1,875	225	421,875	−0.6	455,312.50	−33,437.50
2,000	200	400,000	−0.5	504,000.00	−104,000.00
2,125	175	371,875	−0.41176	555,812.50	−183,937.50
2,250	150	337,500	−0.33333	610,750.00	−273,250.00
2,375	125	296,875	−0.26316	668,812.50	−371,937.50
2,500	100	250,000	−0.2	730,000.00	−480,000.00
2,625	75	196,875	−0.14286	794,312.50	−597,437.50
2,750	50	137,500	−0.09091	861,750.00	−724,250.00
2,875	25	71,875	−0.04348	932,312.50	−860,437.50
3,000	0	0	0	1,006,000.00	−1,006,000.00

Index